INTRODUCTION

Congratulations on purchasing this, the fifth volume of collected *Sinister Dexter* comic strips. We're confident that it will afford your, literally, minutes of reading and re-reading pleasure. Warning: this volume may contain traces of puns, as well as pieces of gratuitous violence and unexpectedly graphic cussing.

This collection typifies one of the essential strengths of *Sinister Dexter*. Like other, long-running *2000 AD* strips, it benefits from a rotating art pool, a mix of styles and approaches that bring different qualities to the tone and style of individual stories. Much like the famous Canadian attitude to matters meteorological ("if you don't like the weather, wait five minutes and there'll be some different weather along to try"), Sinister Dexter keeps refreshing itself by mixing it up on the art front. The variety of art styles also helps to accentuate the eclectic, patchwork, melting pot atmosphere of the city of Downlode.

Two of the mainstay artists of the series are represented here: Simon Davis, who many regard, justifiably, as the definitive SinDex artist; and Andy Clarke, who by this time (the early to mid 1200s, prog wise) had become an increasingly regular and welcome hand. As I've previously noted, their styles couldn't be further apart. Simon is a fully painted craftsman with an unrivalled eye for portrait and character. Andy is a meticulous and detailed master of the black line, with effortless story-telling poise.

Also stepping up to the plate in this collection are the estimable Patrick Goddard and Ian Richardson, both of whom show themselves to be perfectly capable of capturing the cosmopolitan essence of Downlode, and Steve Roberts who, while never an actual 'regular' artist on the series, has nevertheless guested often enough to make a distinct and characterful contribution, usually in single part episodes.

Andy Clarke takes the lion's share of the art chores in this collection, however, and contributes his fine work to what is one of my personal favourite stories, Shrink Rap. The whole 'hitman/gangster consults a psychiatrist' riff is now an established trope, thanks to a long list of variations that begins with the Sopranos, but it seemed like a fresh idea to me back then. The point of 'Shrink Rap', however, isn't that it's a couch story - that's just the delivery vehicle. It's another part

of the accumulating *Sinister Dexter* origin tale, with an emphasis on Dexter's past, and as such forms a sequel to, and development of, the story 'Bullfighting Days' (also drawn by Andy Clarke) that appeared in a previous volume.

Andy's stories also shoulder the burden of the recurring story thread featured in this collection. After the heavyweight, large-scale epic of 'Eurocrash', I decided it would be a healthy idea to switch to more self-contained stories and story arcs for a while, but Tharg was also keen on the idea of upping the SF quotient in the series. As a result, there's what might be called the 'Barf' thread running through this block of stories, an occasional alien-oriented storyline that begins to build up a head of steam here, and eventually pays off in the Simon Davis story 'Sinister Dexter's Off-Lode Experience', which will form the centrepiece of a future collection (and a particularly irreverent space romp it is too).

A final word must be said concerning the ultimate story in the book, a single part, five-pager called 'Bullet Time'. Once again, it fell to Andy Clarke to draw this one, and a very fine job he made of it, though it could equally well have gone to any of the other artists (some stories, particularly the longer arcs are specifically written with particular artist in mind, but the shorter ones and the one shots just tend to be written ready to keep the next free artist busy). 'Bullet Time' is a story told from the point of view of... well, I won't spoil the fun. All I know is, I'm fond of the story and, of all the one-shot SinDex stories I've ever done, it's the one that people most often say is their absolute favourite. It's neat, it's a little different, and, more than anything, I think it captures in five neat pages the essential sidelong, off-kilter, jokey flavour of *Sinister Dexter* as a series.

So place your reading goggles in the upright position, fasten your straitjackets, and extinguish all hope of coming through this without smelling of wild japery and feral puns. Because this is Downlode, where they tend to leave good taste at the hat-check.

Dan Abnett
Maidstone, August 2009

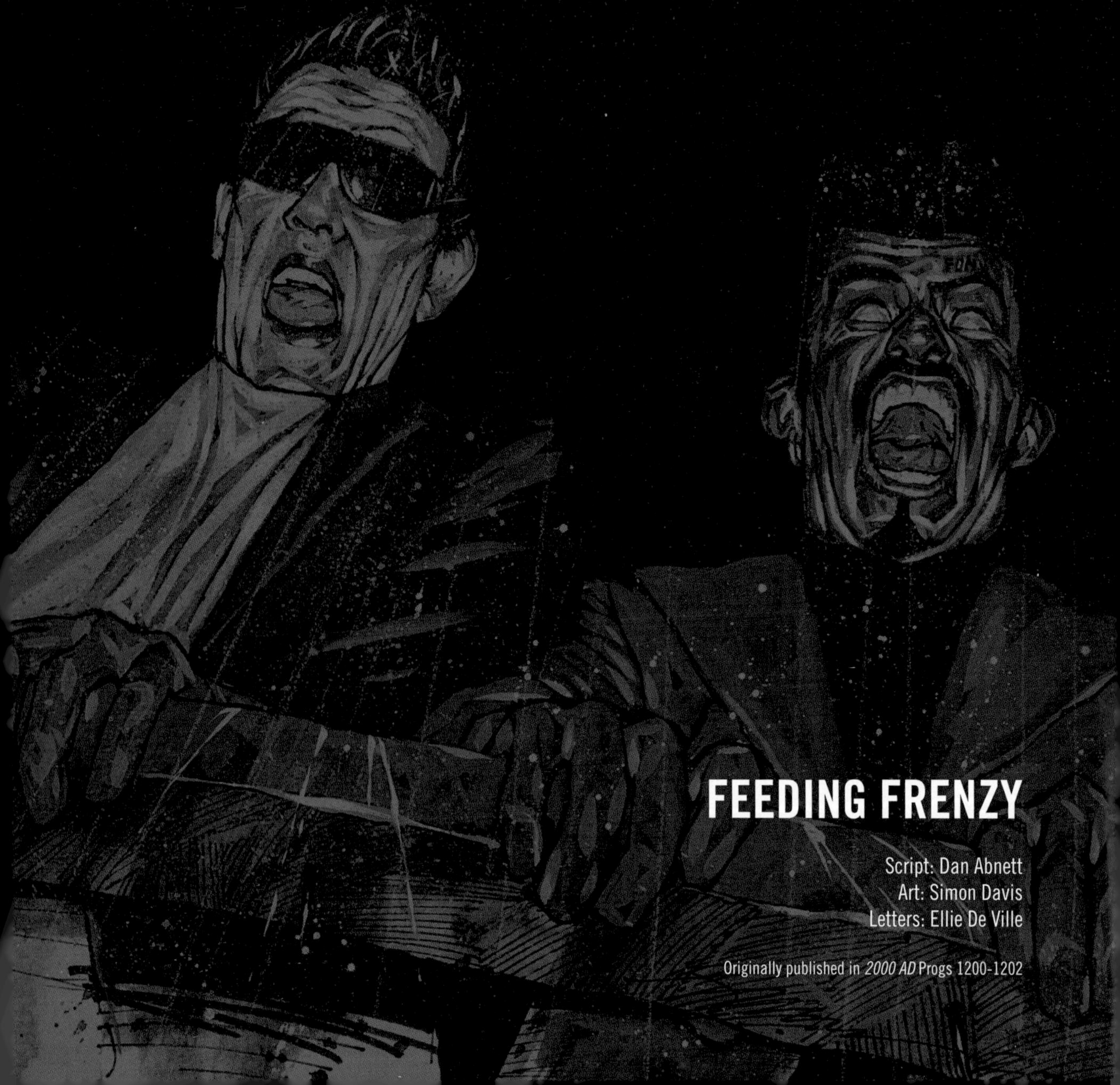

FEEDING FRENZY

Script: Dan Abnett
Art: Simon Davis
Letters: Ellie De Ville

Originally published in *2000 AD* Progs 1200-1202

SINISTER DEXTER

MONEY SHOTS

SINISTER DEXTER CREATED BY DAN ABNETT & DAVID MILLGATE

SINISTER DEXTER

MONEY SHOTS

DAN ABNETT
Writer

ANDY CLARKE ★ NIGEL RAYNOR ★ STEPHEN BASKERVILLE ★ PATRICK GODDARD
SIMON DAVIS ★ STEVE ROBERTS ★ IAN RICHARDSON
Artists

ANDY CLARKE
Cover

REBELLION

Creative Director and CEO: Jason Kingsley
Chief Technical Officer: Chris Kingsley
2000 AD Editor in Chief: Matt Smith
Graphic Design: Simon Parr & Luke Preece
Marketing and PR: Keith Richardson
Repro Assistant: Kathryn Symes

Graphic Novels Editor: Jonathan Oliver
Design: Simon Parr and Luke Preece
Original Commissioning Editor: Andy Diggle

Originally serialised in *2000 AD* Progs 1200-1211, 1220-1228, 2001, 1231-1235, 1243-1248.

Published by Rebellion, Riverside House, Osney Mead, Oxford, OX2 0ES, UK.
www.rebellion.co.uk

ISBN: 978-1-906735-17-3
Printed in Malta by Gutenberg Press
Manufactured in the EU by LPPS Ltd., Wellingborough, NN8 3PJ, UK.
First Printing: October 2009
10 9 8 7 6 5 4 3 2 1

Printed on FSC Accredited Paper

A CIP catalogue record for this book is available from the British Library.

For information on other *2000 AD* graphic novels, or if you have any comments on this book, please email books@2000ADonline.com

To find out more about *2000 AD*, visit www.2000ADonline.com

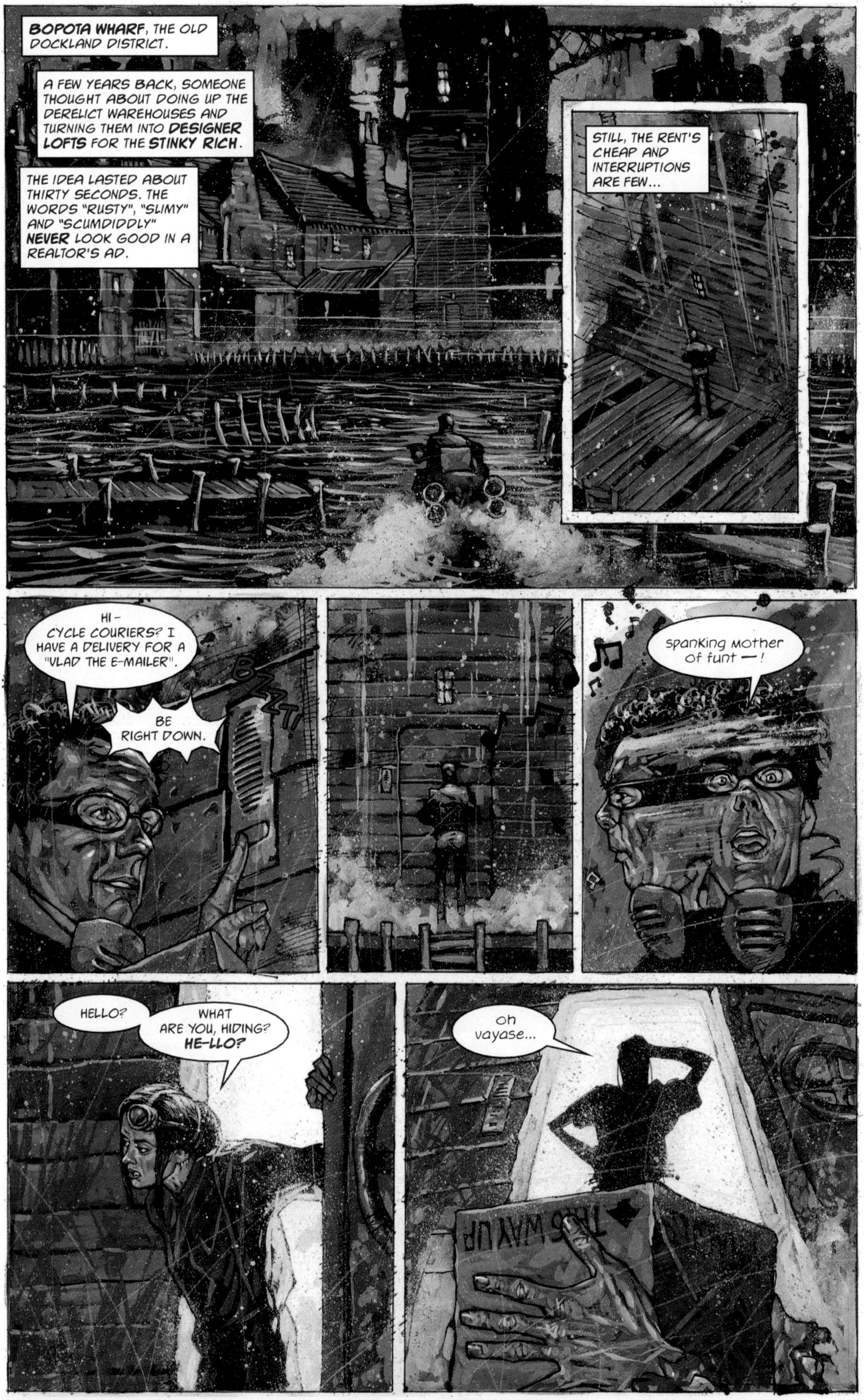
BOPOTA WHARF, THE OLD DOCKLAND DISTRICT.
A FEW YEARS BACK, SOMEONE THOUGHT ABOUT DOING UP THE DERELICT WAREHOUSES AND TURNING THEM INTO DESIGNER LOFTS FOR THE STINKY RICH.
THE IDEA LASTED ABOUT THIRTY SECONDS. THE WORDS "RUSTY", "SLIMY" AND "SCUMDIDDLY" NEVER LOOK GOOD IN A REALTOR'S AD.
STILL, THE RENT'S CHEAP AND INTERRUPTIONS ARE FEW...
HI - CYCLE COURIERS? I HAVE A DELIVERY FOR A "VLAD THE E-MAILER".
BZZT!
BE RIGHT DOWN.
spanking mother of funt —!
HELLO?
WHAT ARE YOU, HIDING? HE-LLO?
oh vayase...
THIS WAY UP

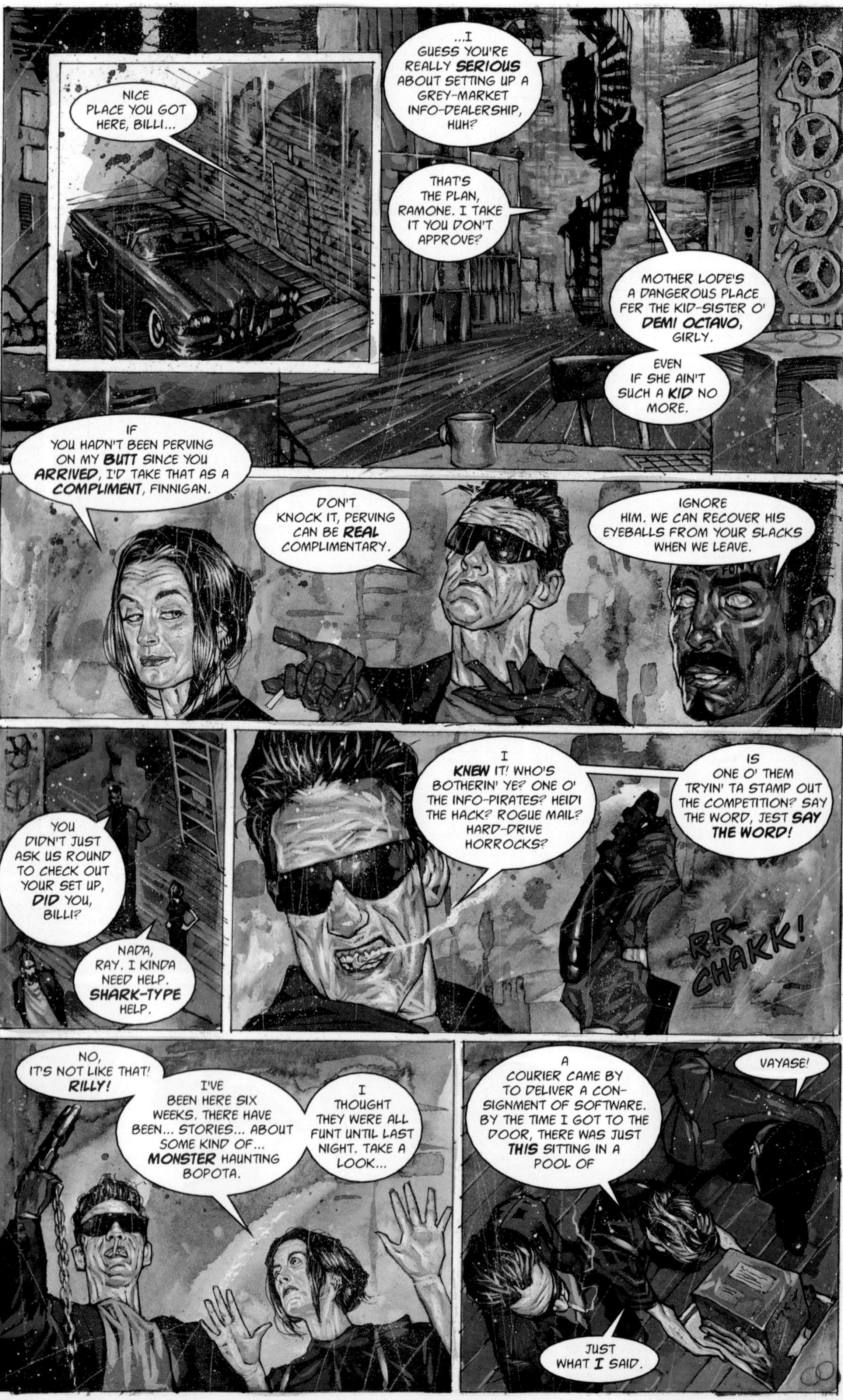
NICE PLACE YOU GOT HERE, BILLI...
...I GUESS YOU'RE REALLY SERIOUS ABOUT SETTING UP A GREY-MARKET INFO-DEALERSHIP, HUH?
THAT'S THE PLAN, RAMONE. I TAKE IT YOU DON'T APPROVE?
MOTHER LODE'S A DANGEROUS PLACE FER THE KID-SISTER O' DEMI OCTAVO, GIRLY.
EVEN IF SHE AIN'T SUCH A KID NO MORE.
IF YOU HADN'T BEEN PERVING ON MY BUTT SINCE YOU ARRIVED, I'D TAKE THAT AS A COMPLIMENT, FINNIGAN.
DON'T KNOCK IT, PERVING CAN BE REAL COMPLIMENTARY.
IGNORE HIM. WE CAN RECOVER HIS EYEBALLS FROM YOUR SLACKS WHEN WE LEAVE.
YOU DIDN'T JUST ASK US ROUND TO CHECK OUT YOUR SET UP, DID YOU, BILLI?
NADA, RAY. I KINDA NEED HELP. SHARK-TYPE HELP.
I KNEW IT! WHO'S BOTHERIN' YE? ONE O' THE INFO-PIRATES? HEIDI THE HACK? ROGUE MAIL? HARD-DRIVE HORROCKS?
IS ONE O' THEM TRYIN' TA STAMP OUT THE COMPETITION? SAY THE WORD, JEST SAY THE WORD!
RR-CHAKK!
NO, IT'S NOT LIKE THAT! RILLY!
I'VE BEEN HERE SIX WEEKS. THERE HAVE BEEN... STORIES... ABOUT SOME KIND OF... MONSTER HAUNTING BOPOTA.
I THOUGHT THEY WERE ALL FUNT UNTIL LAST NIGHT. TAKE A LOOK...
A COURIER CAME BY TO DELIVER A CON-SIGNMENT OF SOFTWARE. BY THE TIME I GOT TO THE DOOR, THERE WAS JUST THIS SITTING IN A POOL OF
VAYASE!
JUST WHAT I SAID.

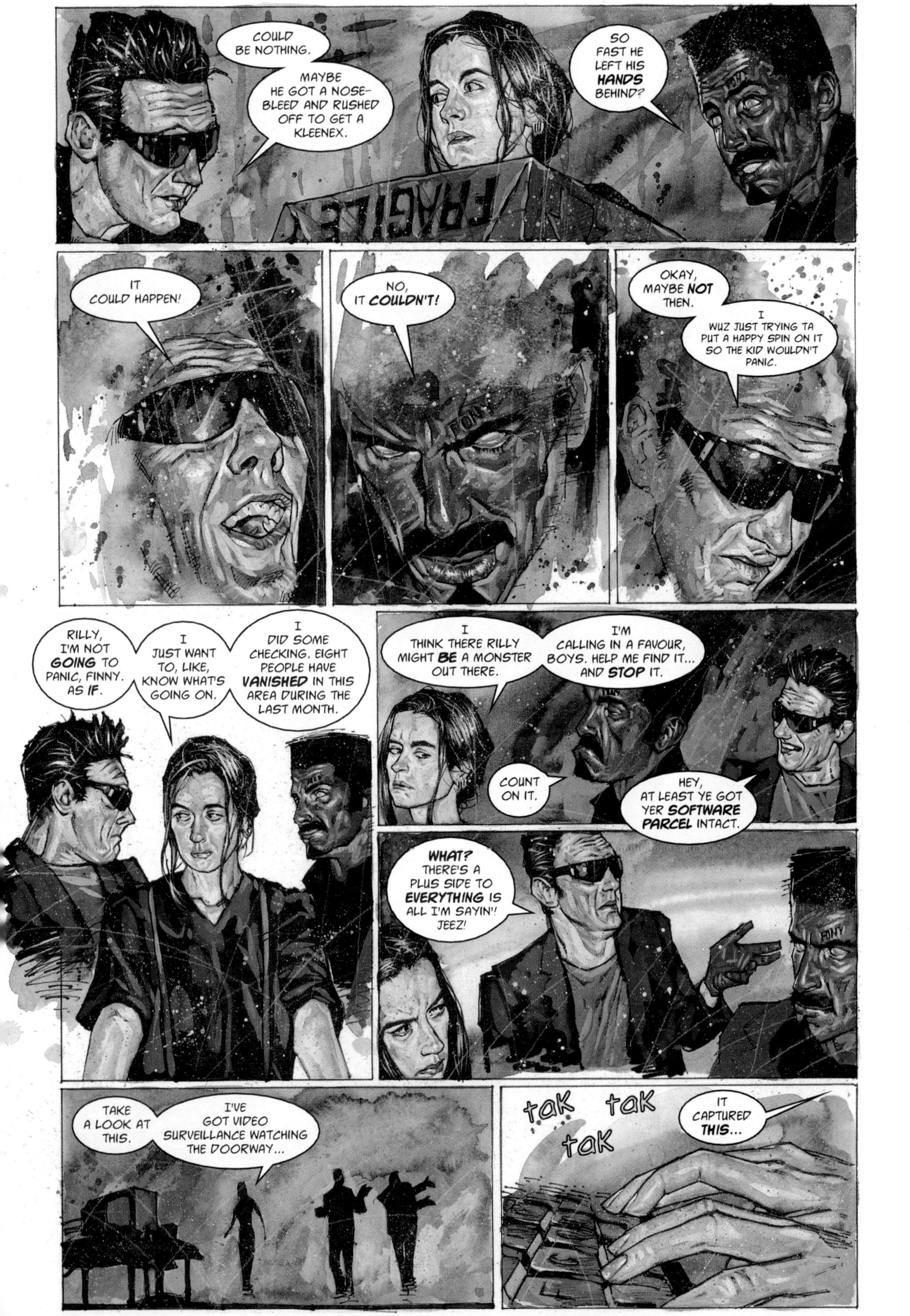
COULD BE NOTHING.
MAYBE HE GOT A NOSE-BLEED AND RUSHED OFF TO GET A KLEENEX.
SO FAST HE LEFT HIS **HANDS** BEHIND?
FRAGILE
IT COULD HAPPEN!
NO, IT **COULDN'T!**
OKAY, MAYBE **NOT** THEN.
I WUZ JUST TRYING TA PUT A HAPPY SPIN ON IT SO THE KID WOULDN'T PANIC.
RILLY, I'M NOT **GOING** TO PANIC, FINNY. AS **IF**.
I JUST WANT TO, LIKE, KNOW WHAT'S GOING ON.
I DID SOME CHECKING. EIGHT PEOPLE HAVE **VANISHED** IN THIS AREA DURING THE LAST MONTH.
I THINK THERE RILLY MIGHT **BE** A MONSTER OUT THERE.
I'M CALLING IN A FAVOUR, BOYS. HELP ME FIND IT... AND **STOP** IT.
COUNT ON IT.
HEY, AT LEAST YE GOT YER **SOFTWARE PARCEL** INTACT.
WHAT? THERE'S A PLUS SIDE TO **EVERYTHING** IS ALL I'M SAYIN'! JEEZ!
TAKE A LOOK AT THIS.
I'VE GOT VIDEO SURVEILLANCE WATCHING THE DOORWAY...
tak tak tak
IT CAPTURED **THIS...**

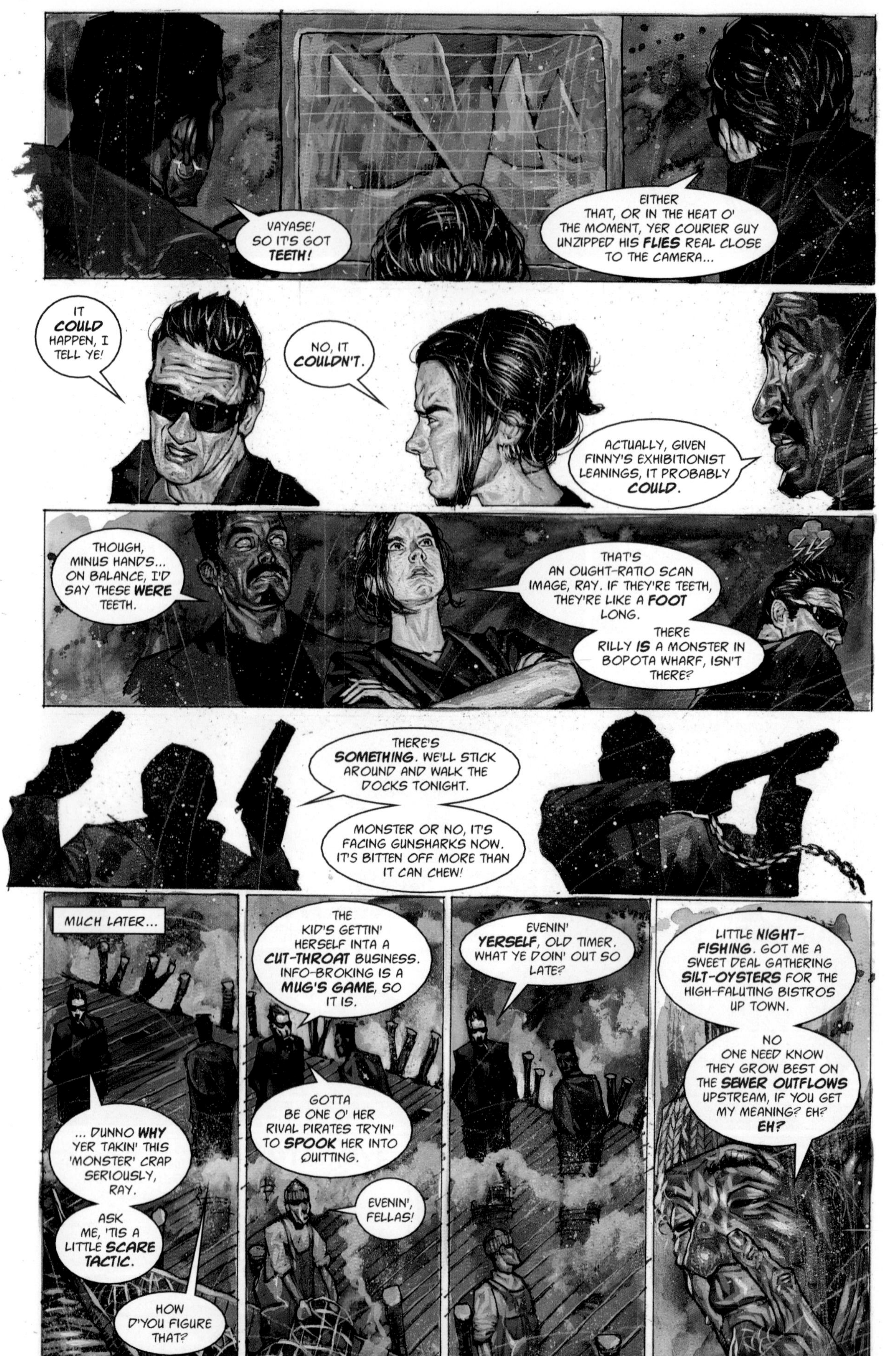
VAYASE! SO IT'S GOT **TEETH!**
EITHER THAT, OR IN THE HEAT O' THE MOMENT, YER COURIER GUY UNZIPPED HIS **FLIES** REAL CLOSE TO THE CAMERA...
IT **COULD** HAPPEN, I TELL YE!
NO, IT **COULDN'T**.
ACTUALLY, GIVEN FINNY'S EXHIBITIONIST LEANINGS, IT PROBABLY **COULD**.
THOUGH, MINUS HANDS... ON BALANCE, I'D SAY THESE **WERE** TEETH.
THAT'S AN OUGHT-RATIO SCAN IMAGE, RAY. IF THEY'RE TEETH, THEY'RE LIKE A **FOOT** LONG.
THERE RILLY **IS** A MONSTER IN BOPOTA WHARF, ISN'T THERE?
THERE'S **SOMETHING**. WE'LL STICK AROUND AND WALK THE DOCKS TONIGHT.
MONSTER OR NO, IT'S FACING GUNSHARKS NOW. IT'S BITTEN OFF MORE THAN IT CAN CHEW!
MUCH LATER...
... DUNNO **WHY** YER TAKIN' THIS 'MONSTER' CRAP SERIOUSLY, RAY.
ASK ME, 'TIS A LITTLE **SCARE TACTIC**.
HOW D'YOU FIGURE THAT?
THE KID'S GETTIN' HERSELF INTA A **CUT-THROAT** BUSINESS. INFO-BROKING IS A **MUG'S GAME**, SO IT IS.
GOTTA BE ONE O' HER RIVAL PIRATES TRYIN' TO **SPOOK** HER INTO QUITTING.
EVENIN', FELLAS!
EVENIN' **YERSELF**, OLD TIMER. WHAT YE DOIN' OUT SO LATE?
LITTLE **NIGHT-FISHING**. GOT ME A SWEET DEAL GATHERING **SILT-OYSTERS** FOR THE HIGH-FALUTING BISTROS UP TOWN.
NO ONE NEED KNOW THEY GROW BEST ON THE **SEWER OUTFLOWS** UPSTREAM, IF YOU GET MY MEANING? EH? **EH?**

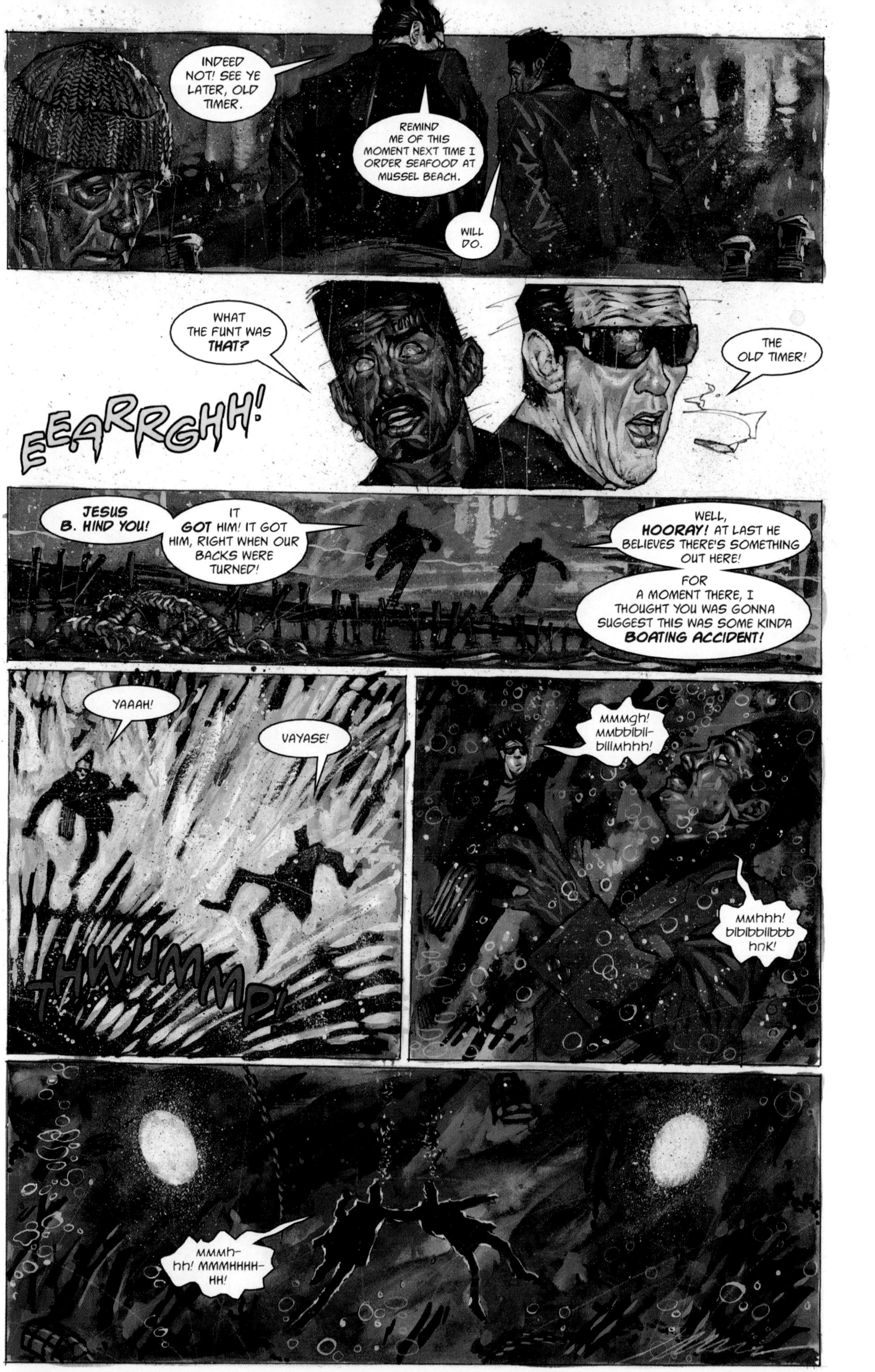
INDEED NOT! SEE YE LATER, OLD TIMER.
REMIND ME OF THIS MOMENT NEXT TIME I ORDER SEAFOOD AT MUSSEL BEACH.
WILL DO.
WHAT THE FUNT WAS THAT?
THE OLD TIMER!
EEARRGHH!
JESUS B. HIND YOU!
IT GOT HIM! IT GOT HIM, RIGHT WHEN OUR BACKS WERE TURNED!
WELL, HOORAY! AT LAST HE BELIEVES THERE'S SOMETHING OUT HERE!
FOR A MOMENT THERE, I THOUGHT YOU WAS GONNA SUGGEST THIS WAS SOME KINDA BOATING ACCIDENT!
YAAAH!
VAYASE!
THWUMMP!
MMMgh! MMbbiblI-blllMhhh!
MMhhh! blblbbllbbb hnk!
MMMh-hh! MMMHHHH-HH!

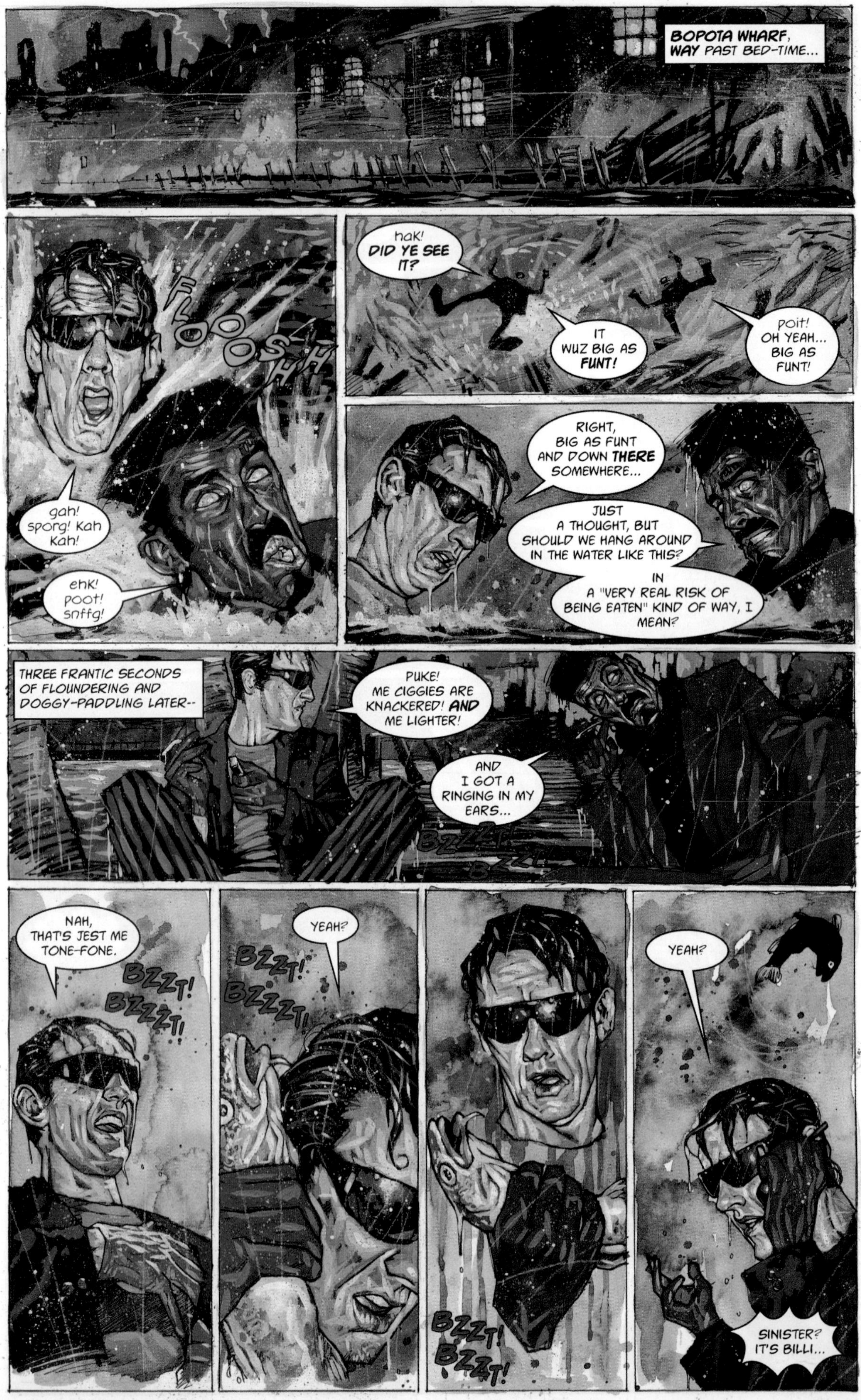
BOPOTA WHARF, WAY PAST BED-TIME...
FLOOSHH
gah! sporg! Kah Kah!
ehk! poot! snffg!
hak! DID YE SEE IT?
IT WUZ BIG AS FUNT!
poit! OH YEAH... BIG AS FUNT!
RIGHT, BIG AS FUNT AND DOWN THERE SOMEWHERE...
JUST A THOUGHT, BUT SHOULD WE HANG AROUND IN THE WATER LIKE THIS?
IN A "VERY REAL RISK OF BEING EATEN" KIND OF WAY, I MEAN?
THREE FRANTIC SECONDS OF FLOUNDERING AND DOGGY-PADDLING LATER--
PUKE! ME CIGGIES ARE KNACKERED! AND ME LIGHTER!
AND I GOT A RINGING IN MY EARS...
NAH, THAT'S JEST ME TONE-FONE.
BZZZT! BZZZZT!
YEAH?
BZZZT! BZZZZT!
BZZT! BZZZT!
YEAH?
SINISTER? IT'S BILLI...

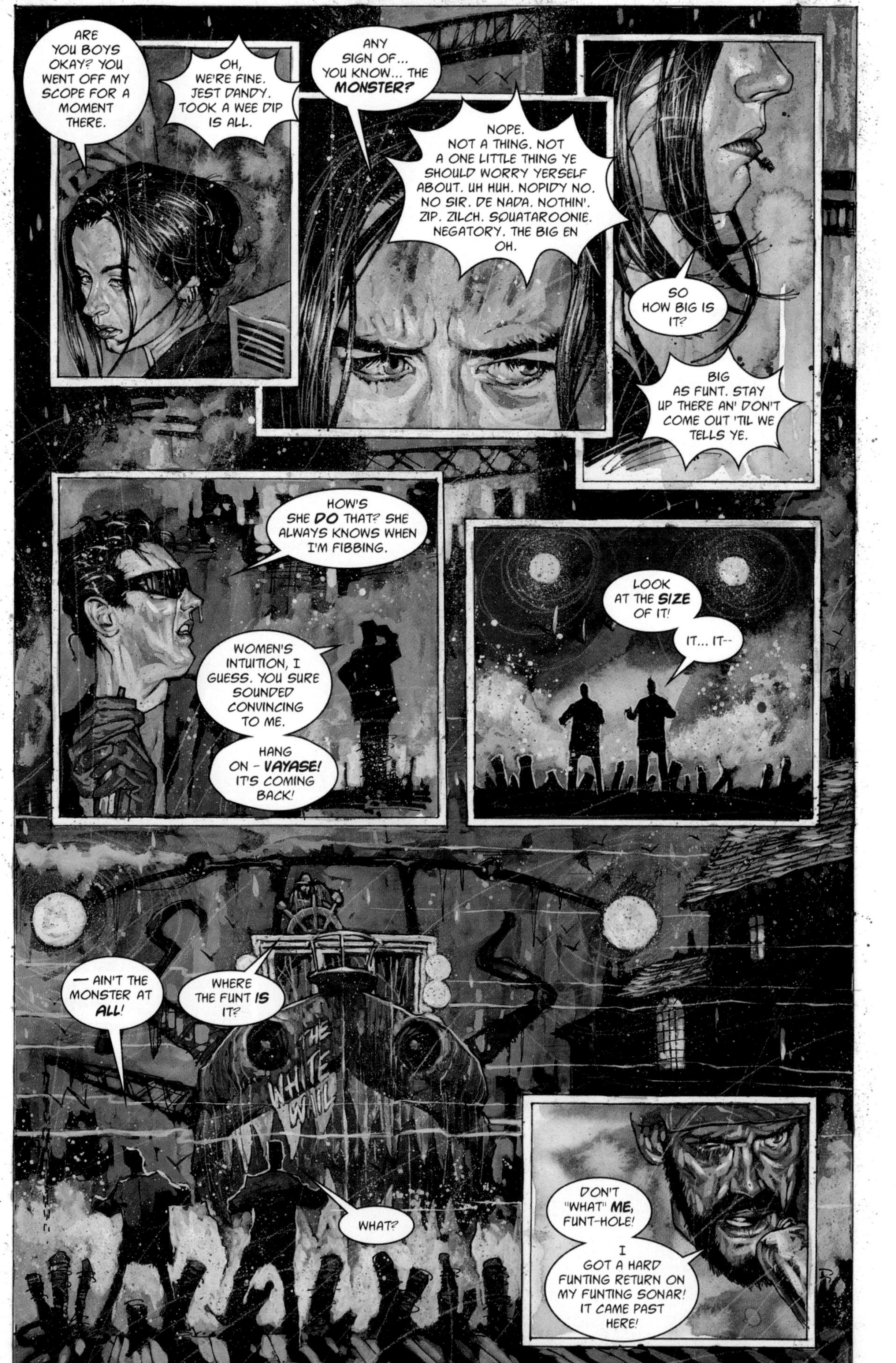
ARE YOU BOYS OKAY? YOU WENT OFF MY SCOPE FOR A MOMENT THERE.
OH, WE'RE FINE. JEST DANDY. TOOK A WEE DIP IS ALL.
ANY SIGN OF... YOU KNOW... THE **MONSTER?**
NOPE. NOT A THING. NOT A ONE LITTLE THING YE SHOULD WORRY YERSELF ABOUT. UH HUH. NOPIDY NO. NO SIR. DE NADA. NOTHIN'. ZIP. ZILCH. SQUATAROONIE. NEGATORY. THE BIG EN OH.
SO HOW BIG IS IT?
BIG AS FUNT. STAY UP THERE AN' DON'T COME OUT 'TIL WE TELLS YE.
HOW'S SHE **DO** THAT? SHE ALWAYS KNOWS WHEN I'M FIBBING.
WOMEN'S INTUITION, I GUESS. YOU SURE SOUNDED CONVINCING TO ME.
HANG ON – **VAYASE!** IT'S COMING BACK!
LOOK AT THE **SIZE** OF IT!
IT... IT--
— AIN'T THE MONSTER AT **ALL**!
WHERE THE FUNT **IS** IT?
THE WHITE WAIL
WHAT?
DON'T "WHAT" **ME**, FUNT-HOLE!
I GOT A HARD FUNTING RETURN ON MY FUNTING SONAR! IT CAME PAST HERE!

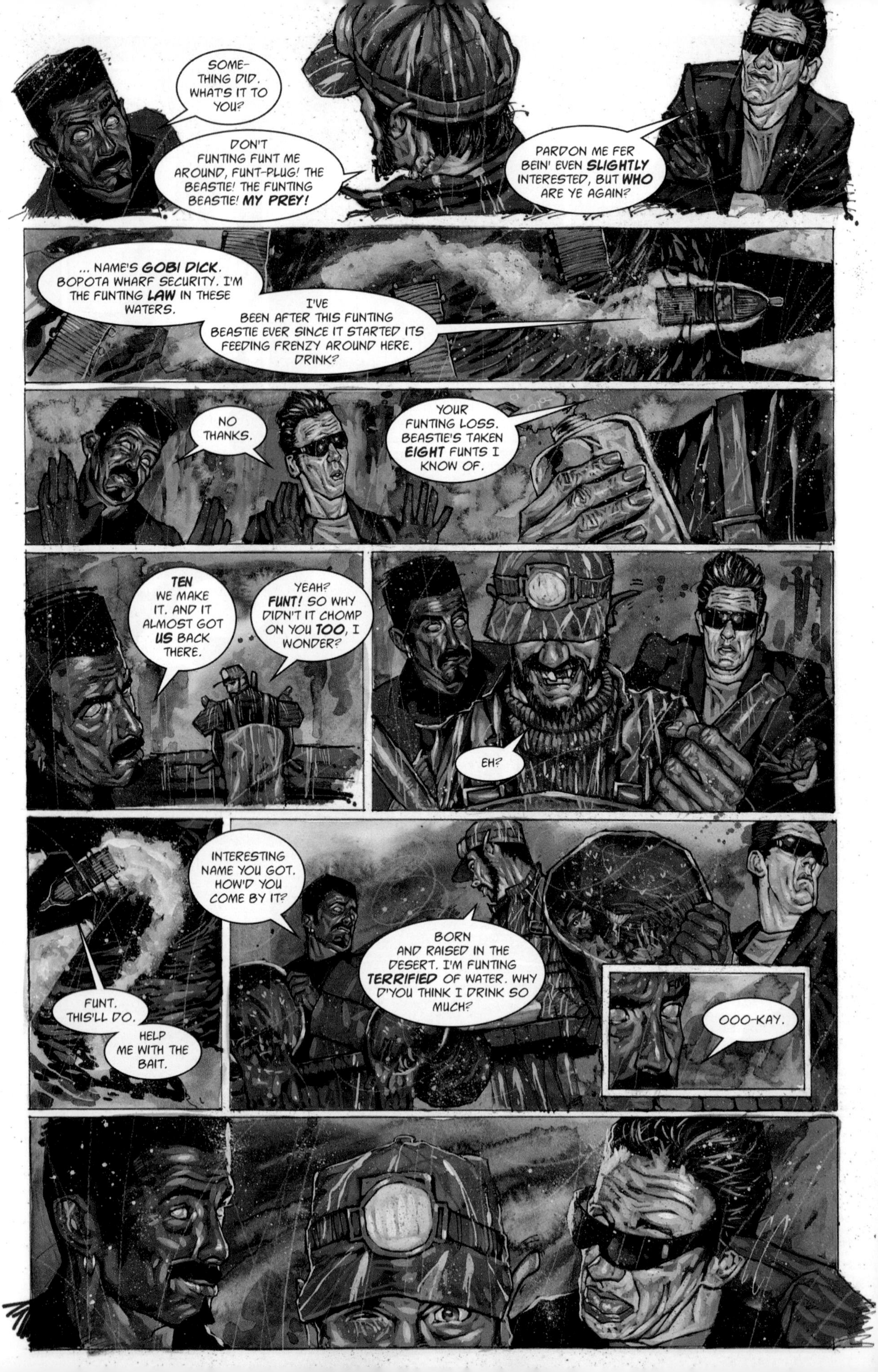
SOMETHING DID. WHAT'S IT TO YOU?
DON'T FUNTING FUNT ME AROUND, FUNT-PLUG! THE BEASTIE! THE FUNTING BEASTIE! MY PREY!
PARDON ME FER BEIN' EVEN SLIGHTLY INTERESTED, BUT WHO ARE YE AGAIN?
... NAME'S GOBI DICK. BOPOTA WHARF SECURITY. I'M THE FUNTING LAW IN THESE WATERS.
I'VE BEEN AFTER THIS FUNTING BEASTIE EVER SINCE IT STARTED ITS FEEDING FRENZY AROUND HERE. DRINK?
NO THANKS.
YOUR FUNTING LOSS. BEASTIE'S TAKEN EIGHT FUNTS I KNOW OF.
TEN WE MAKE IT. AND IT ALMOST GOT US BACK THERE.
YEAH? FUNT! SO WHY DIDN'T IT CHOMP ON YOU TOO, I WONDER?
EH?
FUNT. THIS'LL DO.
HELP ME WITH THE BAIT.
INTERESTING NAME YOU GOT. HOW'D YOU COME BY IT?
BORN AND RAISED IN THE DESERT. I'M FUNTING TERRIFIED OF WATER. WHY D'YOU THINK I DRINK SO MUCH?
OOO-KAY.

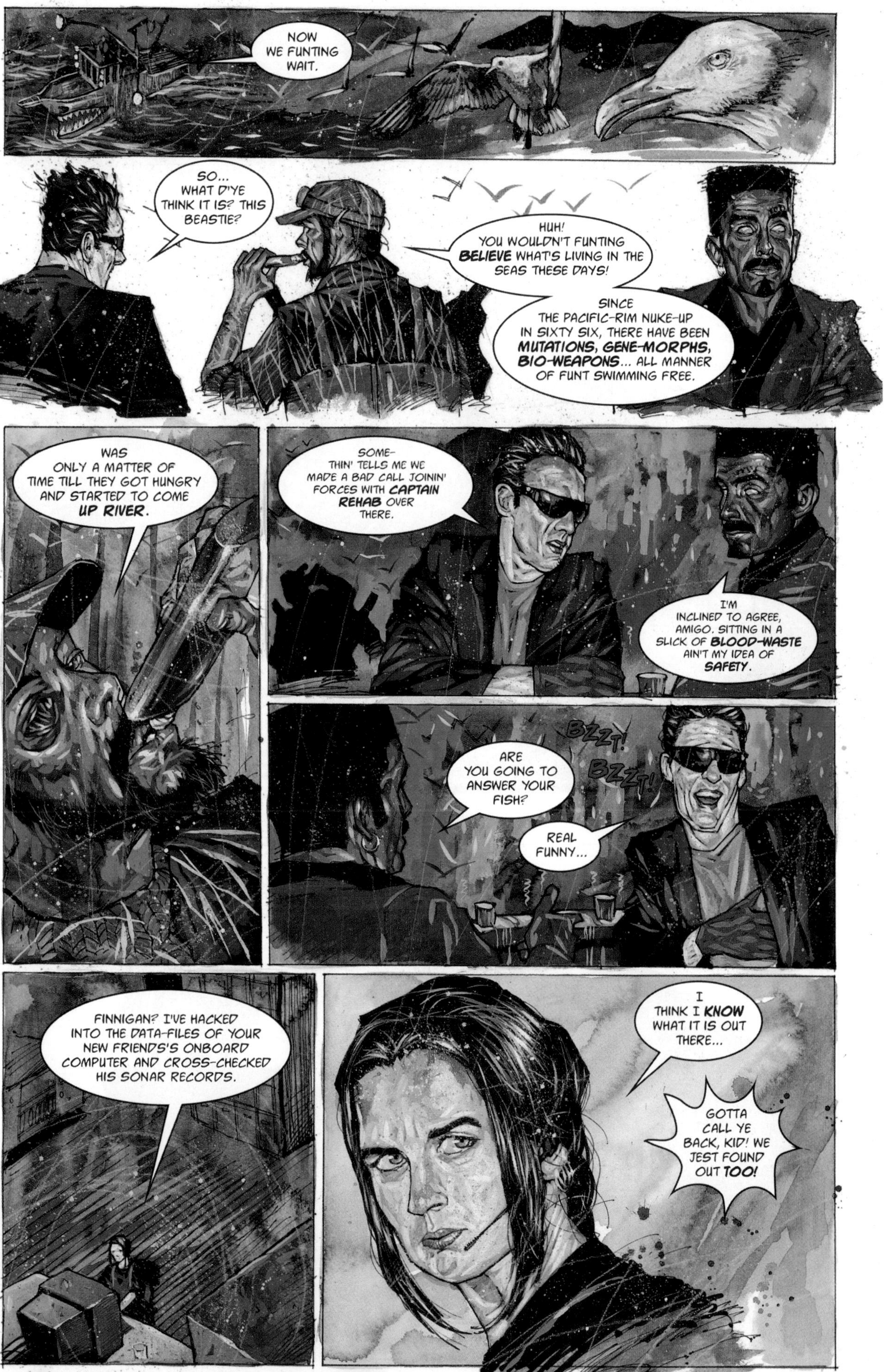
NOW WE FUNTING WAIT.
SO... WHAT D'YE THINK IT IS? THIS BEASTIE?
HUH! YOU WOULDN'T FUNTING **BELIEVE** WHAT'S LIVING IN THE SEAS THESE DAYS!
SINCE THE PACIFIC-RIM NUKE-UP IN SIXTY SIX, THERE HAVE BEEN **MUTATIONS, GENE-MORPHS, BIO-WEAPONS**... ALL MANNER OF FUNT SWIMMING FREE.
WAS ONLY A MATTER OF TIME TILL THEY GOT HUNGRY AND STARTED TO COME **UP RIVER**.
SOME-THIN' TELLS ME WE MADE A BAD CALL JOININ' FORCES WITH **CAPTAIN REHAB** OVER THERE.
I'M INCLINED TO AGREE, AMIGO. SITTING IN A SLICK OF **BLOOD-WASTE** AIN'T MY IDEA OF **SAFETY**.
BZZT! BZZT!
ARE YOU GOING TO ANSWER YOUR FISH?
REAL FUNNY...
FINNIGAN? I'VE HACKED INTO THE DATA-FILES OF YOUR NEW FRIENDS'S ONBOARD COMPUTER AND CROSS-CHECKED HIS SONAR RECORDS.
I THINK I **KNOW** WHAT IT IS OUT THERE...
GOTTA CALL YE BACK, KID! WE JEST FOUND OUT **TOO!**

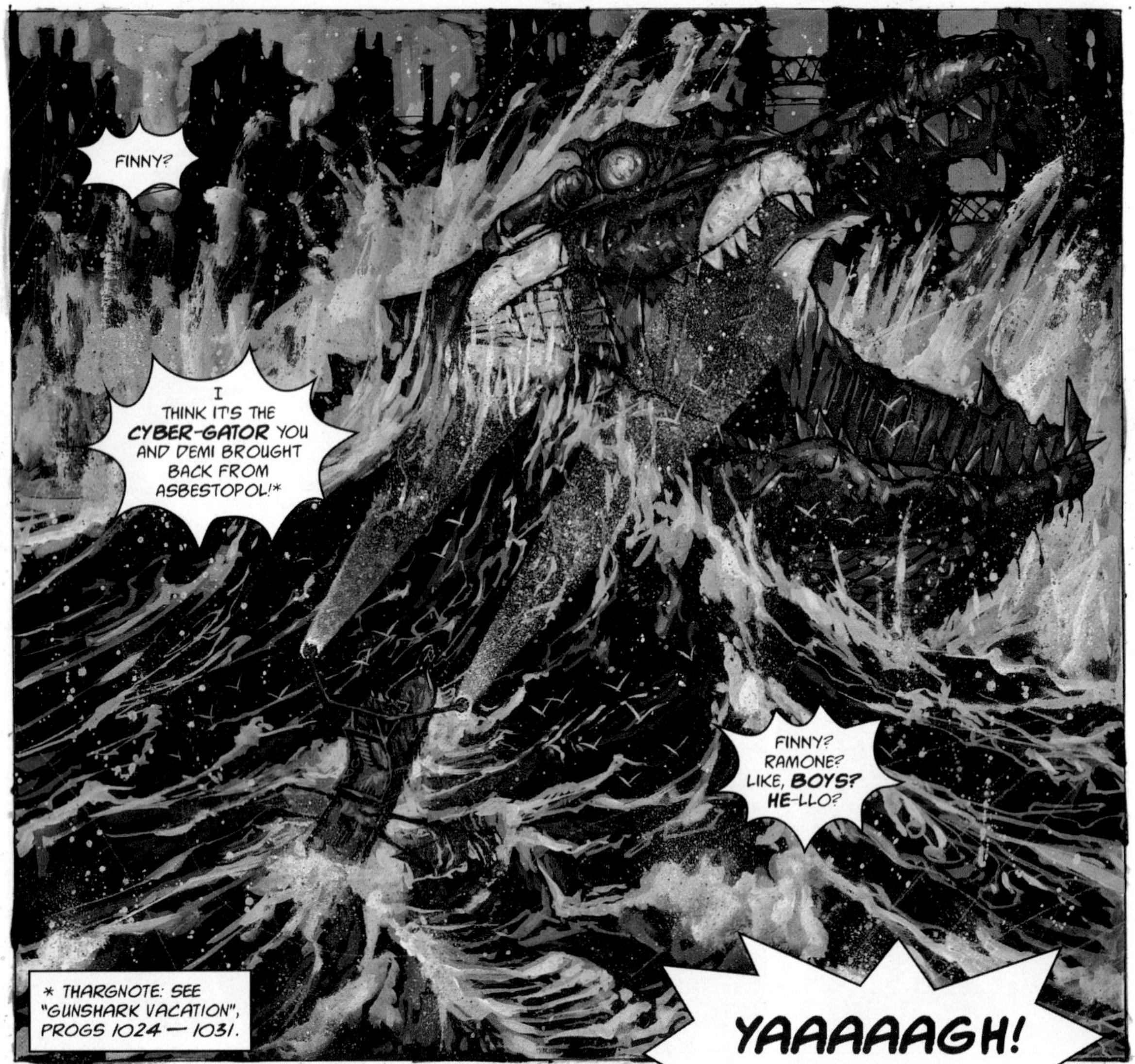
FINNY?
I THINK IT'S THE CYBER-GATOR YOU AND DEMI BROUGHT BACK FROM ASBESTOPOL!*
FINNY? RAMONE? LIKE, BOYS? HE-LLO?
* THARGNOTE: SEE "GUNSHARK VACATION", PROGS 1024 — 1031.

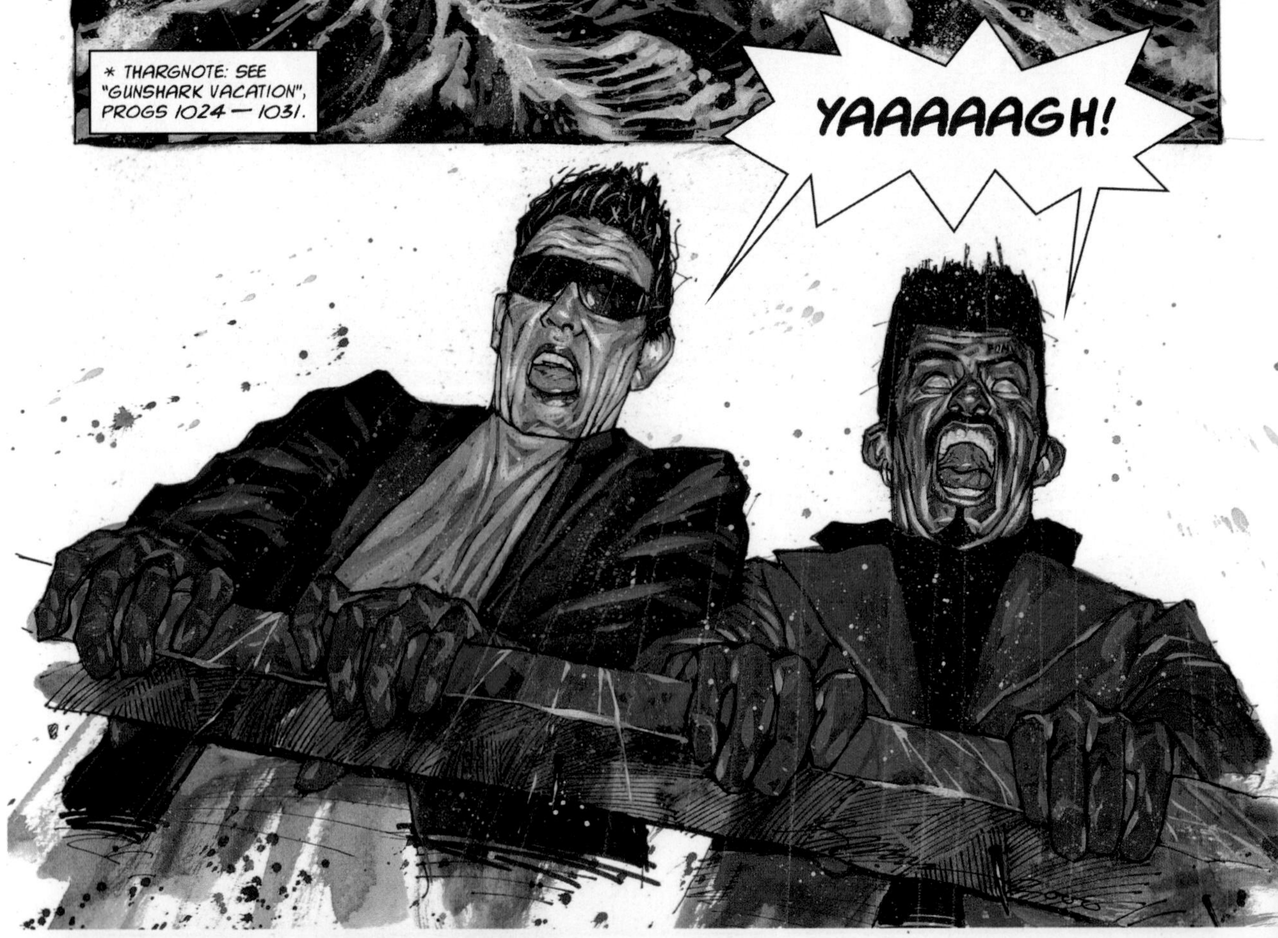
YAAAAAGH!

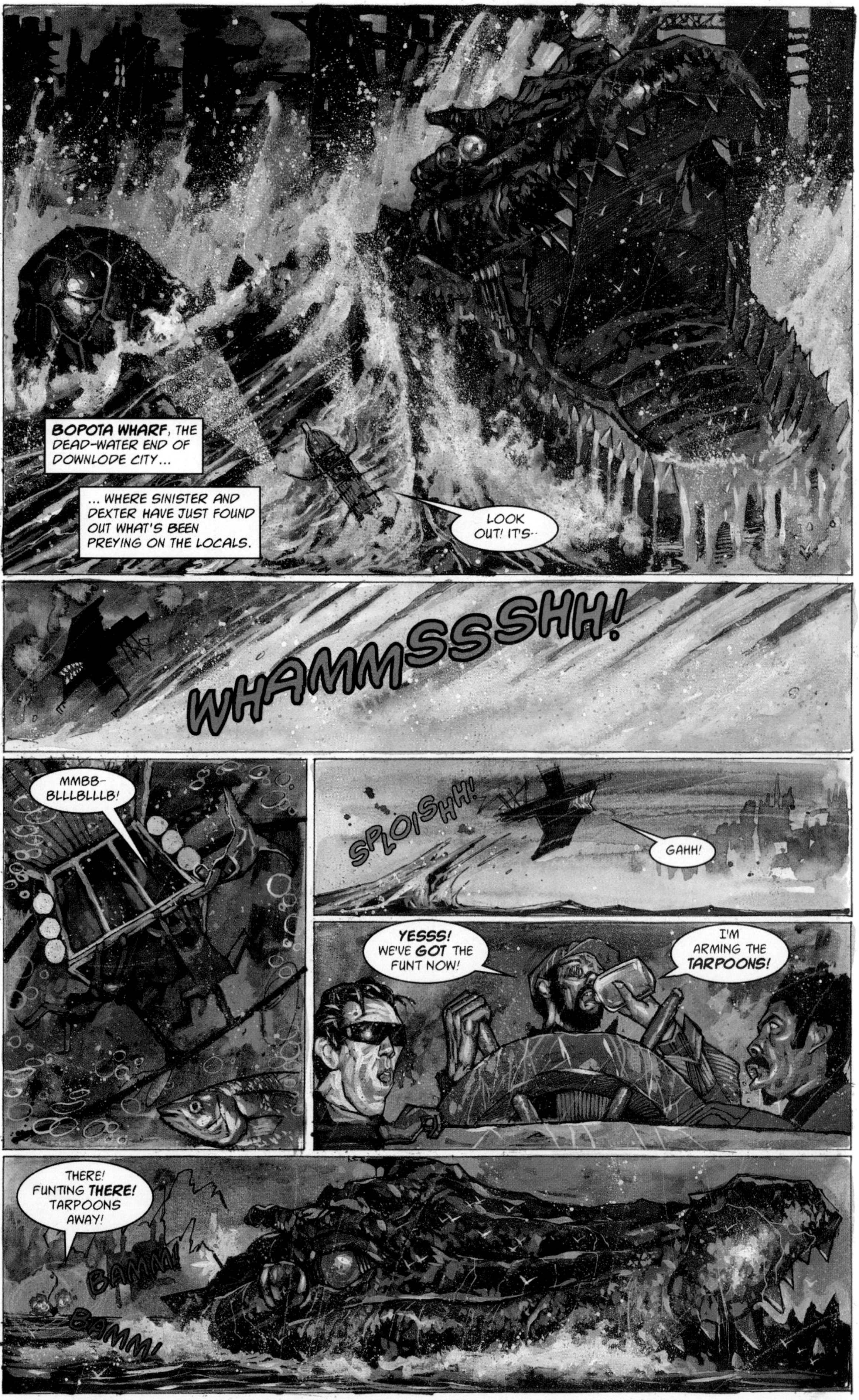
BOPOTA WHARF, THE DEAD-WATER END OF DOWNLODE CITY...
... WHERE SINISTER AND DEXTER HAVE JUST FOUND OUT WHAT'S BEEN PREYING ON THE LOCALS.
LOOK OUT! IT'S--
WHAMMSSSSHH!
MMBB-BLLLBLLLB!
SPLOISHH!
GAHH!
YESSS! WE'VE **GOT** THE FUNT NOW!
I'M ARMING THE **TARPOONS!**
THERE! FUNTING **THERE!** TARPOONS AWAY!
BAMM!
BAMM!

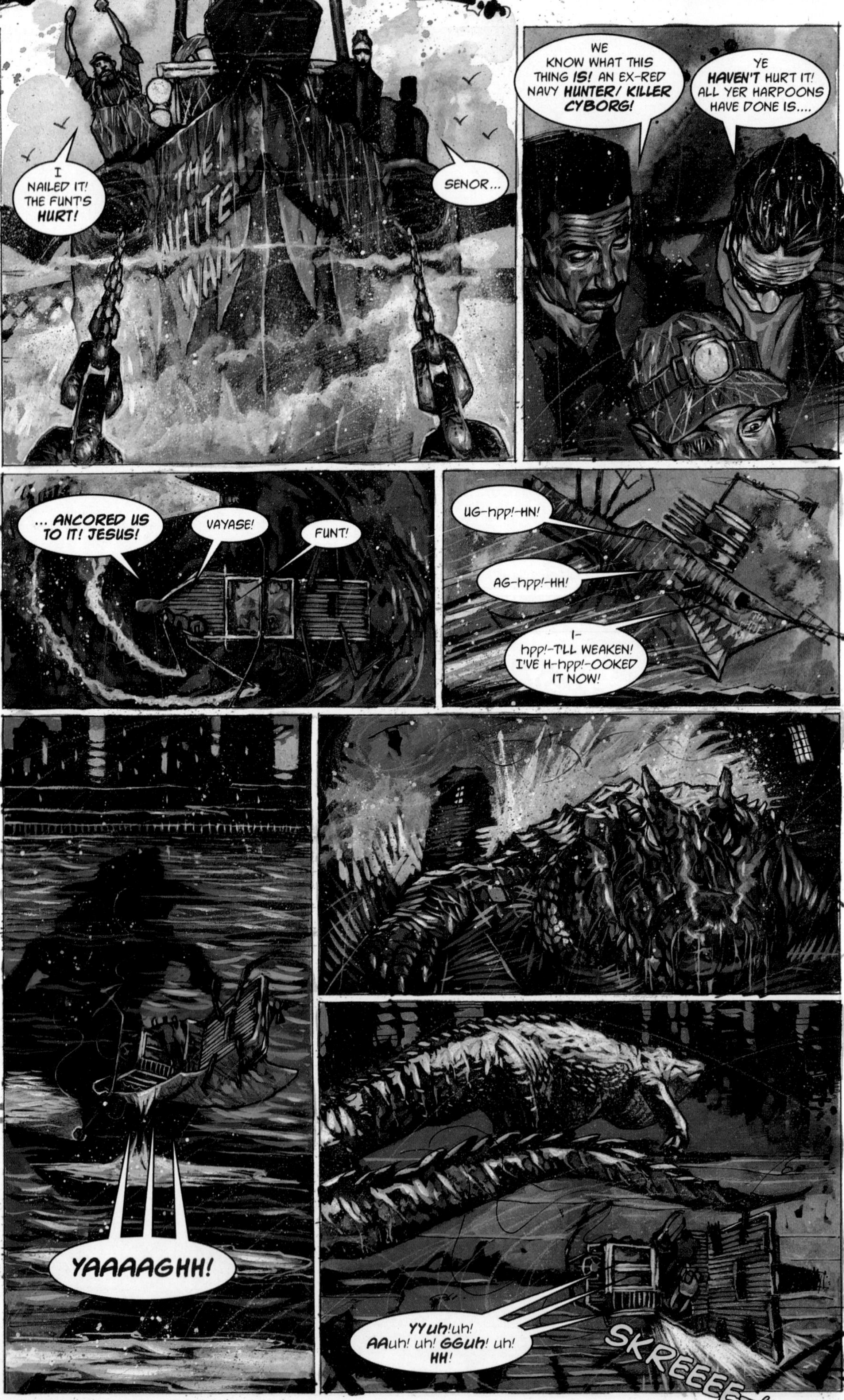

I NAILED IT! THE FUNT'S HURT!
SENOR...
WE KNOW WHAT THIS THING IS! AN EX-RED NAVY HUNTER/ KILLER CYBORG!
YE HAVEN'T HURT IT! ALL YER HARPOONS HAVE DONE IS....
... ANCORED US TO IT! JESUS!
VAYASE!
FUNT!
UG-hpp!-HN!
AG-hpp!-HH!
I-hpp!-T'LL WEAKEN! I'VE H-hpp!-OOKED IT NOW!
YAAAAGHH!
YYuh!uh! AAuh! uh! GGuh! uh! HH!
SKREEEEE-!

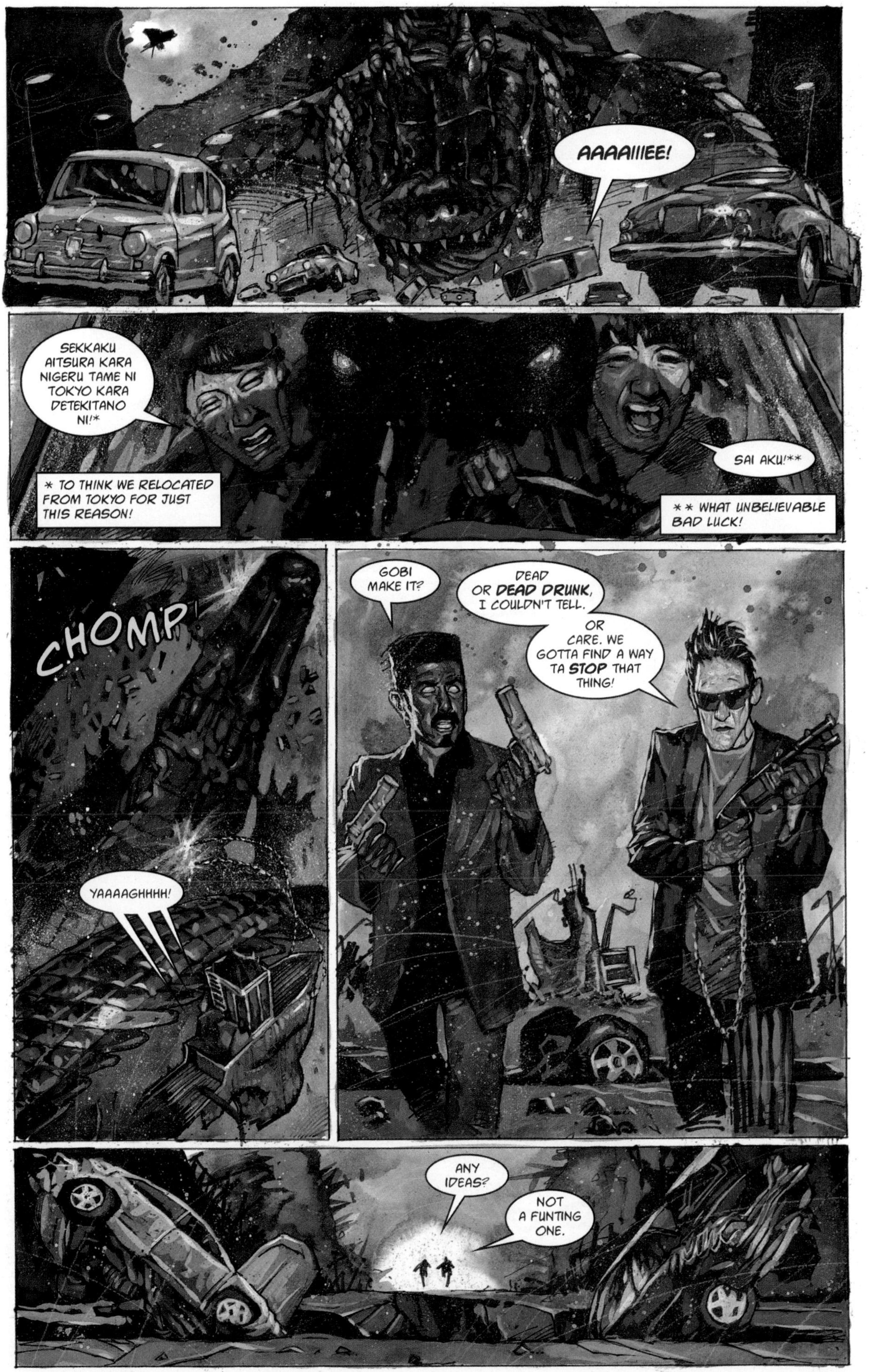
AAAAIIIEE!
SEKKAKU AITSURA KARA NIGERU TAME NI TOKYO KARA DETEKITANO NI!*
SAI AKU!**
* TO THINK WE RELOCATED FROM TOKYO FOR JUST THIS REASON!
** WHAT UNBELIEVABLE BAD LUCK!
CHOMP!
YAAAAGHHHH!
GOBI MAKE IT?
DEAD OR DEAD DRUNK, I COULDN'T TELL.
OR CARE. WE GOTTA FIND A WAY TA STOP THAT THING!
ANY IDEAS?
NOT A FUNTING ONE.

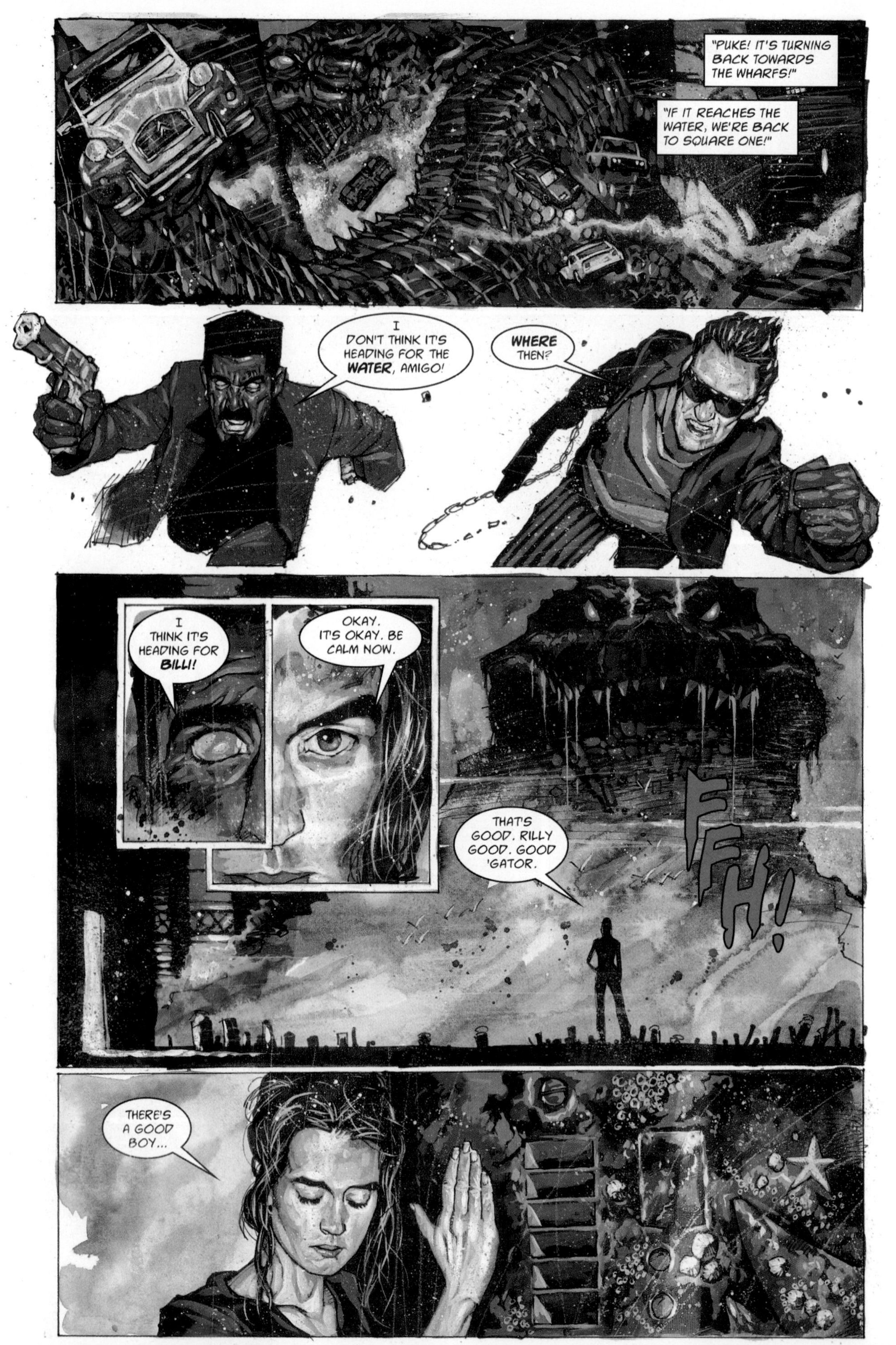
"PUKE! IT'S TURNING BACK TOWARDS THE WHARFS!"
"IF IT REACHES THE WATER, WE'RE BACK TO SQUARE ONE!"
I DON'T THINK IT'S HEADING FOR THE WATER, AMIGO!
WHERE THEN?
I THINK IT'S HEADING FOR BILLI!
OKAY. IT'S OKAY. BE CALM NOW.
THAT'S GOOD. RILLY GOOD. GOOD 'GATOR.
FFH!
THERE'S A GOOD BOY...

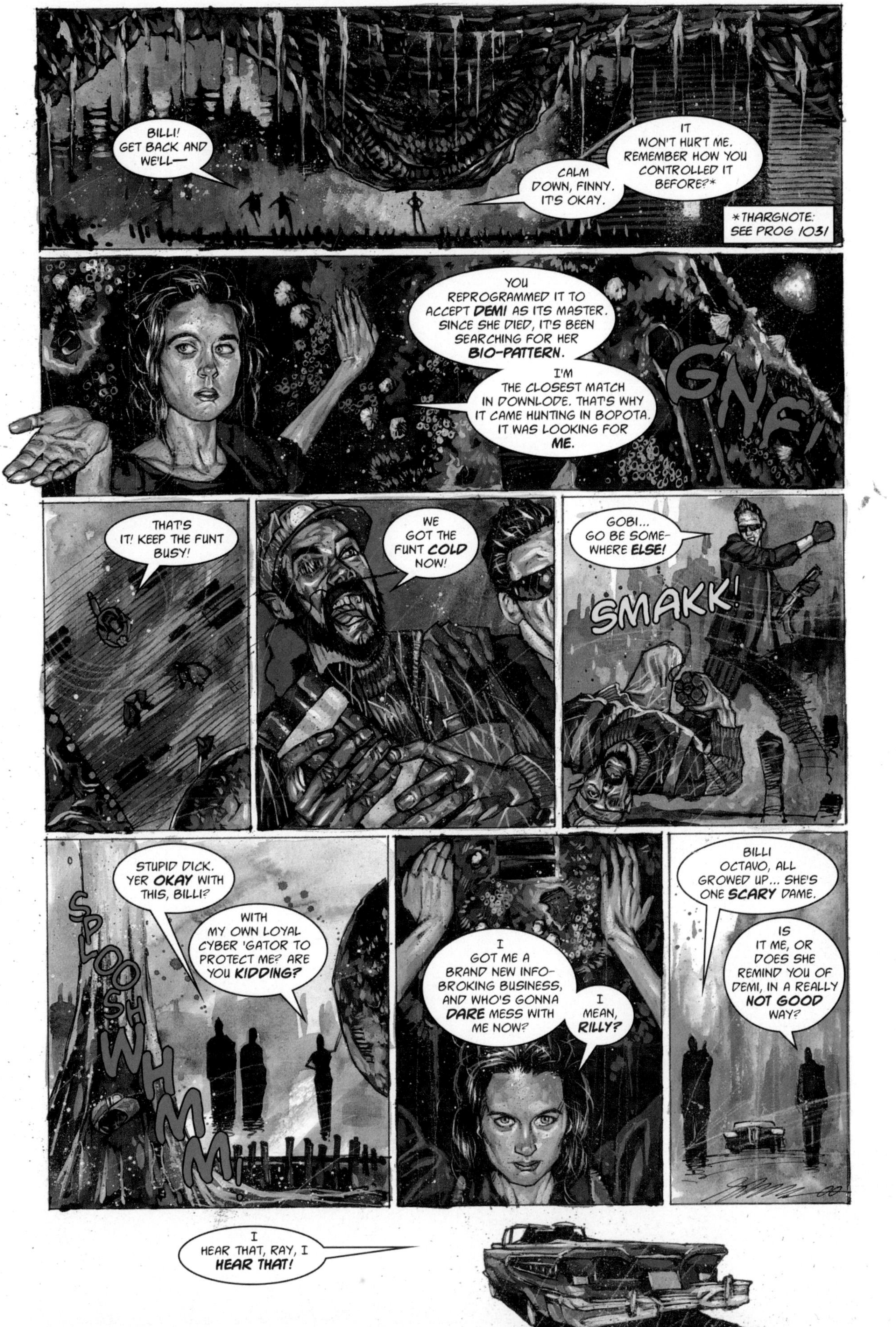
BILLI! GET BACK AND WE'LL—
CALM DOWN, FINNY. IT'S OKAY.
IT WON'T HURT ME. REMEMBER HOW YOU CONTROLLED IT BEFORE?*
*THARGNOTE: SEE PROG 1031
YOU REPROGRAMMED IT TO ACCEPT DEMI AS ITS MASTER. SINCE SHE DIED, IT'S BEEN SEARCHING FOR HER BIO-PATTERN.
I'M THE CLOSEST MATCH IN DOWNLODE. THAT'S WHY IT CAME HUNTING IN BOPOTA. IT WAS LOOKING FOR ME.
GNF!
THAT'S IT! KEEP THE FUNT BUSY!
WE GOT THE FUNT COLD NOW!
GOBI... GO BE SOME-WHERE ELSE!
SMAKK!
SPLOOSH
WHMMM!
STUPID DICK. YER OKAY WITH THIS, BILLI?
WITH MY OWN LOYAL CYBER 'GATOR TO PROTECT ME? ARE YOU KIDDING?
I GOT ME A BRAND NEW INFO-BROKING BUSINESS, AND WHO'S GONNA DARE MESS WITH ME NOW?
I MEAN, RILLY?
BILLI OCTAVO, ALL GROWED UP... SHE'S ONE SCARY DAME.
IS IT ME, OR DOES SHE REMIND YOU OF DEMI, IN A REALLY NOT GOOD WAY?
I HEAR THAT, RAY, I HEAR THAT!

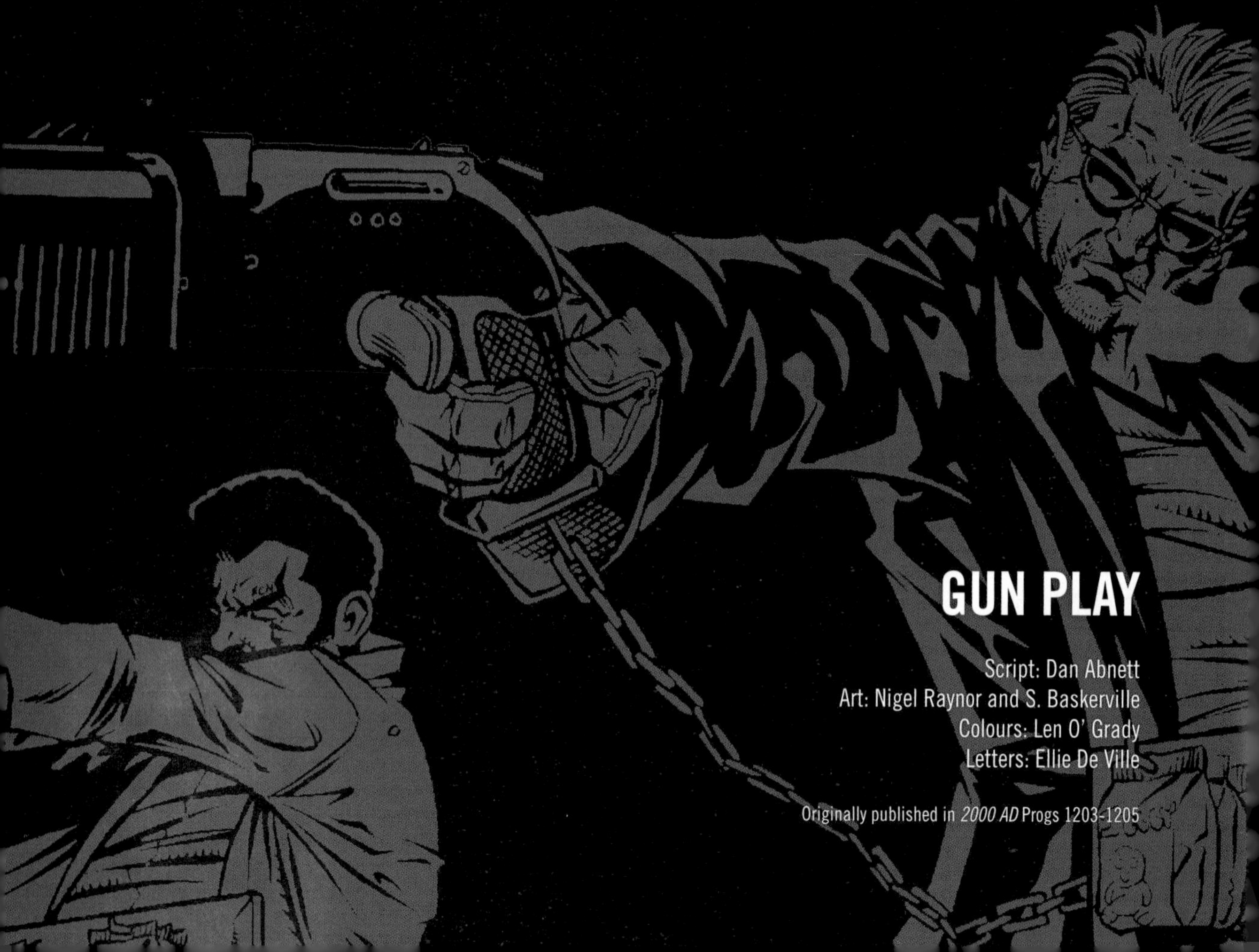

GUN PLAY

Script: Dan Abnett
Art: Nigel Raynor and S. Baskerville
Colours: Len O' Grady
Letters: Ellie De Ville

Originally published in *2000 AD* Progs 1203-1205

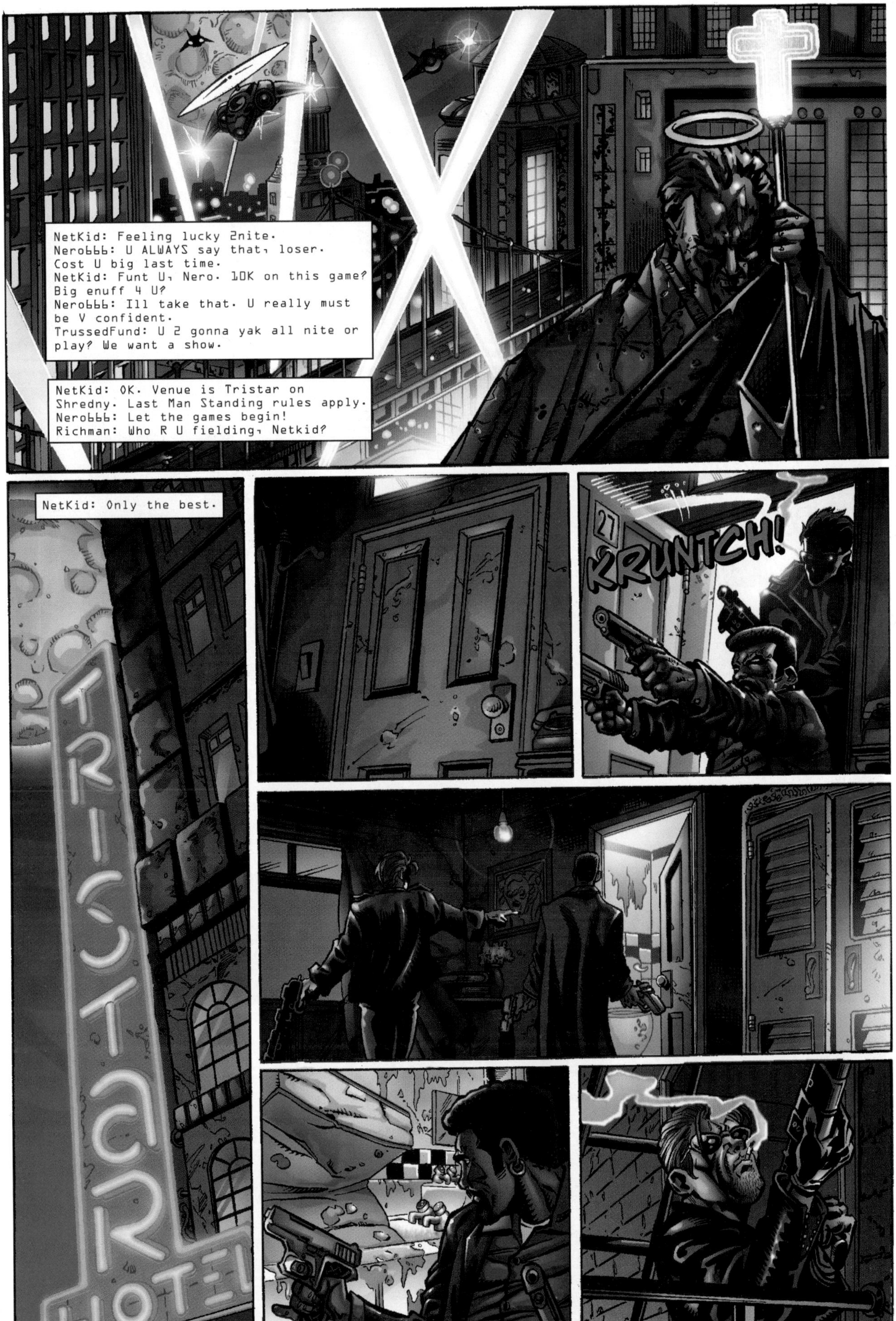
NetKid: Feeling lucky 2nite.
Nero666: U ALWAYS say that, loser. Cost U big last time.
NetKid: Funt U, Nero. 10K on this game? Big enuff 4 U?
Nero666: Ill take that. U really must be V confident.
TrussedFund: U 2 gonna yak all nite or play? We want a show.
NetKid: OK. Venue is Tristar on Shredny. Last Man Standing rules apply.
Nero666: Let the games begin!
Richman: Who R U fielding, Netkid?
NetKid: Only the best.
TRISTAR
HOTEL
27
KRUNTCH!

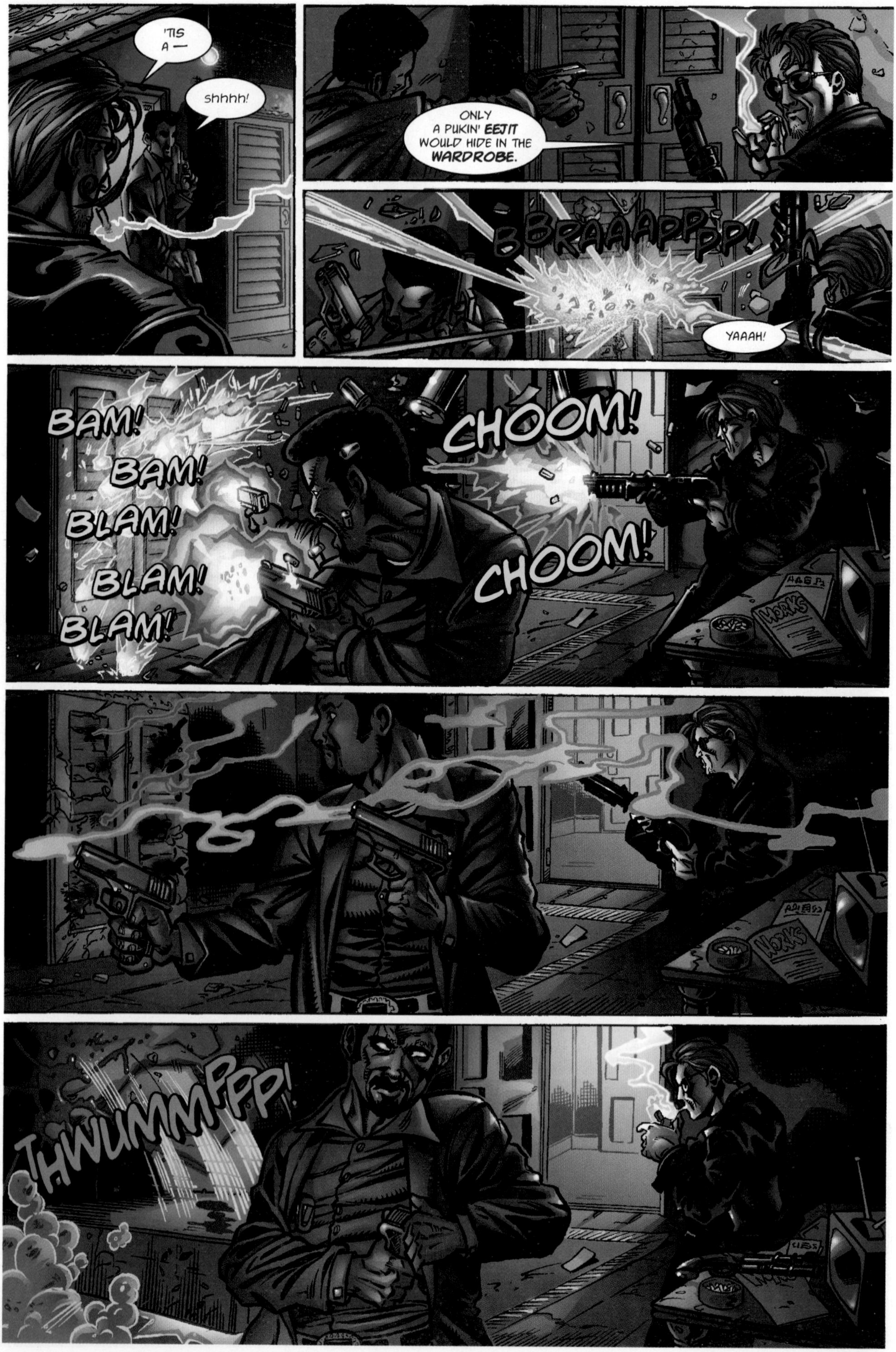
'TIS A —
shhhh!
ONLY A PUKIN' EEJIT WOULD HIDE IN THE WARDROBE.
BBRAAAAPPPP!
YAAAH!
BAM!
BAM!
BLAM!
BLAM!
BLAM!
CHOOM!
CHOOM!
THWUMMPPP!

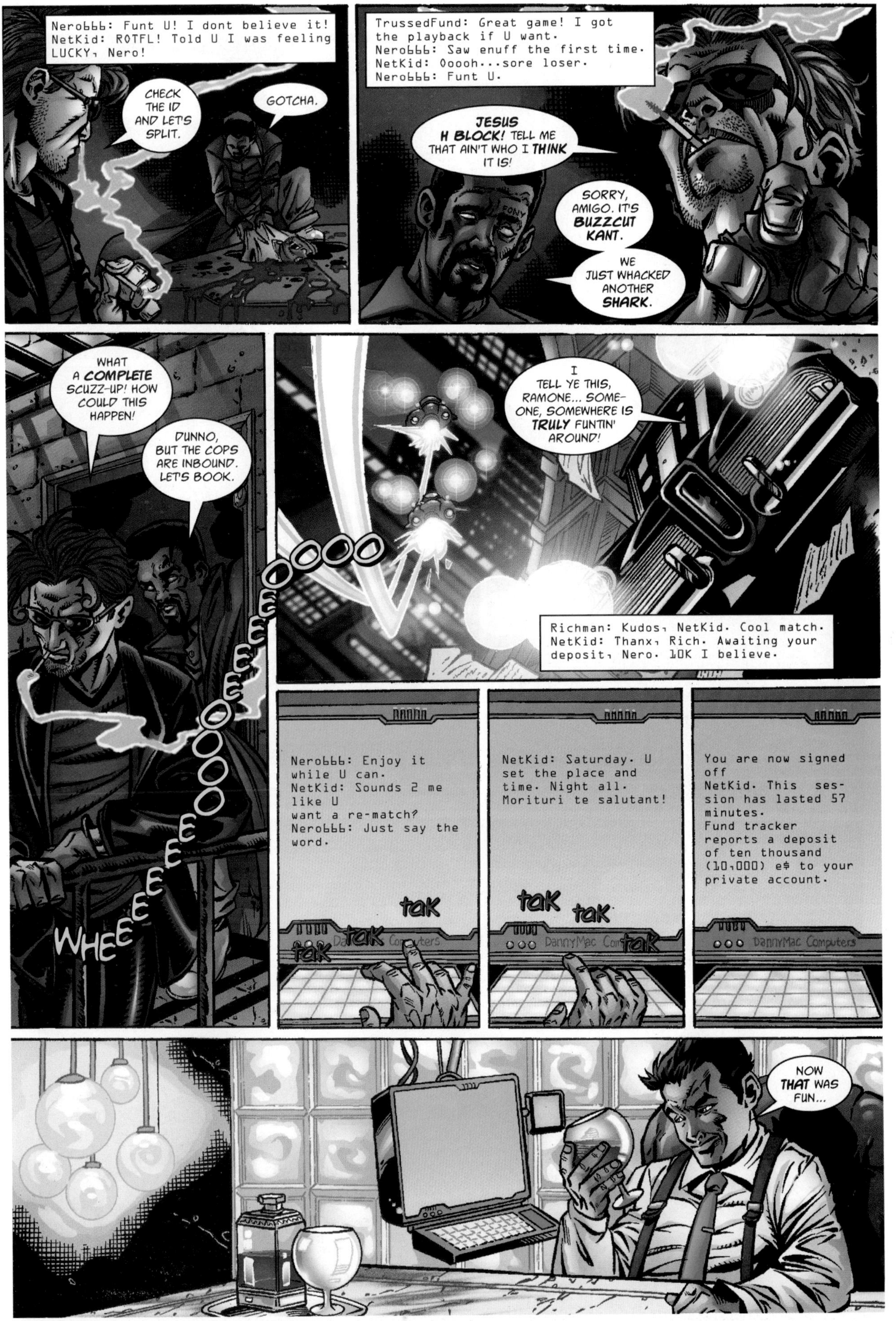

Nero666: Funt U! I dont believe it!
NetKid: ROTFL! Told U I was feeling LUCKY, Nero!
CHECK THE ID AND LET'S SPLIT.
GOTCHA.
TrussedFund: Great game! I got the playback if U want.
Nero666: Saw enuff the first time.
NetKid: Ooooh...sore loser.
Nero666: Funt U.
JESUS H BLOCK! TELL ME THAT AIN'T WHO I THINK IT IS!
SORRY, AMIGO. IT'S BUZZCUT KANT.
WE JUST WHACKED ANOTHER SHARK.
WHAT A COMPLETE SCUZZ-UP! HOW COULD THIS HAPPEN!
DUNNO, BUT THE COPS ARE INBOUND. LET'S BOOK.
WHEEEEEEOOOOOEEEEEEOOOOO
I TELL YE THIS, RAMONE... SOMEONE, SOMEWHERE IS TRULY FUNTIN' AROUND!
Richman: Kudos, NetKid. Cool match.
NetKid: Thanx, Rich. Awaiting your deposit, Nero. 10K I believe.
Nero666: Enjoy it while U can.
NetKid: Sounds 2 me like U want a re-match?
Nero666: Just say the word.
tak tak tak
NetKid: Saturday. U set the place and time. Night all. Morituri te salutant!
tak tak tak
You are now signed off NetKid. This session has lasted 57 minutes. Fund tracker reports a deposit of ten thousand (10,000) e$ to your private account.
DannyMac Computers
NOW THAT WAS FUN...

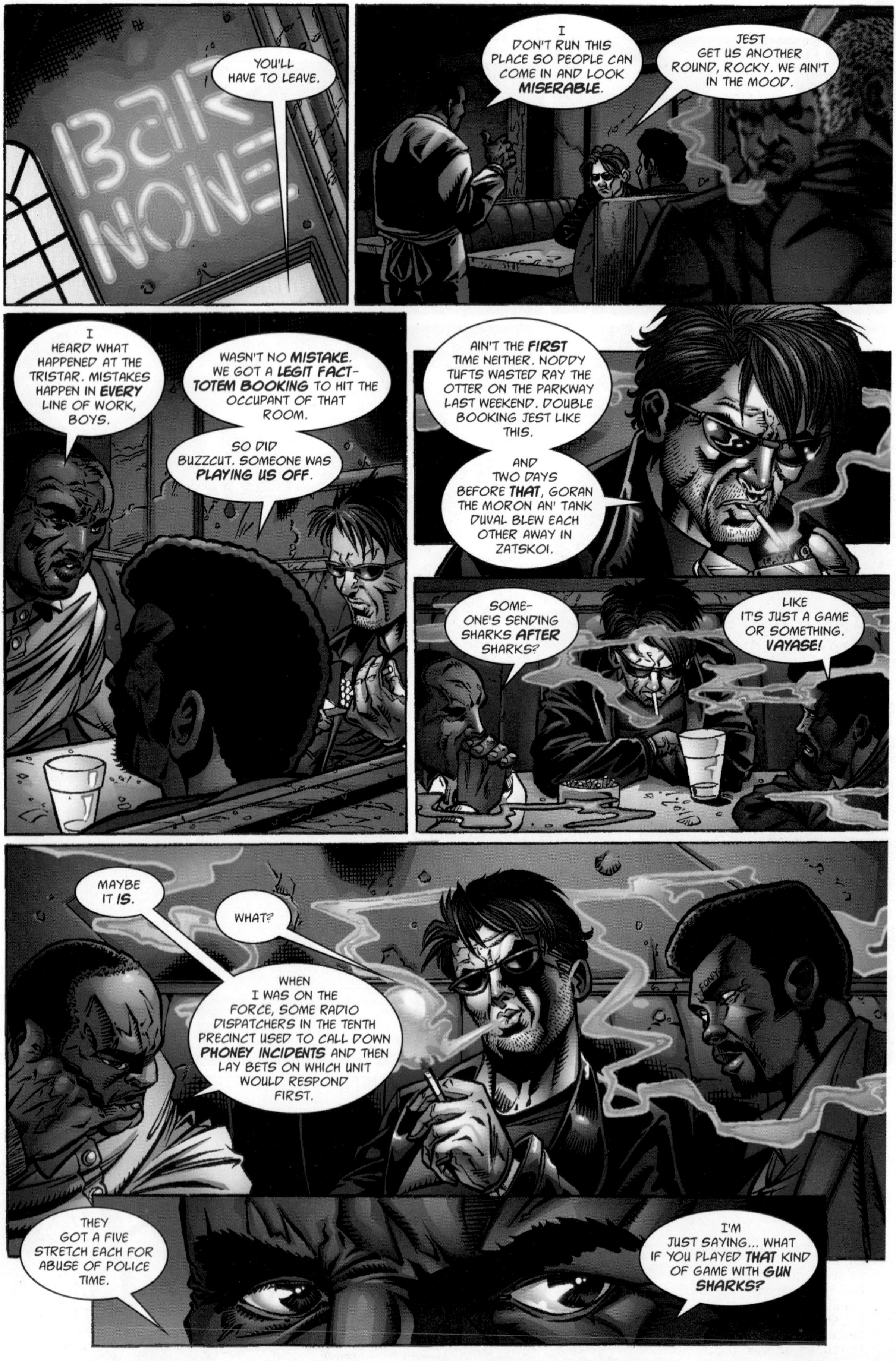

BAR NONE
YOU'LL HAVE TO LEAVE.
I DON'T RUN THIS PLACE SO PEOPLE CAN COME IN AND LOOK **MISERABLE**.
JEST GET US ANOTHER ROUND, ROCKY. WE AIN'T IN THE MOOD.
I HEARD WHAT HAPPENED AT THE TRISTAR. MISTAKES HAPPEN IN **EVERY** LINE OF WORK, BOYS.
WASN'T NO **MISTAKE**. WE GOT A **LEGIT FACT-TOTEM BOOKING** TO HIT THE OCCUPANT OF THAT ROOM.
SO DID BUZZCUT. SOMEONE WAS **PLAYING US OFF**.
AIN'T THE **FIRST** TIME NEITHER. NODDY TUFTS WASTED RAY THE OTTER ON THE PARKWAY LAST WEEKEND. DOUBLE BOOKING JEST LIKE THIS.
AND TWO DAYS BEFORE **THAT**, GORAN THE MORON AN' TANK DUVAL BLEW EACH OTHER AWAY IN ZATSKOI.
SOME-ONE'S SENDING SHARKS **AFTER** SHARKS?
LIKE IT'S JUST A GAME OR SOMETHING. **VAYASE!**
MAYBE IT **IS**.
WHAT?
WHEN I WAS ON THE FORCE, SOME RADIO DISPATCHERS IN THE TENTH PRECINCT USED TO CALL DOWN **PHONEY INCIDENTS** AND THEN LAY BETS ON WHICH UNIT WOULD RESPOND FIRST.
THEY GOT A FIVE STRETCH EACH FOR ABUSE OF POLICE TIME.
I'M JUST SAYING... WHAT IF YOU PLAYED **THAT** KIND OF GAME WITH **GUN SHARKS?**

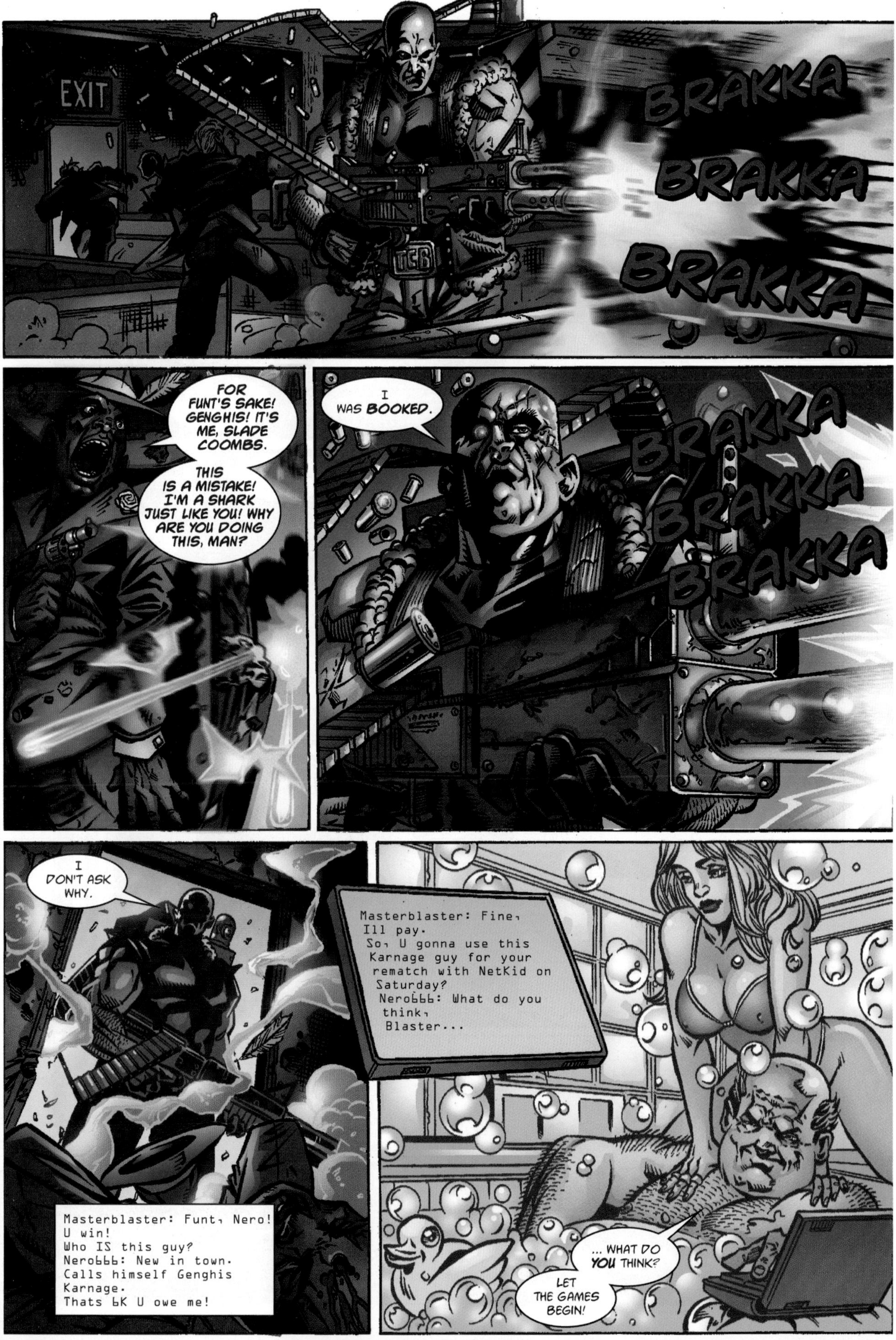
EXIT
BRAKKA
BRAKKA
BRAKKA
FOR FUNT'S SAKE! GENGHIS! IT'S ME, SLADE COOMBS.
THIS IS A MISTAKE! I'M A SHARK JUST LIKE YOU! WHY ARE YOU DOING THIS, MAN?
I WAS BOOKED.
BRAKKA
BRAKKA
BRAKKA
I DON'T ASK WHY.
Masterblaster: Funt, Nero! U win! Who IS this guy?
Nero666: New in town. Calls himself Genghis Karnage. Thats 6K U owe me!
Masterblaster: Fine, Ill pay. So, U gonna use this Karnage guy for your rematch with NetKid on Saturday?
Nero666: What do you think, Blaster...
... WHAT DO YOU THINK?
LET THE GAMES BEGIN!

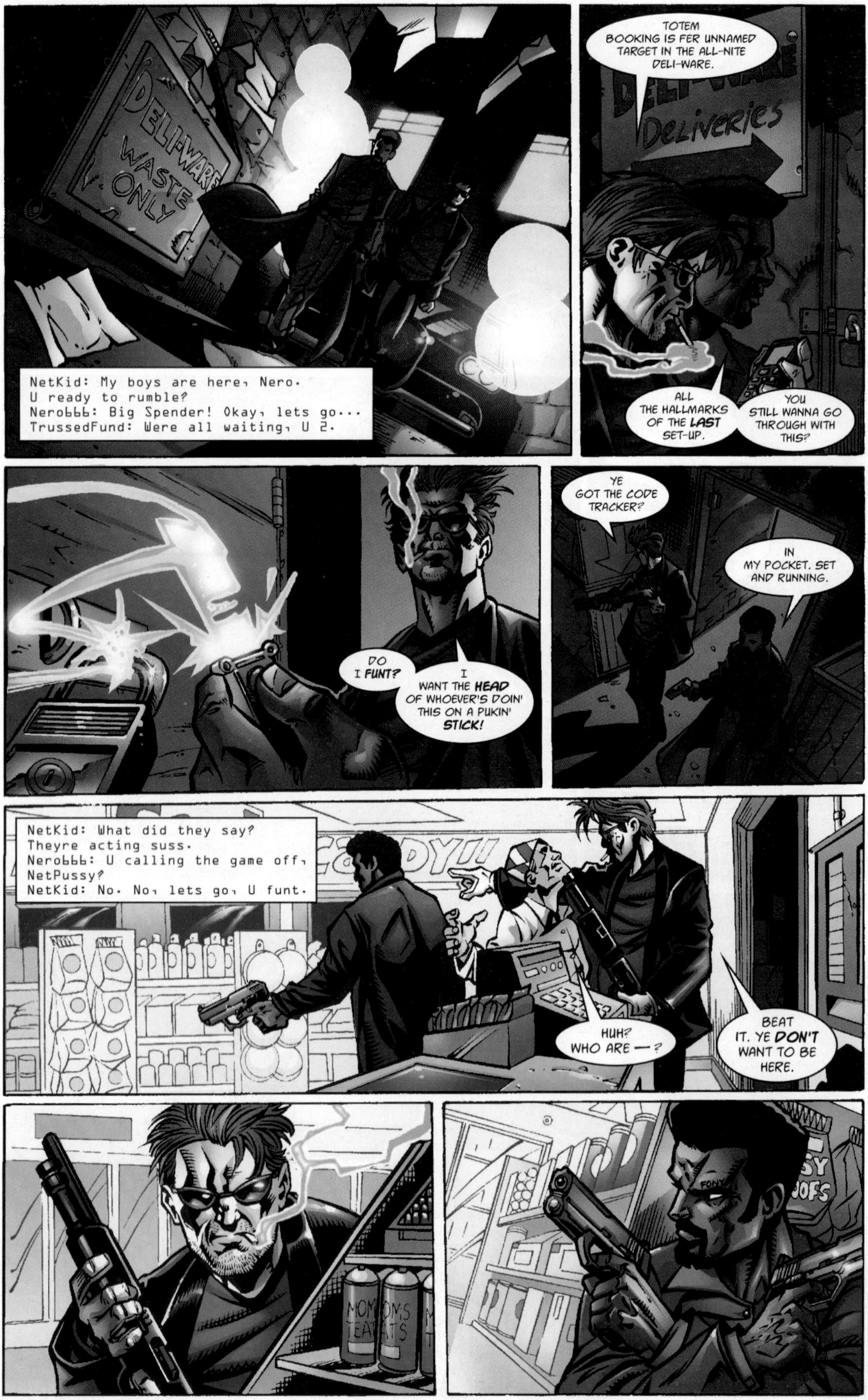
NetKid: My boys are here, Nero.
U ready to rumble?
Nero666: Big Spender! Okay, lets go...
TrussedFund: Were all waiting, U 2.
DELI-WARE WASTE ONLY
TOTEM BOOKING IS FER UNNAMED TARGET IN THE ALL-NITE DELI-WARE.
DELI-WARE Deliveries
ALL THE HALLMARKS OF THE LAST SET-UP.
YOU STILL WANNA GO THROUGH WITH THIS?
DO I FUNT?
I WANT THE HEAD OF WHOEVER'S DOIN' THIS ON A PUKIN' STICK!
YE GOT THE CODE TRACKER?
IN MY POCKET. SET AND RUNNING.
NetKid: What did they say?
Theyre acting suss.
Nero666: U calling the game off,
NetPussy?
NetKid: No. No, lets go, U funt.
HUH? WHO ARE — ?
BEAT IT. YE DON'T WANT TO BE HERE.

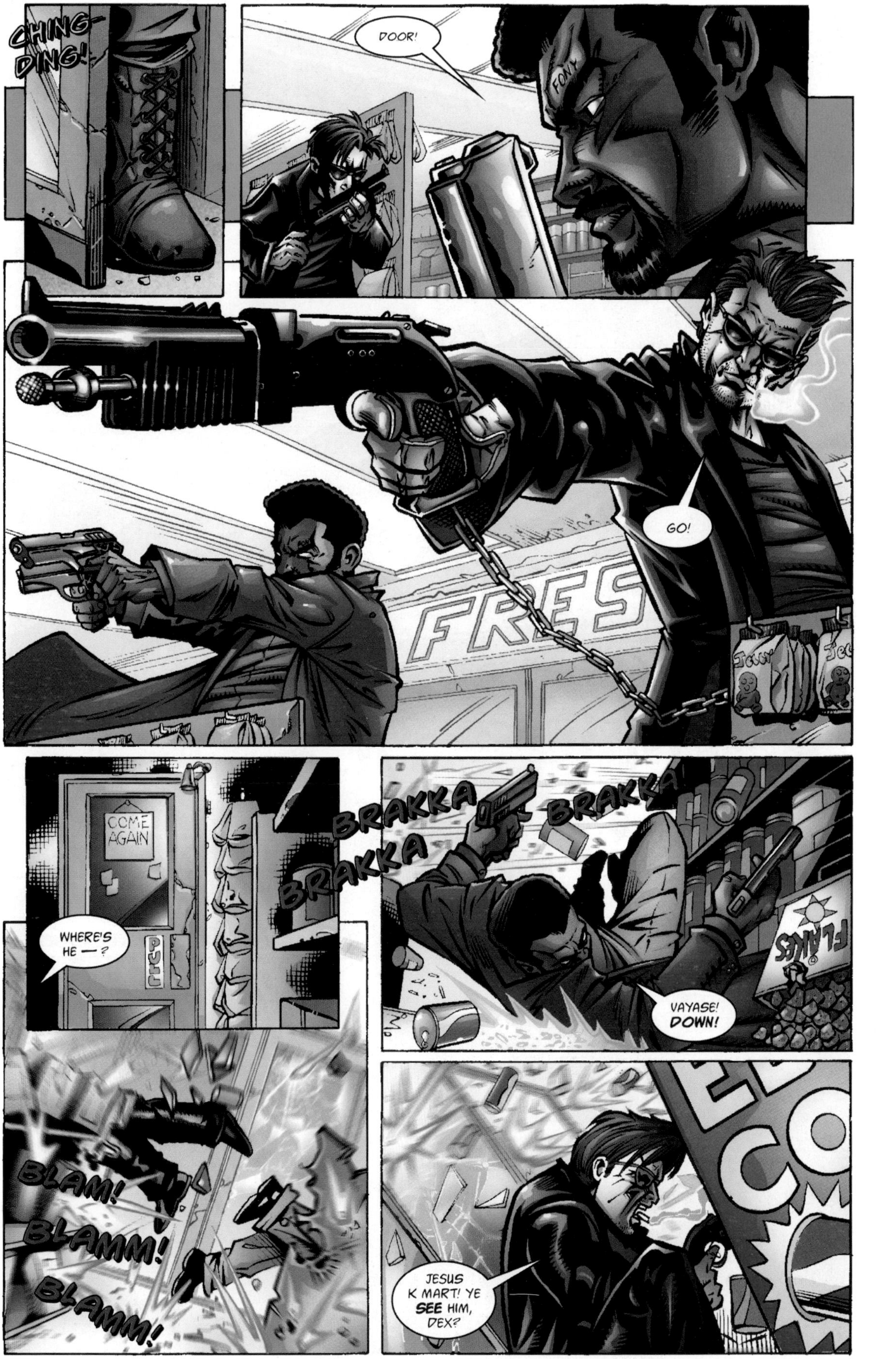
CHING-DING!
DOOR!
FONY
GO!
FRES
COME AGAIN
PULL
WHERE'S HE — ?
BRAKKA
BRAKKA
BRAKKA
FLAKES
VAYASE! DOWN!
BLAM!
BLAMM!
BLAMM!
JESUS K MART! YE SEE HIM, DEX?

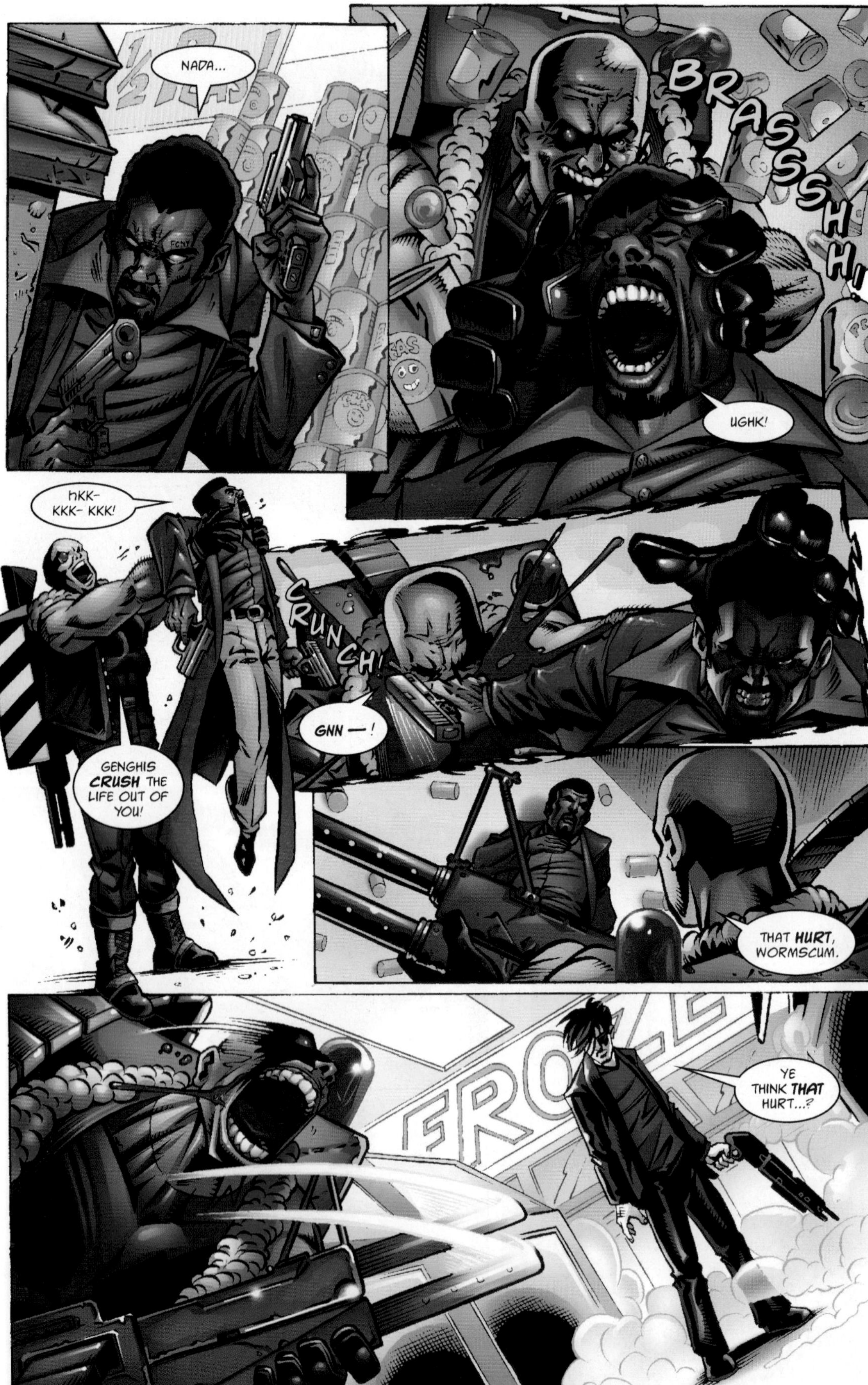
NADA...
BRASSSH!
UGHK!
hKK-
KKK- KKK!
CRUNCH!
GNN —!
GENGHIS CRUSH THE LIFE OUT OF YOU!
THAT HURT, WORMSCUM.
YE THINK THAT HURT...?

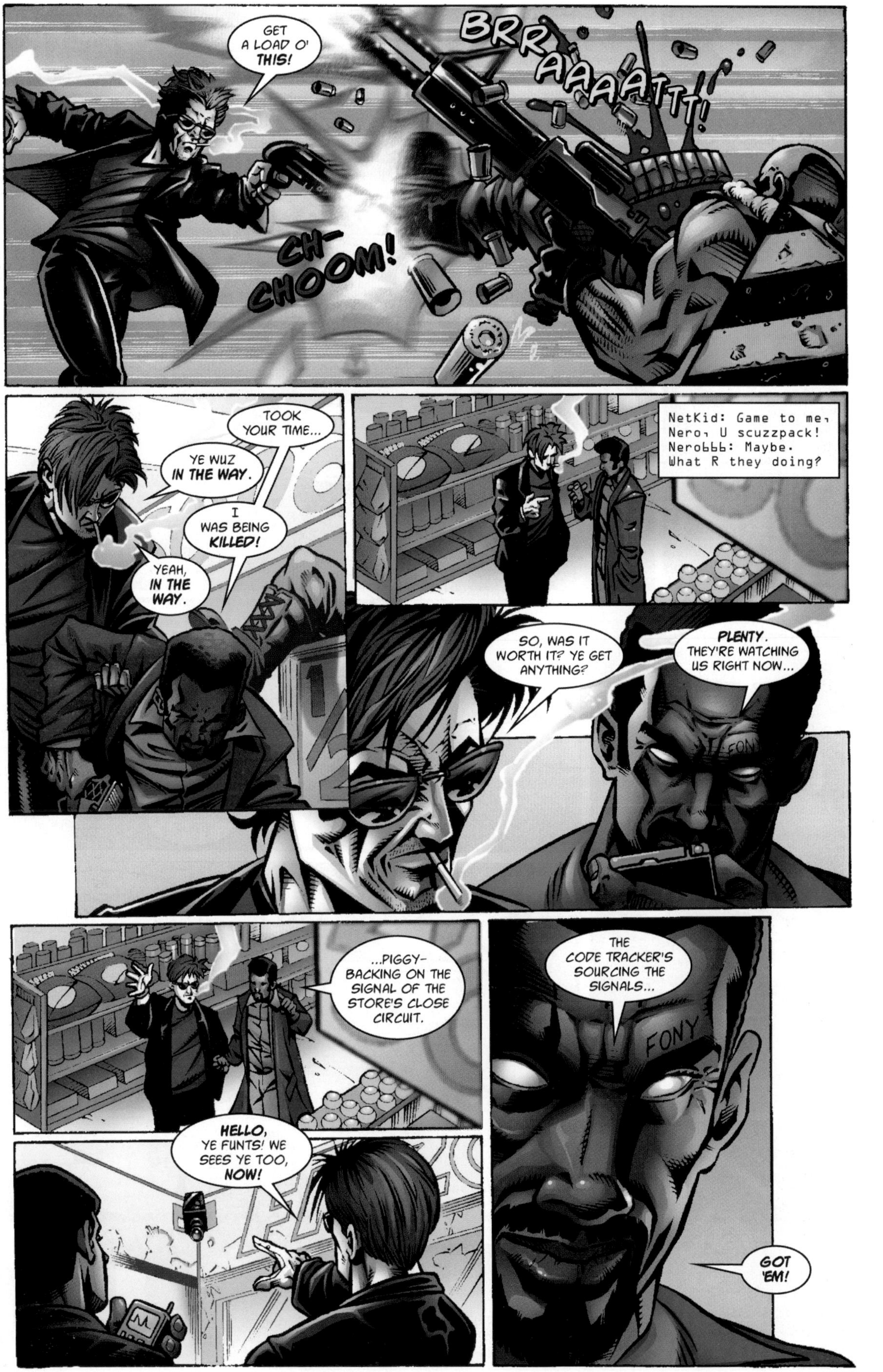
GET A LOAD O' THIS!
BRRAAAATTT!
CH-CHOOM!
TOOK YOUR TIME...
YE WUZ IN THE WAY.
I WAS BEING KILLED!
YEAH, IN THE WAY.
NetKid: Game to me, Nero, U scuzzpack!
Nero666: Maybe. What R they doing?
SO, WAS IT WORTH IT? YE GET ANYTHING?
PLENTY. THEY'RE WATCHING US RIGHT NOW...
...PIGGY-BACKING ON THE SIGNAL OF THE STORE'S CLOSE CIRCUIT.
HELLO, YE FUNTS! WE SEES YE TOO, NOW!
THE CODE TRACKER'S SOURCING THE SIGNALS...
FONY
GOT 'EM!

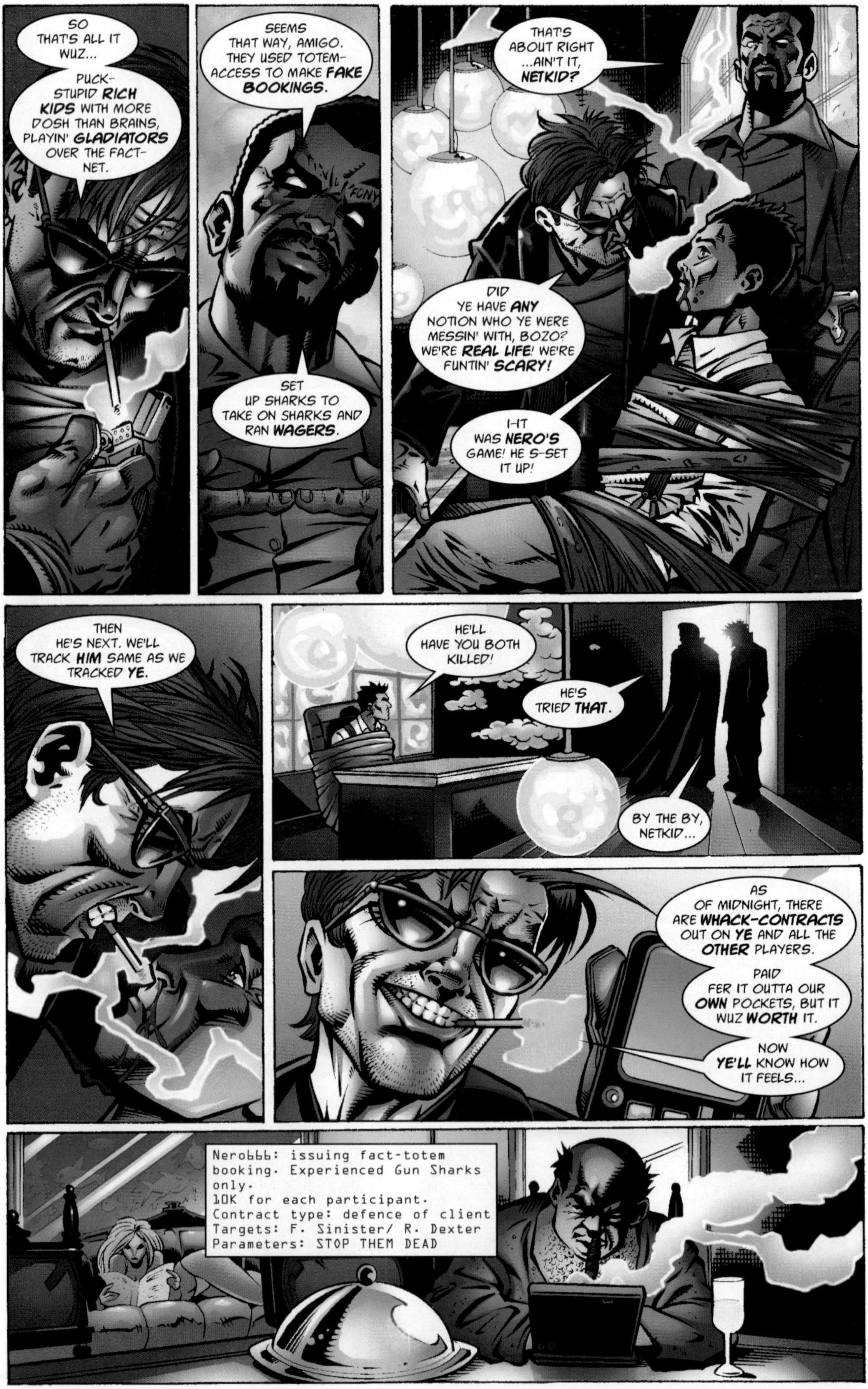

SO THAT'S ALL IT WUZ...
PUCK-STUPID RICH KIDS WITH MORE DOSH THAN BRAINS, PLAYIN' GLADIATORS OVER THE FACT-NET.
SEEMS THAT WAY, AMIGO. THEY USED TOTEM-ACCESS TO MAKE FAKE BOOKINGS.
SET UP SHARKS TO TAKE ON SHARKS AND RAN WAGERS.
THAT'S ABOUT RIGHT ...AIN'T IT, NETKID?
DID YE HAVE ANY NOTION WHO YE WERE MESSIN' WITH, BOZO? WE'RE REAL LIFE! WE'RE FUNTIN' SCARY!
I-IT WAS NERO'S GAME! HE S-SET IT UP!
THEN HE'S NEXT. WE'LL TRACK HIM SAME AS WE TRACKED YE.
HE'LL HAVE YOU BOTH KILLED!
HE'S TRIED THAT.
BY THE BY, NETKID...
AS OF MIDNIGHT, THERE ARE WHACK-CONTRACTS OUT ON YE AND ALL THE OTHER PLAYERS.
PAID FER IT OUTTA OUR OWN POCKETS, BUT IT WUZ WORTH IT.
NOW YE'LL KNOW HOW IT FEELS...
Nero666: issuing fact-totem booking. Experienced Gun Sharks only.
10K for each participant.
Contract type: defence of client
Targets: F. Sinister/ R. Dexter
Parameters: STOP THEM DEAD

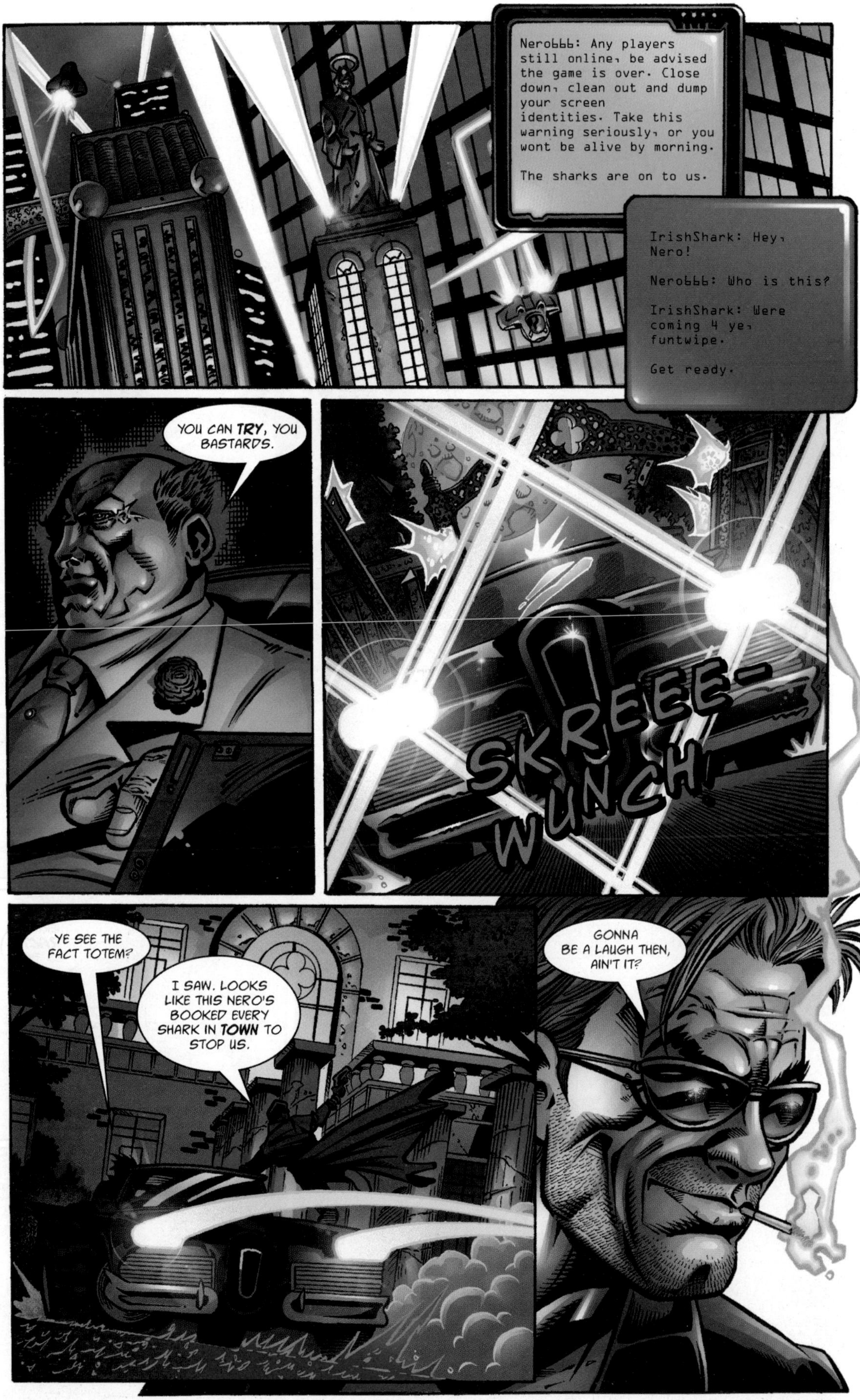
Nero666: Any players still online, be advised the game is over. Close down, clean out and dump your screen identities. Take this warning seriously, or you wont be alive by morning.
The sharks are on to us.
IrishShark: Hey, Nero!
Nero666: Who is this?
IrishShark: Were coming 4 ye, funtwipe.
Get ready.
YOU CAN TRY, YOU BASTARDS.
SKREEE- WUNCH!
YE SEE THE FACT TOTEM?
I SAW. LOOKS LIKE THIS NERO'S BOOKED EVERY SHARK IN TOWN TO STOP US.
GONNA BE A LAUGH THEN, AIN'T IT?

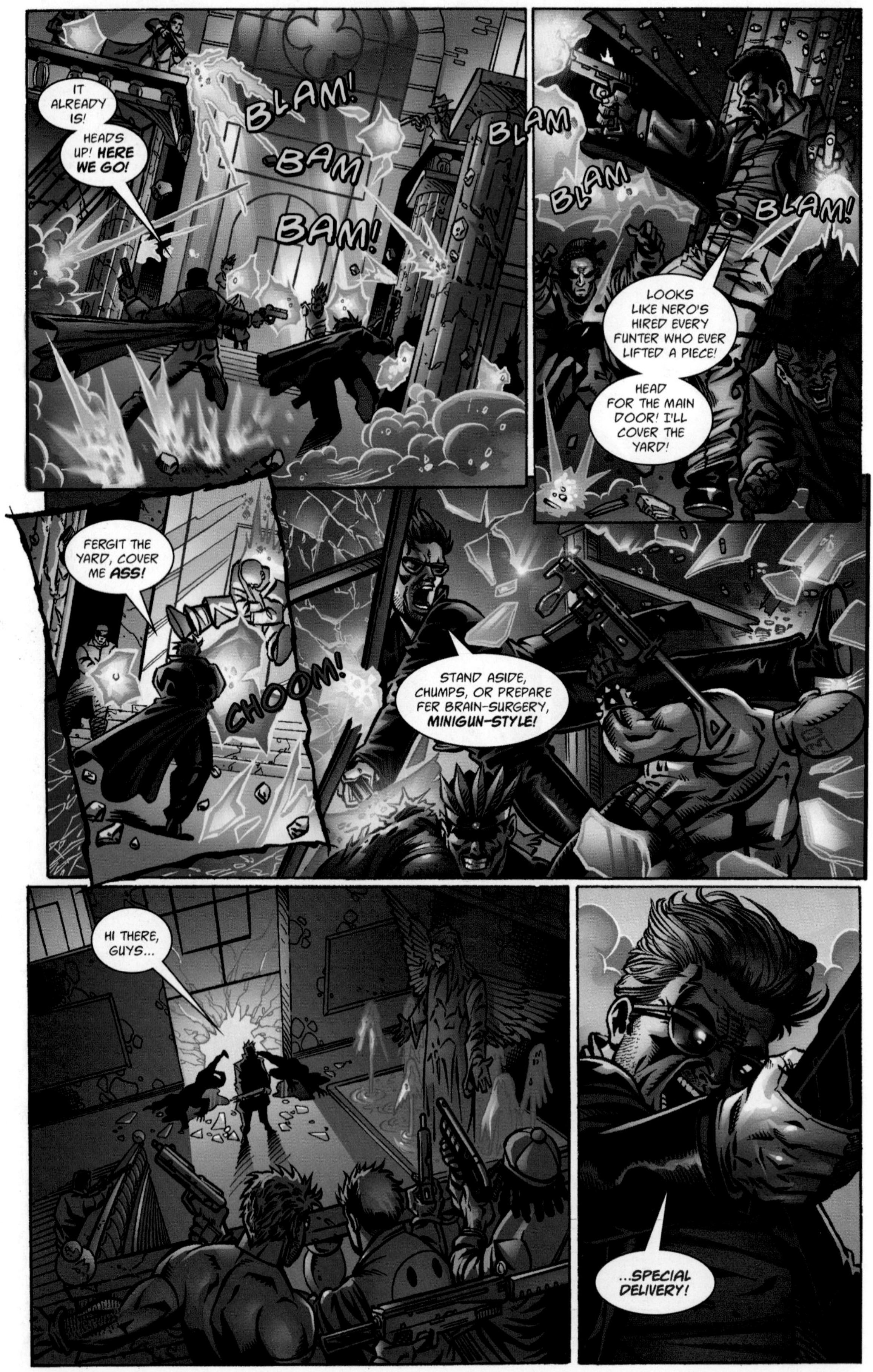
IT ALREADY IS!
HEADS UP! HERE WE GO!
BLAM!
BAM
BAM!
BLAM
BLAM
BLAM!
LOOKS LIKE NERO'S HIRED EVERY FUNTER WHO EVER LIFTED A PIECE!
HEAD FOR THE MAIN DOOR! I'LL COVER THE YARD!
FERGIT THE YARD, COVER ME ASS!
CHOOM!
STAND ASIDE, CHUMPS, OR PREPARE FER BRAIN-SURGERY, MINIGUN-STYLE!
HI THERE, GUYS...
...SPECIAL DELIVERY!

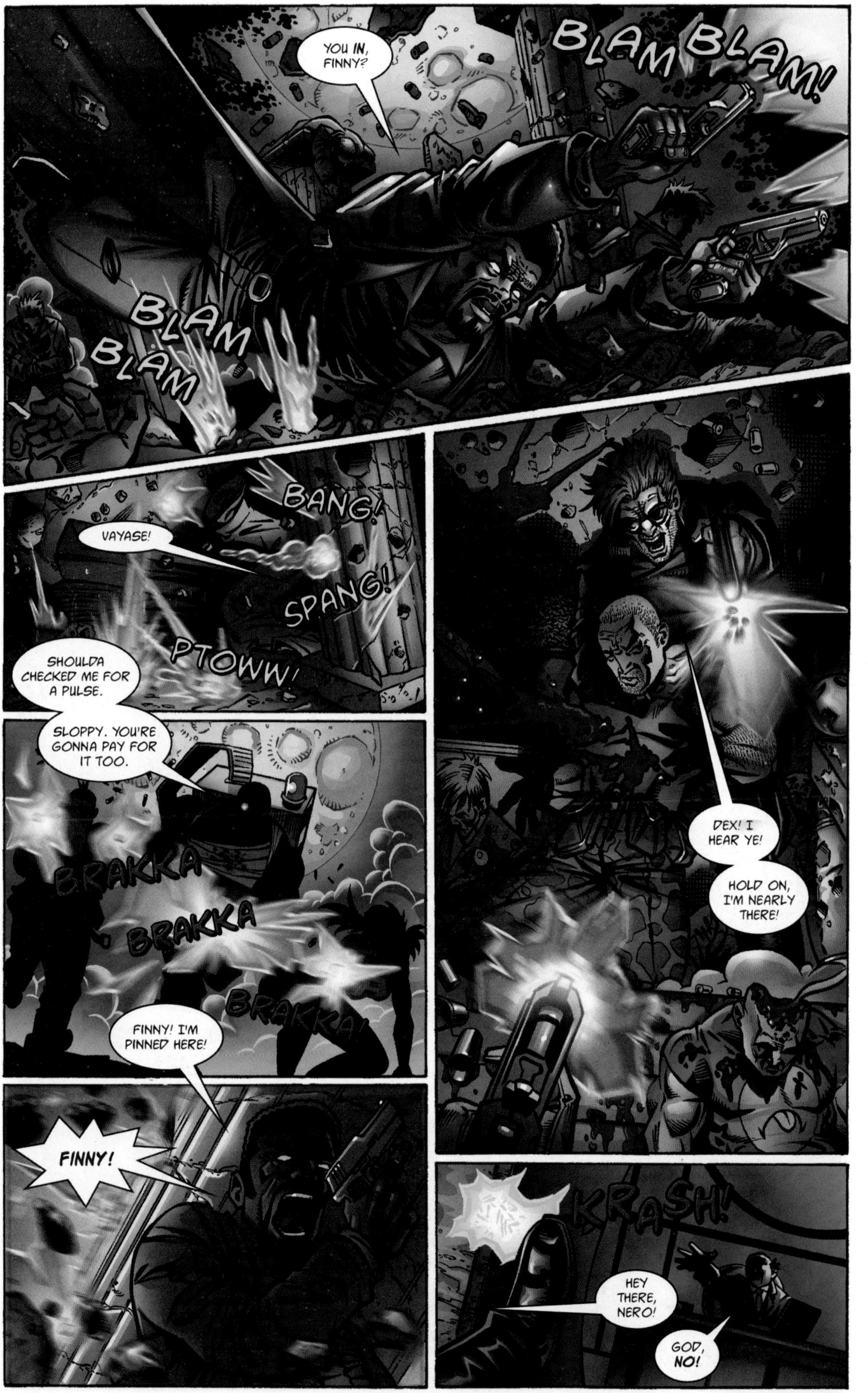
YOU IN, FINNY?
BLAM BLAM!
BLAM BLAM
BANG!
VAYASE!
SPANG!
PTOWW!
SHOULDA CHECKED ME FOR A PULSE.
SLOPPY. YOU'RE GONNA PAY FOR IT TOO.
BRAKKA
BRAKKA
BRAKKA!
FINNY! I'M PINNED HERE!
FINNY!
DEX! I HEAR YE!
HOLD ON, I'M NEARLY THERE!
KRASH!
HEY THERE, NERO!
GOD, NO!

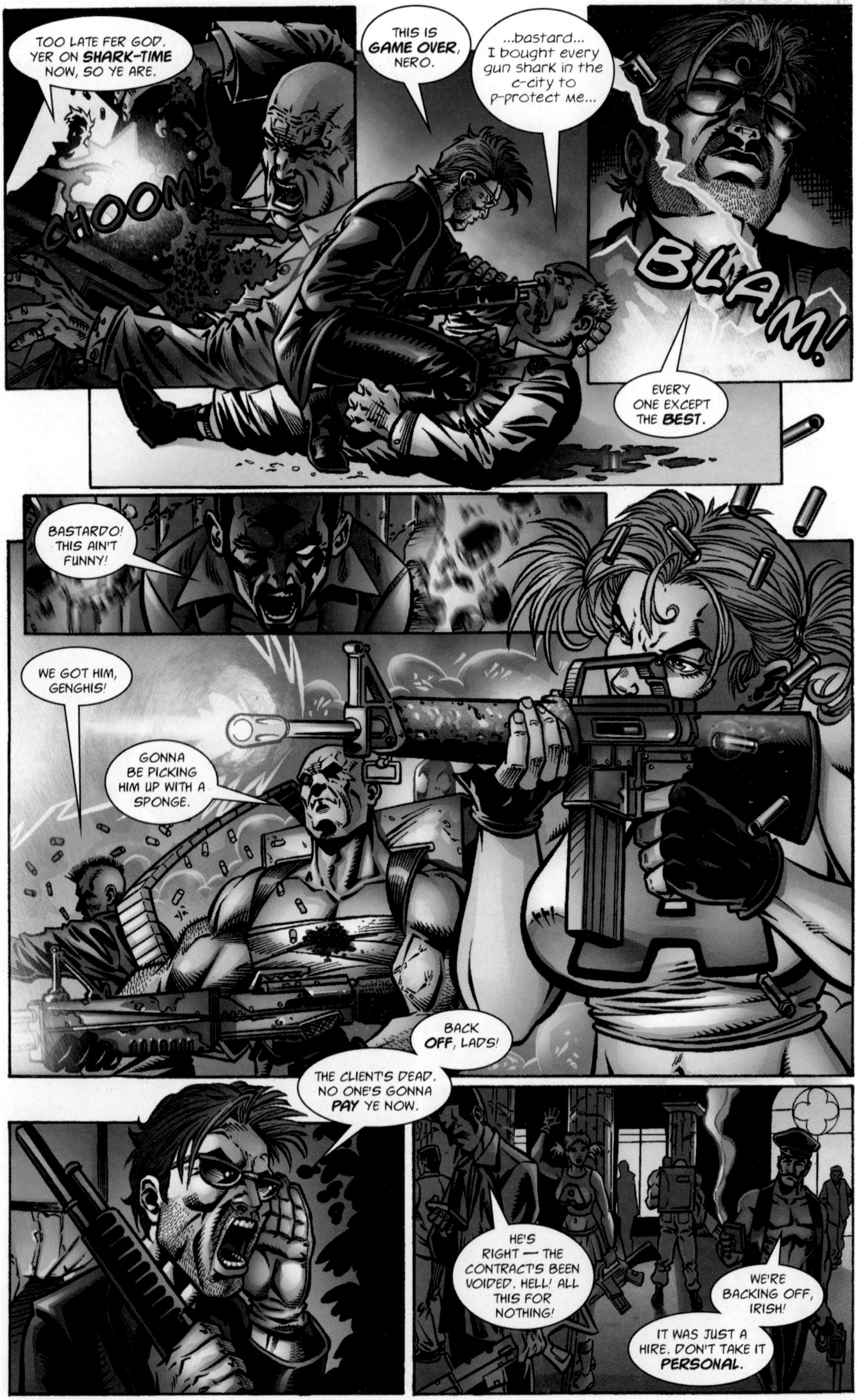

TOO LATE FER GOD. YER ON SHARK-TIME NOW, SO YE ARE.
CHOOM!
THIS IS GAME OVER, NERO.
...bastard... I bought every gun shark in the c-city to p-protect me...
BLAM!
EVERY ONE EXCEPT THE BEST.
BASTARDO! THIS AIN'T FUNNY!
WE GOT HIM, GENGHIS!
GONNA BE PICKING HIM UP WITH A SPONGE.
BACK OFF, LADS!
THE CLIENT'S DEAD. NO ONE'S GONNA PAY YE NOW.
HE'S RIGHT — THE CONTRACT'S BEEN VOIDED. HELL! ALL THIS FOR NOTHING!
WE'RE BACKING OFF, IRISH!
IT WAS JUST A HIRE. DON'T TAKE IT PERSONAL.

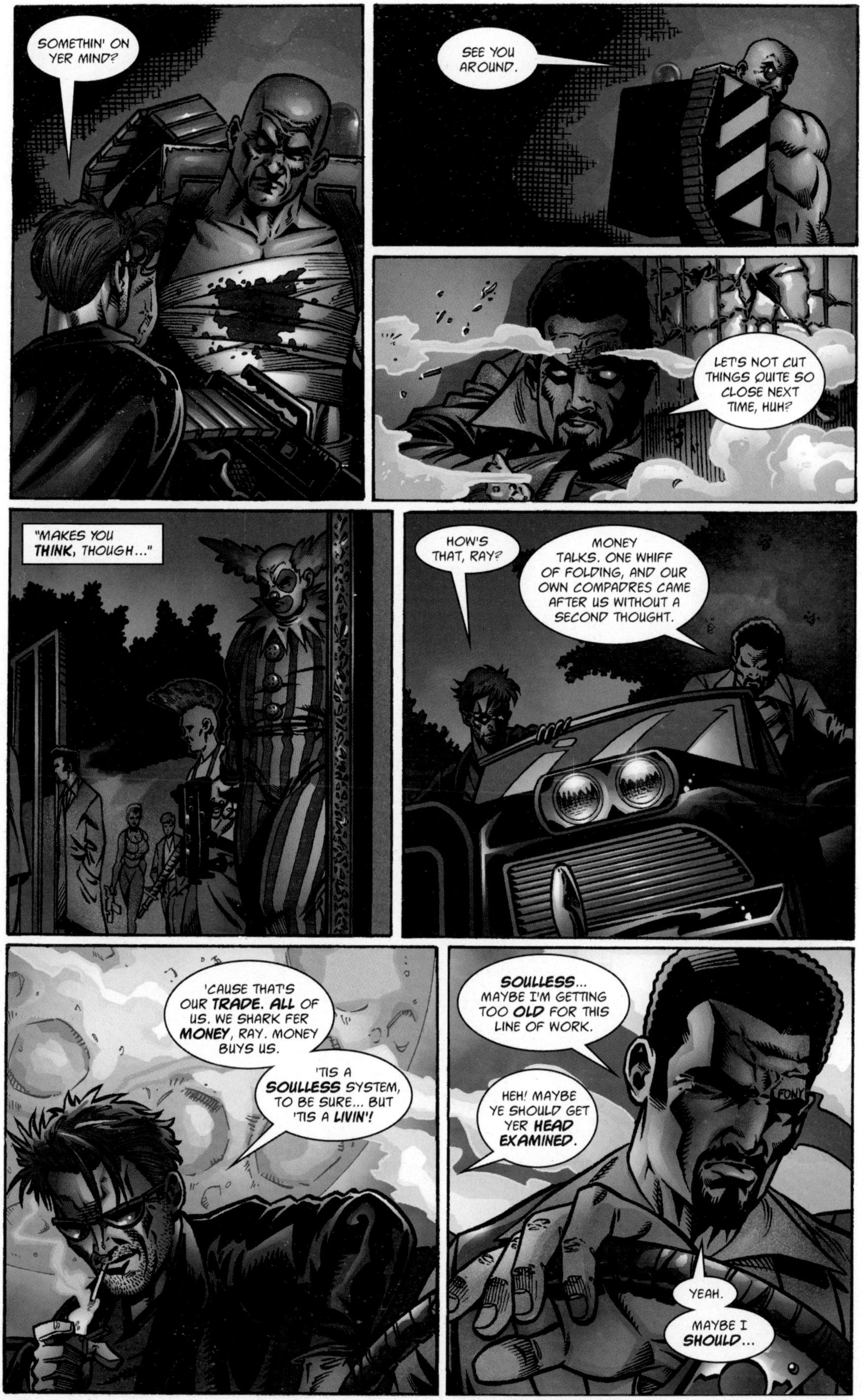
SOMETHIN' ON YER MIND?
SEE YOU AROUND.
LET'S NOT CUT THINGS QUITE SO CLOSE NEXT TIME, HUH?
"MAKES YOU THINK, THOUGH..."
HOW'S THAT, RAY?
MONEY TALKS. ONE WHIFF OF FOLDING, AND OUR OWN COMPADRES CAME AFTER US WITHOUT A SECOND THOUGHT.
'CAUSE THAT'S OUR TRADE. ALL OF US. WE SHARK FER MONEY, RAY. MONEY BUYS US.
'TIS A SOULLESS SYSTEM, TO BE SURE... BUT 'TIS A LIVIN'!
SOULLESS... MAYBE I'M GETTING TOO OLD FOR THIS LINE OF WORK.
HEH! MAYBE YE SHOULD GET YER HEAD EXAMINED.
YEAH.
MAYBE I SHOULD...

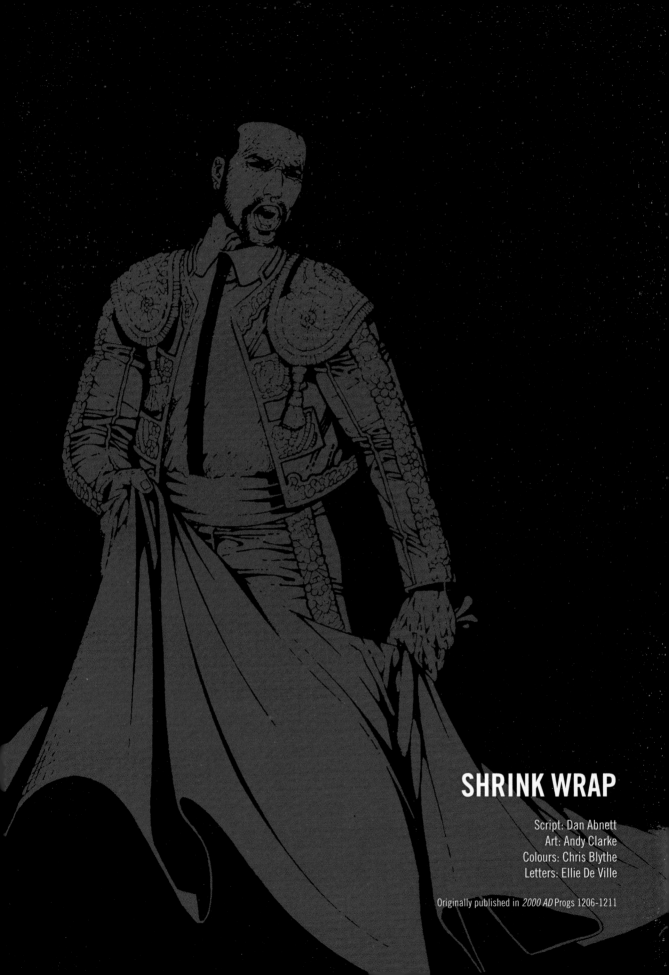

SHRINK WRAP

Script: Dan Abnett
Art: Andy Clarke
Colours: Chris Blythe
Letters: Ellie De Ville

Originally published in *2000 AD* Progs 1206-1211

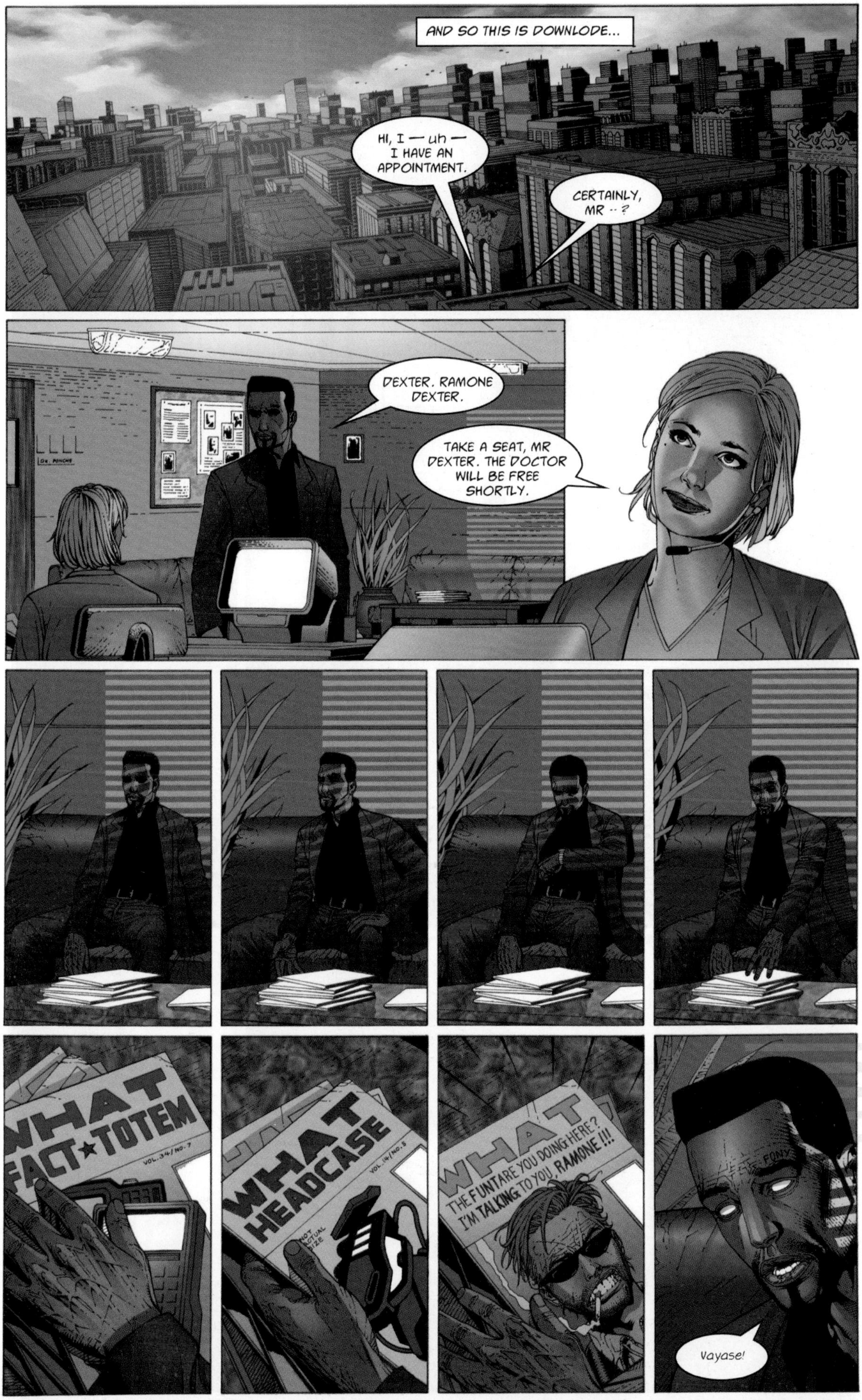
AND SO THIS IS DOWNLODE...
HI, I — uh — I HAVE AN APPOINTMENT.
CERTAINLY, MR -- ?
DEXTER. RAMONE DEXTER.
TAKE A SEAT, MR DEXTER. THE DOCTOR WILL BE FREE SHORTLY.
WHAT
FACT★TOTEM
VOL.34/NO.7
WHAT
HEADCASE
VOL.14/NO.5
NOT ACTUAL SIZE
WHAT
THE FUNT ARE YOU DOING HERE? I'M TALKING TO YOU, RAMONE!!!
Vayase!

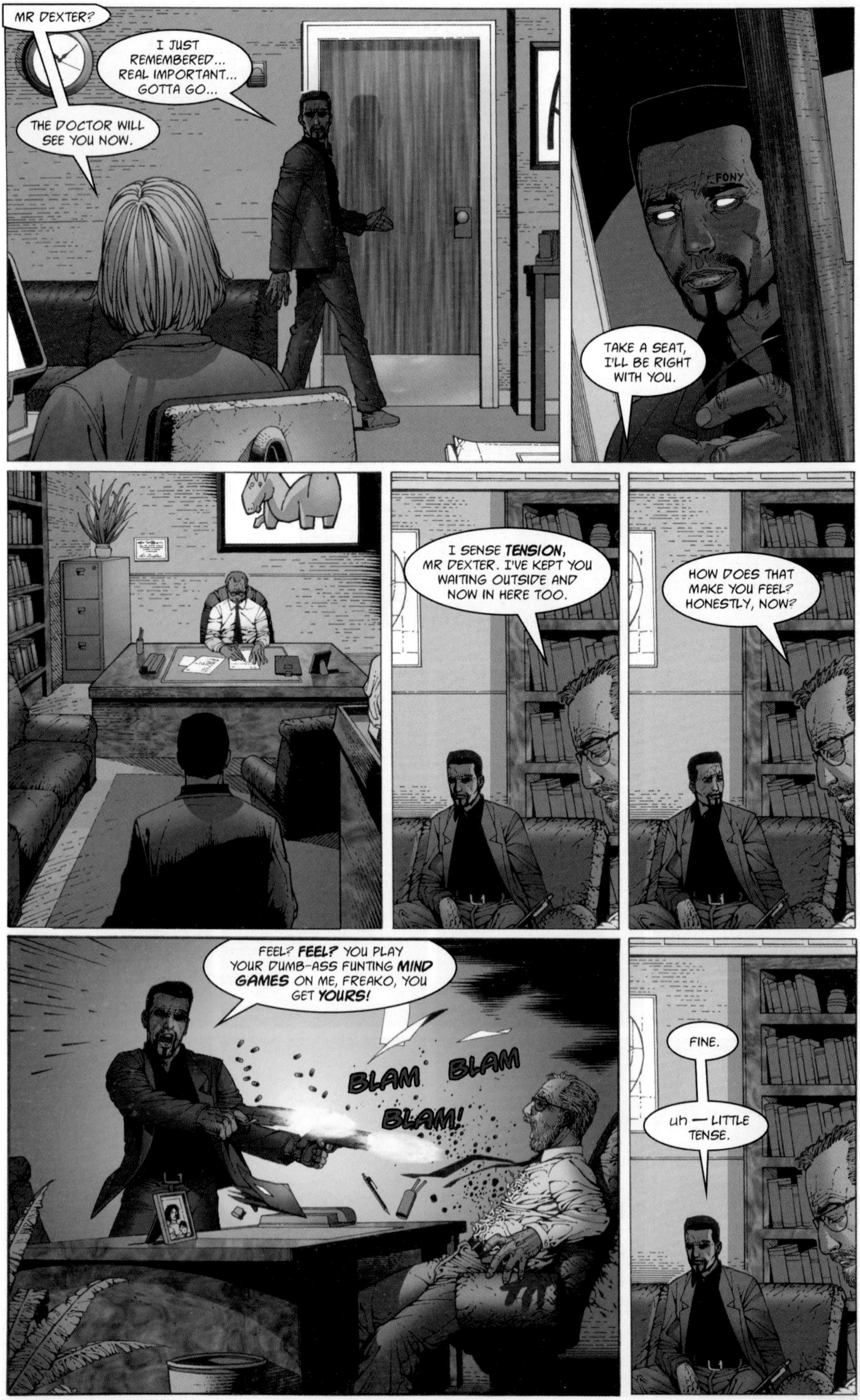
MR DEXTER?
I JUST REMEMBERED... REAL IMPORTANT... GOTTA GO...
THE DOCTOR WILL SEE YOU NOW.
FONY
TAKE A SEAT, I'LL BE RIGHT WITH YOU.
I SENSE TENSION, MR DEXTER. I'VE KEPT YOU WAITING OUTSIDE AND NOW IN HERE TOO.
HOW DOES THAT MAKE YOU FEEL? HONESTLY, NOW?
FEEL? FEEL? YOU PLAY YOUR DUMB-ASS FUNTING MIND GAMES ON ME, FREAKO, YOU GET YOURS!
BLAM BLAM BLAM!
FINE.
uh — LITTLE TENSE.

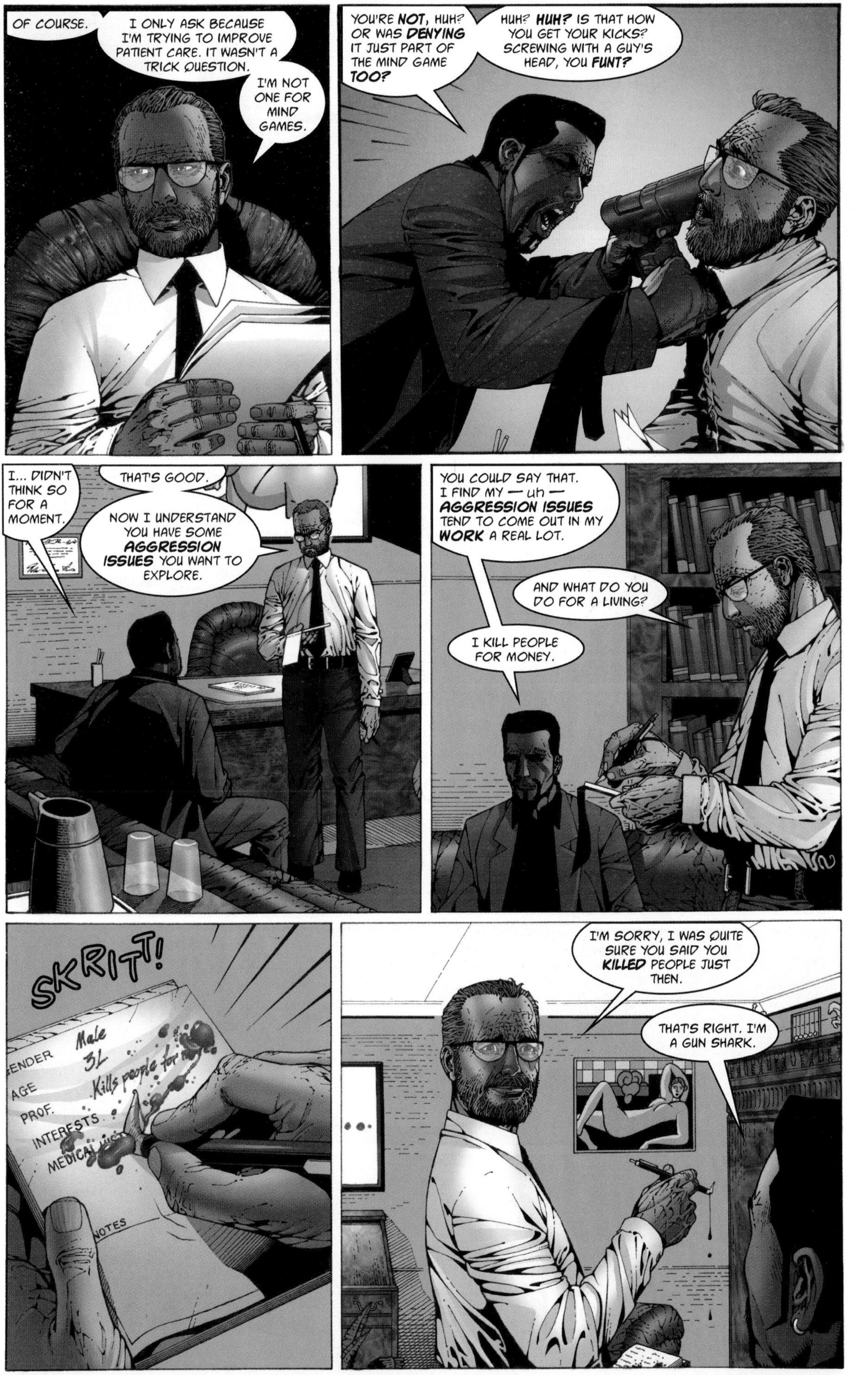
OF COURSE.
I ONLY ASK BECAUSE I'M TRYING TO IMPROVE PATIENT CARE. IT WASN'T A TRICK QUESTION.
I'M NOT ONE FOR MIND GAMES.
YOU'RE NOT, HUH? OR WAS DENYING IT JUST PART OF THE MIND GAME TOO?
HUH? HUH? IS THAT HOW YOU GET YOUR KICKS? SCREWING WITH A GUY'S HEAD, YOU FUNT?
I... DIDN'T THINK SO FOR A MOMENT.
THAT'S GOOD.
NOW I UNDERSTAND YOU HAVE SOME AGGRESSION ISSUES YOU WANT TO EXPLORE.
YOU COULD SAY THAT. I FIND MY — uh — AGGRESSION ISSUES TEND TO COME OUT IN MY WORK A REAL LOT.
AND WHAT DO YOU DO FOR A LIVING?
I KILL PEOPLE FOR MONEY.
SKRITT!
GENDER Male
AGE 3L
PROF. Kills people for
INTERESTS
MEDICAL
NOTES
I'M SORRY, I WAS QUITE SURE YOU SAID YOU KILLED PEOPLE JUST THEN.
THAT'S RIGHT. I'M A GUN SHARK.

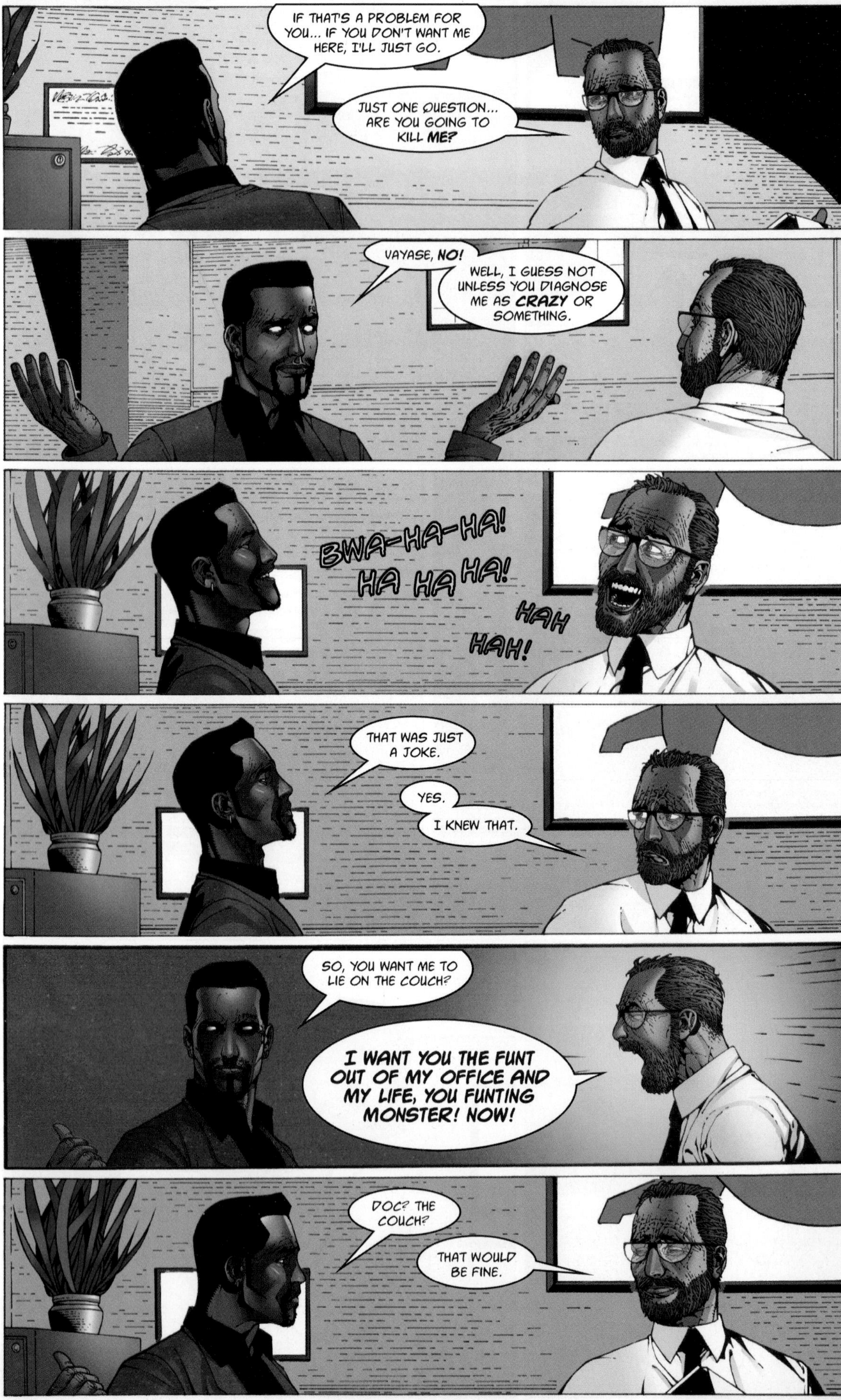

IF THAT'S A PROBLEM FOR YOU... IF YOU DON'T WANT ME HERE, I'LL JUST GO.
JUST ONE QUESTION... ARE YOU GOING TO KILL ME?
VAYASE, NO!
WELL, I GUESS NOT UNLESS YOU DIAGNOSE ME AS CRAZY OR SOMETHING.
BWA-HA-HA! HA HA HA!
HAH HAH!
THAT WAS JUST A JOKE.
YES.
I KNEW THAT.
SO, YOU WANT ME TO LIE ON THE COUCH?
I WANT YOU THE FUNT OUT OF MY OFFICE AND MY LIFE, YOU FUNTING MONSTER! NOW!
DOC? THE COUCH?
THAT WOULD BE FINE.

SO... RAMONE... YOU GREW UP IN **SPANISHTOWN**. WHAT IS YOUR EARLIEST MEMORY?

"THE TV."

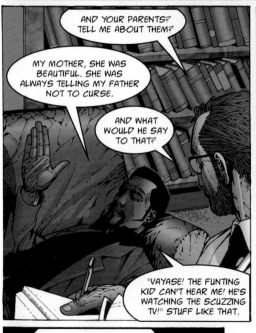

AND YOUR PARENTS? TELL ME ABOUT THEM?

MY MOTHER, SHE WAS BEAUTIFUL. SHE WAS ALWAYS TELLING MY FATHER NOT TO CURSE.

AND WHAT WOULD HE SAY TO THAT?

"VAYASE! THE FUNTING KID CAN'T HEAR ME! HE'S WATCHING THE SCUZZING TV!" STUFF LIKE THAT.

AND WHAT IS YOUR HAPPIEST MEMORY FROM THAT TIME?

"THE TV."

YOUR FATHER? WHAT DO YOU REMEMBER ABOUT HIM?

HE WAS STRONG. HE FOUGHT BULLS IN THE RING.

AND HE **DIED**.

D-DO PAINFUL EMOTIONAL MEMORIES MAKE YOU V-VIOLENT, RAMONE?

NO. WHY?

J-JUST A STANDARD QUESTION...

SO — uhm — **H-HOW** DID YOUR FATHER DIE?

DEXTER'S FIRST SESSION WITH PSYCHIATRIST PONCKS CONTINUES...

MY FATHER AND MOTHER RAN A CANTINA ON ANGUILA STREET, NEAR LA PLAZA DE TOROS.

BUT HE WAS A BULL-FIGHTER?

"OH YEAH. THAT WAS HIS LIFE. HE WAS A MATADOR ESTUPENDO!"

YAY! YAY! COME ON, TORO! COME ON, CRETINO!

GRAA! GRAA!

VAYASE! TOO SLOW, MY LITTLE TORO!

HA HA! YOU'LL BE A BULL-DANCER LIKE YOUR PAPA ONE DAY, EH, LITTLE RAMONE?

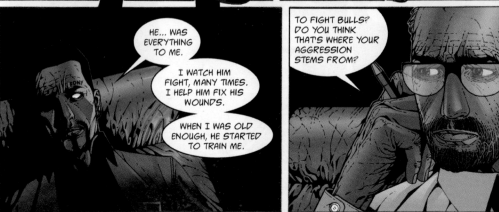

HE... WAS EVERYTHING TO ME.

I WATCH HIM FIGHT, MANY TIMES. I HELP HIM FIX HIS WOUNDS.

WHEN I WAS OLD ENOUGH, HE STARTED TO TRAIN ME.

TO FIGHT BULLS? DO YOU THINK THAT'S WHERE YOUR AGGRESSION STEMS FROM?

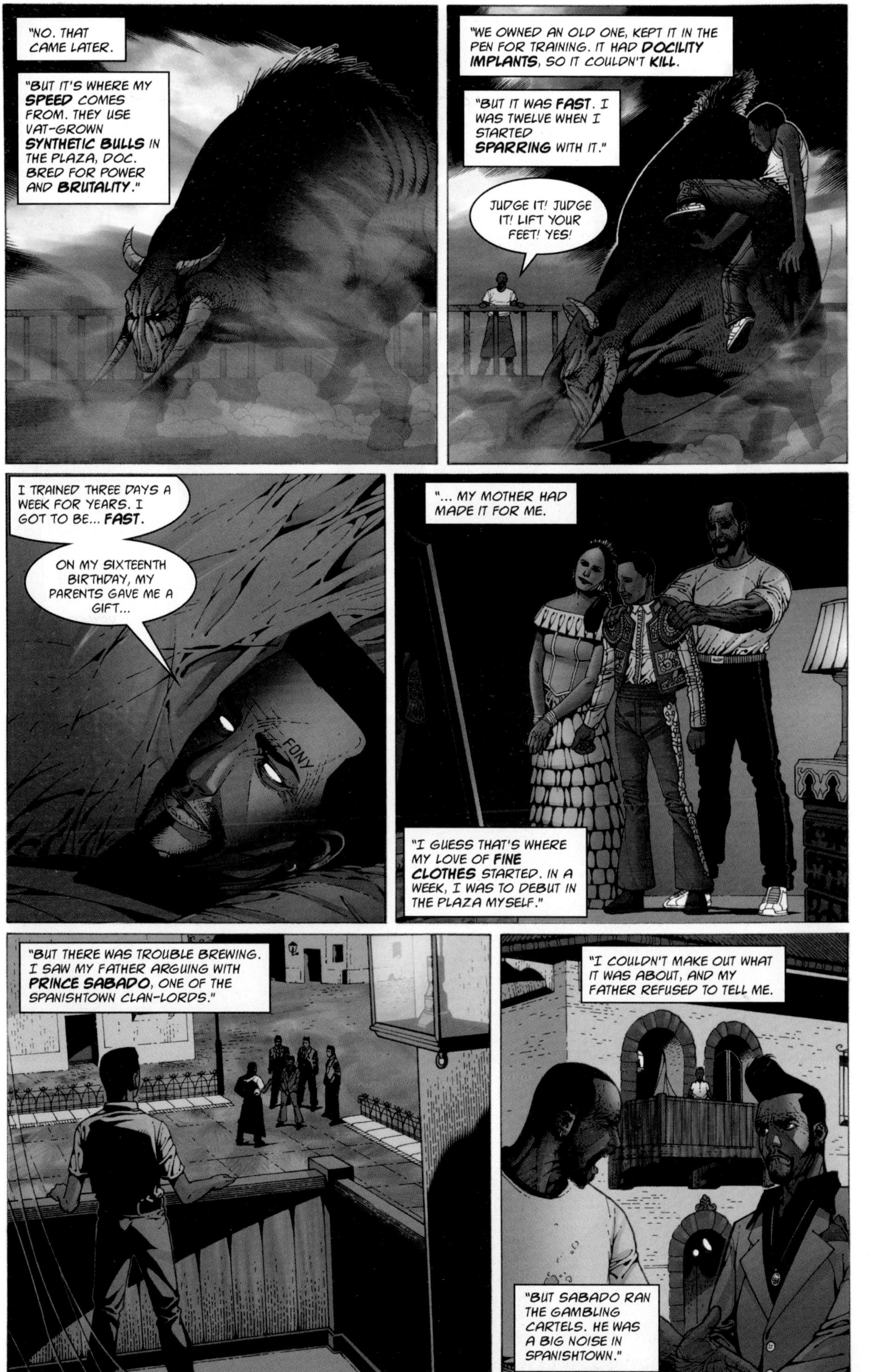
"NO. THAT CAME LATER.
"BUT IT'S WHERE MY SPEED COMES FROM. THEY USE VAT-GROWN SYNTHETIC BULLS IN THE PLAZA, DOC. BRED FOR POWER AND BRUTALITY."
"WE OWNED AN OLD ONE, KEPT IT IN THE PEN FOR TRAINING. IT HAD DOCILITY IMPLANTS, SO IT COULDN'T KILL.
"BUT IT WAS FAST. I WAS TWELVE WHEN I STARTED SPARRING WITH IT."
JUDGE IT! JUDGE IT! LIFT YOUR FEET! YES!
I TRAINED THREE DAYS A WEEK FOR YEARS. I GOT TO BE... FAST.
ON MY SIXTEENTH BIRTHDAY, MY PARENTS GAVE ME A GIFT...
FONY
"... MY MOTHER HAD MADE IT FOR ME.
"I GUESS THAT'S WHERE MY LOVE OF FINE CLOTHES STARTED. IN A WEEK, I WAS TO DEBUT IN THE PLAZA MYSELF."
"BUT THERE WAS TROUBLE BREWING. I SAW MY FATHER ARGUING WITH PRINCE SABADO, ONE OF THE SPANISHTOWN CLAN-LORDS."
"I COULDN'T MAKE OUT WHAT IT WAS ABOUT, AND MY FATHER REFUSED TO TELL ME.
"BUT SABADO RAN THE GAMBLING CARTELS. HE WAS A BIG NOISE IN SPANISHTOWN."

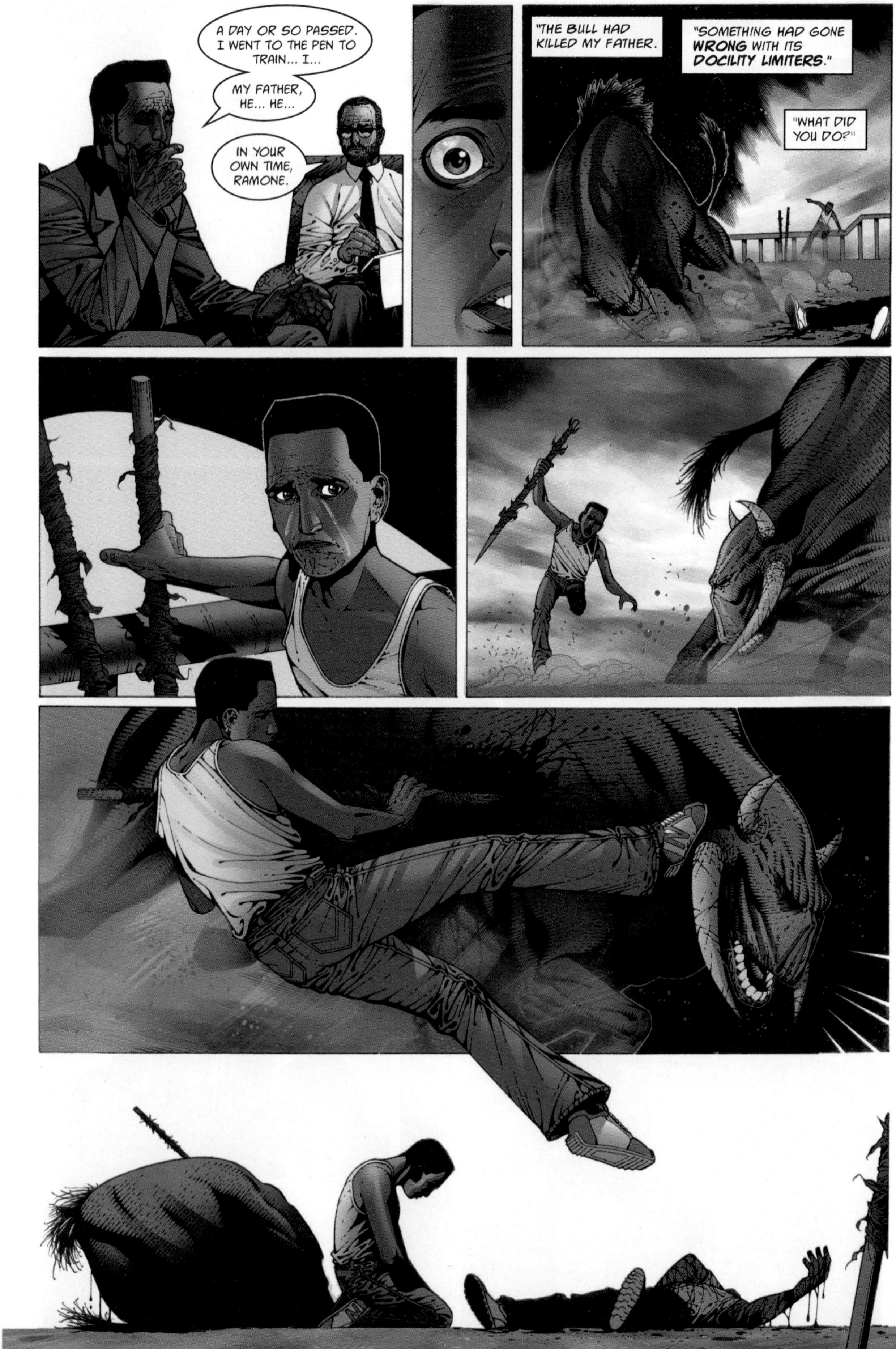
A DAY OR SO PASSED. I WENT TO THE PEN TO TRAIN... I...
MY FATHER, HE... HE...
IN YOUR OWN TIME, RAMONE.
"THE BULL HAD KILLED MY FATHER.
"SOMETHING HAD GONE **WRONG** WITH ITS **DOCILITY LIMITERS**."
"WHAT DID YOU DO?"

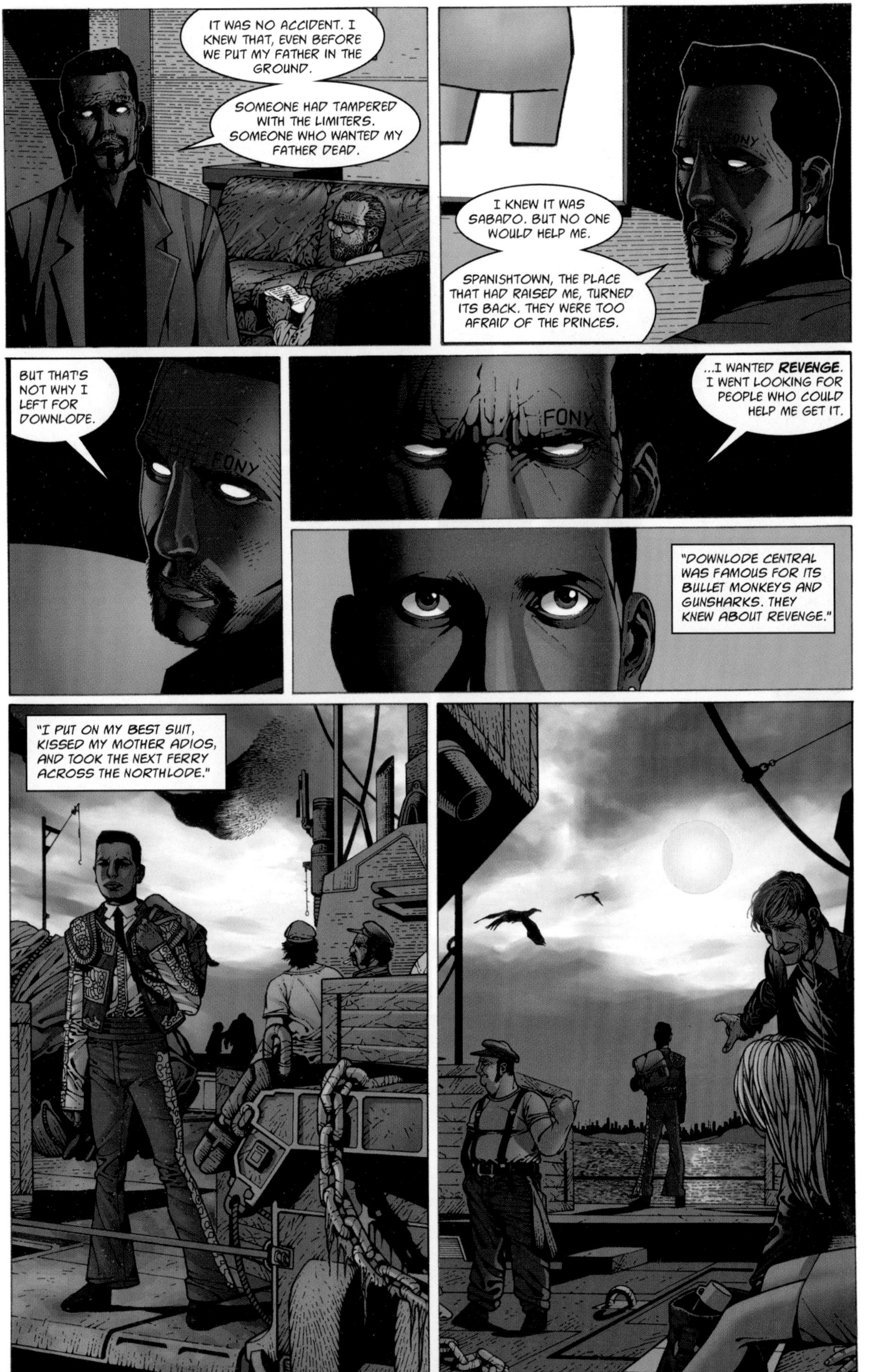
IT WAS NO ACCIDENT. I KNEW THAT, EVEN BEFORE WE PUT MY FATHER IN THE GROUND.
SOMEONE HAD TAMPERED WITH THE LIMITERS. SOMEONE WHO WANTED MY FATHER DEAD.
I KNEW IT WAS SABADO. BUT NO ONE WOULD HELP ME.
SPANISHTOWN, THE PLACE THAT HAD RAISED ME, TURNED ITS BACK. THEY WERE TOO AFRAID OF THE PRINCES.
FONY
BUT THAT'S NOT WHY I LEFT FOR DOWNLODE.
FONY
...I WANTED **REVENGE**. I WENT LOOKING FOR PEOPLE WHO COULD HELP ME GET IT.
"DOWNLODE CENTRAL WAS FAMOUS FOR ITS BULLET MONKEYS AND GUNSHARKS. THEY KNEW ABOUT REVENGE."
"I PUT ON MY BEST SUIT, KISSED MY MOTHER ADIOS, AND TOOK THE NEXT FERRY ACROSS THE NORTHLODE."

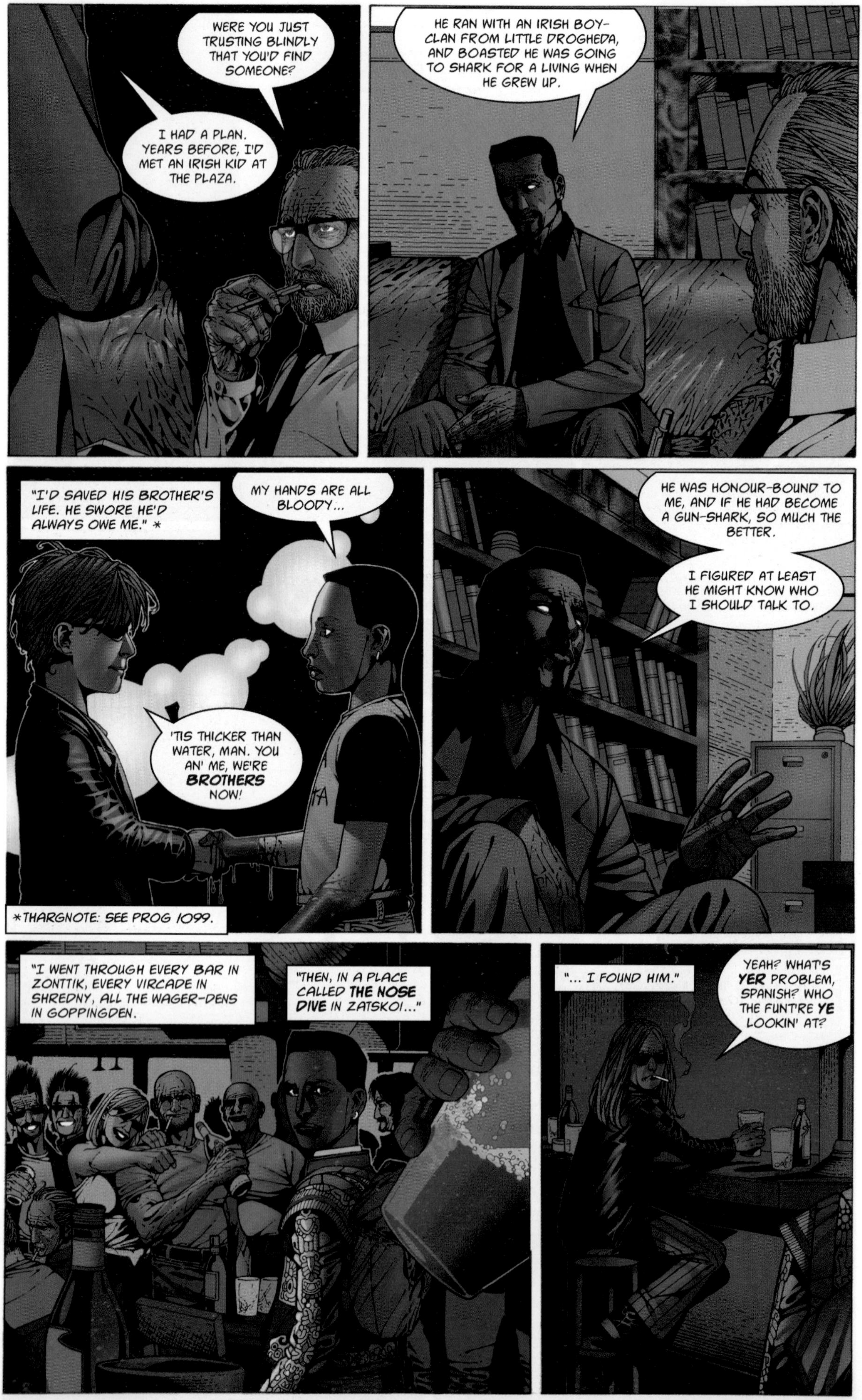
WERE YOU JUST TRUSTING BLINDLY THAT YOU'D FIND SOMEONE?
I HAD A PLAN. YEARS BEFORE, I'D MET AN IRISH KID AT THE PLAZA.
HE RAN WITH AN IRISH BOY-CLAN FROM LITTLE DROGHEDA, AND BOASTED HE WAS GOING TO SHARK FOR A LIVING WHEN HE GREW UP.
"I'D SAVED HIS BROTHER'S LIFE. HE SWORE HE'D ALWAYS OWE ME." *
MY HANDS ARE ALL BLOODY...
'TIS THICKER THAN WATER, MAN. YOU AN' ME, WE'RE **BROTHERS** NOW!
*THARGNOTE: SEE PROG 1099.
HE WAS HONOUR-BOUND TO ME, AND IF HE HAD BECOME A GUN-SHARK, SO MUCH THE BETTER.
I FIGURED AT LEAST HE MIGHT KNOW WHO I SHOULD TALK TO.
"I WENT THROUGH EVERY BAR IN ZONTTIK, EVERY VIRCADE IN SHREDNY, ALL THE WAGER-DENS IN GOPPINGDEN.
"THEN, IN A PLACE CALLED **THE NOSE DIVE** IN ZATSKOI..."
"... I FOUND HIM."
YEAH? WHAT'S **YER** PROBLEM, SPANISH? WHO THE FUNT'RE **YE** LOOKIN' AT?

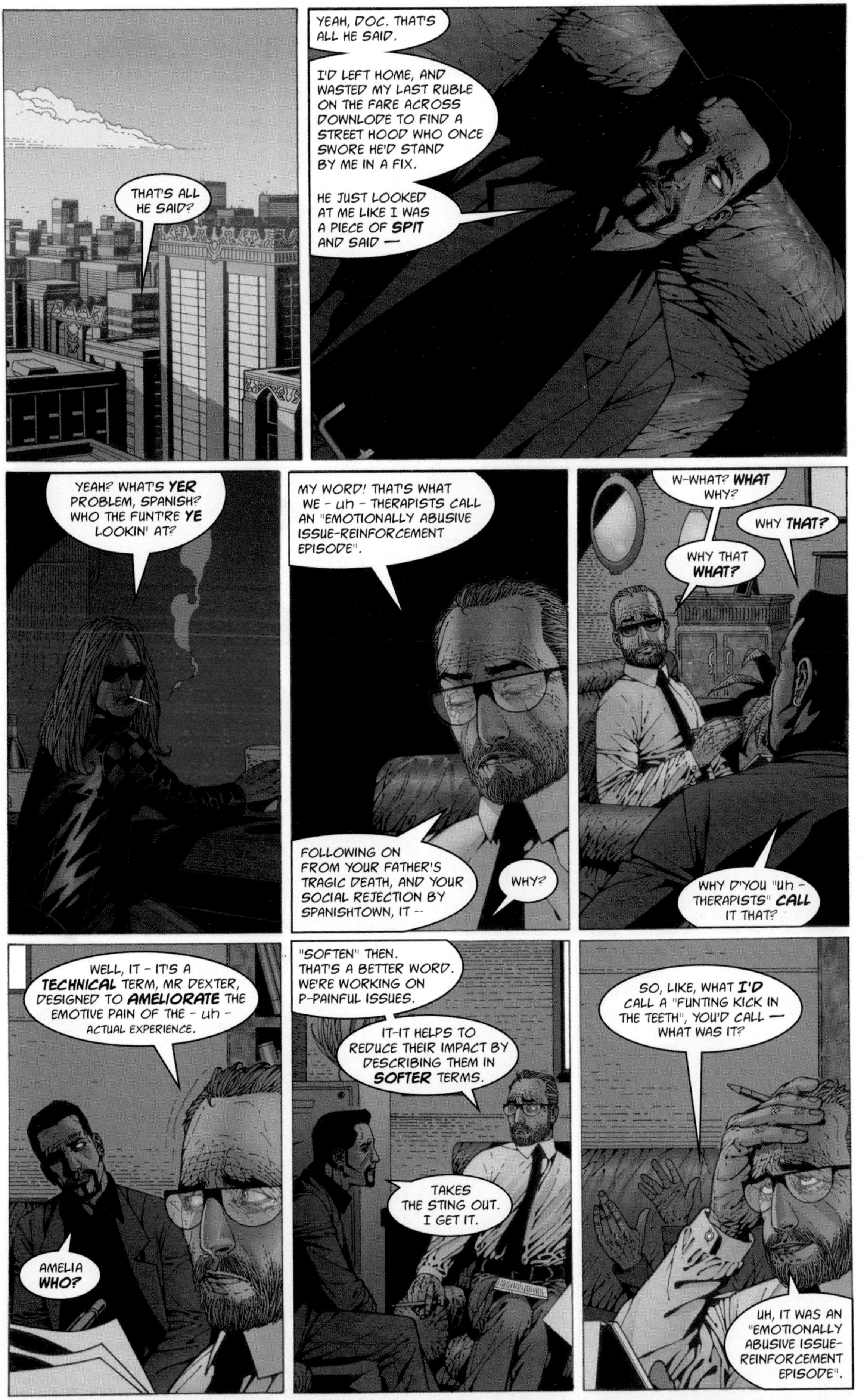
THAT'S ALL HE SAID?
YEAH, DOC. THAT'S ALL HE SAID.
I'D LEFT HOME, AND WASTED MY LAST RUBLE ON THE FARE ACROSS DOWNLODE TO FIND A STREET HOOD WHO ONCE SWORE HE'D STAND BY ME IN A FIX.
HE JUST LOOKED AT ME LIKE I WAS A PIECE OF SPIT AND SAID —
YEAH? WHAT'S YER PROBLEM, SPANISH? WHO THE FUNT'RE YE LOOKIN' AT?
MY WORD! THAT'S WHAT WE - uh - THERAPISTS CALL AN "EMOTIONALLY ABUSIVE ISSUE-REINFORCEMENT EPISODE".
FOLLOWING ON FROM YOUR FATHER'S TRAGIC DEATH, AND YOUR SOCIAL REJECTION BY SPANISHTOWN, IT --
WHY?
W-WHAT? WHAT WHY?
WHY THAT?
WHY THAT WHAT?
WHY D'YOU "uh - THERAPISTS" CALL IT THAT?
WELL, IT - IT'S A TECHNICAL TERM, MR DEXTER, DESIGNED TO AMELIORATE THE EMOTIVE PAIN OF THE - uh - ACTUAL EXPERIENCE.
AMELIA WHO?
"SOFTEN" THEN. THAT'S A BETTER WORD. WE'RE WORKING ON P-PAINFUL ISSUES.
IT-IT HELPS TO REDUCE THEIR IMPACT BY DESCRIBING THEM IN SOFTER TERMS.
TAKES THE STING OUT. I GET IT.
SO, LIKE, WHAT I'D CALL A "FUNTING KICK IN THE TEETH", YOU'D CALL — WHAT WAS IT?
UH, IT WAS AN "EMOTIONALLY ABUSIVE ISSUE-REINFORCEMENT EPISODE".

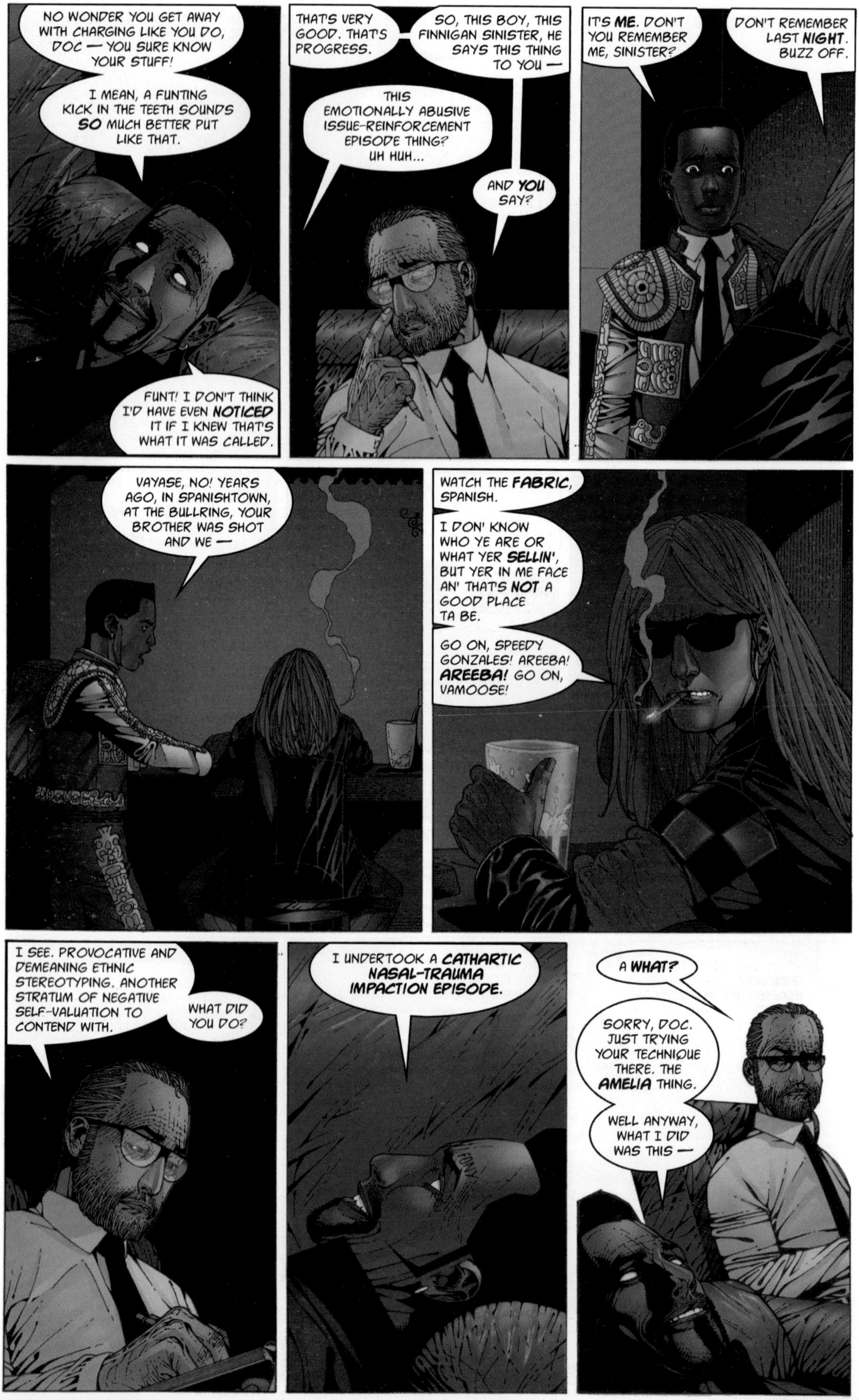
NO WONDER YOU GET AWAY WITH CHARGING LIKE YOU DO, DOC — YOU SURE KNOW YOUR STUFF!
I MEAN, A FUNTING KICK IN THE TEETH SOUNDS SO MUCH BETTER PUT LIKE THAT.
FUNT! I DON'T THINK I'D HAVE EVEN NOTICED IT IF I KNEW THAT'S WHAT IT WAS CALLED.
THAT'S VERY GOOD. THAT'S PROGRESS.
SO, THIS BOY, THIS FINNIGAN SINISTER, HE SAYS THIS THING TO YOU —
THIS EMOTIONALLY ABUSIVE ISSUE-REINFORCEMENT EPISODE THING? UH HUH...
AND YOU SAY?
IT'S ME. DON'T YOU REMEMBER ME, SINISTER?
DON'T REMEMBER LAST NIGHT. BUZZ OFF.
VAYASE, NO! YEARS AGO, IN SPANISHTOWN, AT THE BULLRING, YOUR BROTHER WAS SHOT AND WE —
WATCH THE FABRIC, SPANISH.
I DON' KNOW WHO YE ARE OR WHAT YER SELLIN', BUT YER IN ME FACE AN' THAT'S NOT A GOOD PLACE TA BE.
GO ON, SPEEDY GONZALES! AREEBA! AREEBA! GO ON, VAMOOSE!
I SEE. PROVOCATIVE AND DEMEANING ETHNIC STEREOTYPING. ANOTHER STRATUM OF NEGATIVE SELF-VALUATION TO CONTEND WITH.
WHAT DID YOU DO?
I UNDERTOOK A CATHARTIC NASAL-TRAUMA IMPACTION EPISODE.
A WHAT?
SORRY, DOC. JUST TRYING YOUR TECHNIQUE THERE. THE AMELIA THING.
WELL ANYWAY, WHAT I DID WAS THIS —

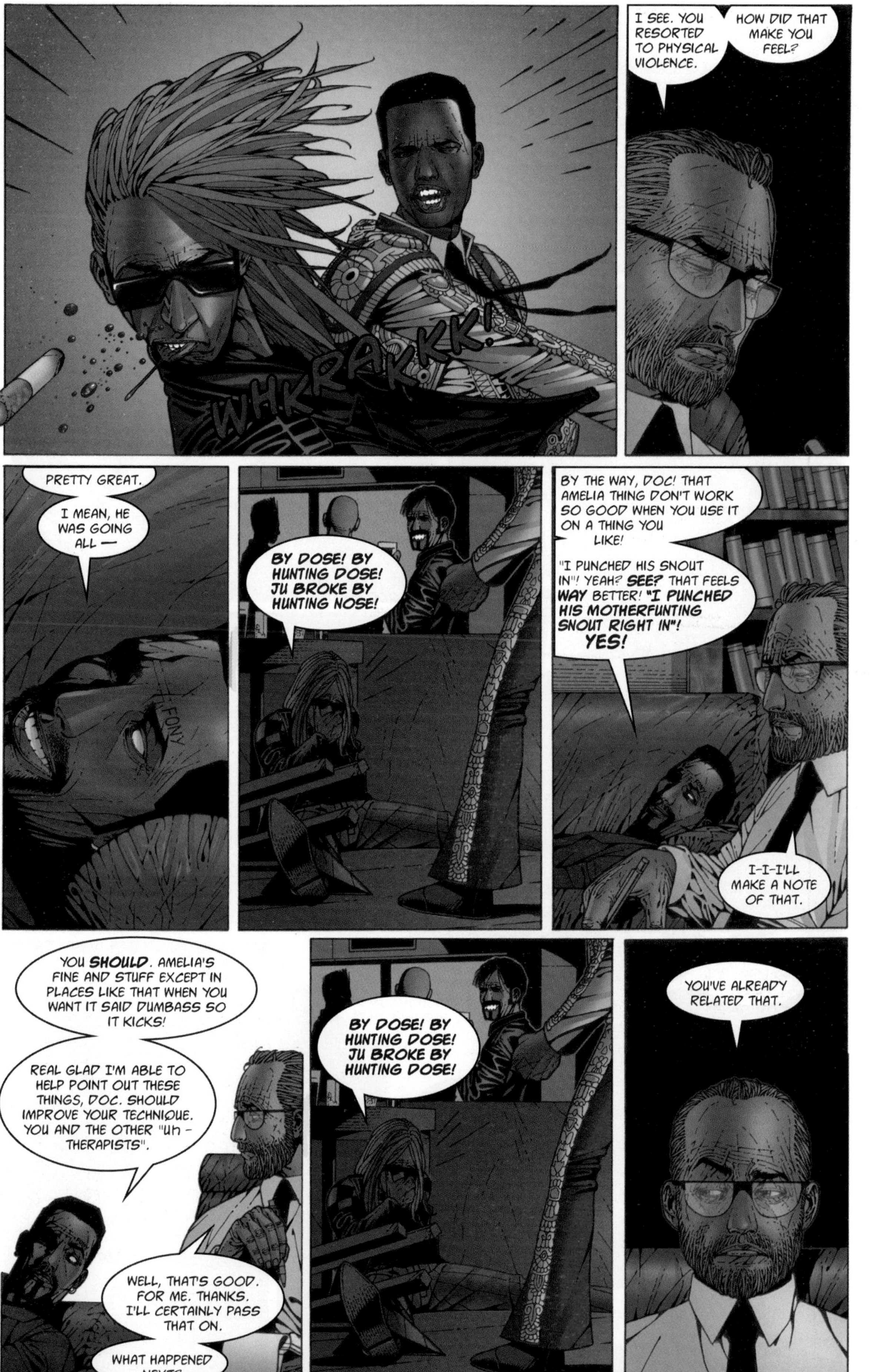
WHKRAKKK!
I SEE. YOU RESORTED TO PHYSICAL VIOLENCE.
HOW DID THAT MAKE YOU FEEL?
PRETTY GREAT.
I MEAN, HE WAS GOING ALL —
FONY
BY DOSE! BY HUNTING DOSE! JU BROKE BY HUNTING NOSE!
BY THE WAY, DOC! THAT AMELIA THING DON'T WORK SO GOOD WHEN YOU USE IT ON A THING YOU LIKE!
"I PUNCHED HIS SNOUT IN"! YEAH? SEE? THAT FEELS WAY BETTER! "I PUNCHED HIS MOTHERFUNTING SNOUT RIGHT IN"! YES!
I-I-I'LL MAKE A NOTE OF THAT.
YOU SHOULD. AMELIA'S FINE AND STUFF EXCEPT IN PLACES LIKE THAT WHEN YOU WANT IT SAID DUMBASS SO IT KICKS!
REAL GLAD I'M ABLE TO HELP POINT OUT THESE THINGS, DOC. SHOULD IMPROVE YOUR TECHNIQUE. YOU AND THE OTHER "UH - THERAPISTS".
WELL, THAT'S GOOD. FOR ME. THANKS. I'LL CERTAINLY PASS THAT ON.
WHAT HAPPENED NEXT?
BY DOSE! BY HUNTING DOSE! JU BROKE BY HUNTING DOSE!
YOU'VE ALREADY RELATED THAT.

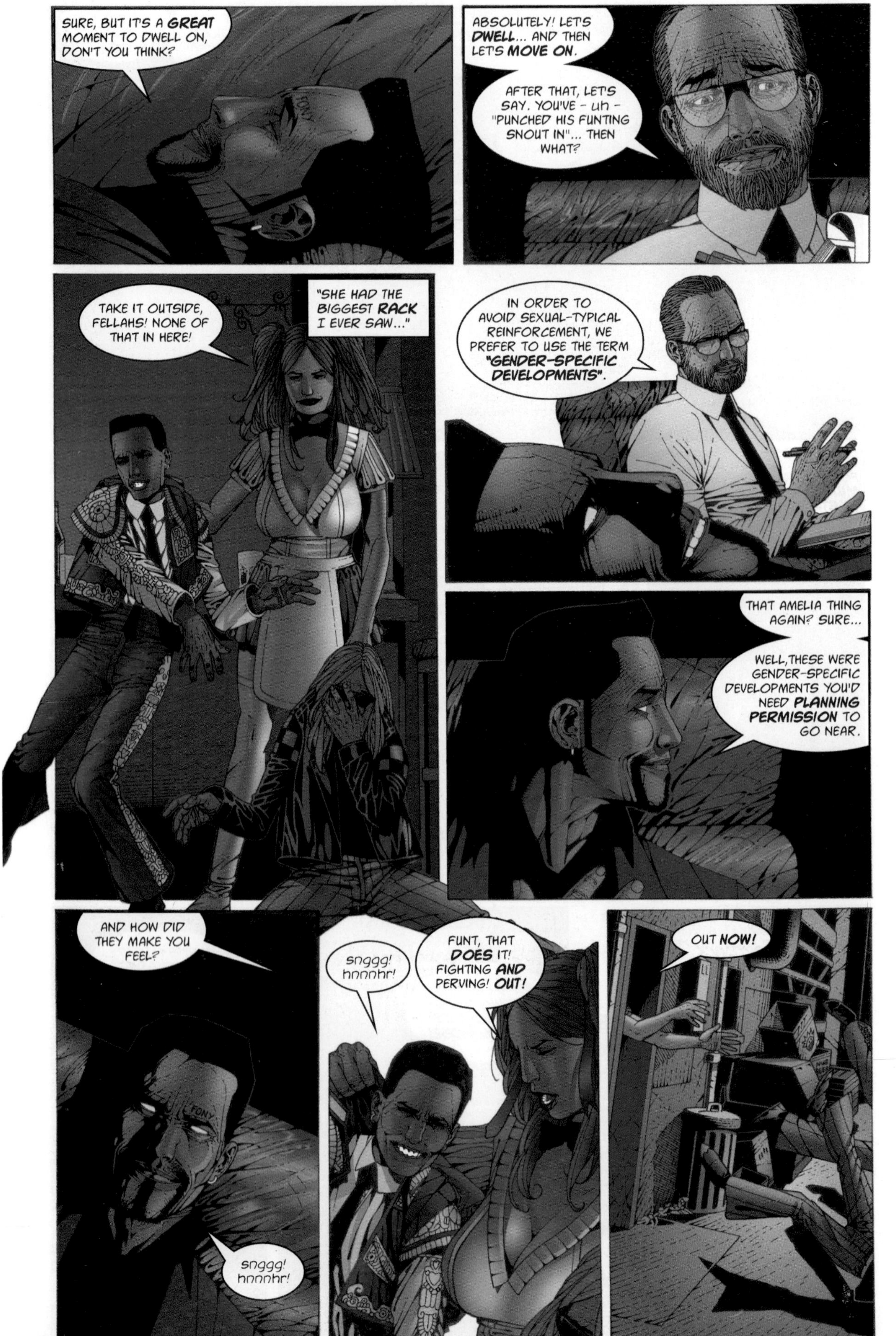
SURE, BUT IT'S A GREAT MOMENT TO DWELL ON, DON'T YOU THINK?
FONY
ABSOLUTELY! LET'S DWELL... AND THEN LET'S MOVE ON.
AFTER THAT, LET'S SAY. YOU'VE - uh - "PUNCHED HIS FUNTING SNOUT IN"... THEN WHAT?
TAKE IT OUTSIDE, FELLAHS! NONE OF THAT IN HERE!
"SHE HAD THE BIGGEST RACK I EVER SAW..."
IN ORDER TO AVOID SEXUAL-TYPICAL REINFORCEMENT, WE PREFER TO USE THE TERM "GENDER-SPECIFIC DEVELOPMENTS".
THAT AMELIA THING AGAIN? SURE...
WELL, THESE WERE GENDER-SPECIFIC DEVELOPMENTS YOU'D NEED PLANNING PERMISSION TO GO NEAR.
AND HOW DID THEY MAKE YOU FEEL?
FONY
snggg! hnnnhr!
snggg! hnnnhr!
FUNT, THAT DOES IT! FIGHTING AND PERVING! OUT!
OUT NOW!

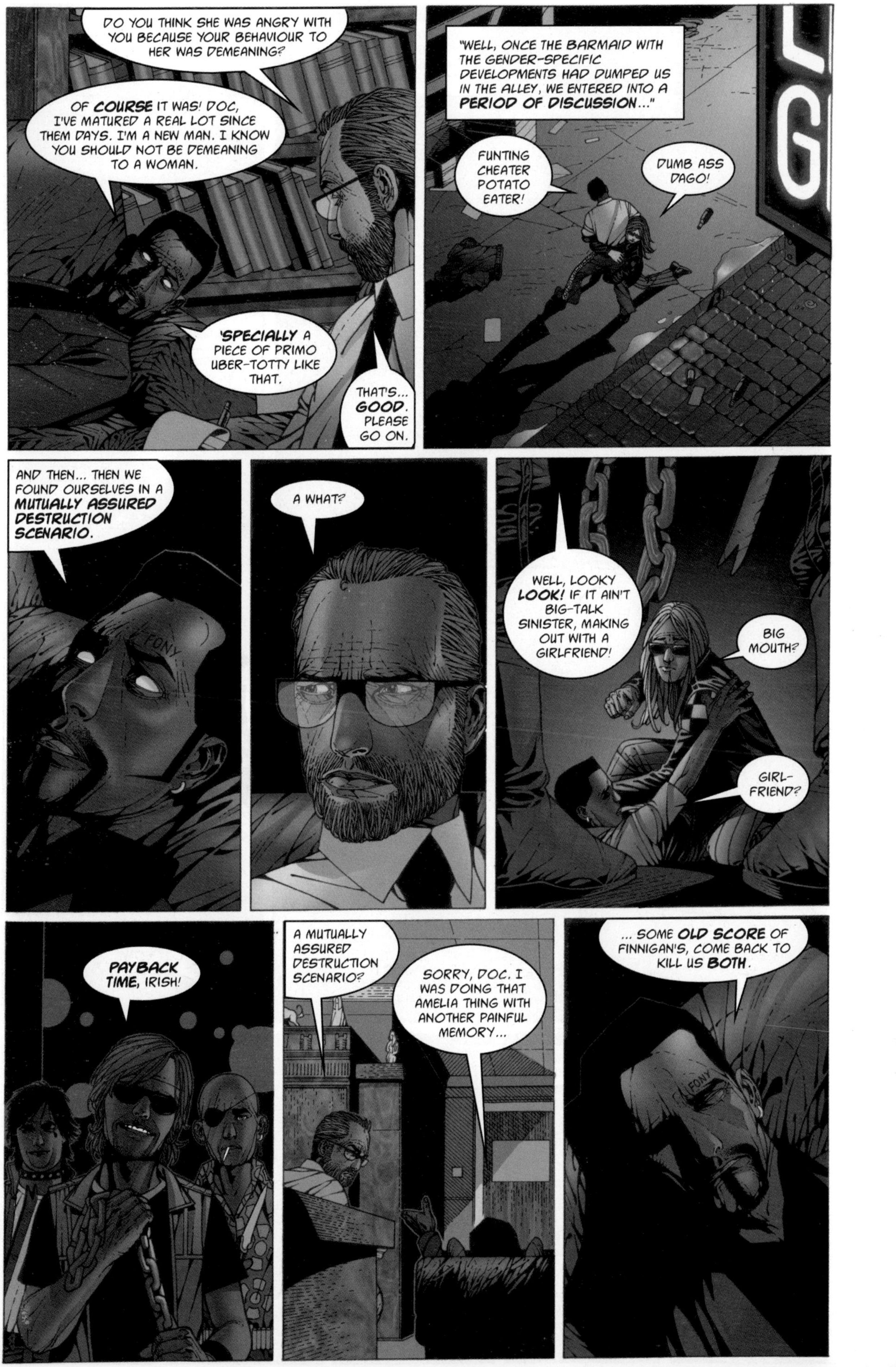
DO YOU THINK SHE WAS ANGRY WITH YOU BECAUSE YOUR BEHAVIOUR TO HER WAS DEMEANING?
OF COURSE IT WAS! DOC, I'VE MATURED A REAL LOT SINCE THEM DAYS. I'M A NEW MAN. I KNOW YOU SHOULD NOT BE DEMEANING TO A WOMAN.
'SPECIALLY A PIECE OF PRIMO UBER-TOTTY LIKE THAT.
THAT'S... GOOD. PLEASE GO ON.
"WELL, ONCE THE BARMAID WITH THE GENDER-SPECIFIC DEVELOPMENTS HAD DUMPED US IN THE ALLEY, WE ENTERED INTO A PERIOD OF DISCUSSION..."
FUNTING CHEATER POTATO EATER!
DUMB ASS DAGO!
AND THEN... THEN WE FOUND OURSELVES IN A MUTUALLY ASSURED DESTRUCTION SCENARIO.
A WHAT?
WELL, LOOKY LOOK! IF IT AIN'T BIG-TALK SINISTER, MAKING OUT WITH A GIRLFRIEND!
BIG MOUTH?
GIRL-FRIEND?
PAYBACK TIME, IRISH!
A MUTUALLY ASSURED DESTRUCTION SCENARIO?
SORRY, DOC. I WAS DOING THAT AMELIA THING WITH ANOTHER PAINFUL MEMORY...
... SOME OLD SCORE OF FINNIGAN'S, COME BACK TO KILL US BOTH.

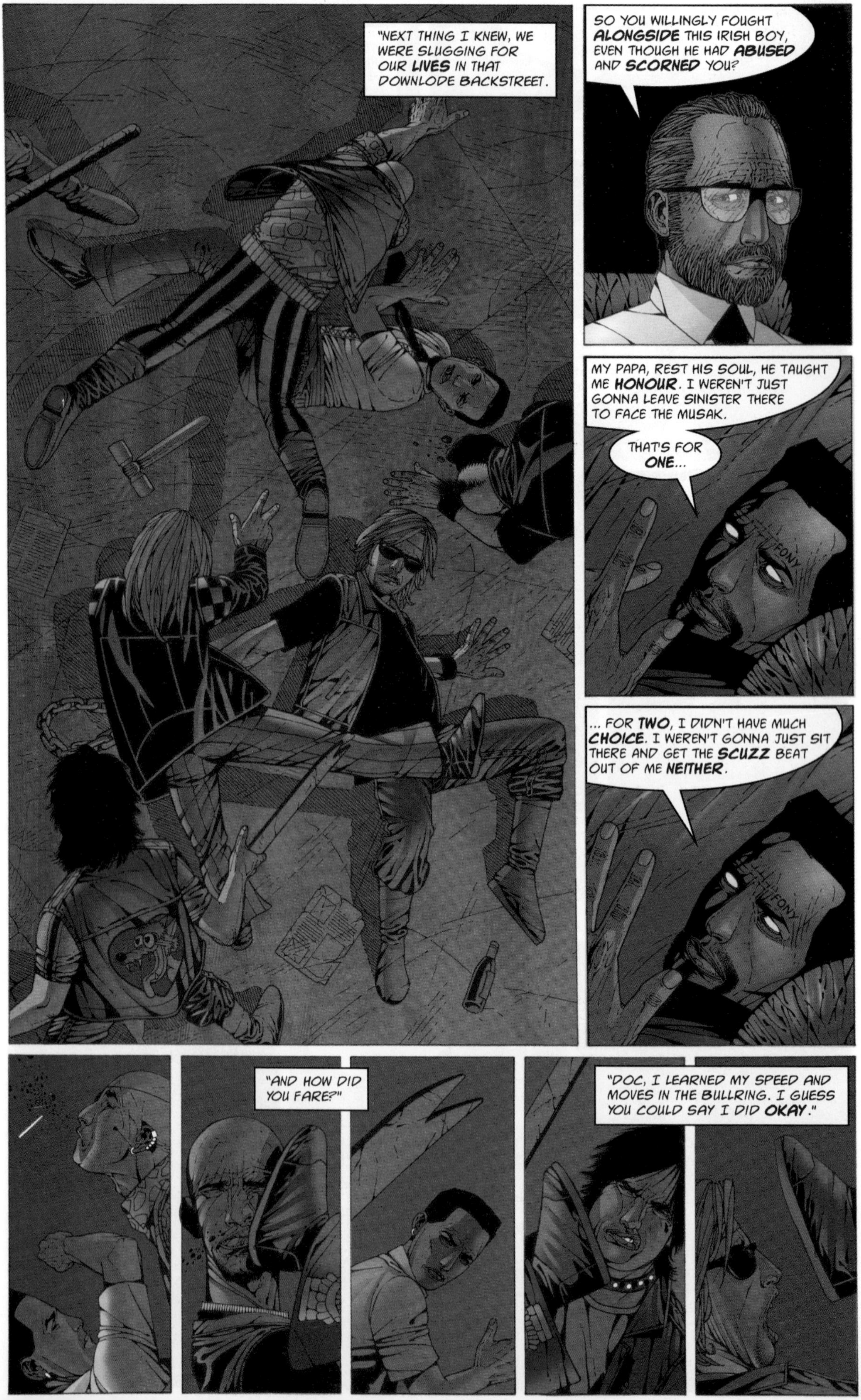
"NEXT THING I KNEW, WE WERE SLUGGING FOR OUR LIVES IN THAT DOWNLODE BACKSTREET.
SO YOU WILLINGLY FOUGHT ALONGSIDE THIS IRISH BOY, EVEN THOUGH HE HAD ABUSED AND SCORNED YOU?
MY PAPA, REST HIS SOUL, HE TAUGHT ME HONOUR. I WEREN'T JUST GONNA LEAVE SINISTER THERE TO FACE THE MUSAK.
THAT'S FOR ONE...
FONY
... FOR TWO, I DIDN'T HAVE MUCH CHOICE. I WEREN'T GONNA JUST SIT THERE AND GET THE SCUZZ BEAT OUT OF ME NEITHER.
"AND HOW DID YOU FARE?"
"DOC, I LEARNED MY SPEED AND MOVES IN THE BULLRING. I GUESS YOU COULD SAY I DID OKAY."

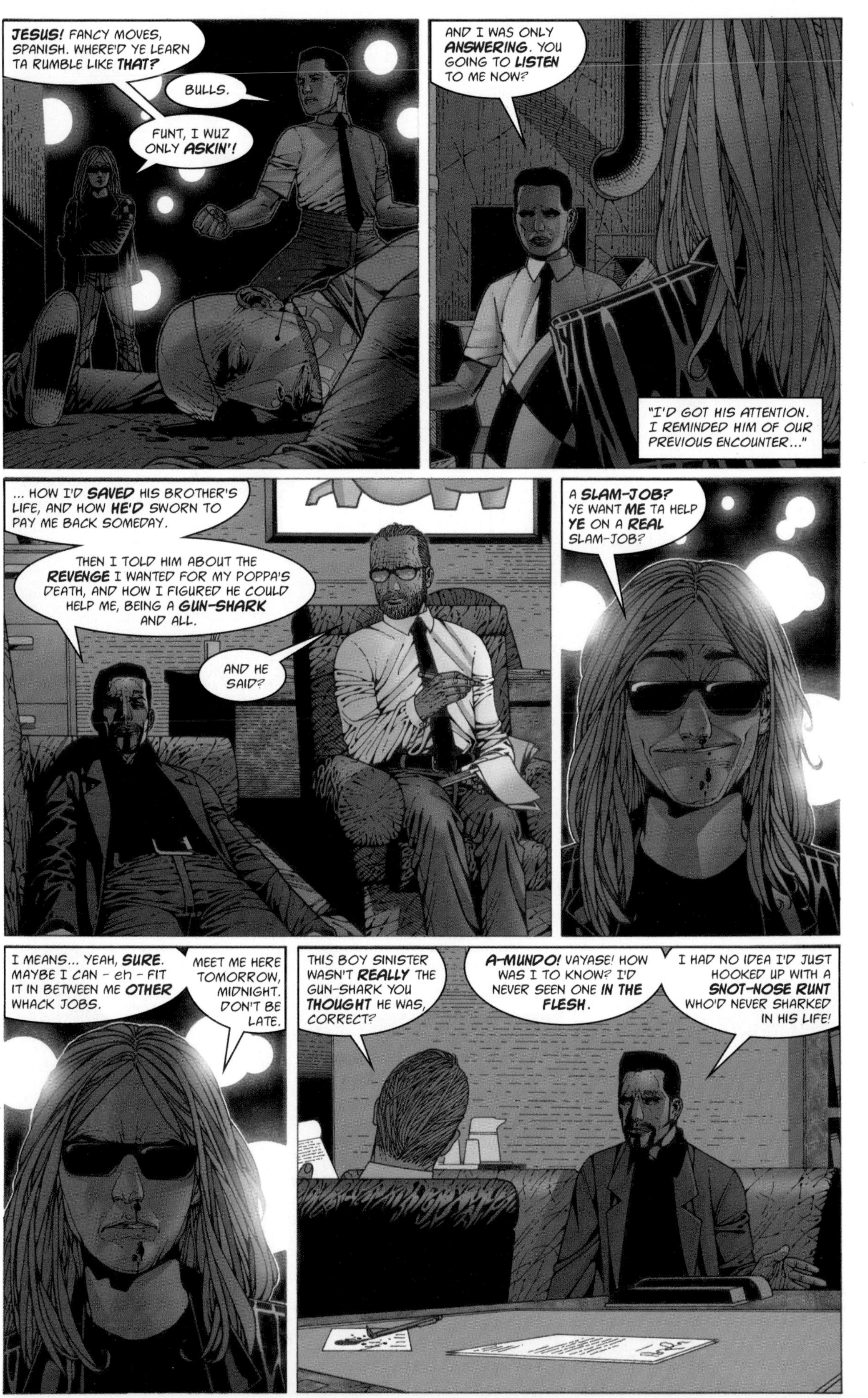
JESUS! FANCY MOVES, SPANISH. WHERE'D YE LEARN TA RUMBLE LIKE THAT?
BULLS.
FUNT, I WUZ ONLY ASKIN'!
AND I WAS ONLY ANSWERING. YOU GOING TO LISTEN TO ME NOW?
"I'D GOT HIS ATTENTION. I REMINDED HIM OF OUR PREVIOUS ENCOUNTER..."
... HOW I'D SAVED HIS BROTHER'S LIFE, AND HOW HE'D SWORN TO PAY ME BACK SOMEDAY.
THEN I TOLD HIM ABOUT THE REVENGE I WANTED FOR MY POPPA'S DEATH, AND HOW I FIGURED HE COULD HELP ME, BEING A GUN-SHARK AND ALL.
AND HE SAID?
A SLAM-JOB? YE WANT ME TA HELP YE ON A REAL SLAM-JOB?
I MEANS... YEAH, SURE. MAYBE I CAN - eh - FIT IT IN BETWEEN ME OTHER WHACK JOBS.
MEET ME HERE TOMORROW, MIDNIGHT. DON'T BE LATE.
THIS BOY SINISTER WASN'T REALLY THE GUN-SHARK YOU THOUGHT HE WAS, CORRECT?
A-MUNDO! VAYASE! HOW WAS I TO KNOW? I'D NEVER SEEN ONE IN THE FLESH.
I HAD NO IDEA I'D JUST HOOKED UP WITH A SNOT-NOSE RUNT WHO'D NEVER SHARKED IN HIS LIFE!

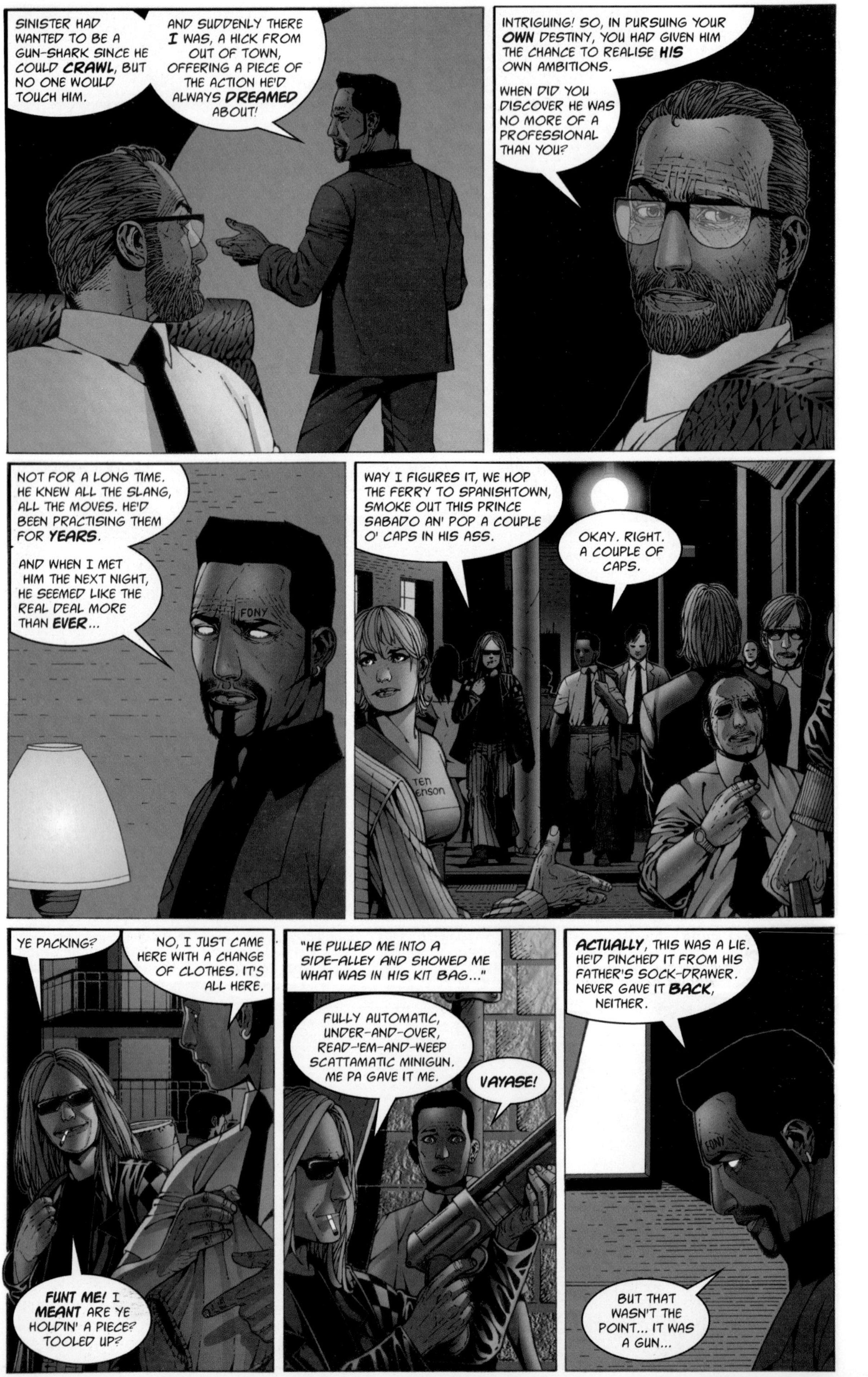
SINISTER HAD WANTED TO BE A GUN-SHARK SINCE HE COULD **CRAWL**, BUT NO ONE WOULD TOUCH HIM.
AND SUDDENLY THERE **I** WAS, A HICK FROM OUT OF TOWN, OFFERING A PIECE OF THE ACTION HE'D ALWAYS **DREAMED** ABOUT!
INTRIGUING! SO, IN PURSUING YOUR **OWN** DESTINY, YOU HAD GIVEN HIM THE CHANCE TO REALISE **HIS** OWN AMBITIONS.
WHEN DID YOU DISCOVER HE WAS NO MORE OF A PROFESSIONAL THAN YOU?
NOT FOR A LONG TIME. HE KNEW ALL THE SLANG, ALL THE MOVES. HE'D BEEN PRACTISING THEM FOR **YEARS**.
AND WHEN I MET HIM THE NEXT NIGHT, HE SEEMED LIKE THE REAL DEAL MORE THAN **EVER**...
WAY I FIGURES IT, WE HOP THE FERRY TO SPANISHTOWN, SMOKE OUT THIS PRINCE SABADO AN' POP A COUPLE O' CAPS IN HIS ASS.
OKAY. RIGHT. A COUPLE OF CAPS.
YE PACKING?
NO, I JUST CAME HERE WITH A CHANGE OF CLOTHES. IT'S ALL HERE.
FUNT ME! I **MEANT** ARE YE HOLDIN' A PIECE? TOOLED UP?
"HE PULLED ME INTO A SIDE-ALLEY AND SHOWED ME WHAT WAS IN HIS KIT BAG..."
FULLY AUTOMATIC, UNDER-AND-OVER, READ-'EM-AND-WEEP SCATTAMATIC MINIGUN. ME PA GAVE IT ME.
VAYASE!
ACTUALLY, THIS WAS A LIE. HE'D PINCHED IT FROM HIS FATHER'S SOCK-DRAWER. NEVER GAVE IT **BACK**, NEITHER.
BUT THAT WASN'T THE POINT... IT WAS A GUN...

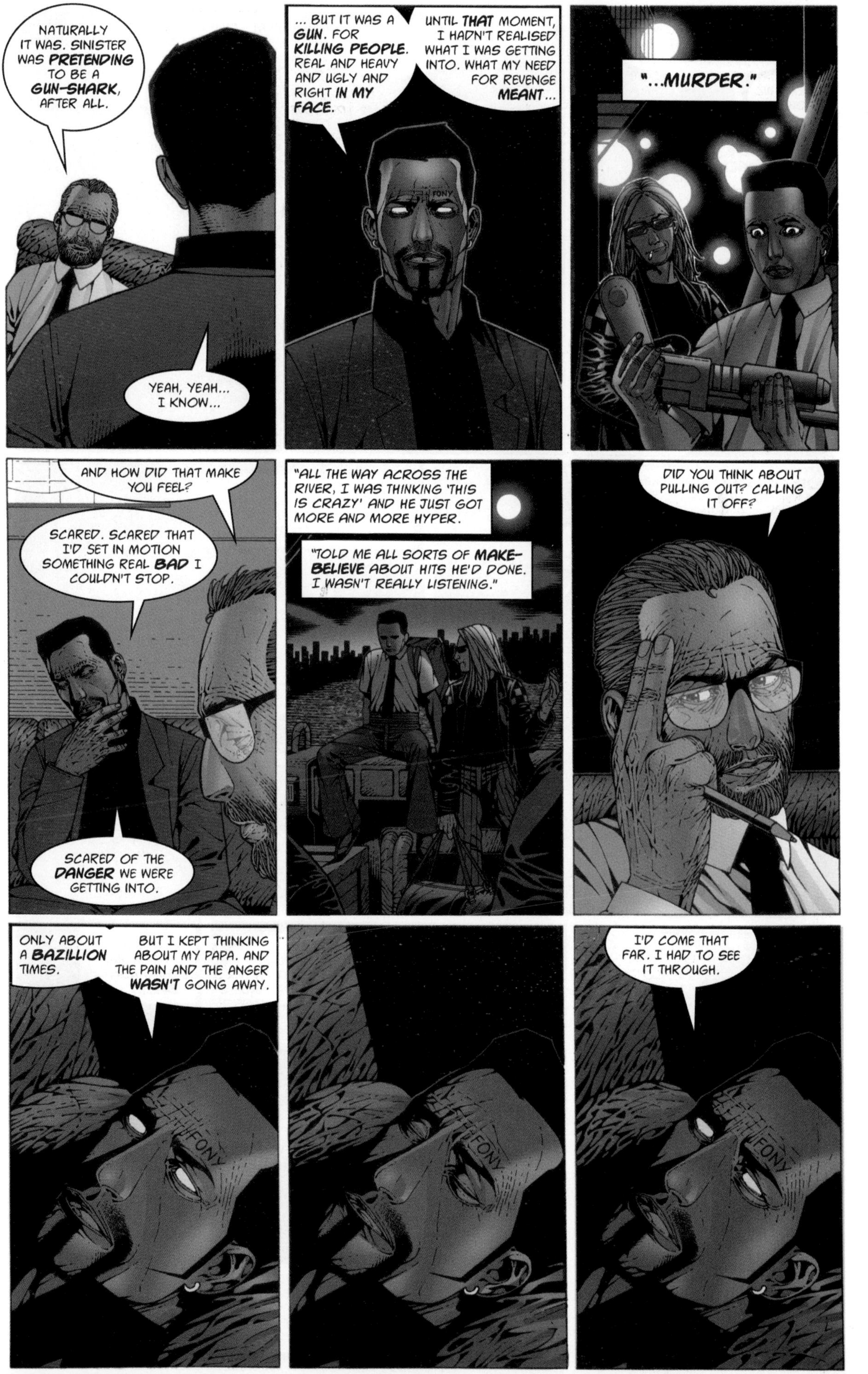

NATURALLY IT WAS. SINISTER WAS PRETENDING TO BE A GUN-SHARK, AFTER ALL.
YEAH, YEAH... I KNOW...
... BUT IT WAS A GUN. FOR KILLING PEOPLE. REAL AND HEAVY AND UGLY AND RIGHT IN MY FACE.
UNTIL THAT MOMENT, I HADN'T REALISED WHAT I WAS GETTING INTO. WHAT MY NEED FOR REVENGE MEANT...
"...MURDER."
AND HOW DID THAT MAKE YOU FEEL?
SCARED. SCARED THAT I'D SET IN MOTION SOMETHING REAL BAD I COULDN'T STOP.
SCARED OF THE DANGER WE WERE GETTING INTO.
"ALL THE WAY ACROSS THE RIVER, I WAS THINKING 'THIS IS CRAZY' AND HE JUST GOT MORE AND MORE HYPER.
"TOLD ME ALL SORTS OF MAKE-BELIEVE ABOUT HITS HE'D DONE. I WASN'T REALLY LISTENING."
DID YOU THINK ABOUT PULLING OUT? CALLING IT OFF?
ONLY ABOUT A BAZILLION TIMES.
BUT I KEPT THINKING ABOUT MY PAPA. AND THE PAIN AND THE ANGER WASN'T GOING AWAY.
I'D COME THAT FAR. I HAD TO SEE IT THROUGH.

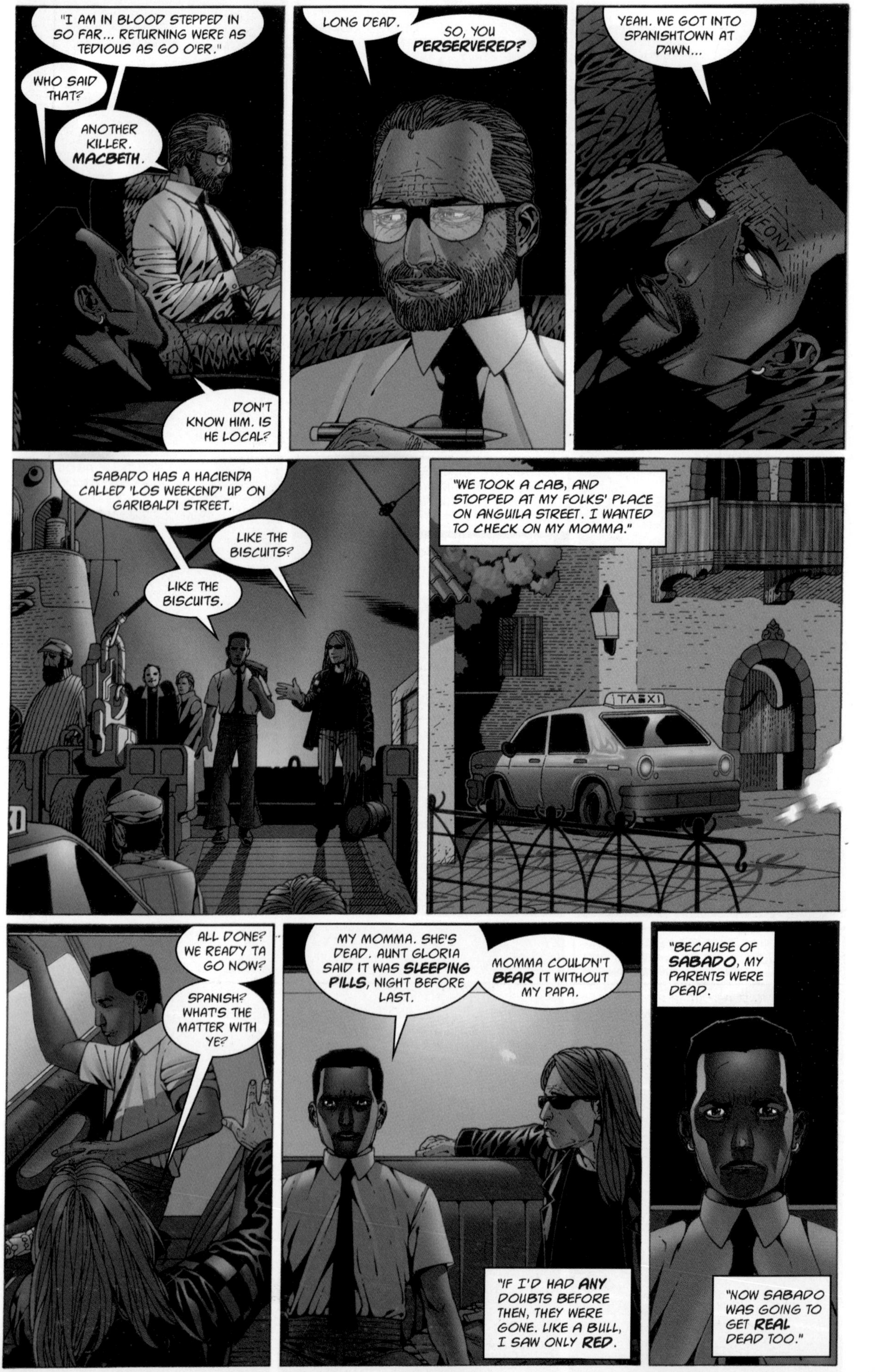
"I AM IN BLOOD STEPPED IN SO FAR... RETURNING WERE AS TEDIOUS AS GO O'ER."
WHO SAID THAT?
ANOTHER KILLER. **MACBETH**.
DON'T KNOW HIM. IS HE LOCAL?
LONG DEAD.
SO, YOU **PERSERVERED?**
YEAH. WE GOT INTO SPANISHTOWN AT DAWN...
SABADO HAS A HACIENDA CALLED 'LOS WEEKEND' UP ON GARIBALDI STREET.
LIKE THE BISCUITS?
LIKE THE BISCUITS.
"WE TOOK A CAB, AND STOPPED AT MY FOLKS' PLACE ON ANGUILA STREET. I WANTED TO CHECK ON MY MOMMA."
TAXI
ALL DONE? WE READY TA GO NOW?
SPANISH? WHAT'S THE MATTER WITH YE?
MY MOMMA. SHE'S DEAD. AUNT GLORIA SAID IT WAS **SLEEPING PILLS**, NIGHT BEFORE LAST.
MOMMA COULDN'T **BEAR** IT WITHOUT MY PAPA.
"IF I'D HAD **ANY** DOUBTS BEFORE THEN, THEY WERE GONE. LIKE A BULL, I SAW ONLY **RED**.
"BECAUSE OF **SABADO**, MY PARENTS WERE DEAD.
"NOW SABADO WAS GOING TO GET **REAL** DEAD TOO."

LET ME **RE-CAP** HERE — YOUR FATHER IS MURDERED, YOUR MOTHER IS DEAD OF A BROKEN HEART...

SO YOU, A TEENAGER PARTNERED WITH AN IRISH HOOLIGAN WHO DREAMS OF BEING A GUN-SHARK, SETS OUT FOR REVENGE.

I JUST **TOLD** YOU ALL THAT, DOC.

WHAT'S WITH THE RE-CAP? LIKE ONE OF THOSE TV THINGS — "PREVIOUSLY ANALYZING DEXTER".

I — uh — JUST LIKE TO MAKE SURE I'M KEEPING UP.

NOW, THIS MAN YOU WERE AFTER, **SABADO**, ONE OF THE CRIME-LORD PRINCES OF SPANISHTOWN.

SURELY HE WAS GOING TO BE **WELL** PROTECTED?

"DEAD RIGHT. HIS HACIENDA WAS CALLED 'LOS WEEKEND'. BIG PLACE, TIGHT AS A **FORTRESS**."

"SABADO HAD ABOUT THIRTY FULL-TIME BULLET-MONKEYS WORKING FOR HIM, HEAVY TYPES RECRUITED FROM THE **MATADOR** GUN-CLANS.

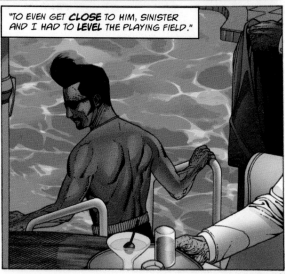

"TO EVEN GET **CLOSE** TO HIM, SINISTER AND I HAD TO **LEVEL** THE PLAYING FIELD."

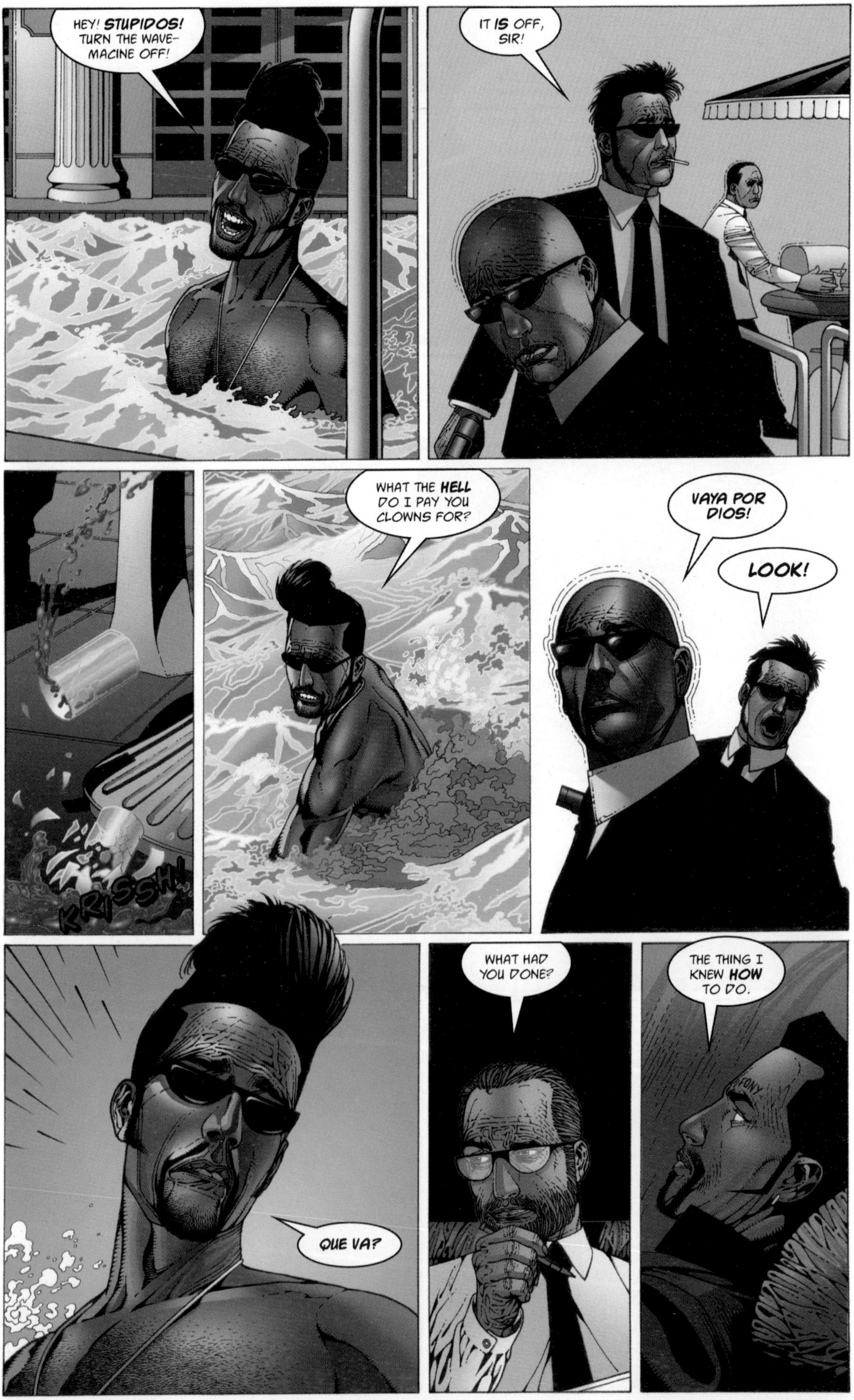
HEY! STUPIDOS! TURN THE WAVE-MACINE OFF!
IT IS OFF, SIR!
KRISSH!
WHAT THE HELL DO I PAY YOU CLOWNS FOR?
VAYA POR DIOS!
LOOK!
QUE VA?
WHAT HAD YOU DONE?
THE THING I KNEW HOW TO DO.

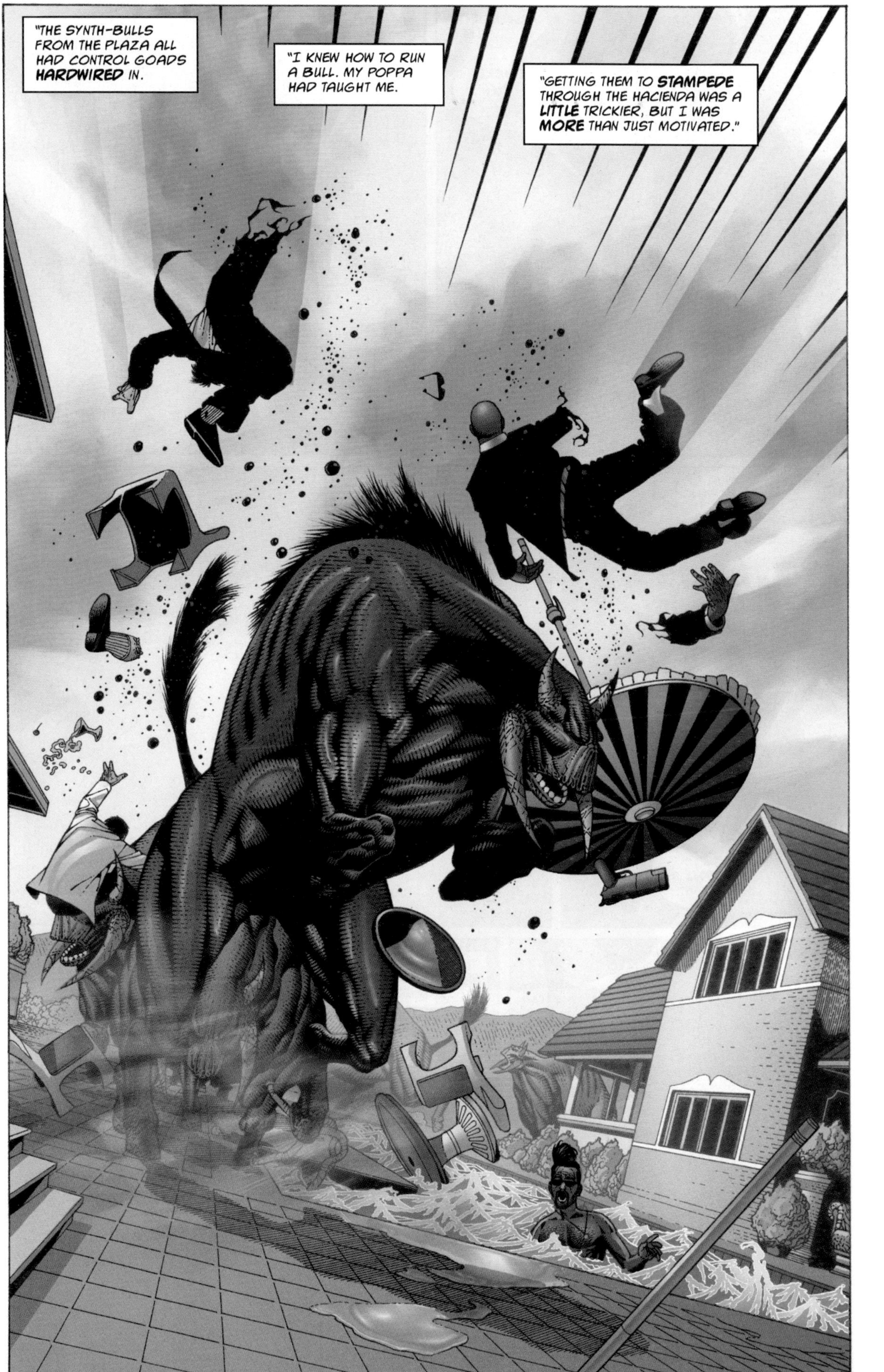
"THE SYNTH-BULLS FROM THE PLAZA ALL HAD CONTROL GOADS **HARDWIRED** IN.
"I KNEW HOW TO RUN A BULL. MY POPPA HAD TAUGHT ME.
"GETTING THEM TO **STAMPEDE** THROUGH THE HACIENDA WAS A **LITTLE** TRICKIER, BUT I WAS **MORE** THAN JUST MOTIVATED."

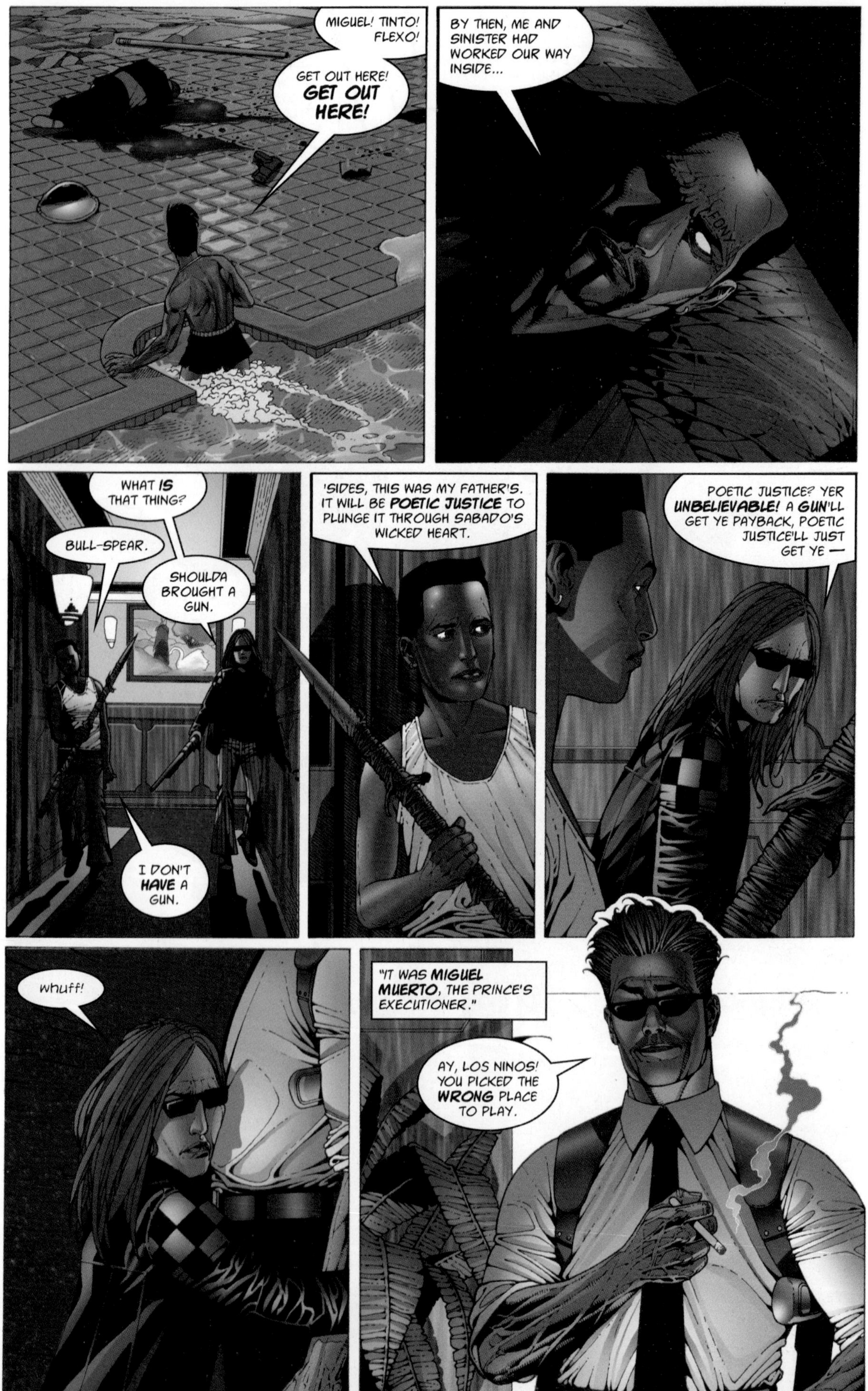
MIGUEL! TINTO! FLEXO!
GET OUT HERE! GET OUT HERE!
BY THEN, ME AND SINISTER HAD WORKED OUR WAY INSIDE...
WHAT IS THAT THING?
BULL-SPEAR.
SHOULDA BROUGHT A GUN.
I DON'T HAVE A GUN.
'SIDES, THIS WAS MY FATHER'S. IT WILL BE POETIC JUSTICE TO PLUNGE IT THROUGH SABADO'S WICKED HEART.
POETIC JUSTICE? YER UNBELIEVABLE! A GUN'LL GET YE PAYBACK, POETIC JUSTICE'LL JUST GET YE —
whuff!
"IT WAS MIGUEL MUERTO, THE PRINCE'S EXECUTIONER."
AY, LOS NINOS! YOU PICKED THE WRONG PLACE TO PLAY.

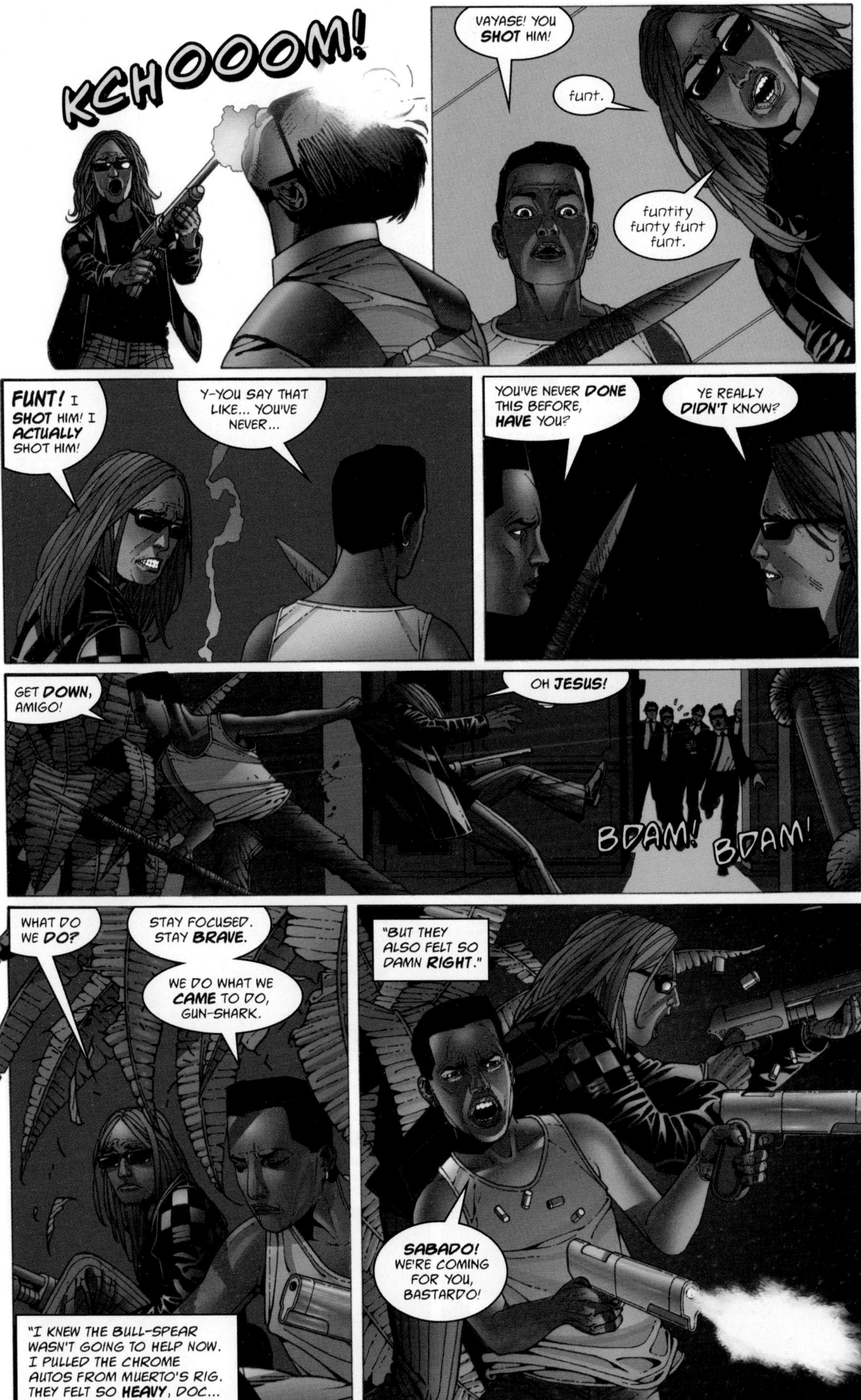
KCHOOOM!
VAYASE! YOU SHOT HIM!
funt.
funtity funty funt funt.
FUNT! I SHOT HIM! I ACTUALLY SHOT HIM!
Y-YOU SAY THAT LIKE... YOU'VE NEVER...
YOU'VE NEVER DONE THIS BEFORE, HAVE YOU?
YE REALLY DIDN'T KNOW?
GET DOWN, AMIGO!
OH JESUS!
BDAM! BDAM!
WHAT DO WE DO?
STAY FOCUSED. STAY BRAVE.
WE DO WHAT WE CAME TO DO, GUN-SHARK.
"I KNEW THE BULL-SPEAR WASN'T GOING TO HELP NOW. I PULLED THE CHROME AUTOS FROM MUERTO'S RIG. THEY FELT SO HEAVY, DOC...
"BUT THEY ALSO FELT SO DAMN RIGHT."
SABADO! WE'RE COMING FOR YOU, BASTARDO!

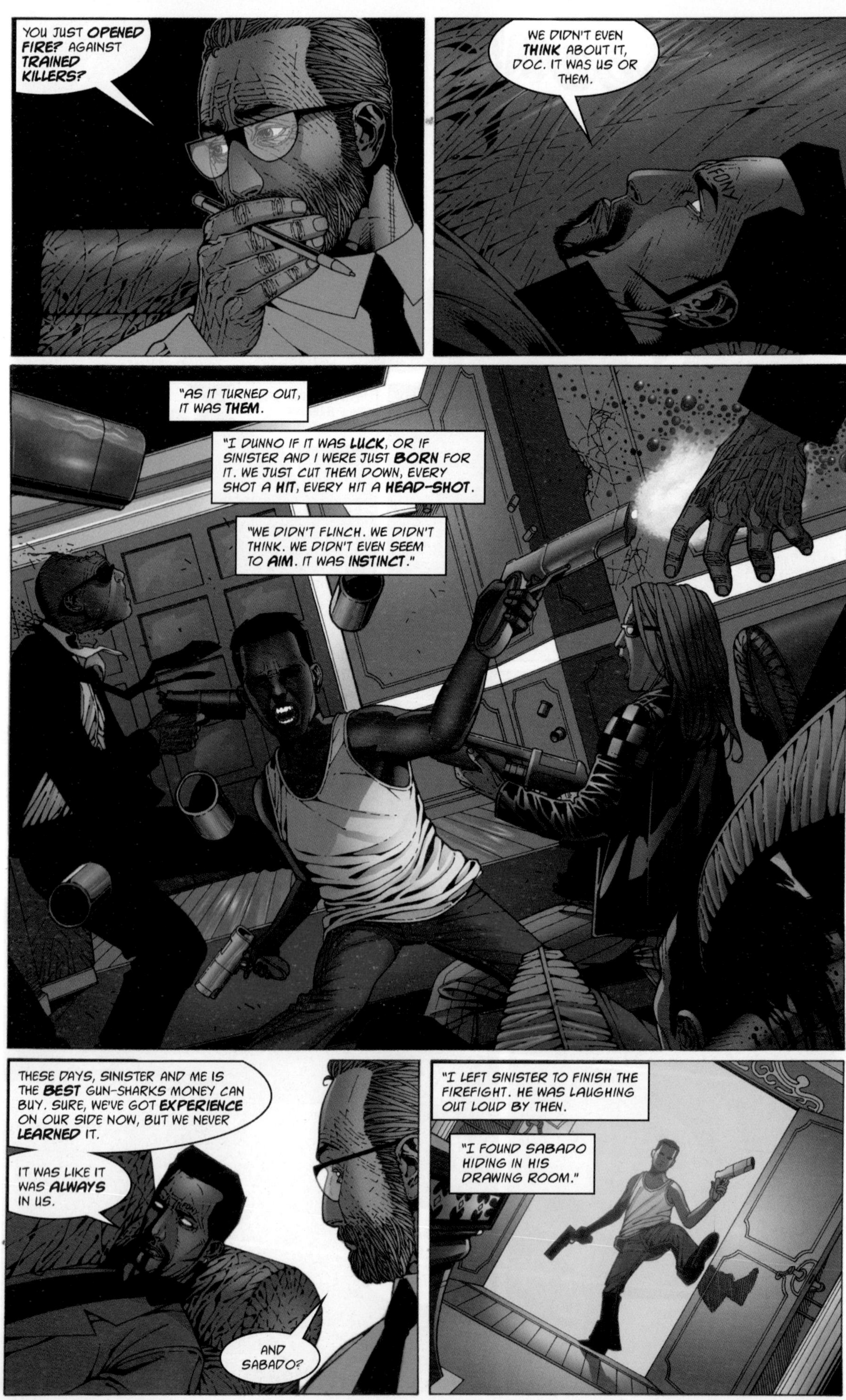

YOU JUST OPENED FIRE? AGAINST TRAINED KILLERS?
WE DIDN'T EVEN THINK ABOUT IT, DOC. IT WAS US OR THEM.
"AS IT TURNED OUT, IT WAS THEM.
"I DUNNO IF IT WAS LUCK, OR IF SINISTER AND I WERE JUST BORN FOR IT. WE JUST CUT THEM DOWN, EVERY SHOT A HIT, EVERY HIT A HEAD-SHOT.
"WE DIDN'T FLINCH. WE DIDN'T THINK. WE DIDN'T EVEN SEEM TO AIM. IT WAS INSTINCT."
THESE DAYS, SINISTER AND ME IS THE BEST GUN-SHARKS MONEY CAN BUY. SURE, WE'VE GOT EXPERIENCE ON OUR SIDE NOW, BUT WE NEVER LEARNED IT.
IT WAS LIKE IT WAS ALWAYS IN US.
AND SABADO?
"I LEFT SINISTER TO FINISH THE FIREFIGHT. HE WAS LAUGHING OUT LOUD BY THEN.
"I FOUND SABADO HIDING IN HIS DRAWING ROOM."

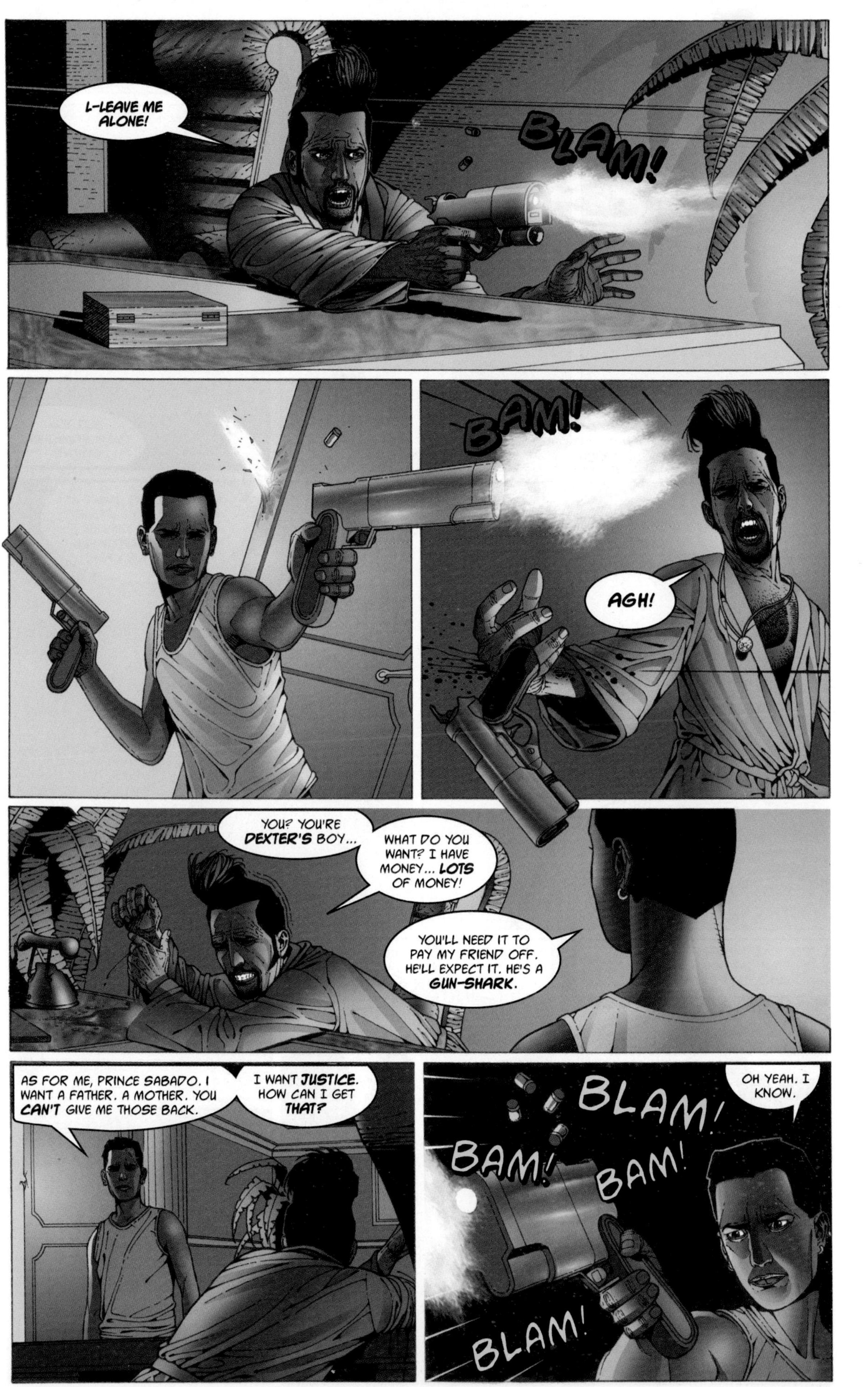
L-LEAVE ME ALONE!
BLAM!
BAM!
AGH!
YOU? YOU'RE **DEXTER'S** BOY...
WHAT DO YOU WANT? I HAVE MONEY... **LOTS** OF MONEY!
YOU'LL NEED IT TO PAY MY FRIEND OFF. HE'LL EXPECT IT. HE'S A **GUN-SHARK**.
AS FOR ME, PRINCE SABADO. I WANT A FATHER. A MOTHER. YOU **CAN'T** GIVE ME THOSE BACK.
I WANT **JUSTICE**. HOW CAN I GET **THAT?**
OH YEAH. I KNOW.
BLAM!
BAM!
BAM!
BLAM!

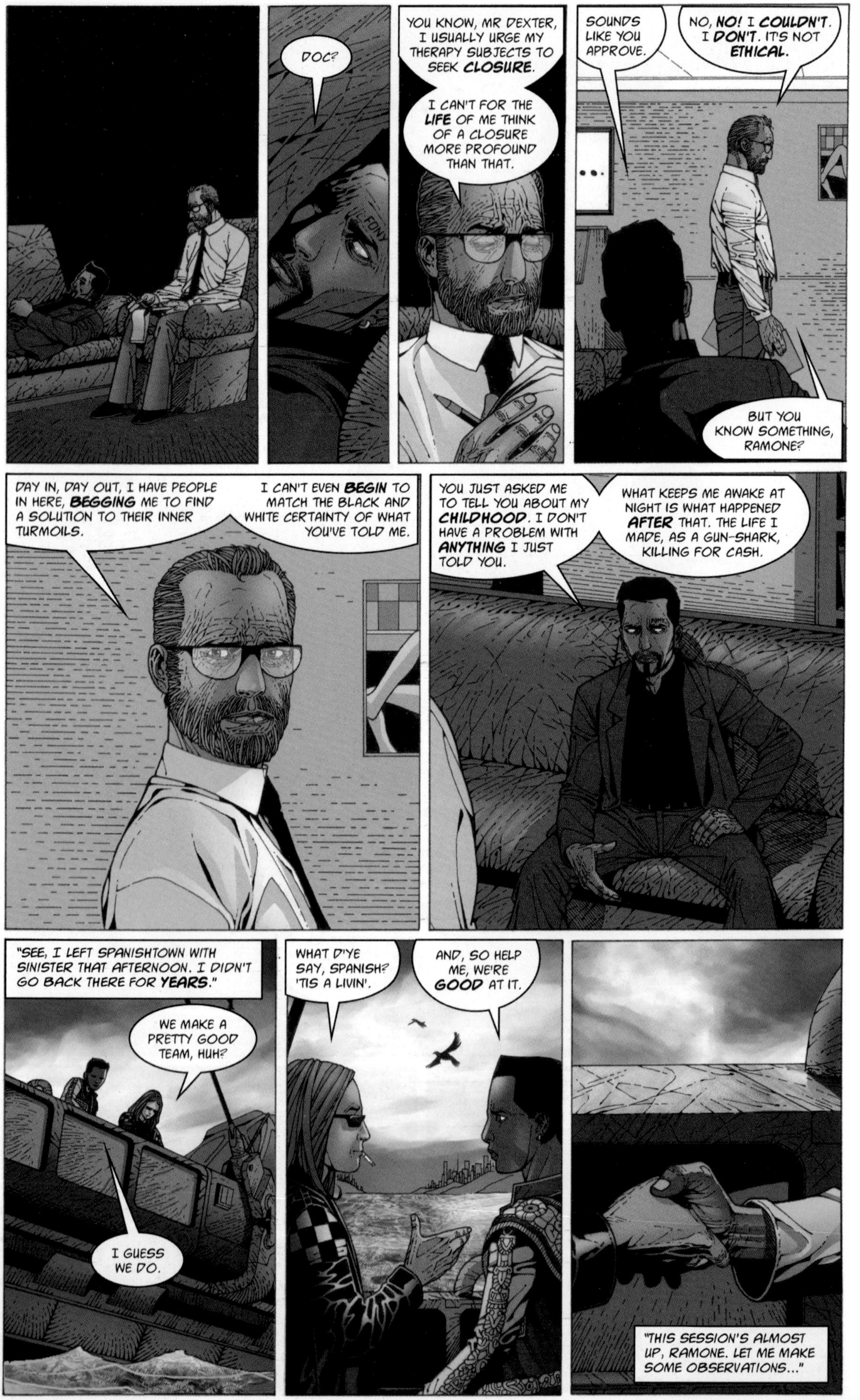
DOC?
YOU KNOW, MR DEXTER, I USUALLY URGE MY THERAPY SUBJECTS TO SEEK CLOSURE.
I CAN'T FOR THE LIFE OF ME THINK OF A CLOSURE MORE PROFOUND THAN THAT.
SOUNDS LIKE YOU APPROVE.
NO, NO! I COULDN'T. I DON'T. IT'S NOT ETHICAL.
BUT YOU KNOW SOMETHING, RAMONE?
DAY IN, DAY OUT, I HAVE PEOPLE IN HERE, BEGGING ME TO FIND A SOLUTION TO THEIR INNER TURMOILS.
I CAN'T EVEN BEGIN TO MATCH THE BLACK AND WHITE CERTAINTY OF WHAT YOU'VE TOLD ME.
YOU JUST ASKED ME TO TELL YOU ABOUT MY CHILDHOOD. I DON'T HAVE A PROBLEM WITH ANYTHING I JUST TOLD YOU.
WHAT KEEPS ME AWAKE AT NIGHT IS WHAT HAPPENED AFTER THAT. THE LIFE I MADE, AS A GUN-SHARK, KILLING FOR CASH.
"SEE, I LEFT SPANISHTOWN WITH SINISTER THAT AFTERNOON. I DIDN'T GO BACK THERE FOR YEARS."
WE MAKE A PRETTY GOOD TEAM, HUH?
I GUESS WE DO.
WHAT D'YE SAY, SPANISH? 'TIS A LIVIN'.
AND, SO HELP ME, WE'RE GOOD AT IT.
"THIS SESSION'S ALMOST UP, RAMONE. LET ME MAKE SOME OBSERVATIONS..."

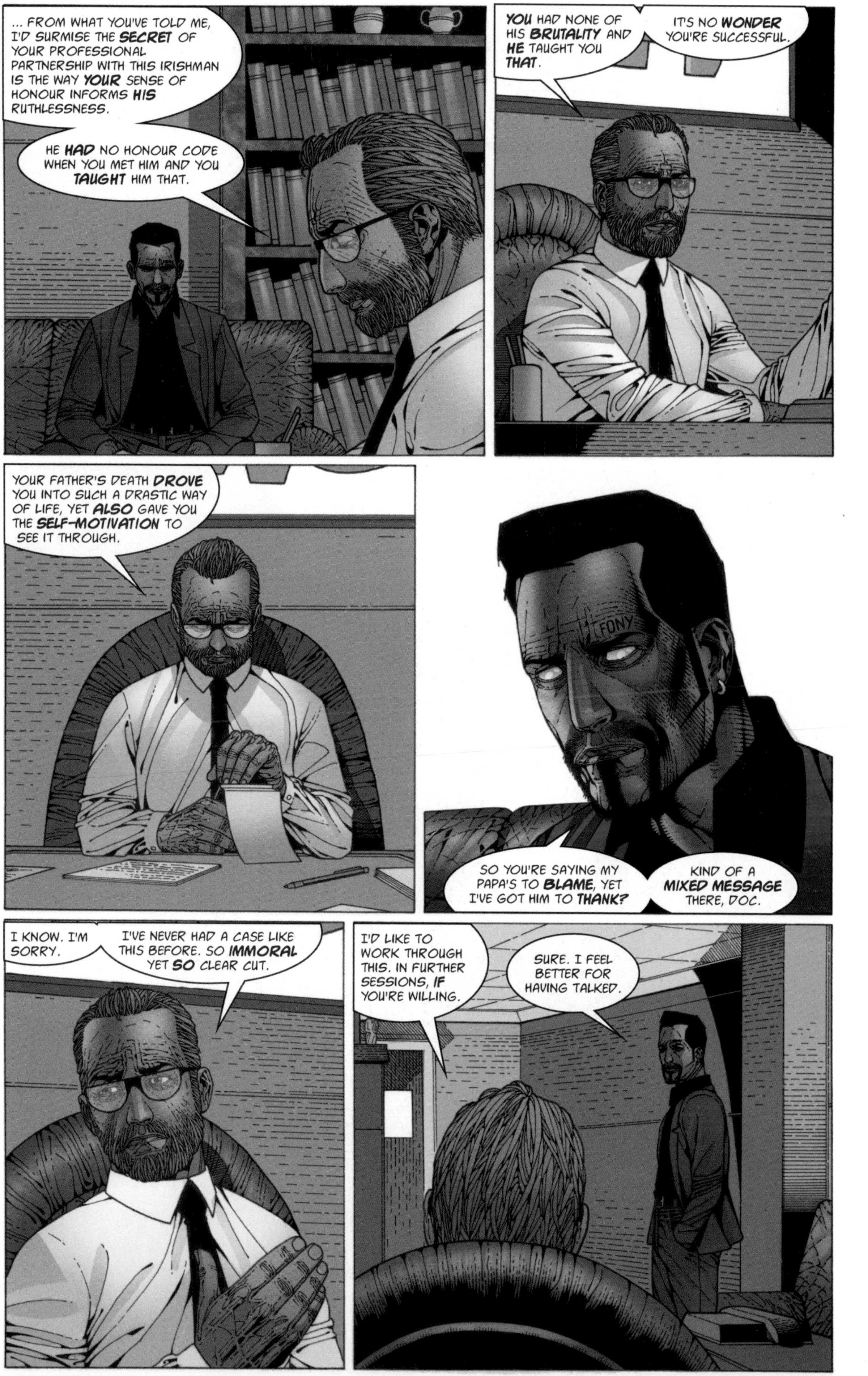
... FROM WHAT YOU'VE TOLD ME, I'D SURMISE THE SECRET OF YOUR PROFESSIONAL PARTNERSHIP WITH THIS IRISHMAN IS THE WAY YOUR SENSE OF HONOUR INFORMS HIS RUTHLESSNESS.
HE HAD NO HONOUR CODE WHEN YOU MET HIM AND YOU TAUGHT HIM THAT.
YOU HAD NONE OF HIS BRUTALITY AND HE TAUGHT YOU THAT.
IT'S NO WONDER YOU'RE SUCCESSFUL.
YOUR FATHER'S DEATH DROVE YOU INTO SUCH A DRASTIC WAY OF LIFE, YET ALSO GAVE YOU THE SELF-MOTIVATION TO SEE IT THROUGH.
FONY
SO YOU'RE SAYING MY PAPA'S TO BLAME, YET I'VE GOT HIM TO THANK?
KIND OF A MIXED MESSAGE THERE, DOC.
I KNOW. I'M SORRY.
I'VE NEVER HAD A CASE LIKE THIS BEFORE. SO IMMORAL YET SO CLEAR CUT.
I'D LIKE TO WORK THROUGH THIS. IN FURTHER SESSIONS, IF YOU'RE WILLING.
SURE. I FEEL BETTER FOR HAVING TALKED.

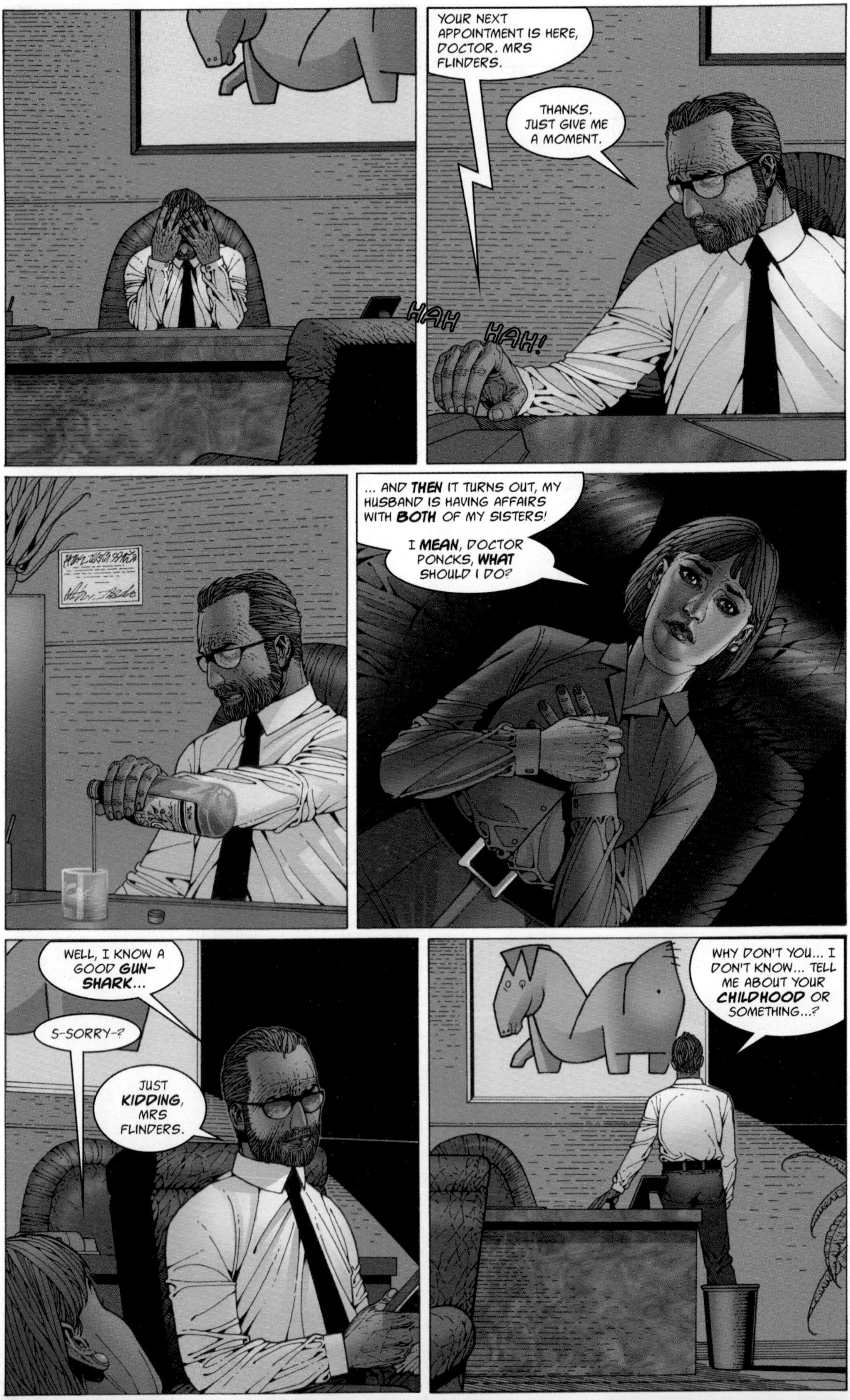

YOUR NEXT APPOINTMENT IS HERE, DOCTOR. MRS FLINDERS.
THANKS. JUST GIVE ME A MOMENT.
HAH HAH!
... AND THEN IT TURNS OUT, MY HUSBAND IS HAVING AFFAIRS WITH BOTH OF MY SISTERS!
I MEAN, DOCTOR PONCKS, WHAT SHOULD I DO?
WELL, I KNOW A GOOD GUN-SHARK...
S-SORRY-?
JUST KIDDING, MRS FLINDERS.
WHY DON'T YOU... I DON'T KNOW... TELL ME ABOUT YOUR CHILDHOOD OR SOMETHING...?

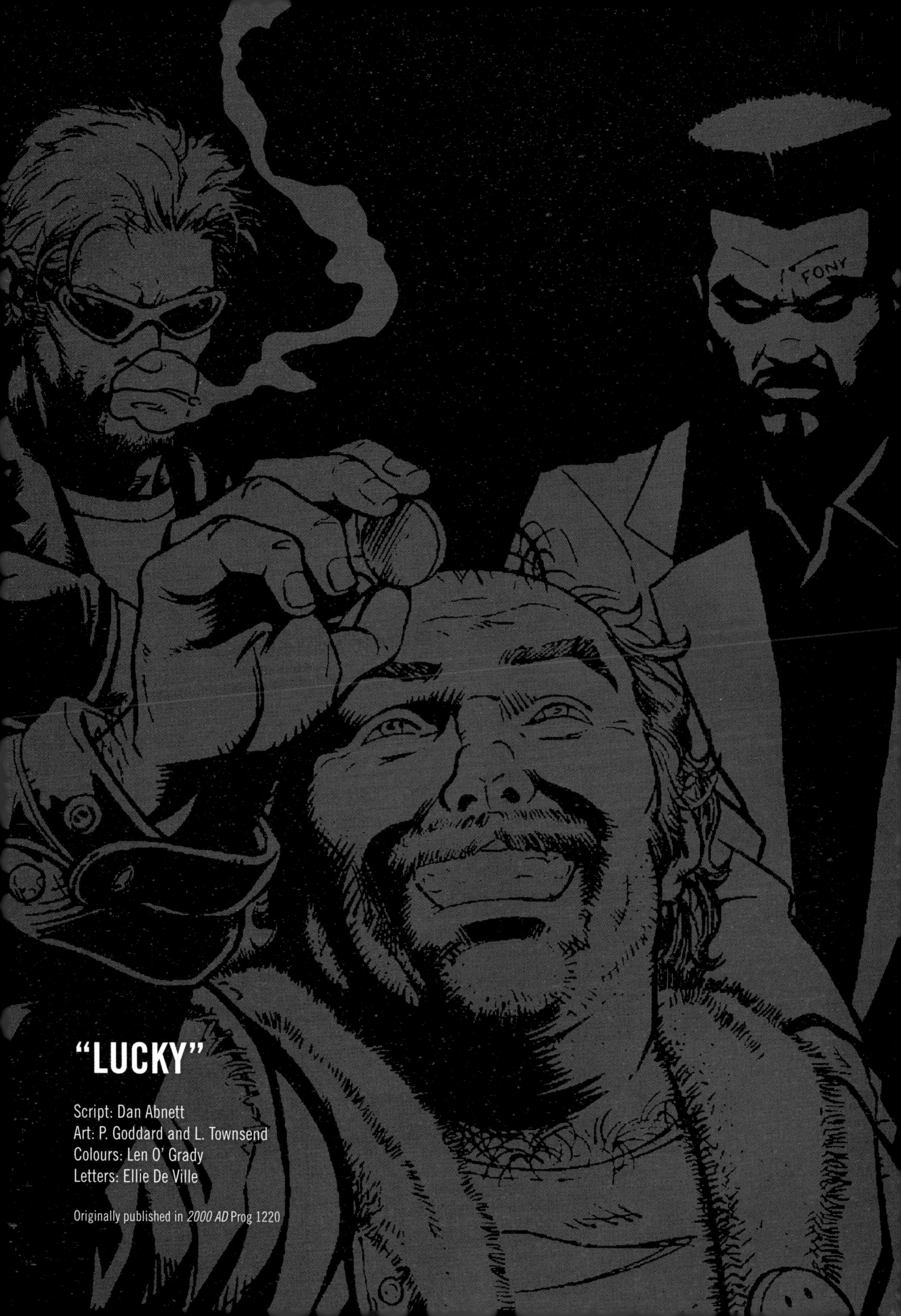
FONY

"LUCKY"

Script: Dan Abnett
Art: P. Goddard and L. Townsend
Colours: Len O' Grady
Letters: Ellie De Ville

Originally published in *2000 AD* Prog 1220

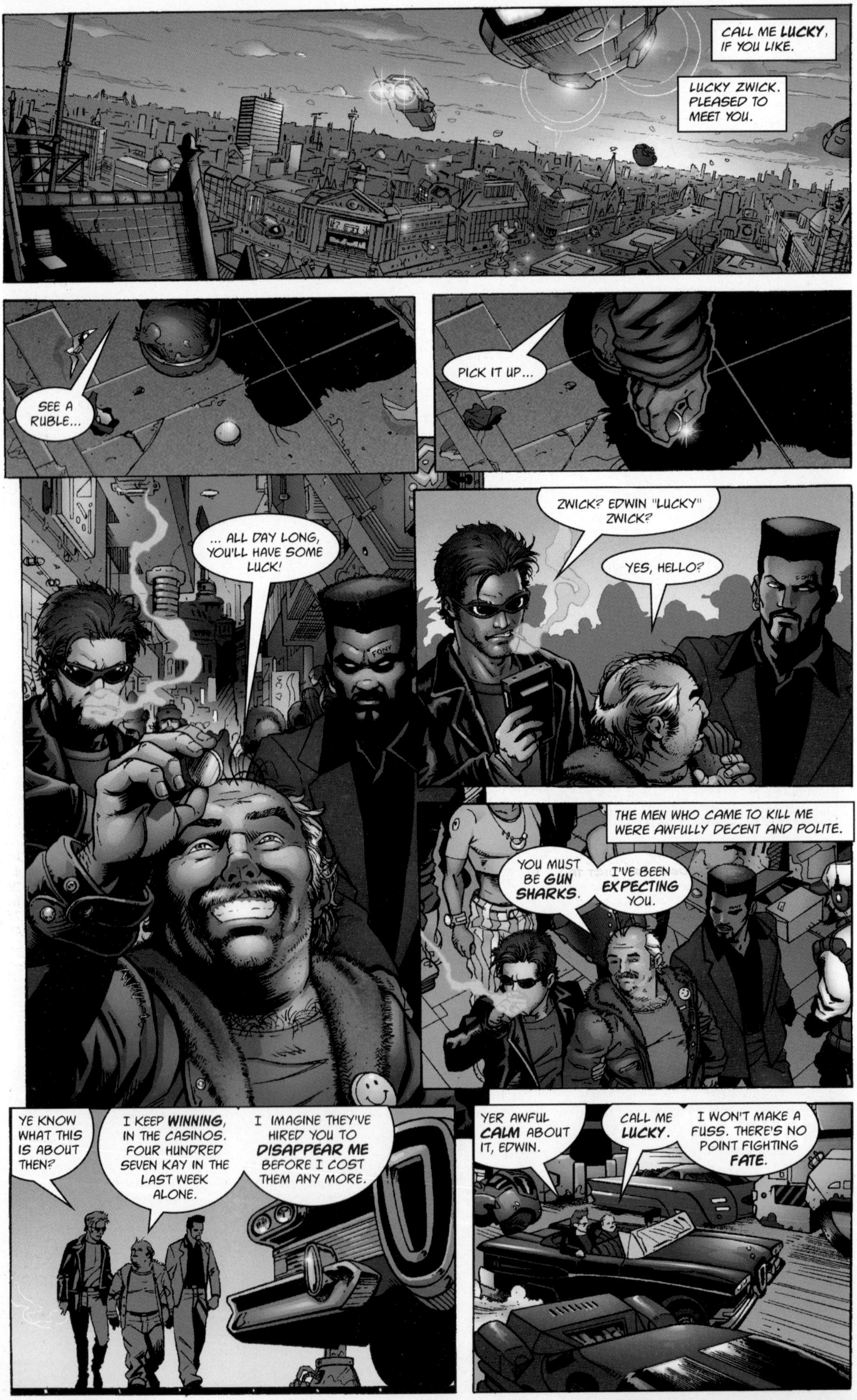
CALL ME **LUCKY**, IF YOU LIKE.
LUCKY ZWICK. PLEASED TO MEET YOU.
SEE A RUBLE...
PICK IT UP...
... ALL DAY LONG, YOU'LL HAVE SOME LUCK!
ZWICK? EDWIN "LUCKY" ZWICK?
YES, HELLO?
THE MEN WHO CAME TO KILL ME WERE AWFULLY DECENT AND POLITE.
YOU MUST BE **GUN SHARKS**.
I'VE BEEN **EXPECTING** YOU.
YE KNOW WHAT THIS IS ABOUT THEN?
I KEEP **WINNING**, IN THE CASINOS. FOUR HUNDRED SEVEN KAY IN THE LAST WEEK ALONE.
I IMAGINE THEY'VE HIRED YOU TO **DISAPPEAR ME** BEFORE I COST THEM ANY MORE.
YER AWFUL **CALM** ABOUT IT, EDWIN.
CALL ME **LUCKY**.
I WON'T MAKE A FUSS. THERE'S NO POINT FIGHTING **FATE**.

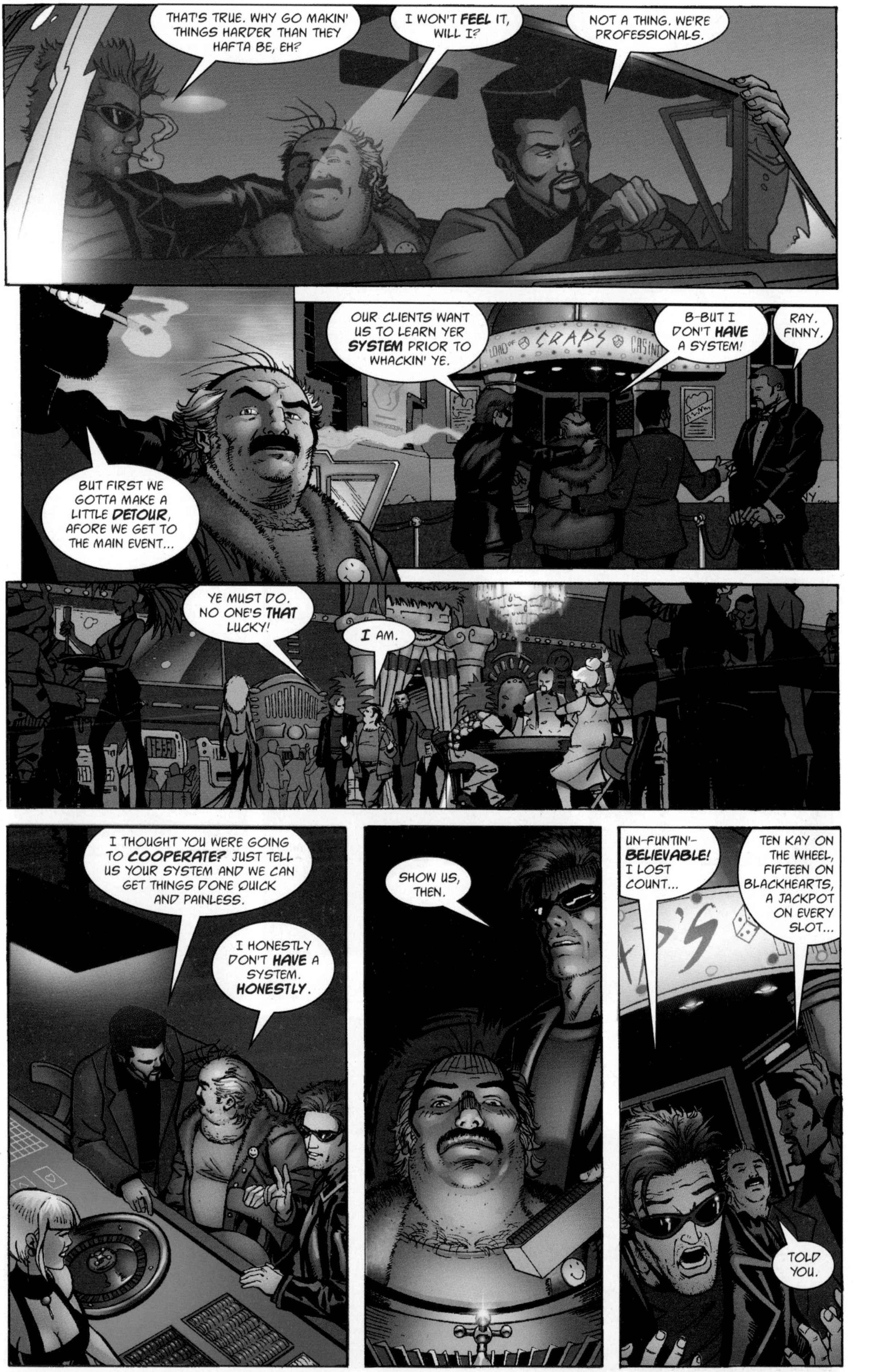
THAT'S TRUE. WHY GO MAKIN' THINGS HARDER THAN THEY HAFTA BE, EH?
I WON'T **FEEL** IT, WILL I?
NOT A THING. WE'RE PROFESSIONALS.
OUR CLIENTS WANT US TO LEARN YER **SYSTEM** PRIOR TO WHACKIN' YE.
B-BUT I DON'T **HAVE** A SYSTEM!
RAY. FINNY.
BUT FIRST WE GOTTA MAKE A LITTLE **DETOUR**, AFORE WE GET TO THE MAIN EVENT...
YE MUST DO. NO ONE'S **THAT** LUCKY!
I AM.
I THOUGHT YOU WERE GOING TO **COOPERATE?** JUST TELL US YOUR SYSTEM AND WE CAN GET THINGS DONE QUICK AND PAINLESS.
I HONESTLY DON'T **HAVE** A SYSTEM. **HONESTLY**.
SHOW US, THEN.
UN-FUNTIN'-**BELIEVABLE!** I LOST COUNT...
TEN KAY ON THE WHEEL, FIFTEEN ON BLACKHEARTS, A JACKPOT ON EVERY SLOT...
TOLD YOU.

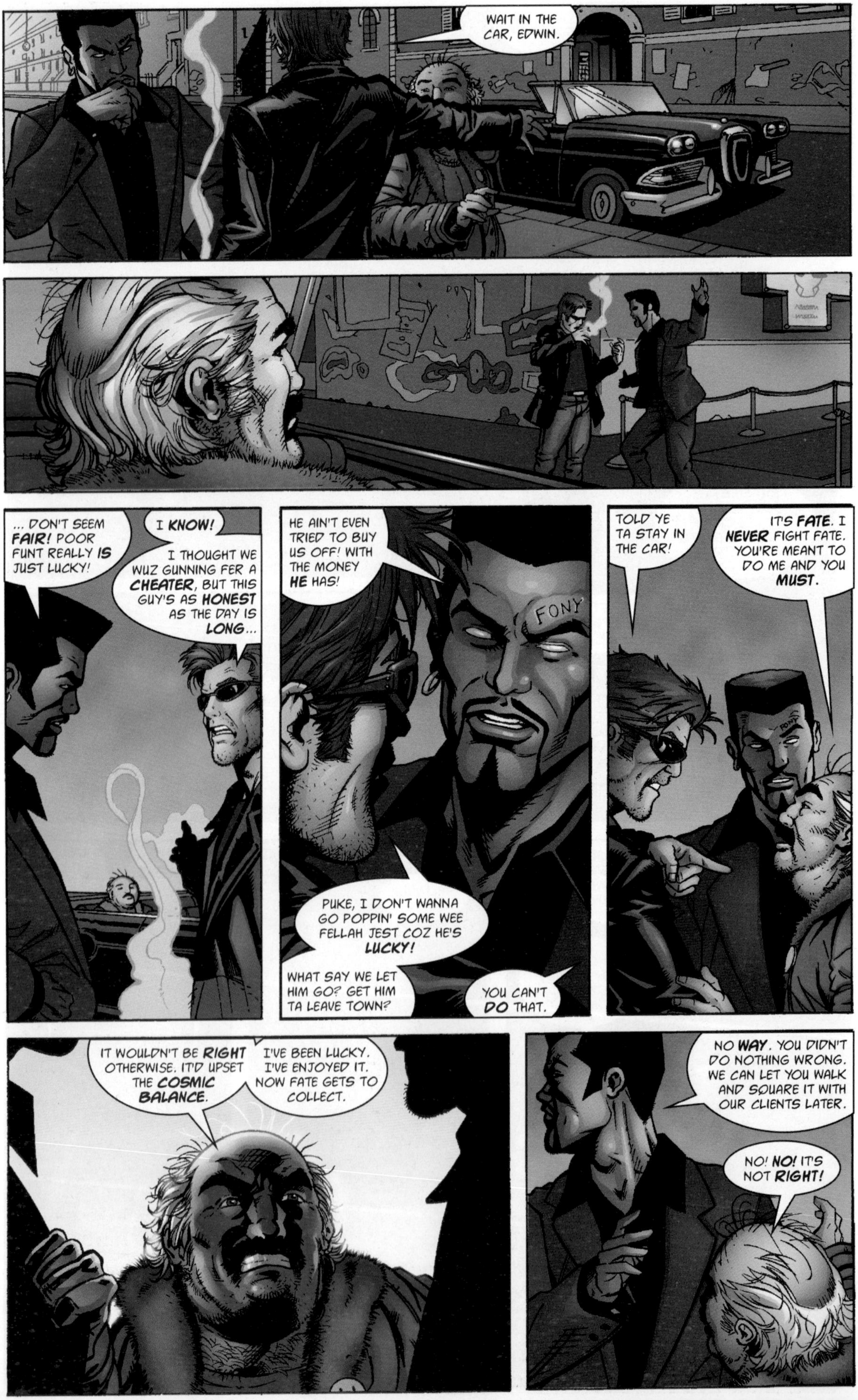
WAIT IN THE CAR, EDWIN.
... DON'T SEEM FAIR! POOR FUNT REALLY IS JUST LUCKY!
I KNOW!
I THOUGHT WE WUZ GUNNING FER A CHEATER, BUT THIS GUY'S AS HONEST AS THE DAY IS LONG...
HE AIN'T EVEN TRIED TO BUY US OFF! WITH THE MONEY HE HAS!
FONY
PUKE, I DON'T WANNA GO POPPIN' SOME WEE FELLAH JEST COZ HE'S LUCKY!
WHAT SAY WE LET HIM GO? GET HIM TA LEAVE TOWN?
YOU CAN'T DO THAT.
TOLD YE TA STAY IN THE CAR!
IT'S FATE. I NEVER FIGHT FATE. YOU'RE MEANT TO DO ME AND YOU MUST.
IT WOULDN'T BE RIGHT OTHERWISE. IT'D UPSET THE COSMIC BALANCE.
I'VE BEEN LUCKY. I'VE ENJOYED IT. NOW FATE GETS TO COLLECT.
NO WAY. YOU DIDN'T DO NOTHING WRONG. WE CAN LET YOU WALK AND SQUARE IT WITH OUR CLIENTS LATER.
NO! NO! IT'S NOT RIGHT!

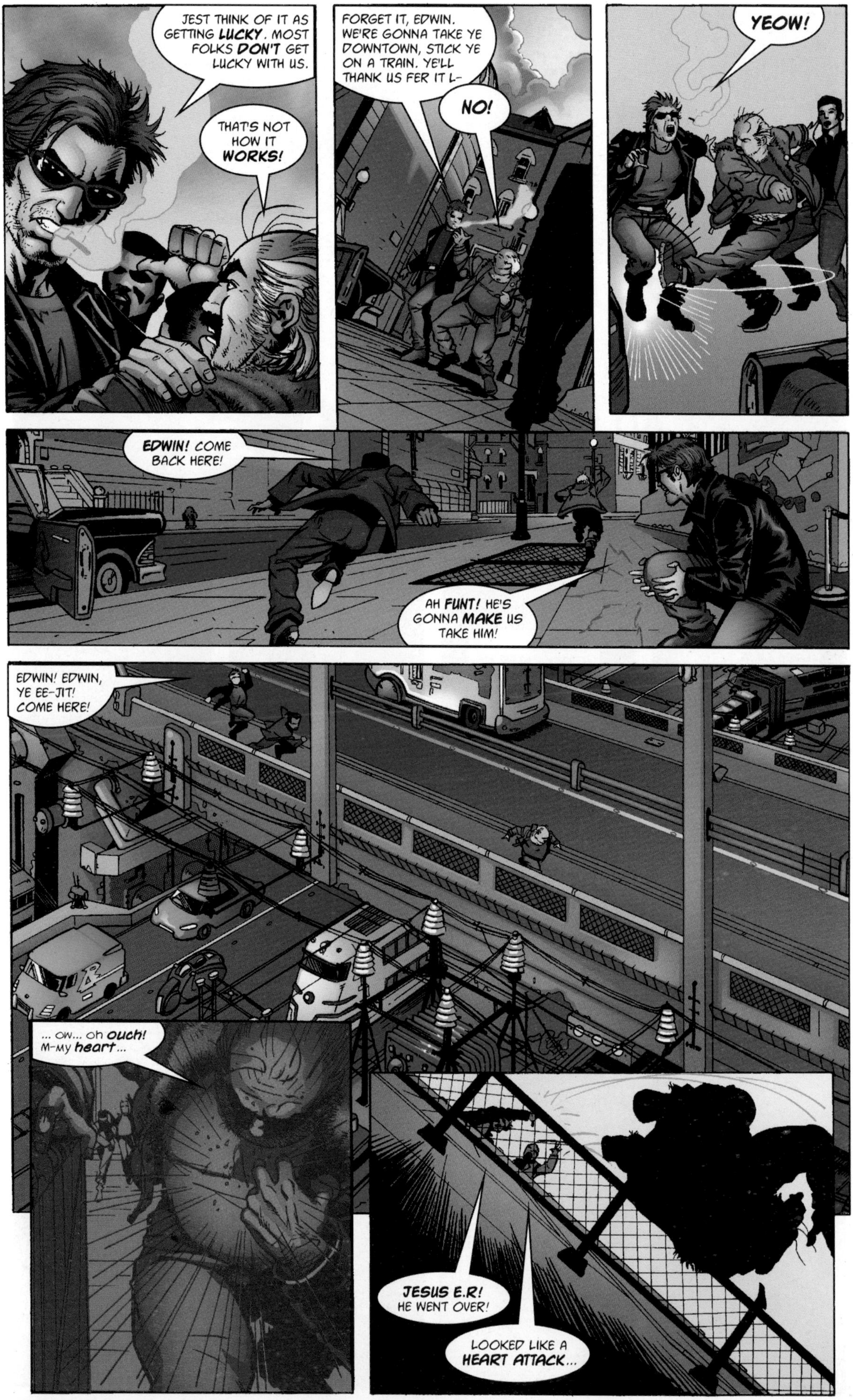

JEST THINK OF IT AS GETTING **LUCKY**. MOST FOLKS **DON'T** GET LUCKY WITH US.
THAT'S NOT HOW IT **WORKS!**
FORGET IT, EDWIN. WE'RE GONNA TAKE YE DOWNTOWN, STICK YE ON A TRAIN. YE'LL THANK US FER IT L-
NO!
YEOW!
EDWIN! COME BACK HERE!
AH **FUNT!** HE'S GONNA **MAKE** US TAKE HIM!
EDWIN! EDWIN, YE EE-JIT! COME HERE!
... OW... OH *OUCH!* M-MY *HEART*...
JESUS E.R! HE WENT OVER!
LOOKED LIKE A **HEART ATTACK**...

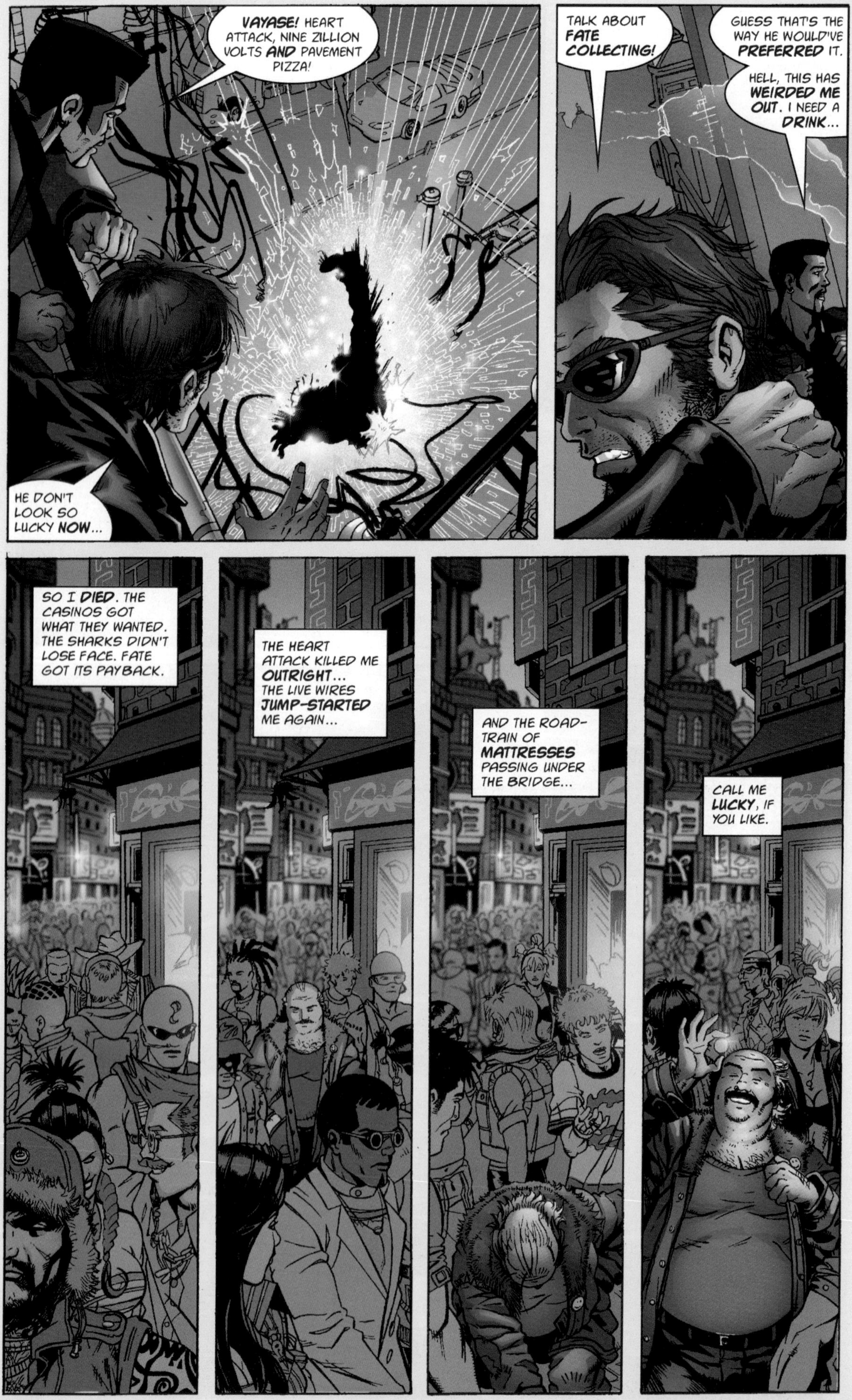

VAYASE! HEART ATTACK, NINE ZILLION VOLTS AND PAVEMENT PIZZA!
HE DON'T LOOK SO LUCKY NOW...
TALK ABOUT FATE COLLECTING!
GUESS THAT'S THE WAY HE WOULD'VE PREFERRED IT.
HELL, THIS HAS WEIRDED ME OUT. I NEED A DRINK...
SO I DIED. THE CASINOS GOT WHAT THEY WANTED. THE SHARKS DIDN'T LOSE FACE. FATE GOT ITS PAYBACK.
THE HEART ATTACK KILLED ME OUTRIGHT... THE LIVE WIRES JUMP-STARTED ME AGAIN...
AND THE ROAD-TRAIN OF MATTRESSES PASSING UNDER THE BRIDGE...
CALL ME LUCKY, IF YOU LIKE.

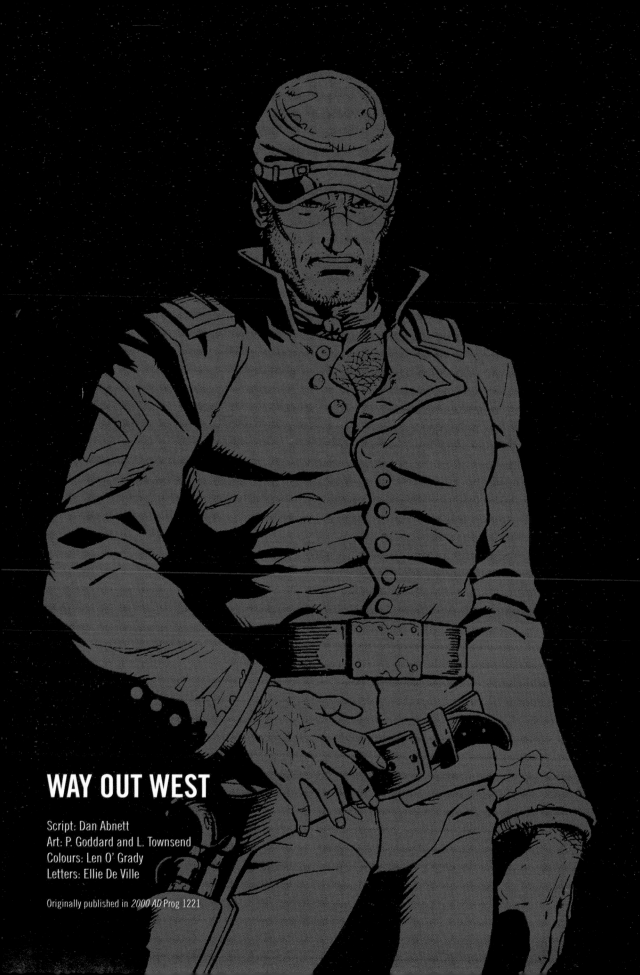

WAY OUT WEST

Script: Dan Abnett
Art: P. Goddard and L. Townsend
Colours: Len O' Grady
Letters: Ellie De Ville

Originally published in *2000 AD* Prog 1221

IT WAS THE FINAL DAYS OF **THE OLD WEST**. THE MODERN WORLD DIDN'T NEED A **WILD FRONTIER** ANYMORE.

ITS TIME HAD COME.

BUT IN THE DUSTY STREETS OF THE LAST CHANCE TOWN BEFORE NOWHERE, TIME MOVED SLOW, **RELUCTANT**, CRAWLING LIKE A DROWSY FLY ON A MULE'S WITHERS.

AND THE LAST OF THE **LEGENDS** LINGERED.

REB BATTLER HAD FOUGHT AT GETTYSBURG, AT APOTOMAC WOOD, AT CLANCYVILLE.

HE'D FOUGHT A THOUSAND TIMES IN A THOUSAND PLACES, HIS NAVY MODEL COLT WREATHING THE AIR WITH GUNSMOKE.

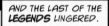

NOW THE OLD WEST WAS FINISHED. BUT REB WASN'T GOING WITHOUT A **FIGHT**.

NO SIR.

TROUBLE'S COMIN'.

LOAD UP.

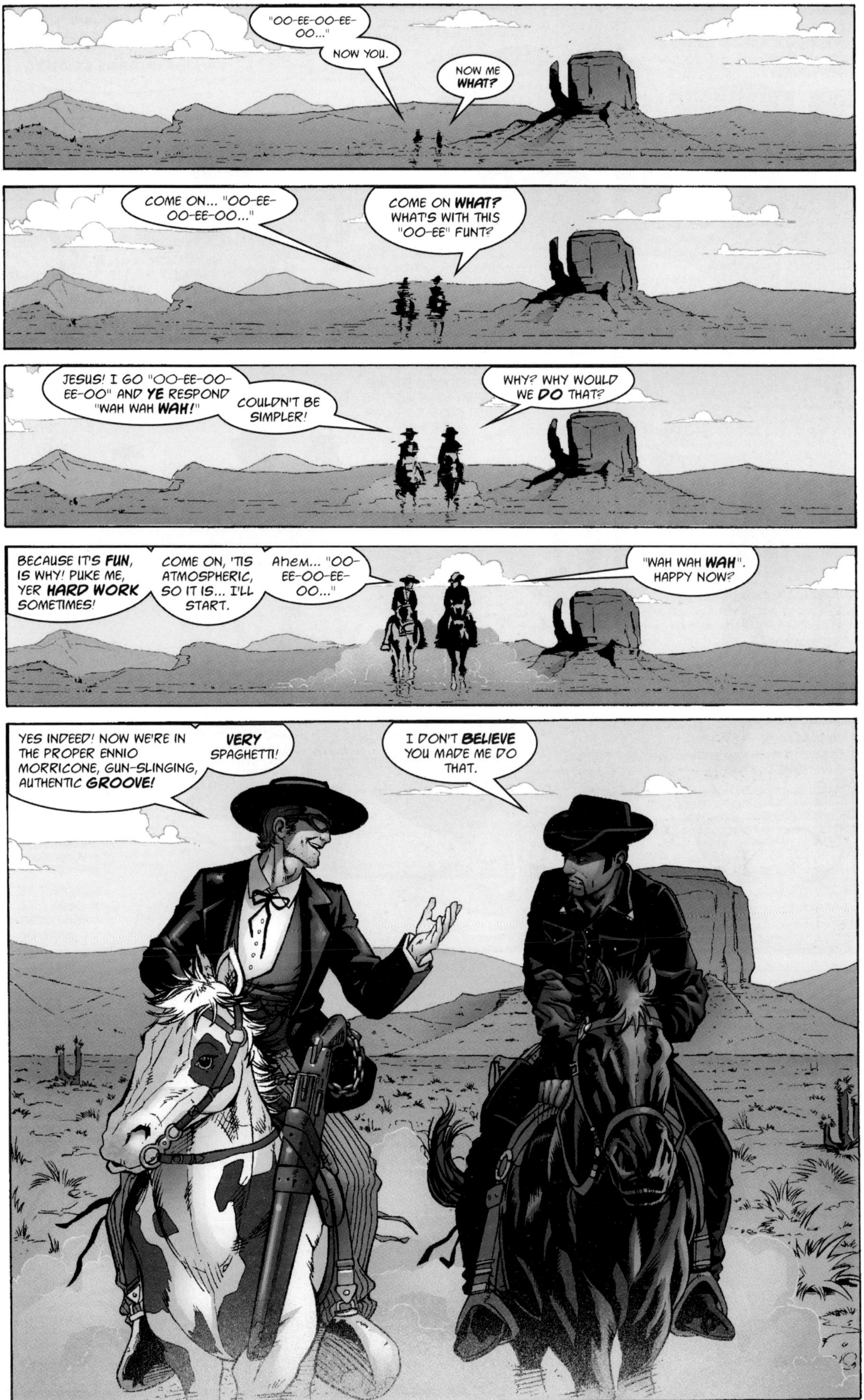
"OO-EE-OO-EE-OO..."
NOW YOU.
NOW ME WHAT?
COME ON... "OO-EE-OO-EE-OO..."
COME ON WHAT? WHAT'S WITH THIS "OO-EE" FUNT?
JESUS! I GO "OO-EE-OO-EE-OO" AND YE RESPOND "WAH WAH WAH!"
COULDN'T BE SIMPLER!
WHY? WHY WOULD WE DO THAT?
BECAUSE IT'S FUN, IS WHY! PUKE ME, YER HARD WORK SOMETIMES!
COME ON, 'TIS ATMOSPHERIC, SO IT IS... I'LL START.
AHEM... "OO-EE-OO-EE-OO..."
"WAH WAH WAH". HAPPY NOW?
YES INDEED! NOW WE'RE IN THE PROPER ENNIO MORRICONE, GUN-SLINGING, AUTHENTIC GROOVE!
VERY SPAGHETTI!
I DON'T BELIEVE YOU MADE ME DO THAT.

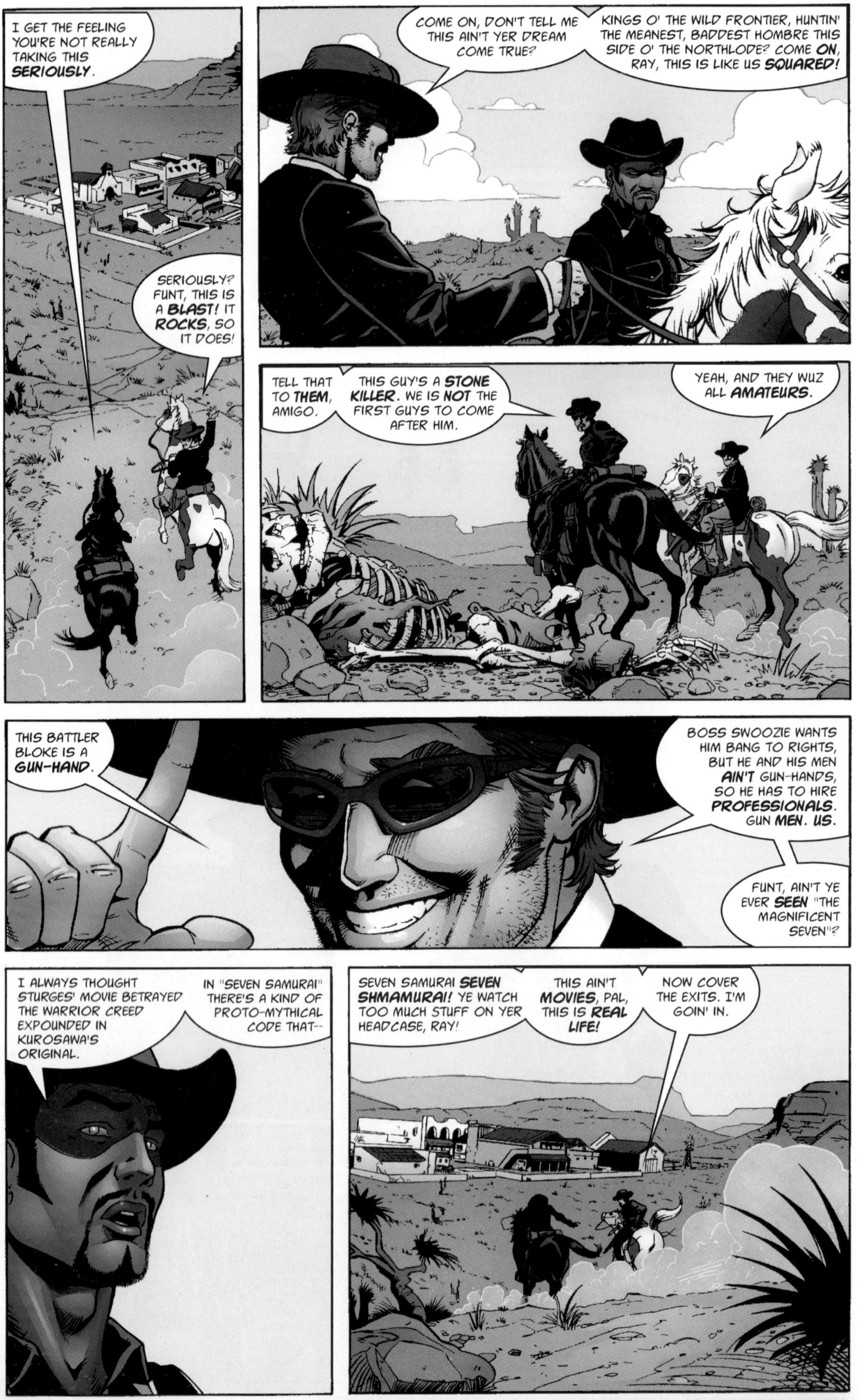

I GET THE FEELING YOU'RE NOT REALLY TAKING THIS **SERIOUSLY**.
SERIOUSLY? FUNT, THIS IS A **BLAST!** IT **ROCKS**, SO IT DOES!
COME ON, DON'T TELL ME THIS AIN'T YER DREAM COME TRUE?
KINGS O' THE WILD FRONTIER, HUNTIN' THE MEANEST, BADDEST HOMBRE THIS SIDE O' THE NORTHLODE? COME **ON**, RAY, THIS IS LIKE US **SQUARED!**
TELL THAT TO **THEM**, AMIGO.
THIS GUY'S A **STONE KILLER**. WE IS **NOT** THE FIRST GUYS TO COME AFTER HIM.
YEAH, AND THEY WUZ ALL **AMATEURS**.
THIS BATTLER BLOKE IS A **GUN-HAND**.
BOSS SWOOZIE WANTS HIM BANG TO RIGHTS, BUT HE AND HIS MEN **AIN'T** GUN-HANDS, SO HE HAS TO HIRE **PROFESSIONALS**. GUN **MEN**. **US**.
FUNT, AIN'T YE EVER **SEEN** "THE MAGNIFICENT SEVEN"?
I ALWAYS THOUGHT STURGES' MOVIE BETRAYED THE WARRIOR CREED EXPOUNDED IN KUROSAWA'S ORIGINAL.
IN "SEVEN SAMURAI" THERE'S A KIND OF PROTO-MYTHICAL CODE THAT--
SEVEN SAMURAI **SEVEN SHMAMURAI!** YE WATCH TOO MUCH STUFF ON YER HEADCASE, RAY!
THIS AIN'T **MOVIES**, PAL, THIS IS **REAL LIFE!**
NOW COVER THE EXITS. I'M GOIN' IN.

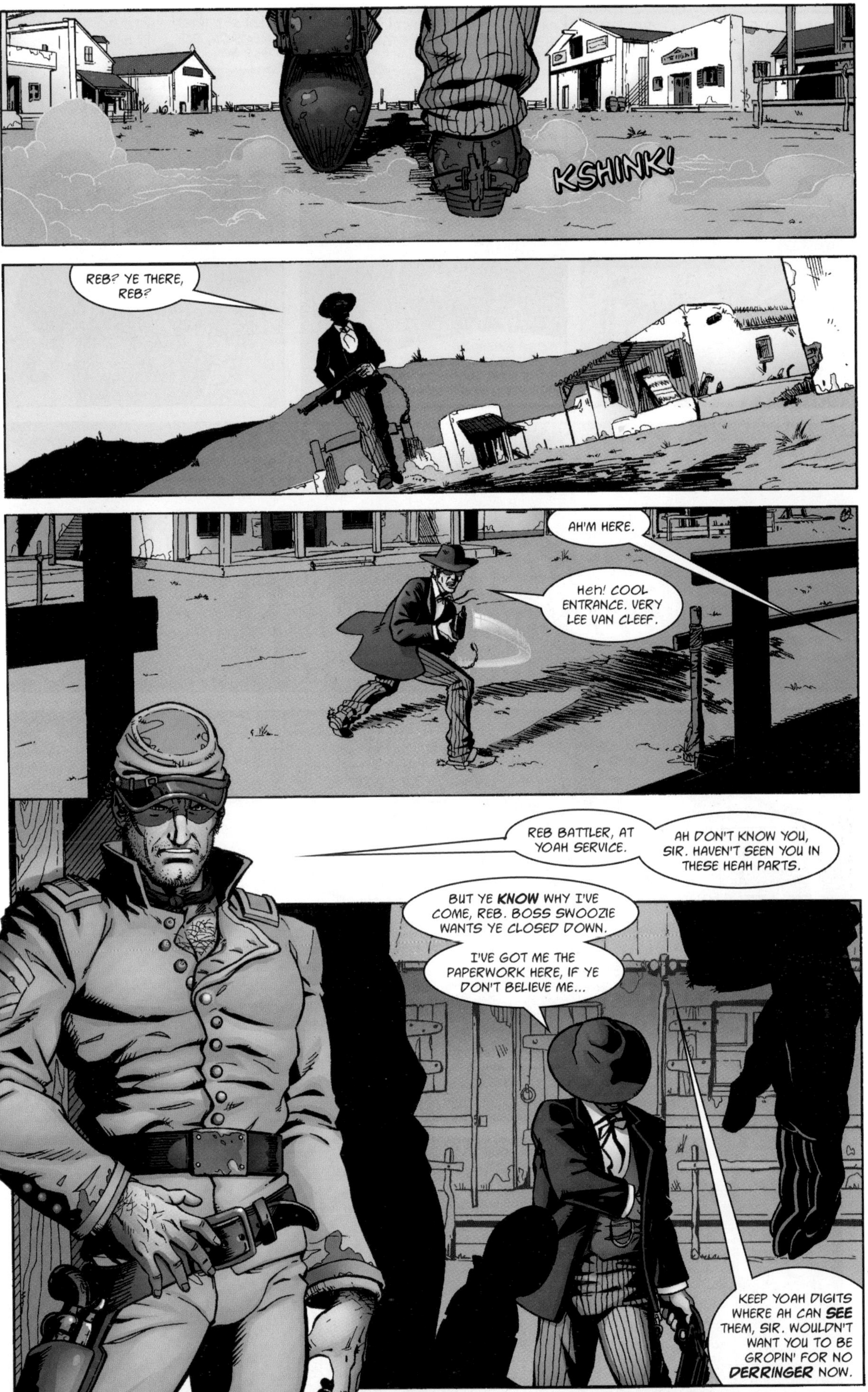
KSHINK!
REB? YE THERE, REB?
AH'M HERE.
Heh! COOL ENTRANCE. VERY LEE VAN CLEEF.
REB BATTLER, AT YOAH SERVICE.
AH DON'T KNOW YOU, SIR. HAVEN'T SEEN YOU IN THESE HEAH PARTS.
BUT YE **KNOW** WHY I'VE COME, REB. BOSS SWOOZIE WANTS YE CLOSED DOWN.
I'VE GOT ME THE PAPERWORK HERE, IF YE DON'T BELIEVE ME...
KEEP YOAH DIGITS WHERE AH CAN **SEE** THEM, SIR. WOULDN'T WANT YOU TO BE GROPIN' FOR NO **DERRINGER** NOW.

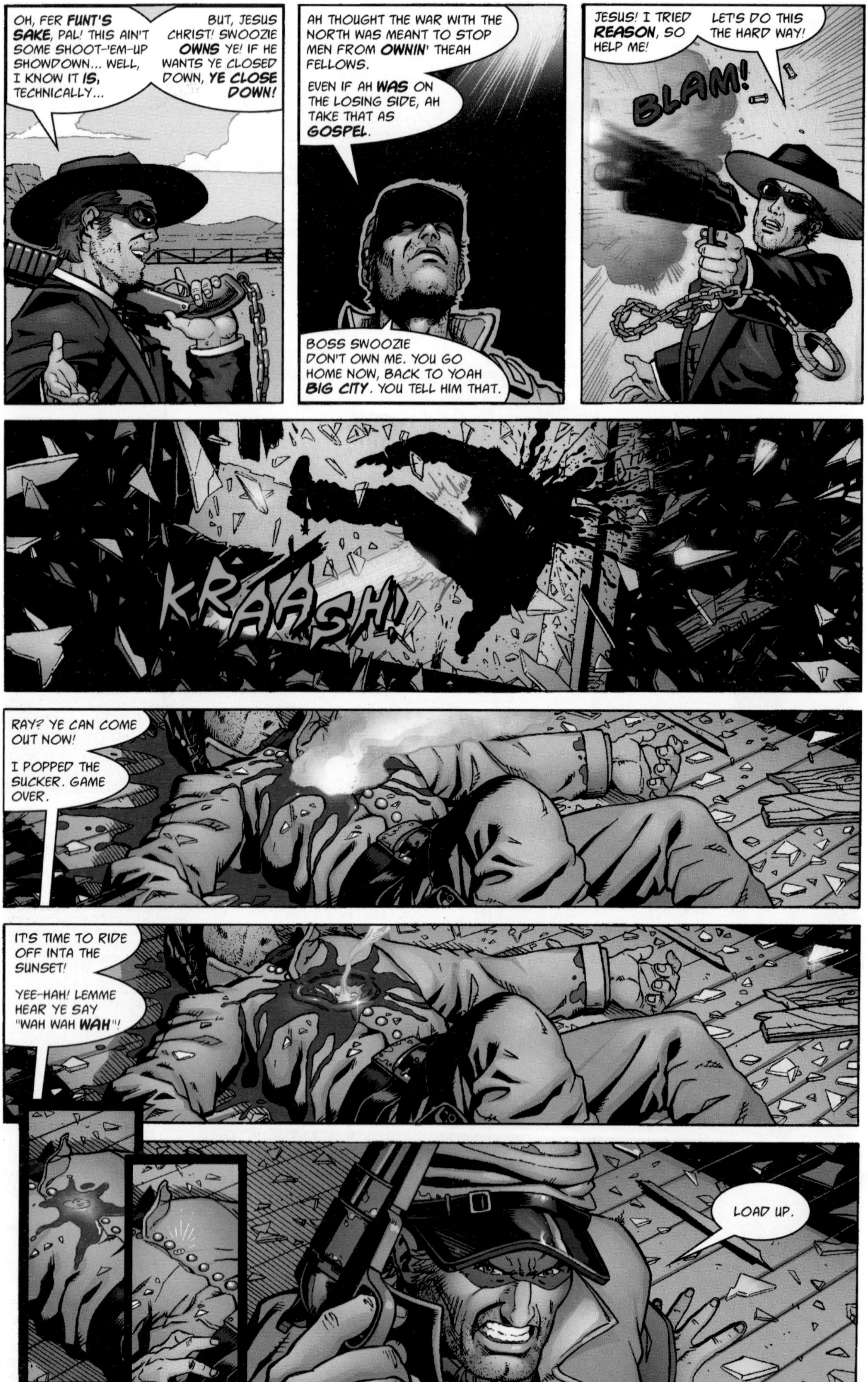
OH, FER FUNT'S SAKE, PAL! THIS AIN'T SOME SHOOT-'EM-UP SHOWDOWN... WELL, I KNOW IT IS, TECHNICALLY...
BUT, JESUS CHRIST! SWOOZIE OWNS YE! IF HE WANTS YE CLOSED DOWN, YE CLOSE DOWN!
AH THOUGHT THE WAR WITH THE NORTH WAS MEANT TO STOP MEN FROM OWNIN' THEAH FELLOWS.
EVEN IF AH WAS ON THE LOSING SIDE, AH TAKE THAT AS GOSPEL.
BOSS SWOOZIE DON'T OWN ME. YOU GO HOME NOW, BACK TO YOAH BIG CITY. YOU TELL HIM THAT.
JESUS! I TRIED REASON, SO HELP ME!
LET'S DO THIS THE HARD WAY!
BLAM!
KRAASH!
RAY? YE CAN COME OUT NOW!
I POPPED THE SUCKER. GAME OVER.
IT'S TIME TO RIDE OFF INTA THE SUNSET!
YEE-HAH! LEMME HEAR YE SAY "WAH WAH WAH"!
LOAD UP.

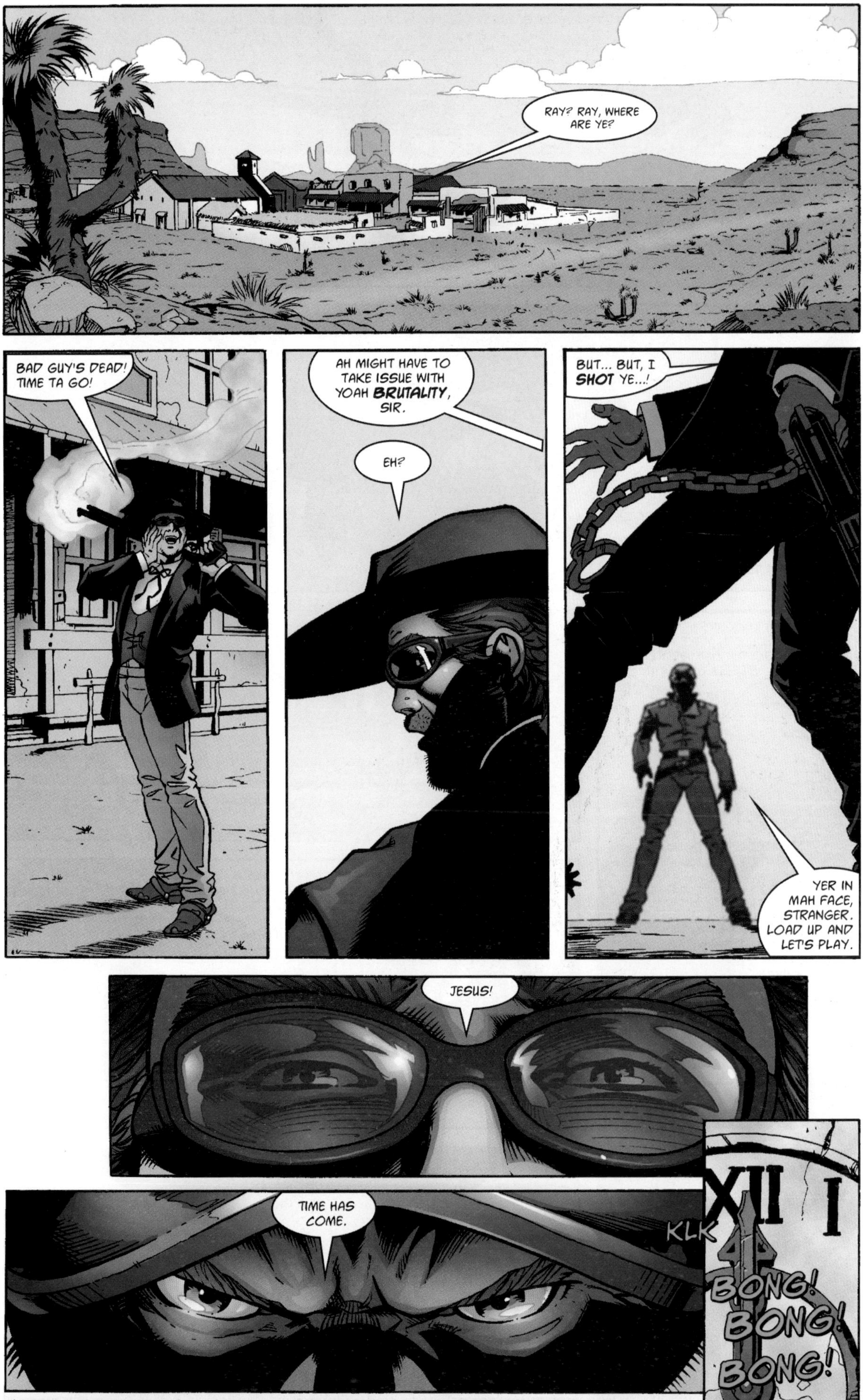
RAY? RAY, WHERE ARE YE?
BAD GUY'S DEAD! TIME TA GO!
AH MIGHT HAVE TO TAKE ISSUE WITH YOAH BRUTALITY, SIR.
EH?
BUT... BUT, I SHOT YE...!
YER IN MAH FACE, STRANGER. LOAD UP AND LET'S PLAY.
JESUS!
TIME HAS COME.
KLK
XII I
BONG! BONG! BONG!

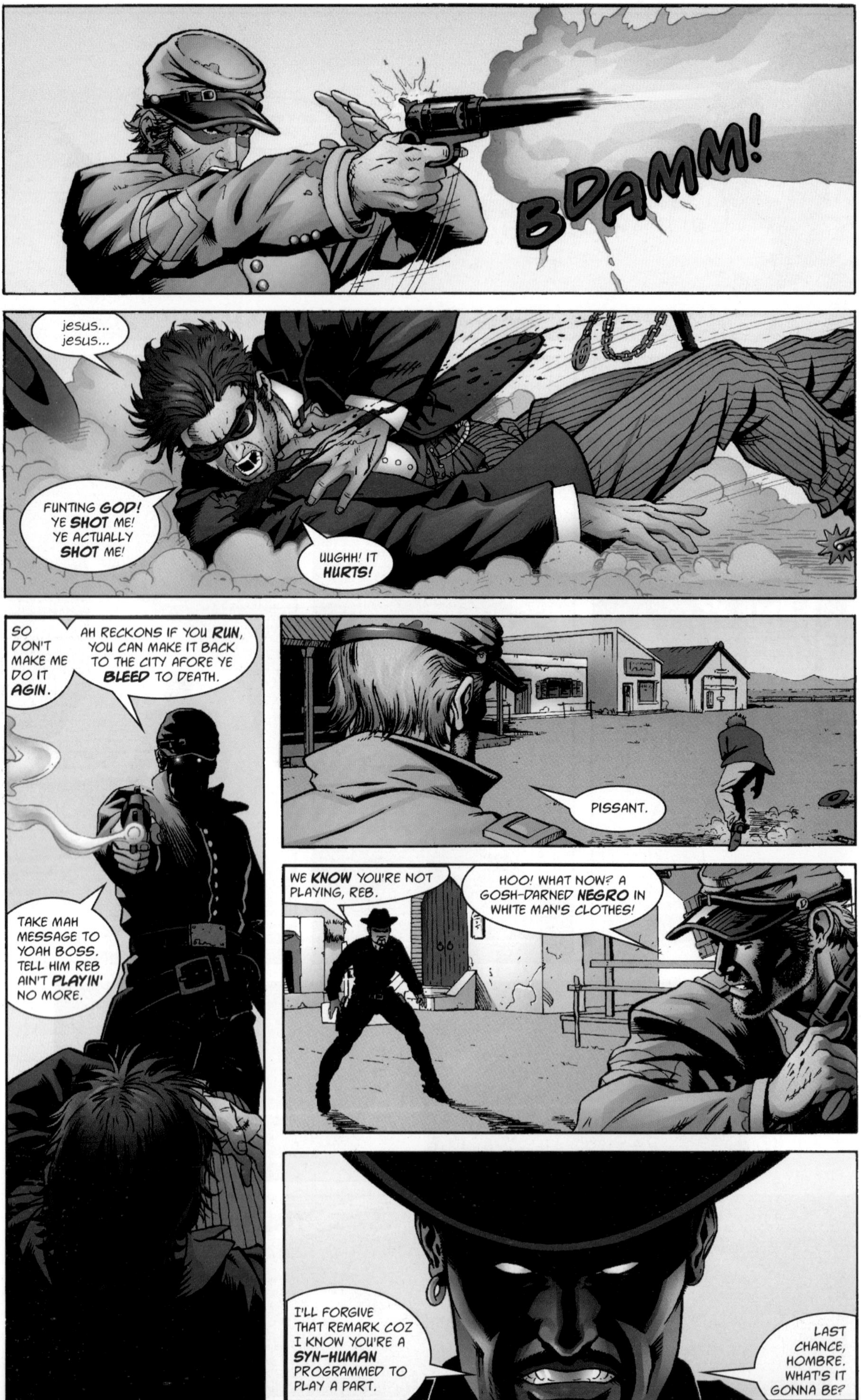
BDAMM!
jesus... jesus...
FUNTING GOD! YE SHOT ME! YE ACTUALLY SHOT ME!
UUGHH! IT HURTS!
SO DON'T MAKE ME DO IT AGIN.
AH RECKONS IF YOU RUN, YOU CAN MAKE IT BACK TO THE CITY AFORE YE BLEED TO DEATH.
TAKE MAH MESSAGE TO YOAH BOSS. TELL HIM REB AIN'T PLAYIN' NO MORE.
PISSANT.
WE KNOW YOU'RE NOT PLAYING, REB.
HOO! WHAT NOW? A GOSH-DARNED NEGRO IN WHITE MAN'S CLOTHES!
I'LL FORGIVE THAT REMARK COZ I KNOW YOU'RE A SYN-HUMAN PROGRAMMED TO PLAY A PART.
LAST CHANCE, HOMBRE. WHAT'S IT GONNA BE?

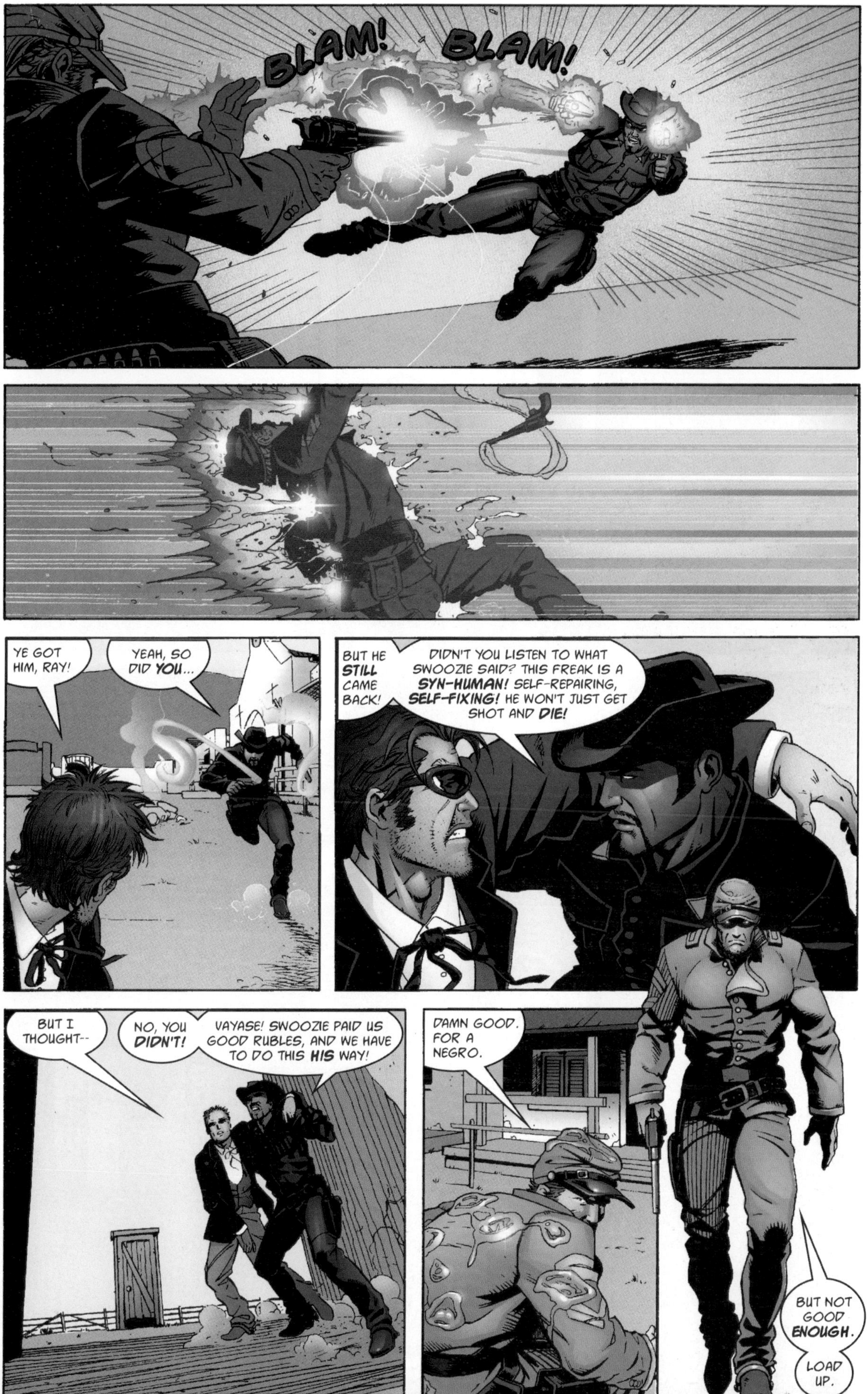
BLAM! BLAM!
YE GOT HIM, RAY!
YEAH, SO DID YOU...
BUT HE STILL CAME BACK!
DIDN'T YOU LISTEN TO WHAT SWOOZIE SAID? THIS FREAK IS A SYN-HUMAN! SELF-REPAIRING, SELF-FIXING! HE WON'T JUST GET SHOT AND DIE!
BUT I THOUGHT--
NO, YOU DIDN'T!
VAYASE! SWOOZIE PAID US GOOD RUBLES, AND WE HAVE TO DO THIS HIS WAY!
DAMN GOOD. FOR A NEGRO.
BUT NOT GOOD ENOUGH.
LOAD UP.

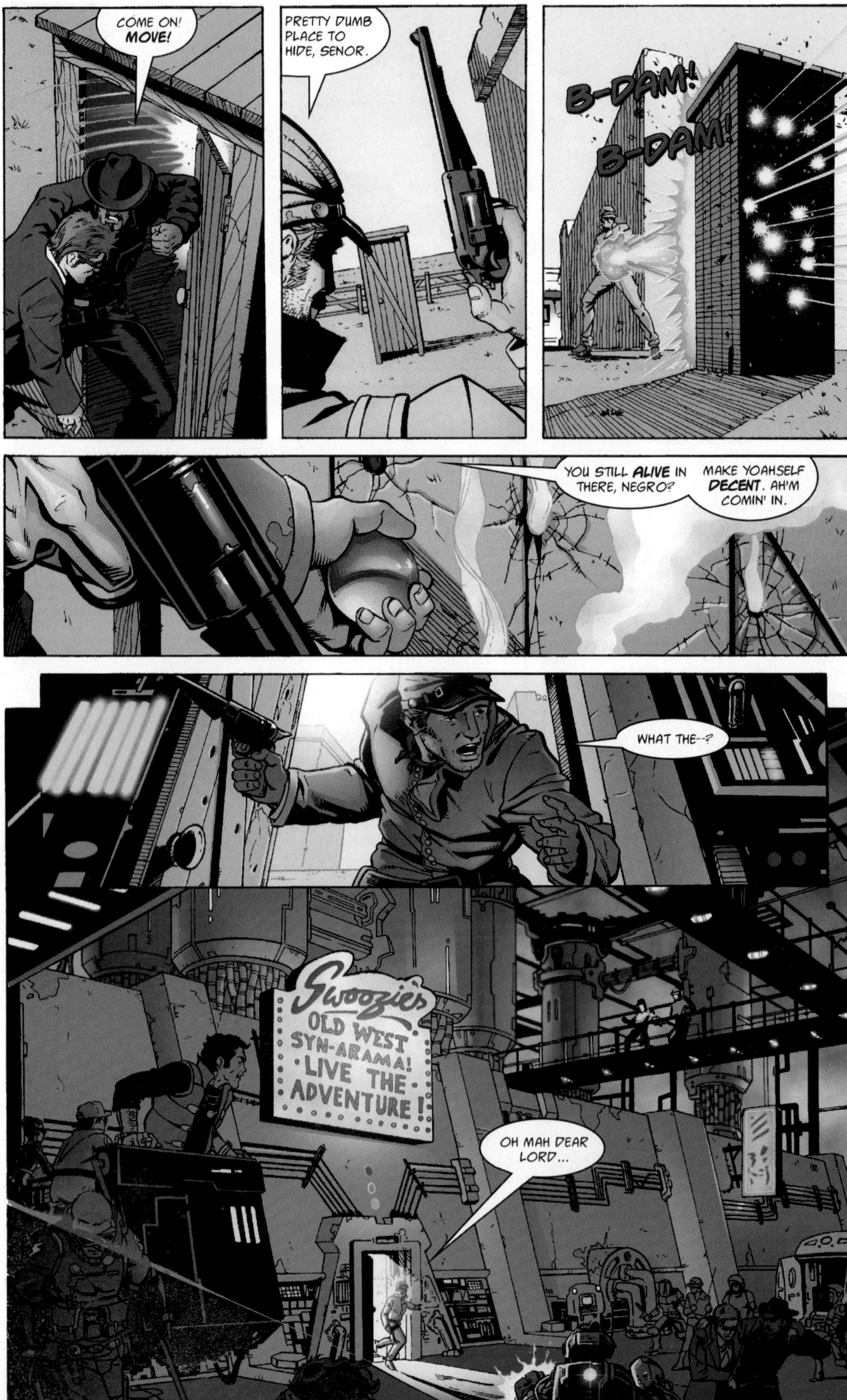
COME ON! **MOVE!**
PRETTY DUMB PLACE TO HIDE, SENOR.
B-DAM!
B-DAM!
YOU STILL **ALIVE** IN THERE, NEGRO?
MAKE YOAHSELF **DECENT**. AH'M COMIN' IN.
WHAT THE--?
Swoozie's OLD WEST SYN-ARAMA! LIVE THE ADVENTURE!
OH MAH DEAR LORD...

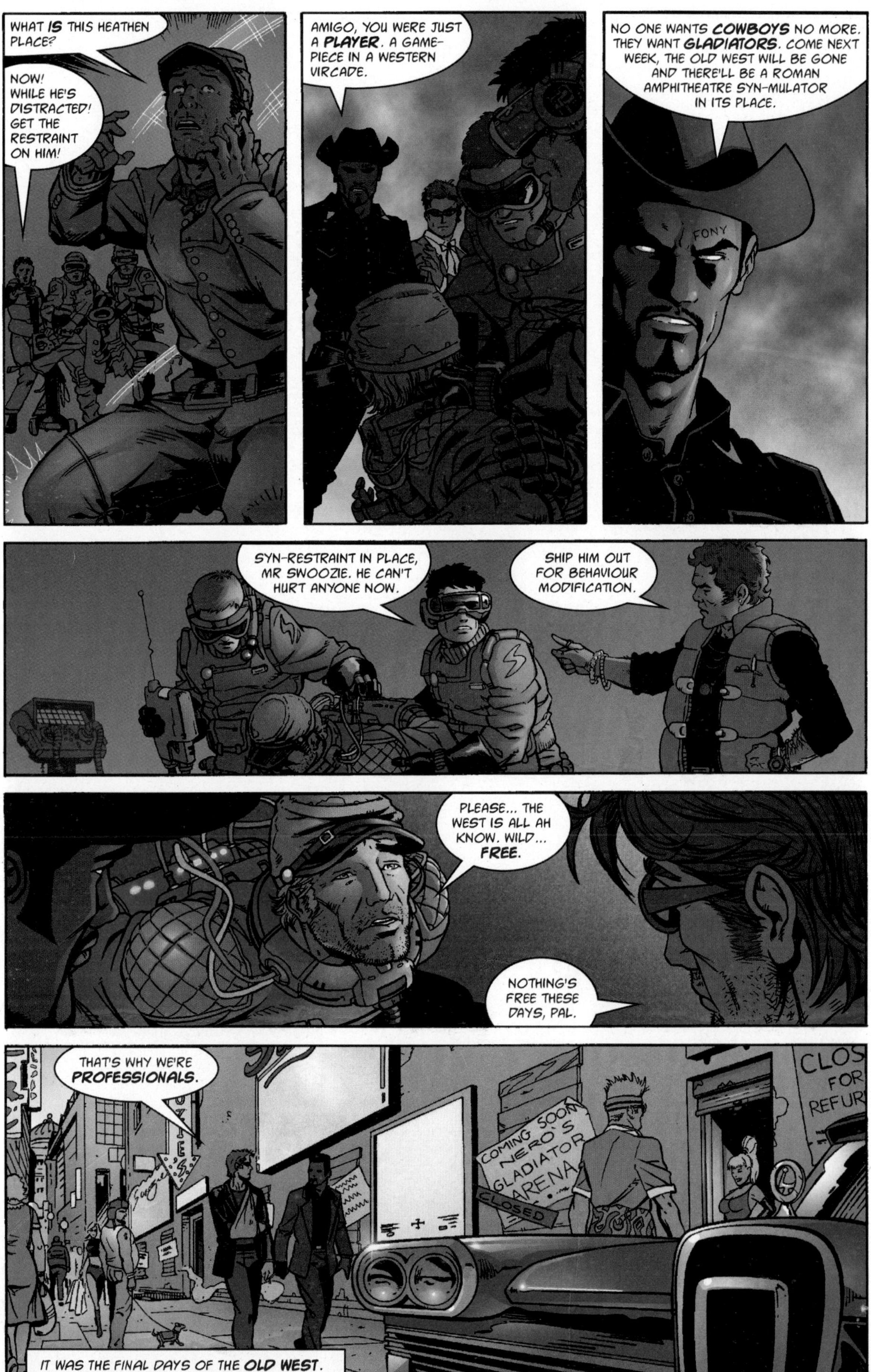
WHAT **IS** THIS HEATHEN PLACE?
NOW! WHILE HE'S DISTRACTED! GET THE RESTRAINT ON HIM!
AMIGO, YOU WERE JUST A **PLAYER**. A GAME-PIECE IN A WESTERN VIRCADE.
NO ONE WANTS **COWBOYS** NO MORE. THEY WANT **GLADIATORS**. COME NEXT WEEK, THE OLD WEST WILL BE GONE AND THERE'LL BE A ROMAN AMPHITHEATRE SYN-MULATOR IN ITS PLACE.
FONY
SYN-RESTRAINT IN PLACE, MR SWOOZIE. HE CAN'T HURT ANYONE NOW.
SHIP HIM OUT FOR BEHAVIOUR MODIFICATION.
PLEASE... THE WEST IS ALL AH KNOW. WILD... **FREE**.
NOTHING'S FREE THESE DAYS, PAL.
THAT'S WHY WE'RE **PROFESSIONALS**.
COMING SOON NERO'S GLADIATOR ARENA
CLOSED
IT WAS THE FINAL DAYS OF THE **OLD WEST**. THINGS HAD CHANGED. THE MODERN WORLD DIDN'T NEED A **WILD FRONTIER** ANYMORE.

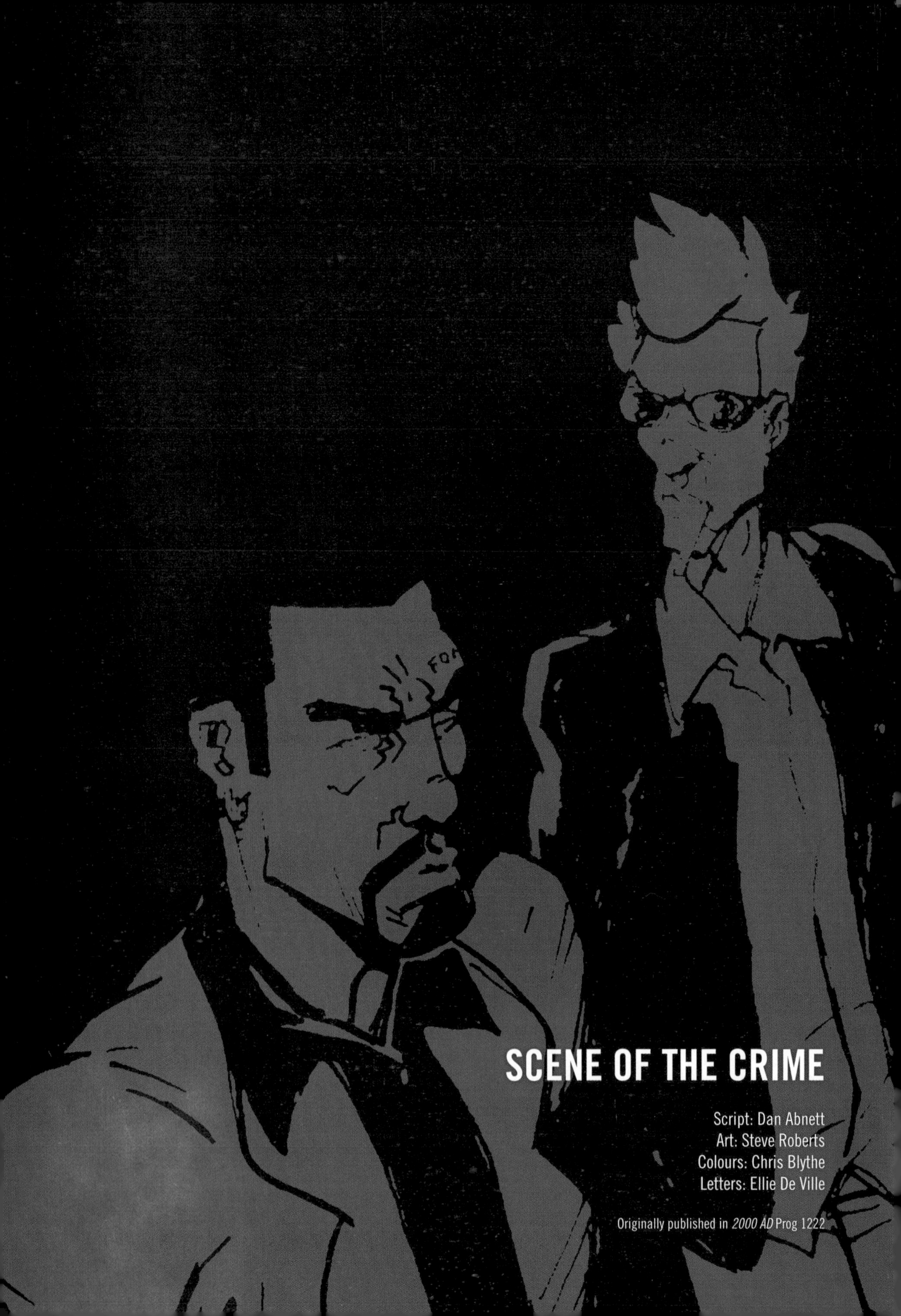

SCENE OF THE CRIME

Script: Dan Abnett
Art: Steve Roberts
Colours: Chris Blythe
Letters: Ellie De Ville

Originally published in *2000 AD* Prog 1222

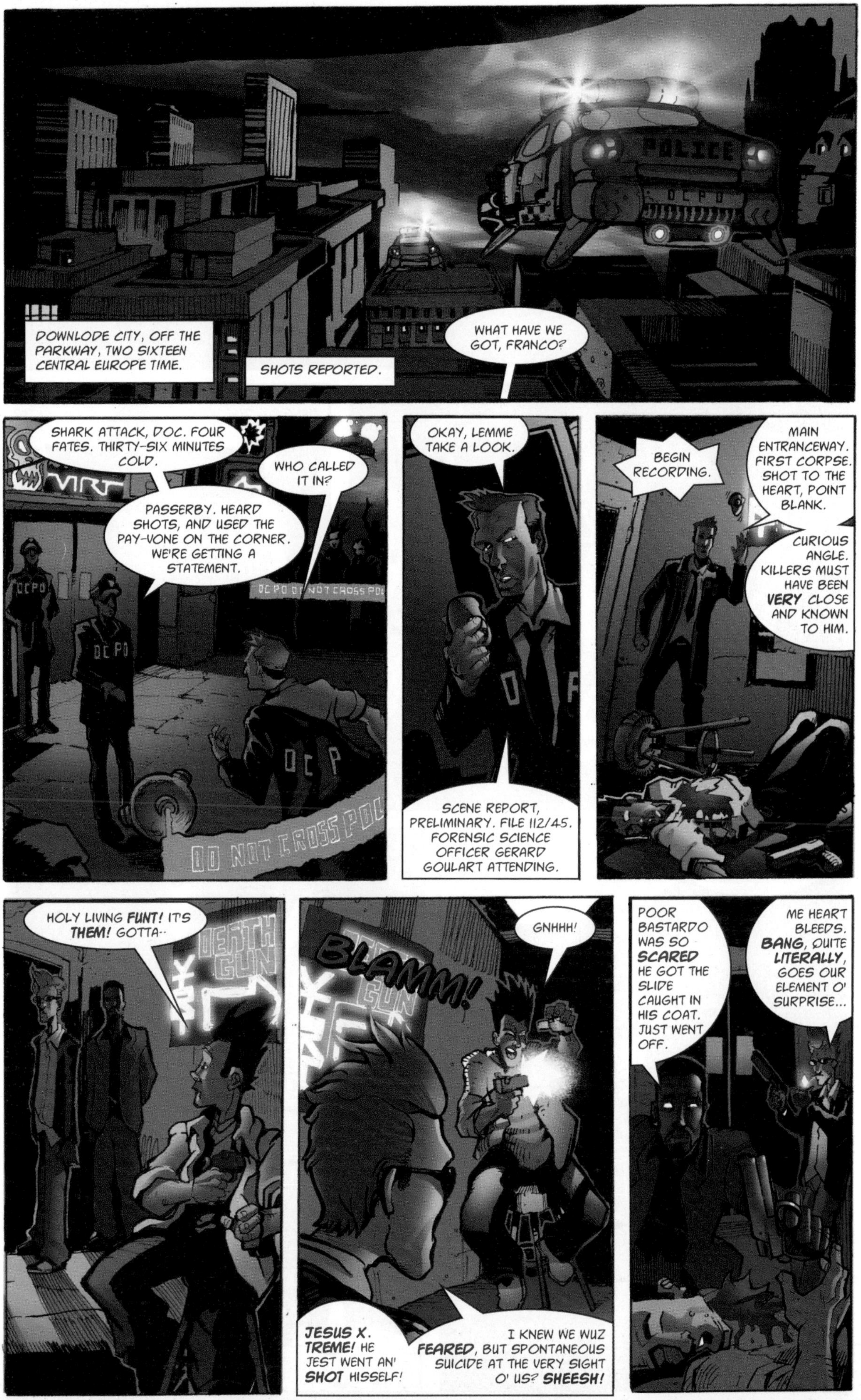

DOWNLODE CITY, OFF THE PARKWAY, TWO SIXTEEN CENTRAL EUROPE TIME.
SHOTS REPORTED.
WHAT HAVE WE GOT, FRANCO?
POLICE
DCPD
SHARK ATTACK, DOC. FOUR FATES. THIRTY-SIX MINUTES COLD.
WHO CALLED IT IN?
PASSERBY. HEARD SHOTS, AND USED THE PAY-VONE ON THE CORNER. WE'RE GETTING A STATEMENT.
DO NOT CROSS POL
OKAY, LEMME TAKE A LOOK.
SCENE REPORT, PRELIMINARY. FILE 112/45. FORENSIC SCIENCE OFFICER GERARD GOULART ATTENDING.
BEGIN RECORDING.
MAIN ENTRANCEWAY. FIRST CORPSE. SHOT TO THE HEART, POINT BLANK.
CURIOUS ANGLE. KILLERS MUST HAVE BEEN VERY CLOSE AND KNOWN TO HIM.
HOLY LIVING FUNT! IT'S THEM! GOTTA--
DEATH GUN
BLAMM!
GNHHH!
JESUS X. TREME! HE JEST WENT AN' SHOT HISSELF!
I KNEW WE WUZ FEARED, BUT SPONTANEOUS SUICIDE AT THE VERY SIGHT O' US? SHEESH!
POOR BASTARDO WAS SO SCARED HE GOT THE SLIDE CAUGHT IN HIS COAT. JUST WENT OFF.
ME HEART BLEEDS. BANG, QUITE LITERALLY, GOES OUR ELEMENT O' SURPRISE...

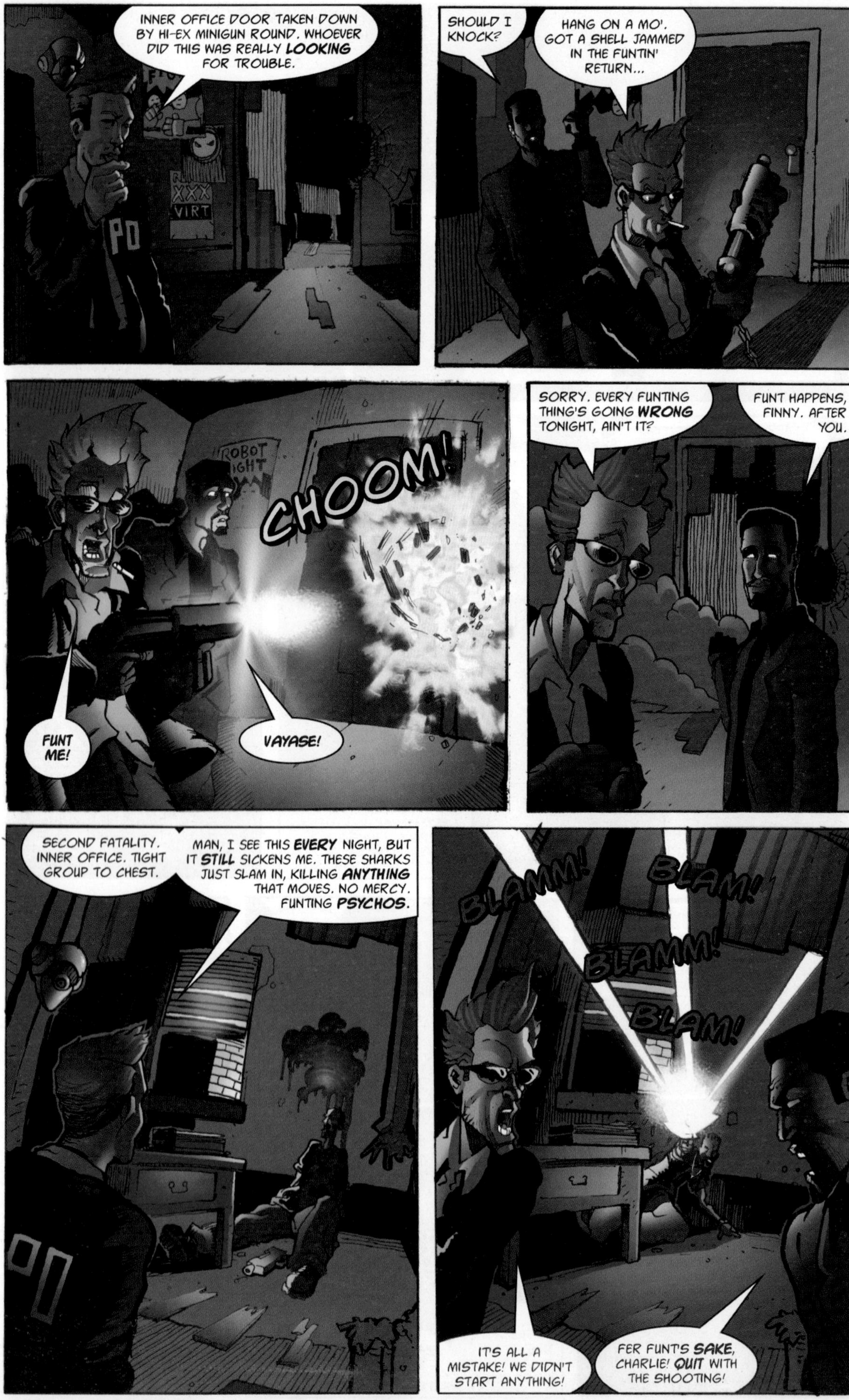

INNER OFFICE DOOR TAKEN DOWN BY HI-EX MINIGUN ROUND. WHOEVER DID THIS WAS REALLY **LOOKING** FOR TROUBLE.
SHOULD I KNOCK?
HANG ON A MO'. GOT A SHELL JAMMED IN THE FUNTIN' RETURN...
CHOOM!
FUNT ME!
VAYASE!
SORRY. EVERY FUNTING THING'S GOING **WRONG** TONIGHT, AIN'T IT?
FUNT HAPPENS, FINNY. AFTER YOU.
SECOND FATALITY. INNER OFFICE. TIGHT GROUP TO CHEST.
MAN, I SEE THIS **EVERY** NIGHT, BUT IT **STILL** SICKENS ME. THESE SHARKS JUST SLAM IN, KILLING **ANYTHING** THAT MOVES. NO MERCY. FUNTING **PSYCHOS**.
BLAMM!
BLAM!
BLAMM!
BLAM!
IT'S ALL A MISTAKE! WE DIDN'T START ANYTHING!
FER FUNT'S **SAKE**, CHARLIE! **QUIT** WITH THE SHOOTING!

HE **AIN'T** HEARIN' US. WE GOT NO CHOICE.

BLAMM!

BLAM!

P-TING!

I HATE THAT, AMIGO.

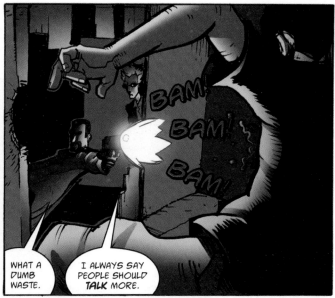

BAM!

BAM!

BAM!

WHAT A DUMB WASTE.

I ALWAYS SAY PEOPLE SHOULD **TALK** MORE.

MAIN VIRCADE HALL. VIRT GAME-BOYS TO EACH SIDE, MOST STILL ACTIVE.

THE SHARKS MUST HAVE MADE A SYSTEMATIC SWEEP AND DRIVEN OUT THE PUNTERS SO THEY COULD GET THE PLACE TO THEMSELVES.

HEY! HEY!

PUKE, I CAN'T HEAR MESSELF **THINK** OVER THIS NOISE.

HOLA EVERYONE! WE'RE LOOKING FOR JEFFY HUANG!

AHA. **THAT** GOT YER ATTENTION. NOW, NO-ONE HAS TA **PANIC**, BUT··

WHEAAY!

GNUFF!

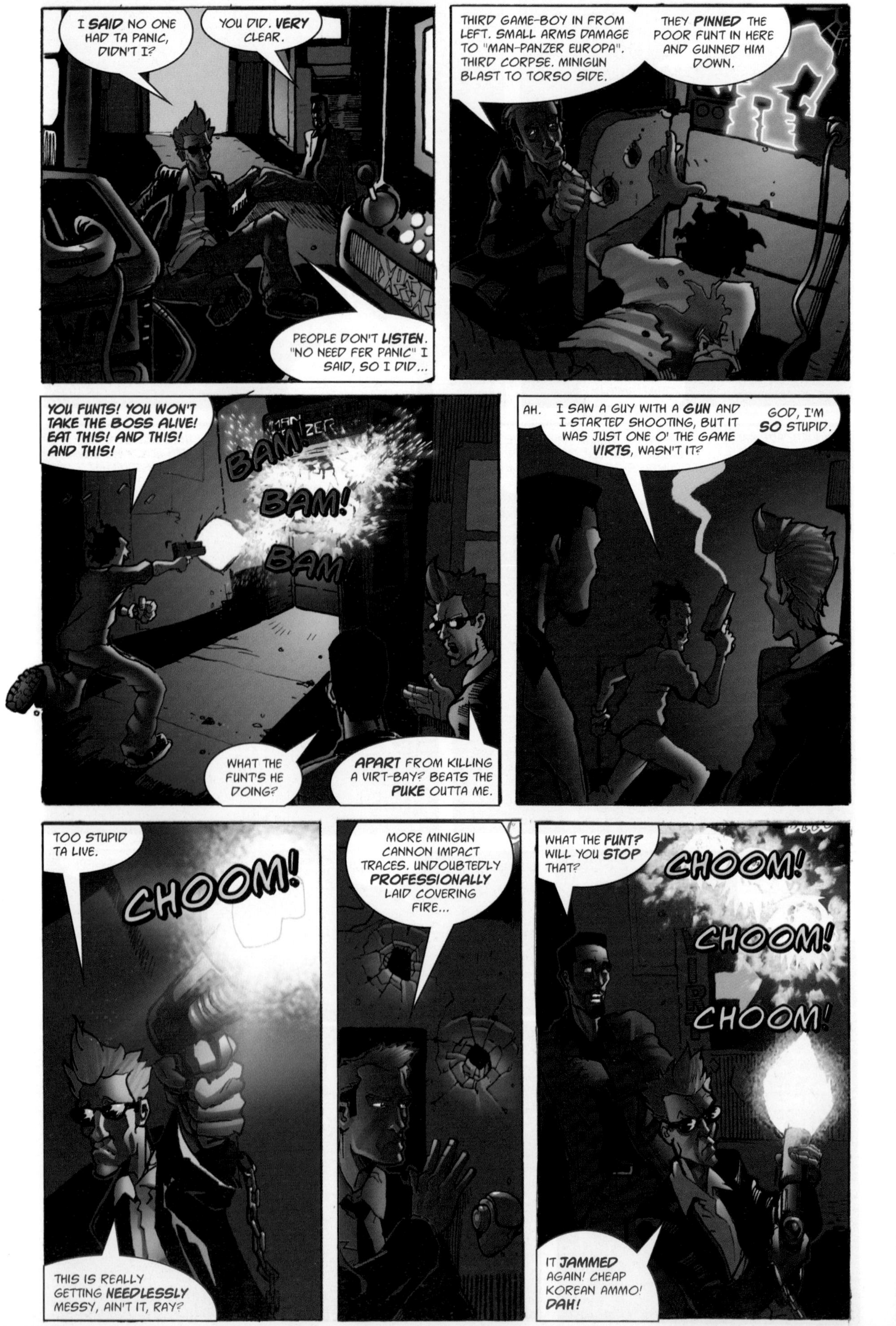

I SAID NO ONE HAD TA PANIC, DIDN'T I?
YOU DID. VERY CLEAR.
PEOPLE DON'T LISTEN. "NO NEED FER PANIC" I SAID, SO I DID...
THIRD GAME-BOY IN FROM LEFT. SMALL ARMS DAMAGE TO "MAN-PANZER EUROPA". THIRD CORPSE. MINIGUN BLAST TO TORSO SIDE.
THEY PINNED THE POOR FUNT IN HERE AND GUNNED HIM DOWN.
YOU FUNTS! YOU WON'T TAKE THE BOSS ALIVE! EAT THIS! AND THIS! AND THIS!
BAM!
BAM!
BAM!
WHAT THE FUNT'S HE DOING?
APART FROM KILLING A VIRT-BAY? BEATS THE PUKE OUTTA ME.
AH.
I SAW A GUY WITH A GUN AND I STARTED SHOOTING, BUT IT WAS JUST ONE O' THE GAME VIRTS, WASN'T IT?
GOD, I'M SO STUPID.
TOO STUPID TA LIVE.
CHOOM!
THIS IS REALLY GETTING NEEDLESSLY MESSY, AIN'T IT, RAY?
MORE MINIGUN CANNON IMPACT TRACES. UNDOUBTEDLY PROFESSIONALLY LAID COVERING FIRE...
WHAT THE FUNT? WILL YOU STOP THAT?
CHOOM!
CHOOM!
CHOOM!
IT JAMMED AGAIN! CHEAP KOREAN AMMO! DAH!

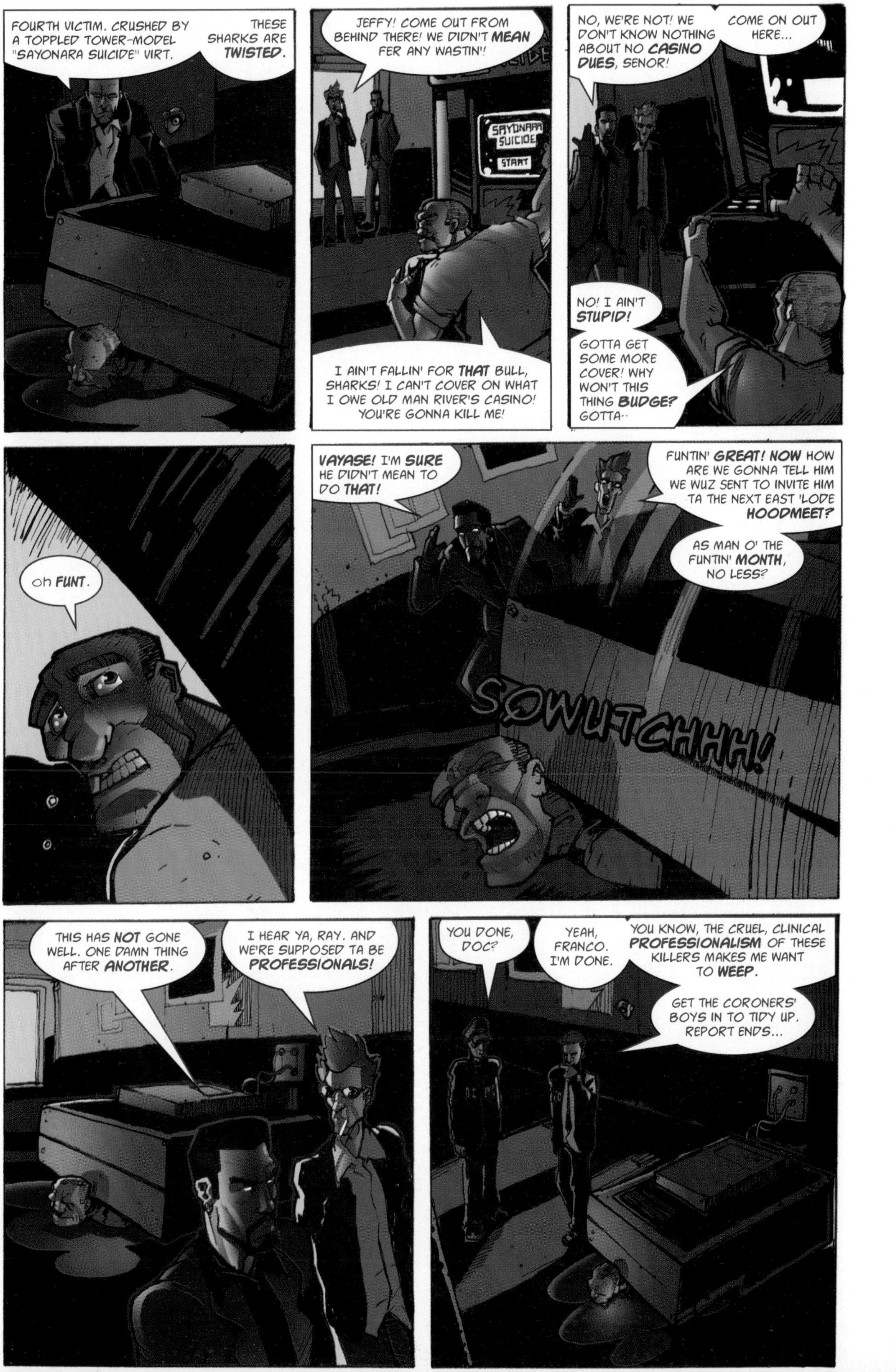
FOURTH VICTIM. CRUSHED BY A TOPPLED TOWER-MODEL "SAYONARA SUICIDE" VIRT.
THESE SHARKS ARE **TWISTED**.
JEFFY! COME OUT FROM BEHIND THERE! WE DIDN'T **MEAN** FER ANY WASTIN'!
SAYONARA SUICIDE
START
I AIN'T FALLIN' FOR **THAT** BULL, SHARKS! I CAN'T COVER ON WHAT I OWE OLD MAN RIVER'S CASINO! YOU'RE GONNA KILL ME!
NO, WE'RE NOT! WE DON'T KNOW NOTHING ABOUT NO **CASINO DUES**, SENOR!
COME ON OUT HERE...
NO! I AIN'T **STUPID!**
GOTTA GET SOME MORE COVER! WHY WON'T THIS THING **BUDGE?** GOTTA--
oh **FUNT**.
VAYASE! I'M **SURE** HE DIDN'T MEAN TO DO **THAT!**
FUNTIN' **GREAT! NOW** HOW ARE WE GONNA TELL HIM WE WUZ SENT TO INVITE HIM TA THE NEXT EAST 'LODE **HOODMEET?**
AS MAN O' THE FUNTIN' **MONTH**, NO LESS?
SQWUTCHHH!
THIS HAS **NOT** GONE WELL. ONE DAMN THING AFTER **ANOTHER**.
I HEAR YA, RAY. AND WE'RE SUPPOSED TA BE **PROFESSIONALS!**
YOU DONE, DOC?
YEAH, FRANCO. I'M DONE.
YOU KNOW, THE CRUEL, CLINICAL **PROFESSIONALISM** OF THESE KILLERS MAKES ME WANT TO **WEEP**.
GET THE CORONERS' BOYS IN TO TIDY UP. REPORT ENDS...

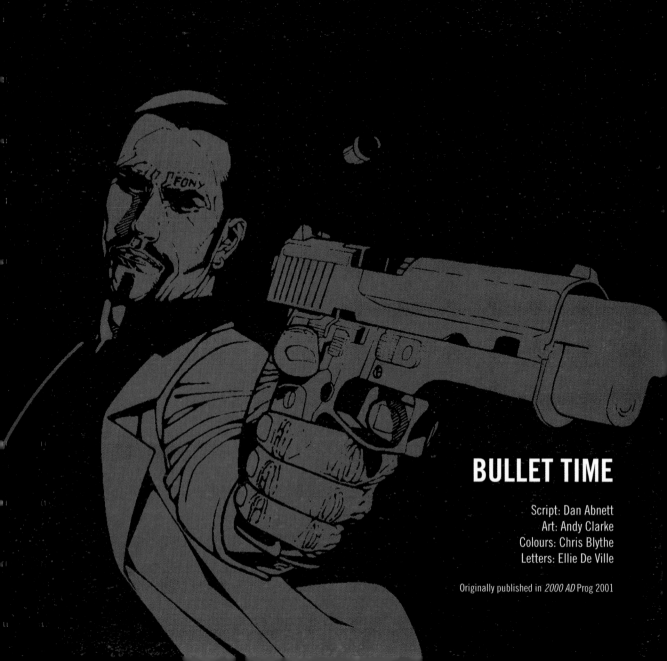

BULLET TIME

Script: Dan Abnett
Art: Andy Clarke
Colours: Chris Blythe
Letters: Ellie De Ville

Originally published in *2000 AD* Prog 2001

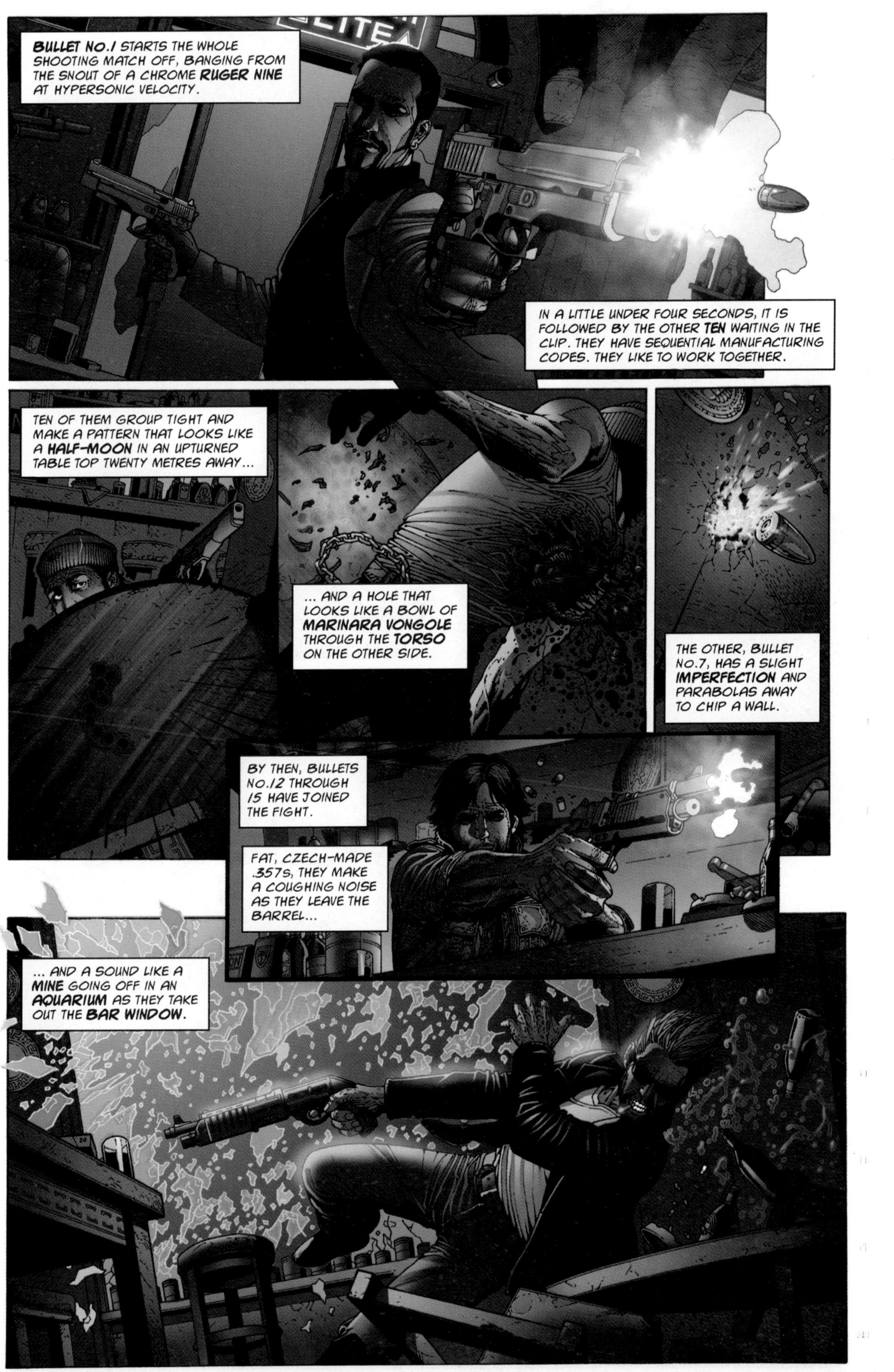
ELITE
BULLET NO.1 STARTS THE WHOLE SHOOTING MATCH OFF, BANGING FROM THE SNOUT OF A CHROME RUGER NINE AT HYPERSONIC VELOCITY.
IN A LITTLE UNDER FOUR SECONDS, IT IS FOLLOWED BY THE OTHER TEN WAITING IN THE CLIP. THEY HAVE SEQUENTIAL MANUFACTURING CODES. THEY LIKE TO WORK TOGETHER.
TEN OF THEM GROUP TIGHT AND MAKE A PATTERN THAT LOOKS LIKE A HALF-MOON IN AN UPTURNED TABLE TOP TWENTY METRES AWAY...
... AND A HOLE THAT LOOKS LIKE A BOWL OF MARINARA VONGOLE THROUGH THE TORSO ON THE OTHER SIDE.
THE OTHER, BULLET NO.7, HAS A SLIGHT IMPERFECTION AND PARABOLAS AWAY TO CHIP A WALL.
BY THEN, BULLETS NO.12 THROUGH 15 HAVE JOINED THE FIGHT.
FAT, CZECH-MADE .357S, THEY MAKE A COUGHING NOISE AS THEY LEAVE THE BARREL...
... AND A SOUND LIKE A MINE GOING OFF IN AN AQUARIUM AS THEY TAKE OUT THE BAR WINDOW.

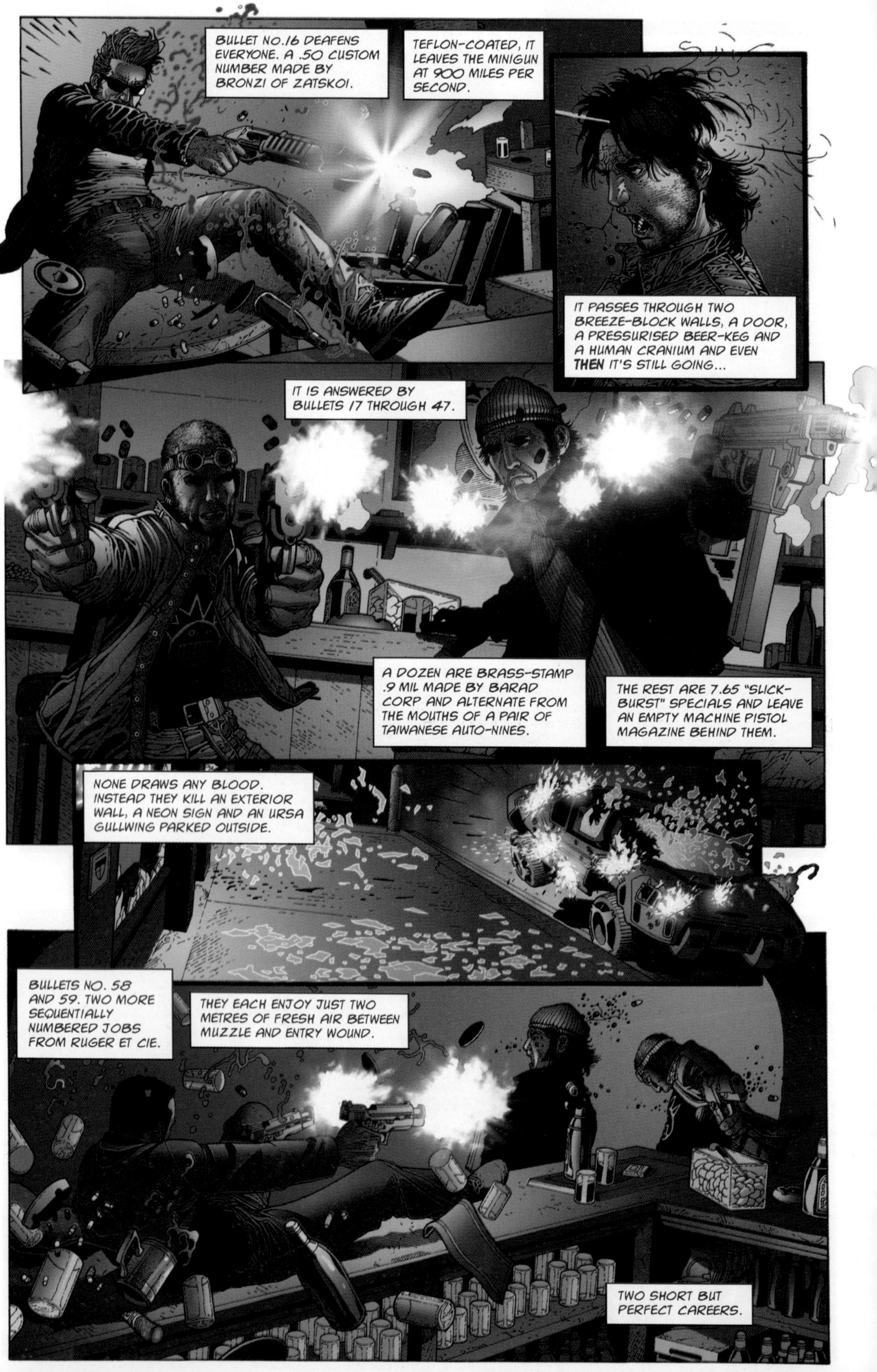

BULLET NO.16 DEAFENS EVERYONE. A .50 CUSTOM NUMBER MADE BY BRONZI OF ZATSKOI.
TEFLON-COATED, IT LEAVES THE MINIGUN AT 900 MILES PER SECOND.
IT PASSES THROUGH TWO BREEZE-BLOCK WALLS, A DOOR, A PRESSURISED BEER-KEG AND A HUMAN CRANIUM AND EVEN THEN IT'S STILL GOING...
IT IS ANSWERED BY BULLETS 17 THROUGH 47.
A DOZEN ARE BRASS-STAMP .9 MIL MADE BY BARAD CORP AND ALTERNATE FROM THE MOUTHS OF A PAIR OF TAIWANESE AUTO-NINES.
THE REST ARE 7.65 "SLICK-BURST" SPECIALS AND LEAVE AN EMPTY MACHINE PISTOL MAGAZINE BEHIND THEM.
NONE DRAWS ANY BLOOD. INSTEAD THEY KILL AN EXTERIOR WALL, A NEON SIGN AND AN URSA GULLWING PARKED OUTSIDE.
BULLETS NO. 58 AND 59. TWO MORE SEQUENTIALLY NUMBERED JOBS FROM RUGER ET CIE.
THEY EACH ENJOY JUST TWO METRES OF FRESH AIR BETWEEN MUZZLE AND ENTRY WOUND.
TWO SHORT BUT PERFECT CAREERS.

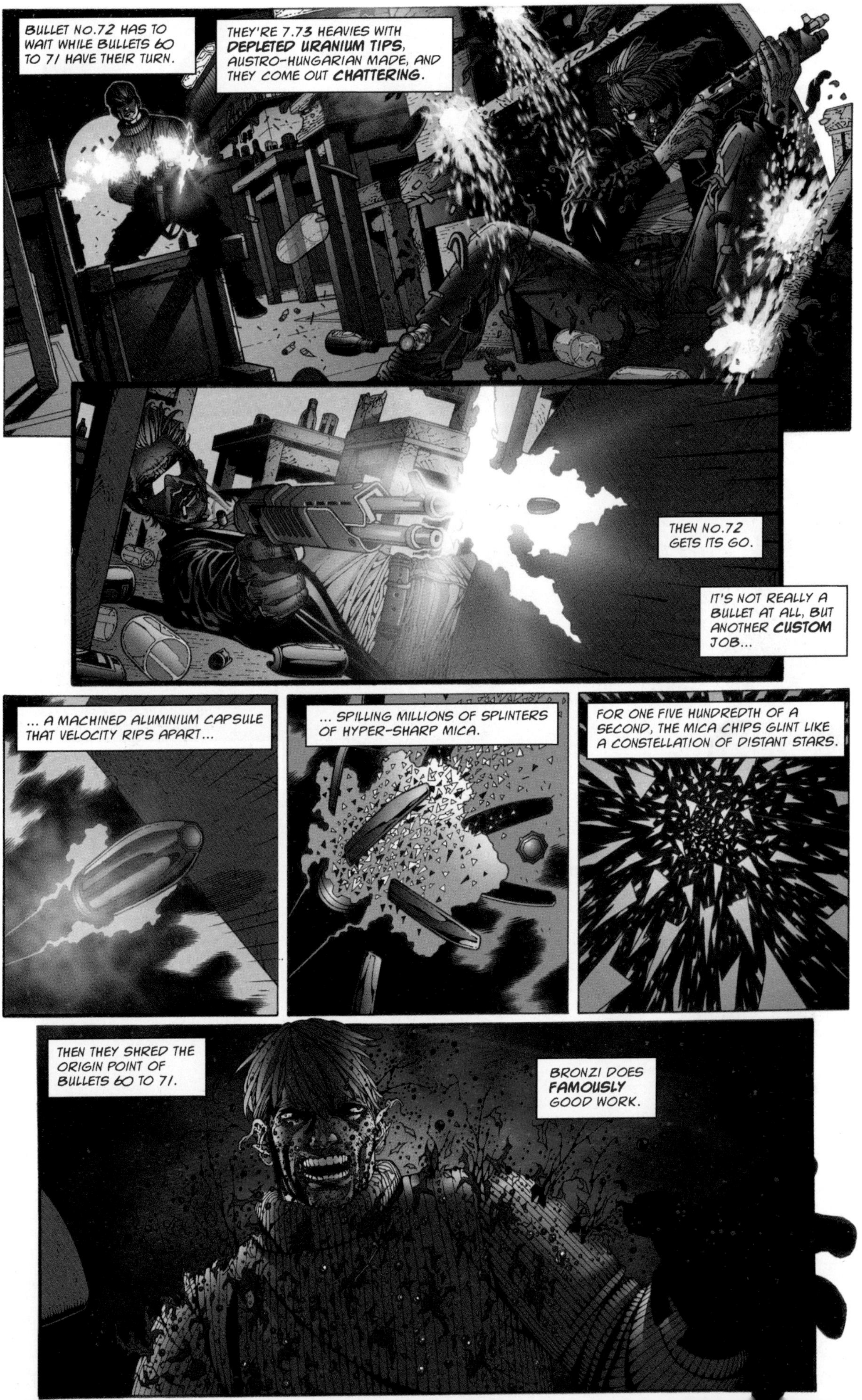
BULLET NO.72 HAS TO WAIT WHILE BULLETS 60 TO 71 HAVE THEIR TURN.
THEY'RE 7.73 HEAVIES WITH **DEPLETED URANIUM TIPS**, AUSTRO-HUNGARIAN MADE, AND THEY COME OUT **CHATTERING**.
THEN NO.72 GETS ITS GO.
IT'S NOT REALLY A BULLET AT ALL, BUT ANOTHER **CUSTOM** JOB...
... A MACHINED ALUMINIUM CAPSULE THAT VELOCITY RIPS APART...
... SPILLING MILLIONS OF SPLINTERS OF HYPER-SHARP MICA.
FOR ONE FIVE HUNDREDTH OF A SECOND, THE MICA CHIPS GLINT LIKE A CONSTELLATION OF DISTANT STARS.
THEN THEY SHRED THE ORIGIN POINT OF BULLETS 60 TO 71.
BRONZI DOES **FAMOUSLY** GOOD WORK.

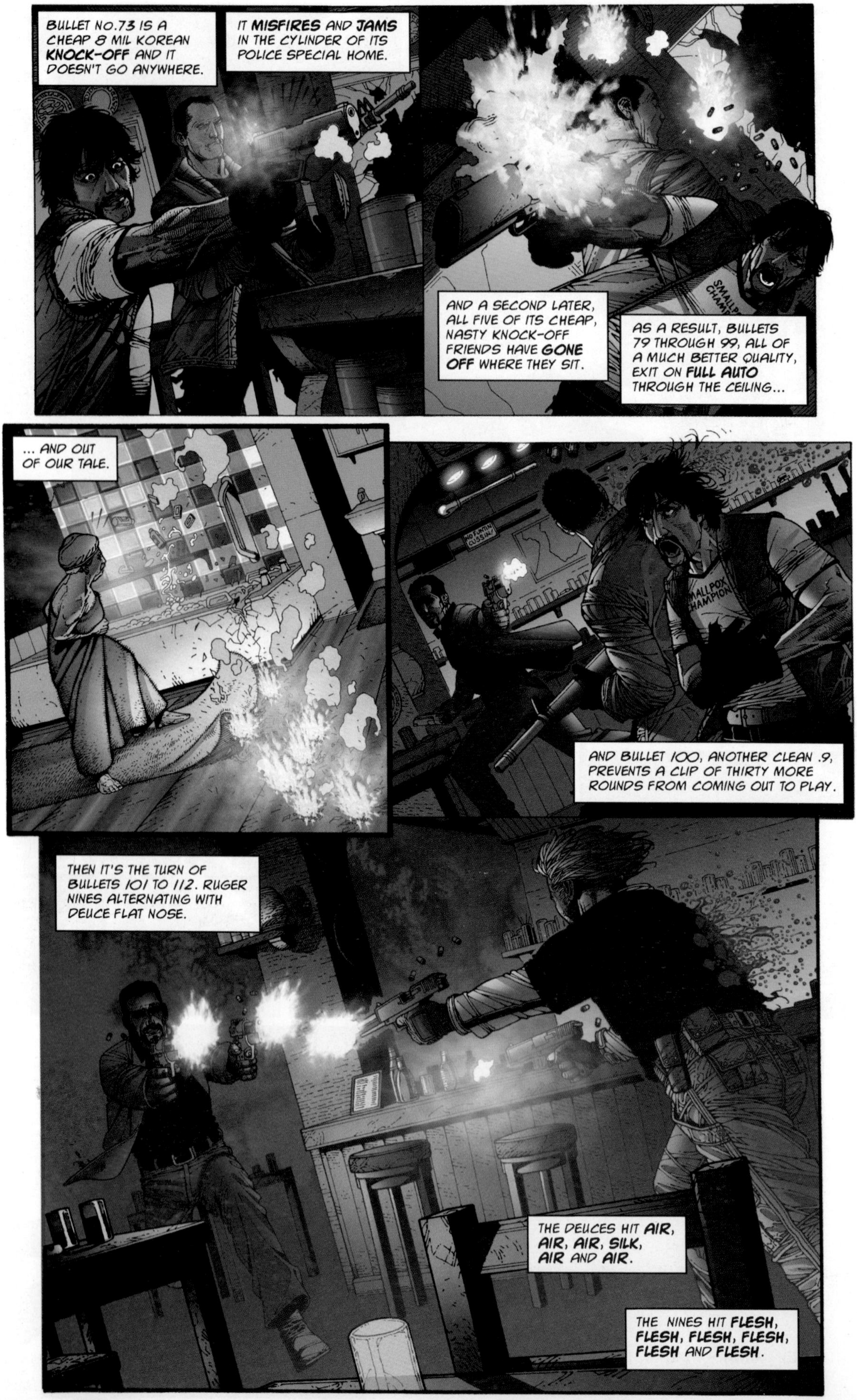
BULLET NO.73 IS A CHEAP 8 MIL KOREAN KNOCK-OFF AND IT DOESN'T GO ANYWHERE.
IT MISFIRES AND JAMS IN THE CYLINDER OF ITS POLICE SPECIAL HOME.
AND A SECOND LATER, ALL FIVE OF ITS CHEAP, NASTY KNOCK-OFF FRIENDS HAVE GONE OFF WHERE THEY SIT.
AS A RESULT, BULLETS 79 THROUGH 99, ALL OF A MUCH BETTER QUALITY, EXIT ON FULL AUTO THROUGH THE CEILING...
... AND OUT OF OUR TALE.
SMALLPOX CHAMPION
AND BULLET 100, ANOTHER CLEAN .9, PREVENTS A CLIP OF THIRTY MORE ROUNDS FROM COMING OUT TO PLAY.
THEN IT'S THE TURN OF BULLETS 101 TO 112. RUGER NINES ALTERNATING WITH DEUCE FLAT NOSE.
THE DEUCES HIT AIR, AIR, AIR, SILK, AIR AND AIR.
THE NINES HIT FLESH, FLESH, FLESH, FLESH, FLESH AND FLESH.

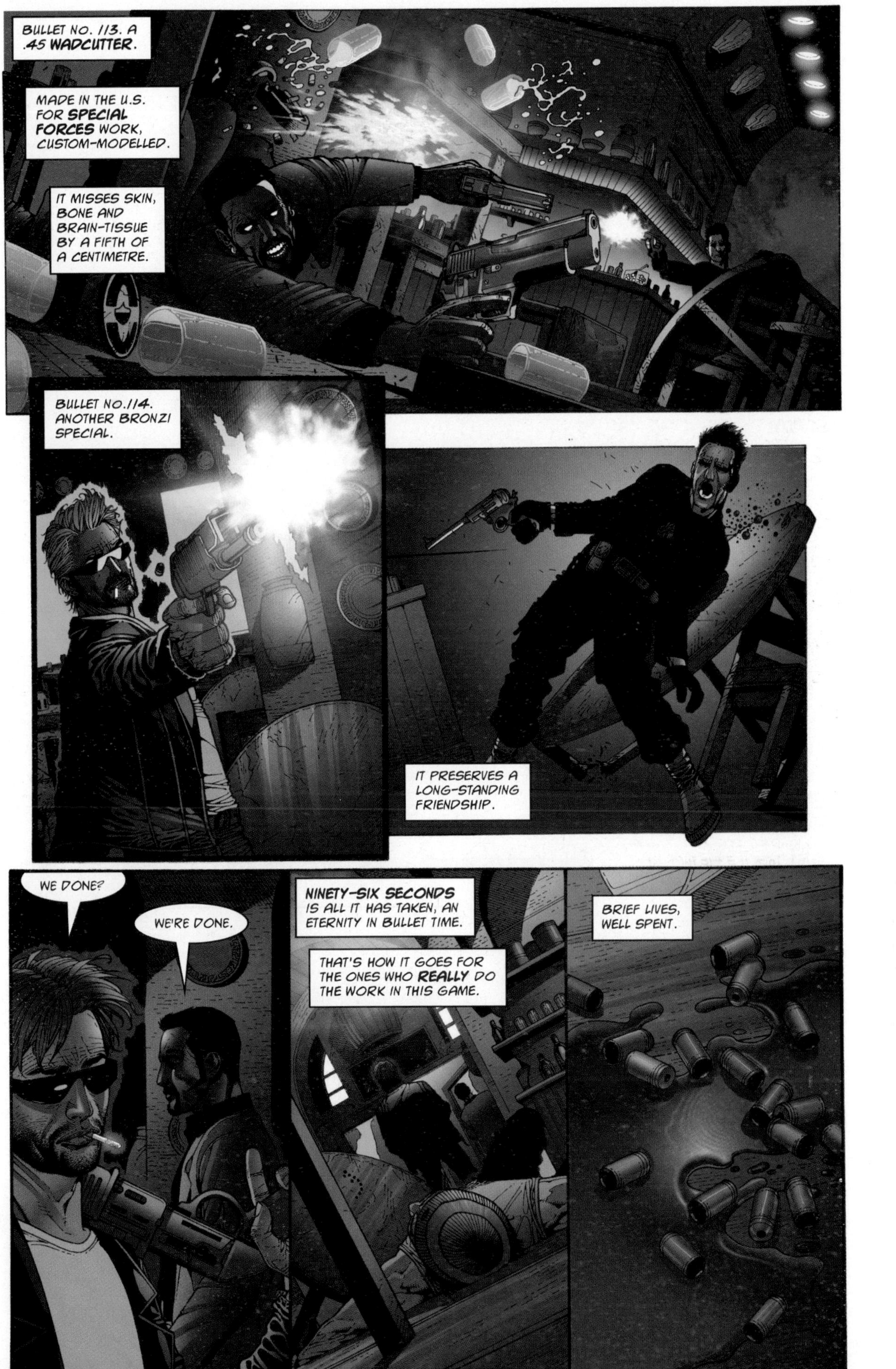
BULLET NO. 113. A .45 WADCUTTER.
MADE IN THE U.S. FOR SPECIAL FORCES WORK, CUSTOM-MODELLED.
IT MISSES SKIN, BONE AND BRAIN-TISSUE BY A FIFTH OF A CENTIMETRE.
BULLET NO. 114. ANOTHER BRONZI SPECIAL.
IT PRESERVES A LONG-STANDING FRIENDSHIP.
WE DONE?
WE'RE DONE.
NINETY-SIX SECONDS IS ALL IT HAS TAKEN, AN ETERNITY IN BULLET TIME.
THAT'S HOW IT GOES FOR THE ONES WHO REALLY DO THE WORK IN THIS GAME.
BRIEF LIVES, WELL SPENT.

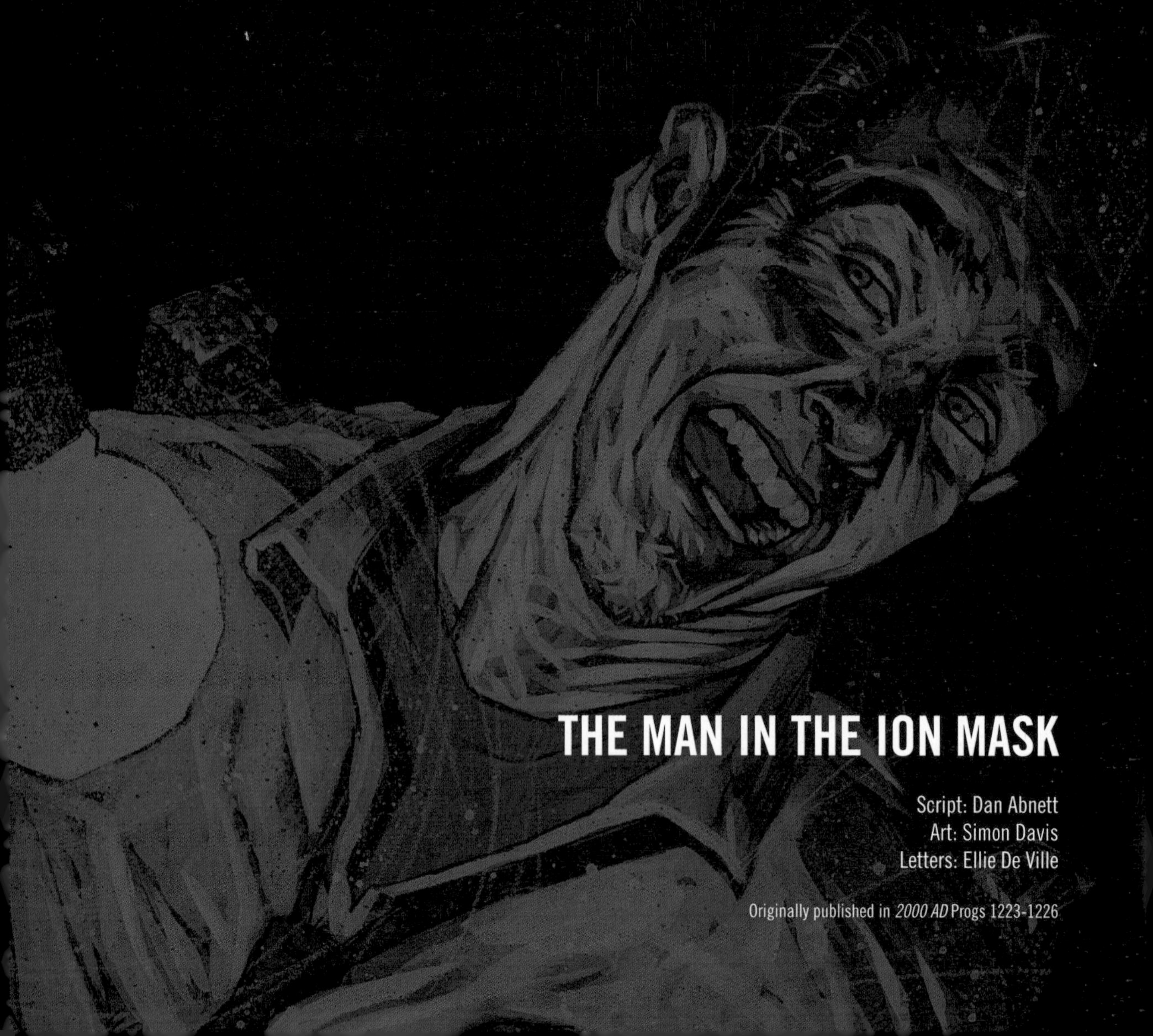

THE MAN IN THE ION MASK

Script: Dan Abnett
Art: Simon Davis
Letters: Ellie De Ville

Originally published in *2000 AD* Progs 1223-1226

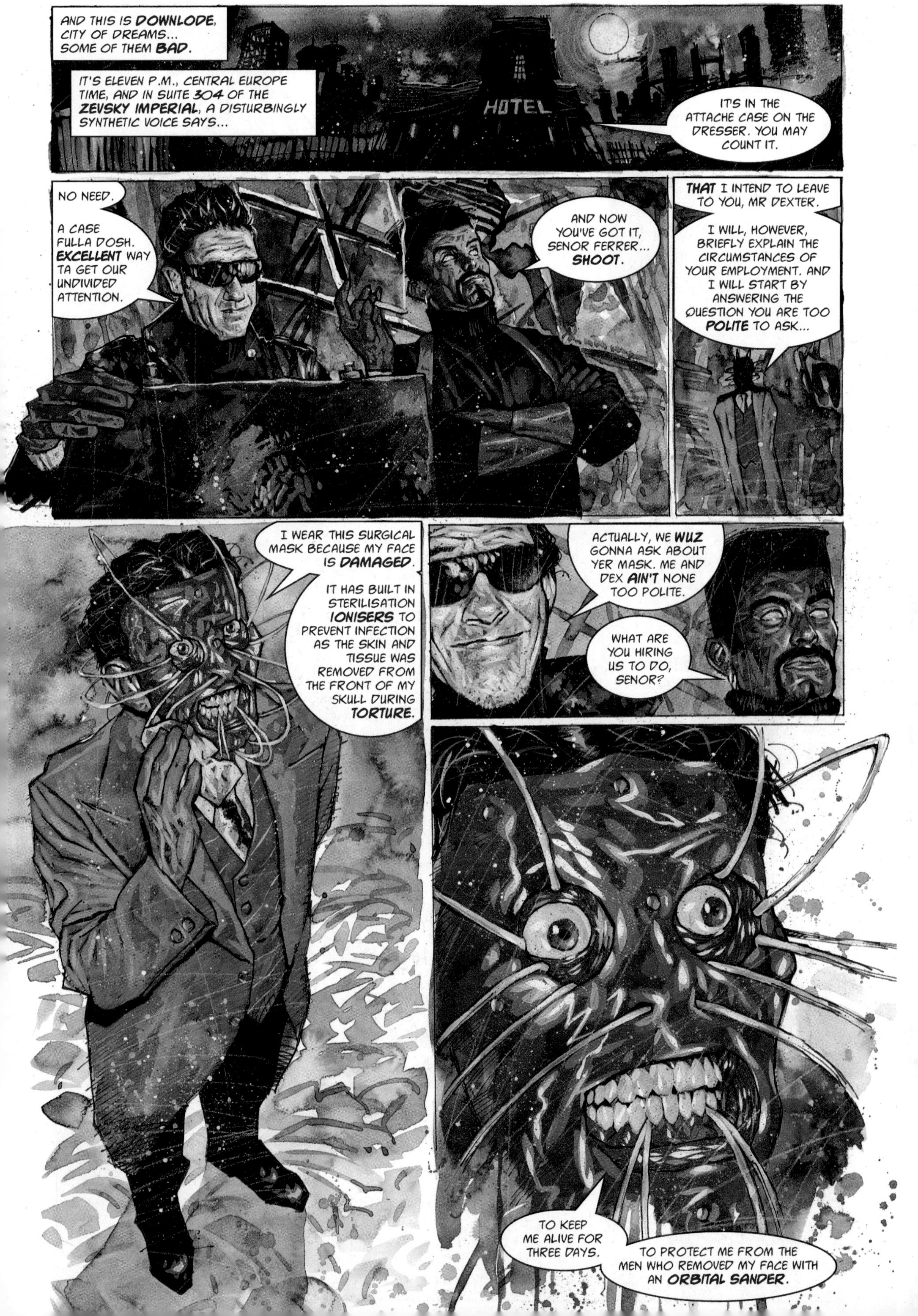
AND THIS IS DOWNLODE, CITY OF DREAMS... SOME OF THEM BAD.
IT'S ELEVEN P.M., CENTRAL EUROPE TIME, AND IN SUITE 304 OF THE ZEVSKY IMPERIAL, A DISTURBINGLY SYNTHETIC VOICE SAYS...
HOTEL
IT'S IN THE ATTACHE CASE ON THE DRESSER. YOU MAY COUNT IT.
NO NEED.
A CASE FULLA DOSH. EXCELLENT WAY TA GET OUR UNDIVIDED ATTENTION.
AND NOW YOU'VE GOT IT, SENOR FERRER... SHOOT.
THAT I INTEND TO LEAVE TO YOU, MR DEXTER.
I WILL, HOWEVER, BRIEFLY EXPLAIN THE CIRCUMSTANCES OF YOUR EMPLOYMENT. AND I WILL START BY ANSWERING THE QUESTION YOU ARE TOO POLITE TO ASK...
I WEAR THIS SURGICAL MASK BECAUSE MY FACE IS DAMAGED.
IT HAS BUILT IN STERILISATION IONISERS TO PREVENT INFECTION AS THE SKIN AND TISSUE WAS REMOVED FROM THE FRONT OF MY SKULL DURING TORTURE.
ACTUALLY, WE WUZ GONNA ASK ABOUT YER MASK. ME AND DEX AIN'T NONE TOO POLITE.
WHAT ARE YOU HIRING US TO DO, SENOR?
TO KEEP ME ALIVE FOR THREE DAYS.
TO PROTECT ME FROM THE MEN WHO REMOVED MY FACE WITH AN ORBITAL SANDER.

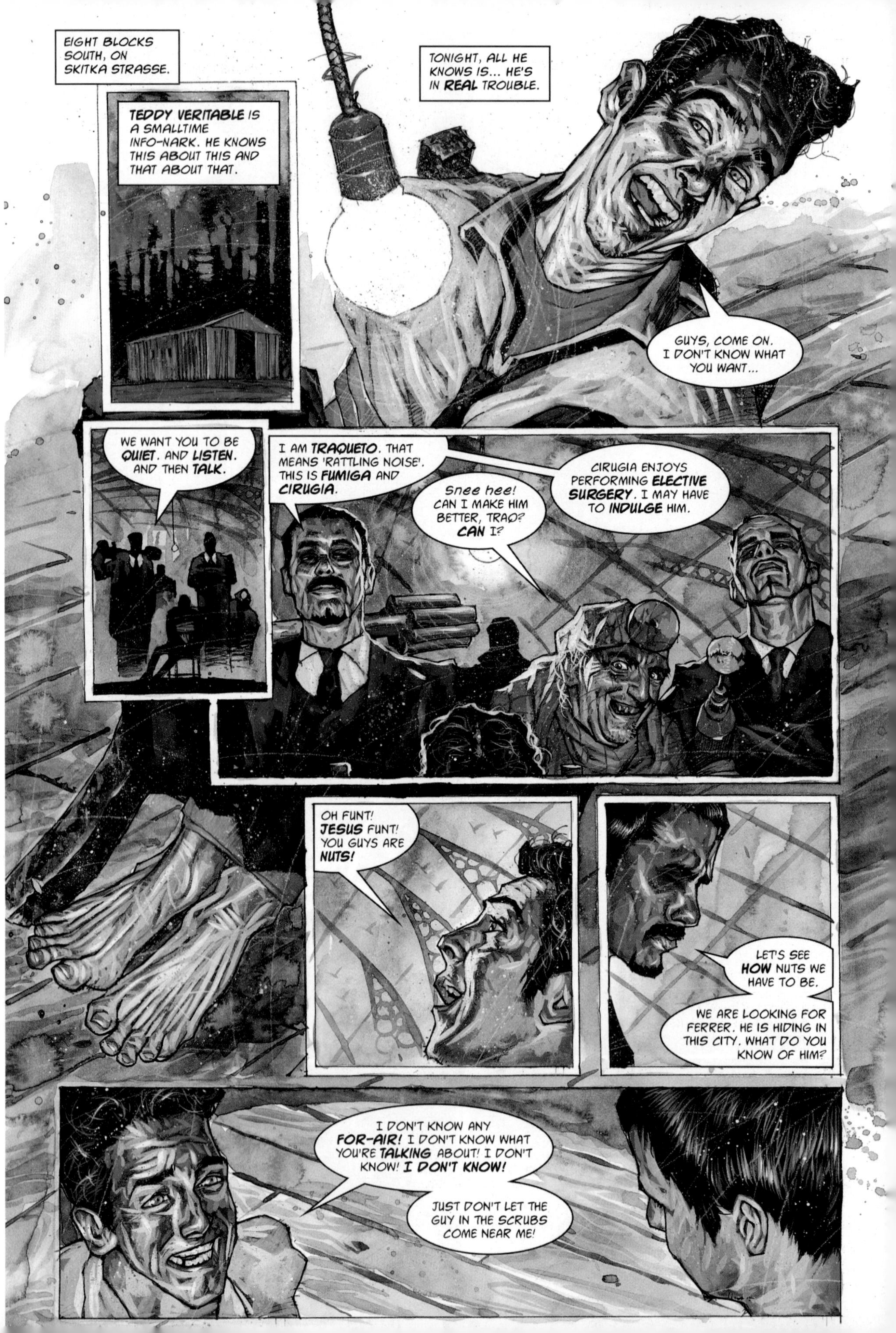
EIGHT BLOCKS SOUTH, ON SKITKA STRASSE.
TEDDY VERITABLE IS A SMALLTIME INFO-NARK. HE KNOWS THIS ABOUT THIS AND THAT ABOUT THAT.
TONIGHT, ALL HE KNOWS IS... HE'S IN REAL TROUBLE.
GUYS, COME ON. I DON'T KNOW WHAT YOU WANT...
WE WANT YOU TO BE QUIET. AND LISTEN. AND THEN TALK.
I AM TRAQUETO. THAT MEANS 'RATTLING NOISE'. THIS IS FUMIGA AND CIRUGIA.
Snee hee! CAN I MAKE HIM BETTER, TRAQ? CAN I?
CIRUGIA ENJOYS PERFORMING ELECTIVE SURGERY. I MAY HAVE TO INDULGE HIM.
OH FUNT! JESUS FUNT! YOU GUYS ARE NUTS!
LET'S SEE HOW NUTS WE HAVE TO BE.
WE ARE LOOKING FOR FERRER. HE IS HIDING IN THIS CITY. WHAT DO YOU KNOW OF HIM?
I DON'T KNOW ANY FOR-AIR! I DON'T KNOW WHAT YOU'RE TALKING ABOUT! I DON'T KNOW! I DON'T KNOW!
JUST DON'T LET THE GUY IN THE SCRUBS COME NEAR ME!

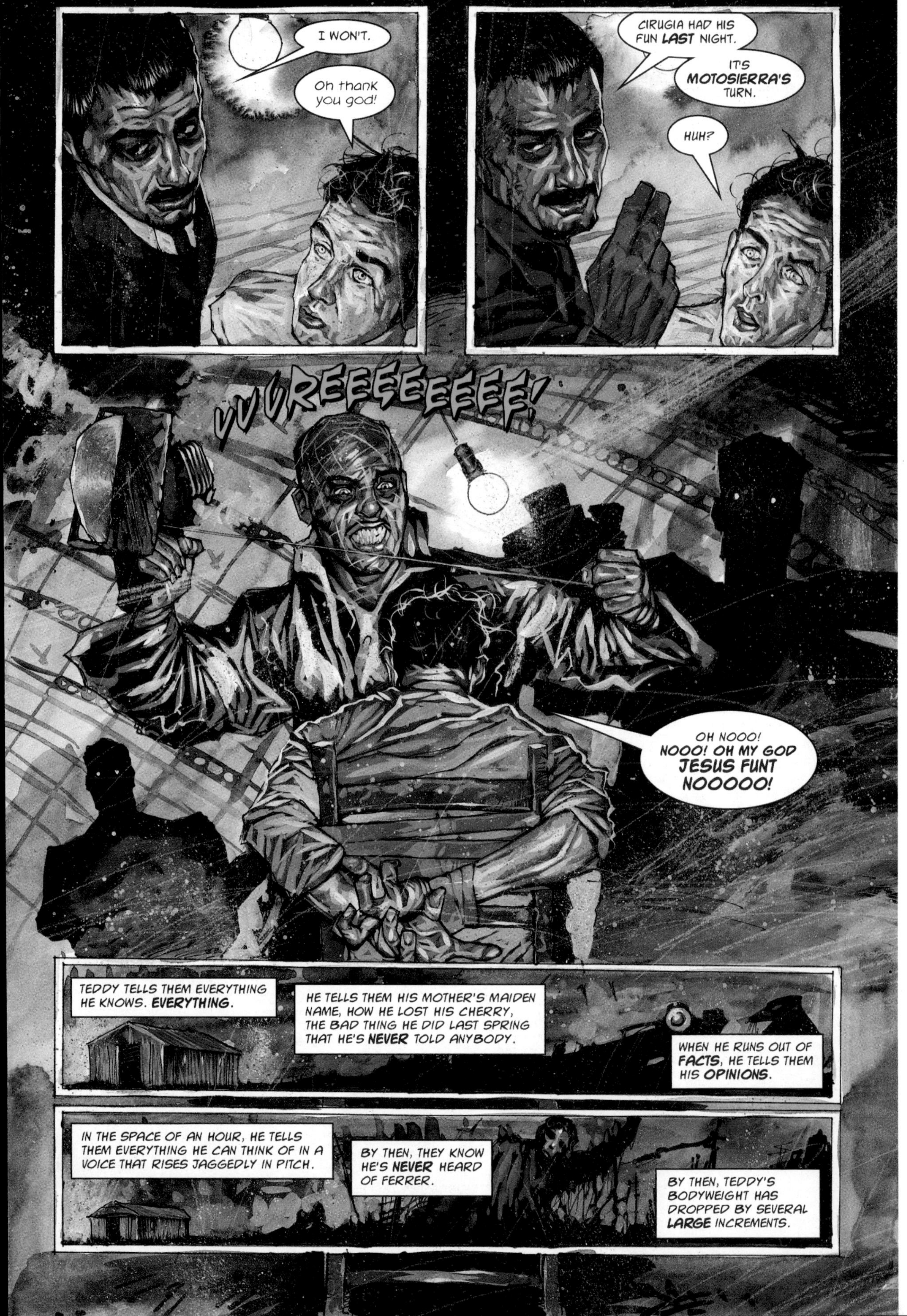

I WON'T.
Oh thank you god!
CIRUGIA HAD HIS FUN LAST NIGHT.
IT'S MOTOSIERRA'S TURN.
HUH?
VVVREEEEEEEEEE!
OH NOOO! NOOO! OH MY GOD JESUS FUNT NOOOOO!
TEDDY TELLS THEM EVERYTHING HE KNOWS. EVERYTHING.
HE TELLS THEM HIS MOTHER'S MAIDEN NAME, HOW HE LOST HIS CHERRY, THE BAD THING HE DID LAST SPRING THAT HE'S NEVER TOLD ANYBODY.
WHEN HE RUNS OUT OF FACTS, HE TELLS THEM HIS OPINIONS.
IN THE SPACE OF AN HOUR, HE TELLS THEM EVERYTHING HE CAN THINK OF IN A VOICE THAT RISES JAGGEDLY IN PITCH.
BY THEN, THEY KNOW HE'S NEVER HEARD OF FERRER.
BY THEN, TEDDY'S BODYWEIGHT HAS DROPPED BY SEVERAL LARGE INCREMENTS.

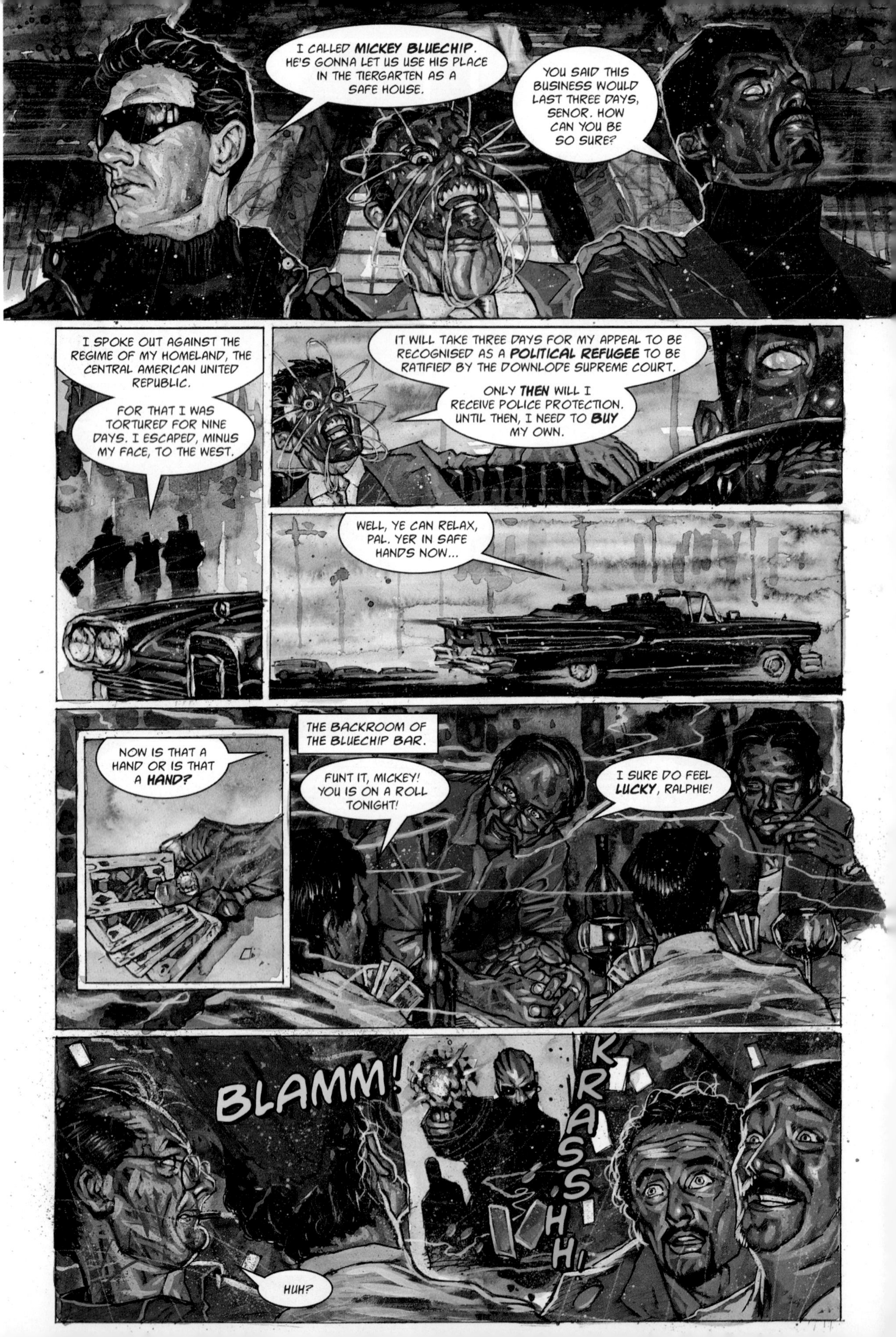
I CALLED **MICKEY BLUECHIP**. HE'S GONNA LET US USE HIS PLACE IN THE TIERGARTEN AS A SAFE HOUSE.
YOU SAID THIS BUSINESS WOULD LAST THREE DAYS, SENOR. HOW CAN YOU BE SO SURE?
I SPOKE OUT AGAINST THE REGIME OF MY HOMELAND, THE CENTRAL AMERICAN UNITED REPUBLIC.
FOR THAT I WAS TORTURED FOR NINE DAYS. I ESCAPED, MINUS MY FACE, TO THE WEST.
IT WILL TAKE THREE DAYS FOR MY APPEAL TO BE RECOGNISED AS A **POLITICAL REFUGEE** TO BE RATIFIED BY THE DOWNLODE SUPREME COURT.
ONLY **THEN** WILL I RECEIVE POLICE PROTECTION. UNTIL THEN, I NEED TO **BUY** MY OWN.
WELL, YE CAN RELAX, PAL. YER IN SAFE HANDS NOW...
THE BACKROOM OF THE BLUECHIP BAR.
NOW IS THAT A HAND OR IS THAT A **HAND?**
FUNT IT, MICKEY! YOU IS ON A ROLL TONIGHT!
I SURE DO FEEL **LUCKY**, RALPHIE!
BLAMM!
KRASSHH
HUH?

WHAT-- WHAT THE...

FUNT ME! *FUNT ME!* HE JUST SHOT *RALPHIE* IN THE HEAD!

AND JEFFY! YOU JUST WENT AND SHOT JEFFY *TOO!*

SO HE *DID.* FUMIGA IS SOMEWHAT... *INDISCRIMINATE.*

BLAMM!

WE WAS *ONLY* PLAYING CARDS.

AND NOW YOU ARE ONLY ANSWERING QUESTIONS, MICKEY BLUECHIP.

DON'T CRY FOR HELP. EVERYONE IN YOUR BAR HAS SOILED THEIR PANTS AND RUN AWAY.

FERRER. WHERE IS HE?

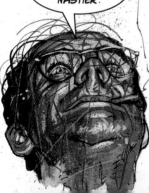

FUNT, THAT'S *EASY!* HE'S IN THE TIERGARTEN. I'LL GIVE YOU THE *ADDRESS* AND EVERYTHING.

THERE'S NO NEED TO GET ANY *NASTIER.*

CIRUGIA? REMOVE MR BLUECHIP'S EARS, SPLEEN AND KNEECAPS.

Snee hee! Y-YEAH! *Y-YES!*

B-B-B-BUT *WAIT!* I *SAID* I'D TELL YOU! *I SAID I'D TELL YOU!*

I KNOW. BUT WHERE IS THE FUN IN *THAT?*

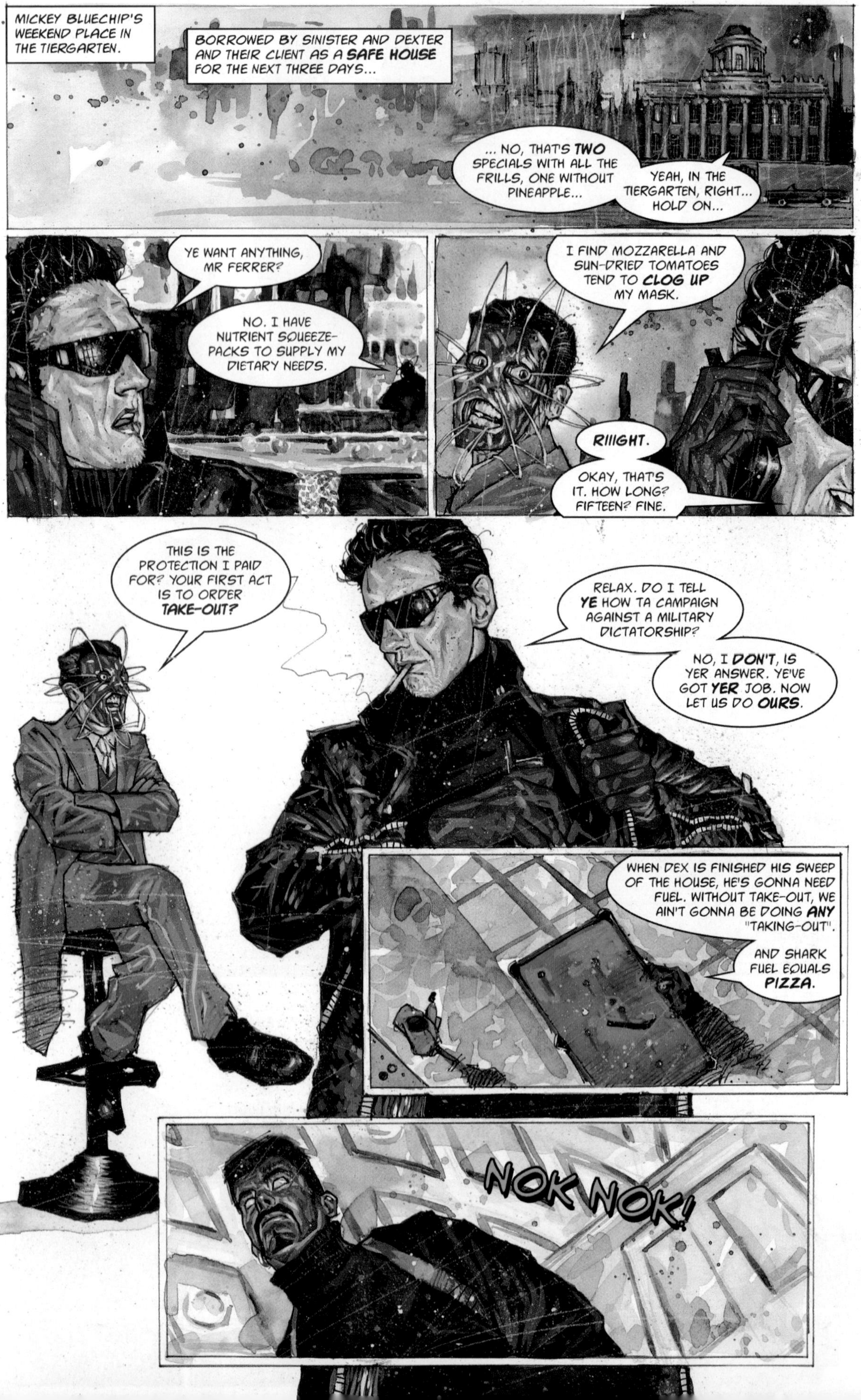

MICKEY BLUECHIP'S WEEKEND PLACE IN THE TIERGARTEN.
BORROWED BY SINISTER AND DEXTER AND THEIR CLIENT AS A SAFE HOUSE FOR THE NEXT THREE DAYS...
... NO, THAT'S TWO SPECIALS WITH ALL THE FRILLS, ONE WITHOUT PINEAPPLE...
YEAH, IN THE TIERGARTEN, RIGHT... HOLD ON...
YE WANT ANYTHING, MR FERRER?
NO. I HAVE NUTRIENT SQUEEZE-PACKS TO SUPPLY MY DIETARY NEEDS.
I FIND MOZZARELLA AND SUN-DRIED TOMATOES TEND TO CLOG UP MY MASK.
RIIIGHT.
OKAY, THAT'S IT. HOW LONG? FIFTEEN? FINE.
THIS IS THE PROTECTION I PAID FOR? YOUR FIRST ACT IS TO ORDER TAKE-OUT?
RELAX. DO I TELL YE HOW TA CAMPAIGN AGAINST A MILITARY DICTATORSHIP?
NO, I DON'T, IS YER ANSWER. YE'VE GOT YER JOB. NOW LET US DO OURS.
WHEN DEX IS FINISHED HIS SWEEP OF THE HOUSE, HE'S GONNA NEED FUEL. WITHOUT TAKE-OUT, WE AIN'T GONNA BE DOING ANY "TAKING-OUT".
AND SHARK FUEL EQUALS PIZZA.
NOK NOK!

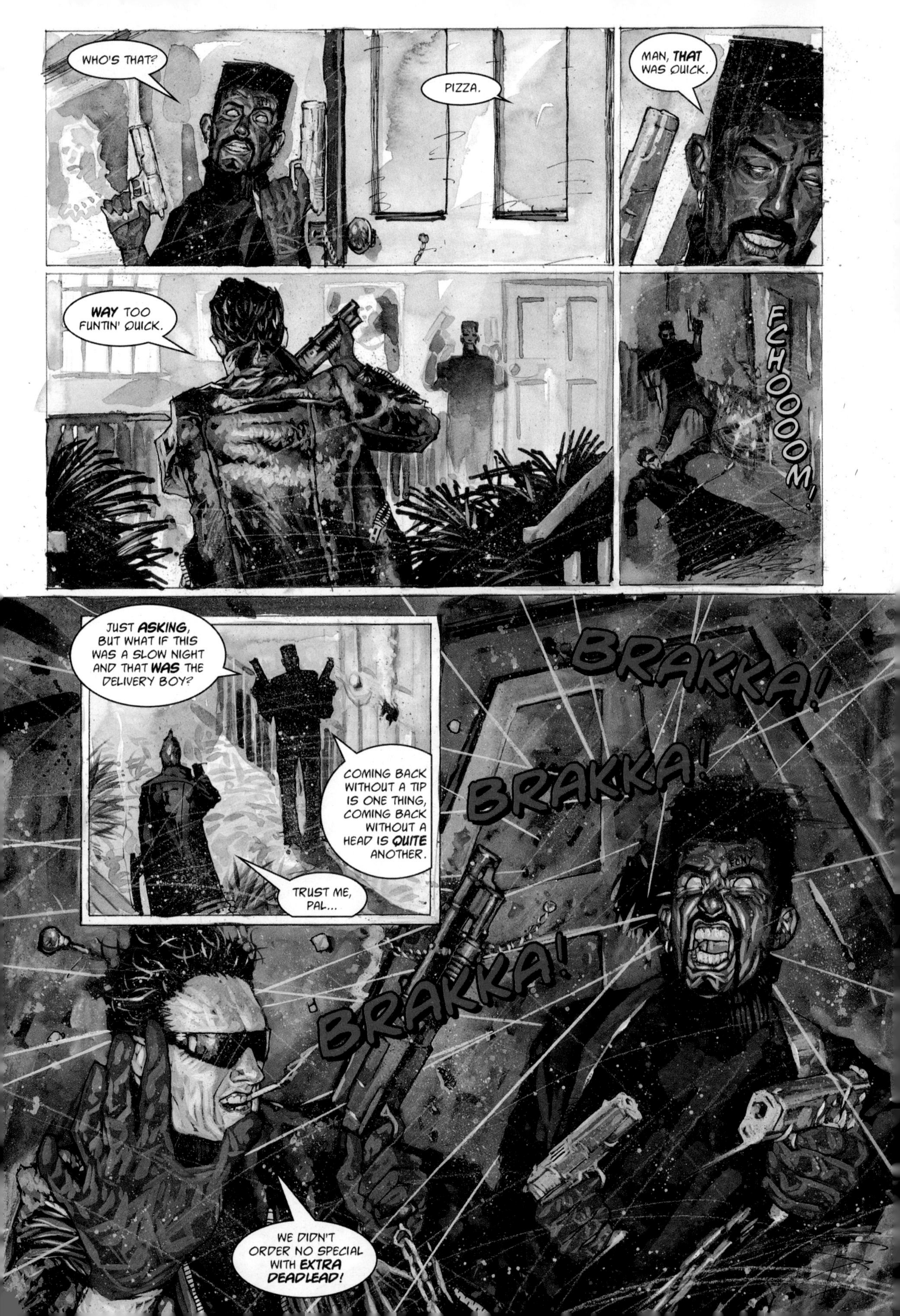
WHO'S THAT?
PIZZA.
MAN, THAT WAS QUICK.
WAY TOO FUNTIN' QUICK.
FCHOOOOOM,
JUST ASKING, BUT WHAT IF THIS WAS A SLOW NIGHT AND THAT WAS THE DELIVERY BOY?
COMING BACK WITHOUT A TIP IS ONE THING, COMING BACK WITHOUT A HEAD IS QUITE ANOTHER.
TRUST ME, PAL...
BRAKKA!
BRAKKA!
BRAKKA!
WE DIDN'T ORDER NO SPECIAL WITH EXTRA DEADLEAD!

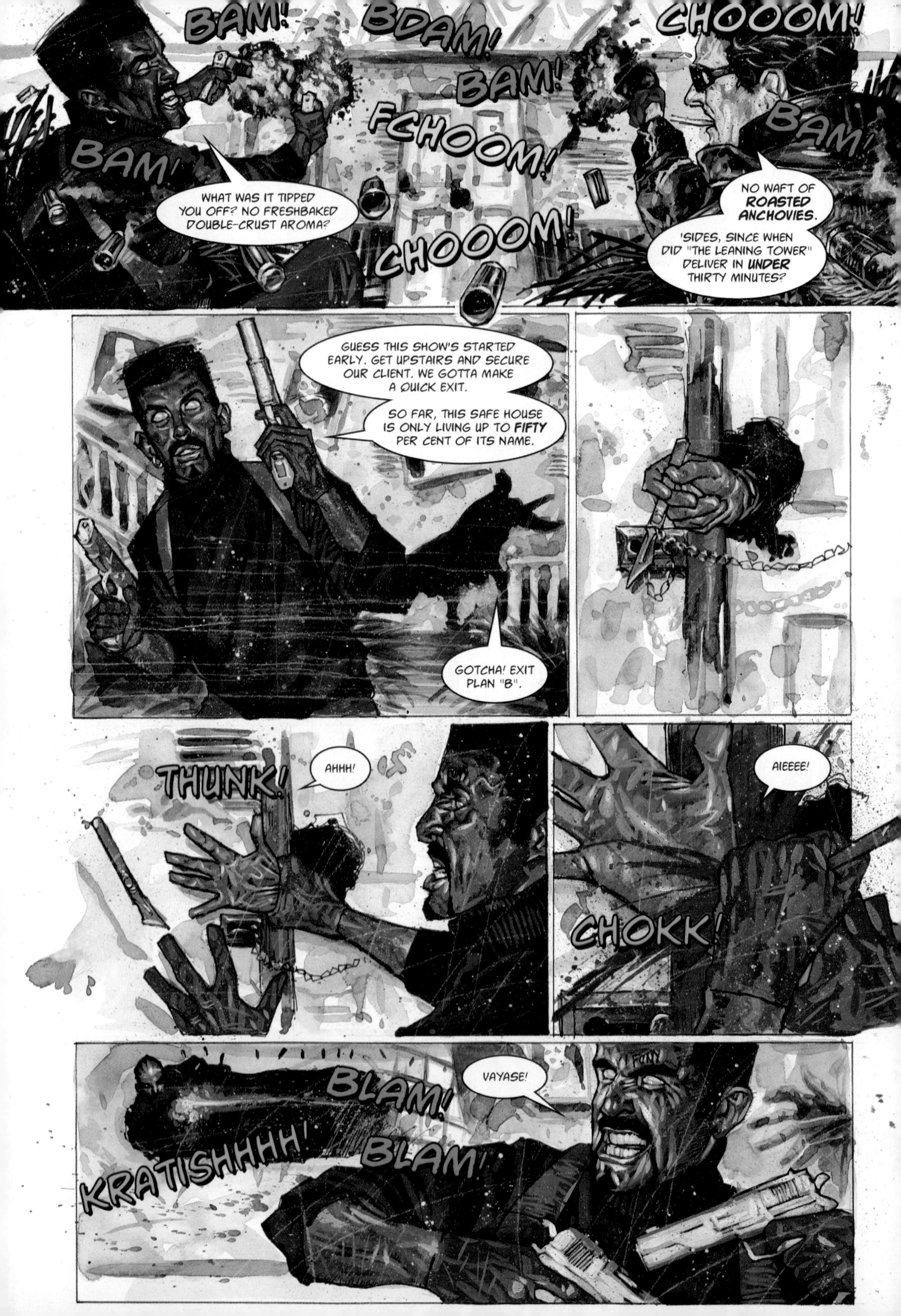
BAM!
BDAM!
CHOOOM!
BAM!
BAM
FCHOOOM!
BAM
WHAT WAS IT TIPPED YOU OFF? NO FRESHBAKED DOUBLE-CRUST AROMA?
CHOOOOM!
NO WAFT OF **ROASTED ANCHOVIES**.
'SIDES, SINCE WHEN DID "THE LEANING TOWER" DELIVER IN **UNDER** THIRTY MINUTES?
GUESS THIS SHOW'S STARTED EARLY. GET UPSTAIRS AND SECURE OUR CLIENT. WE GOTTA MAKE A QUICK EXIT.
SO FAR, THIS SAFE HOUSE IS ONLY LIVING UP TO **FIFTY** PER CENT OF ITS NAME.
GOTCHA! EXIT PLAN "B".
THUNK!
AHHH!
AIEEEE!
CHOKK!
VAYASE!
BLAM!
BLAM
KRATISHHHH!

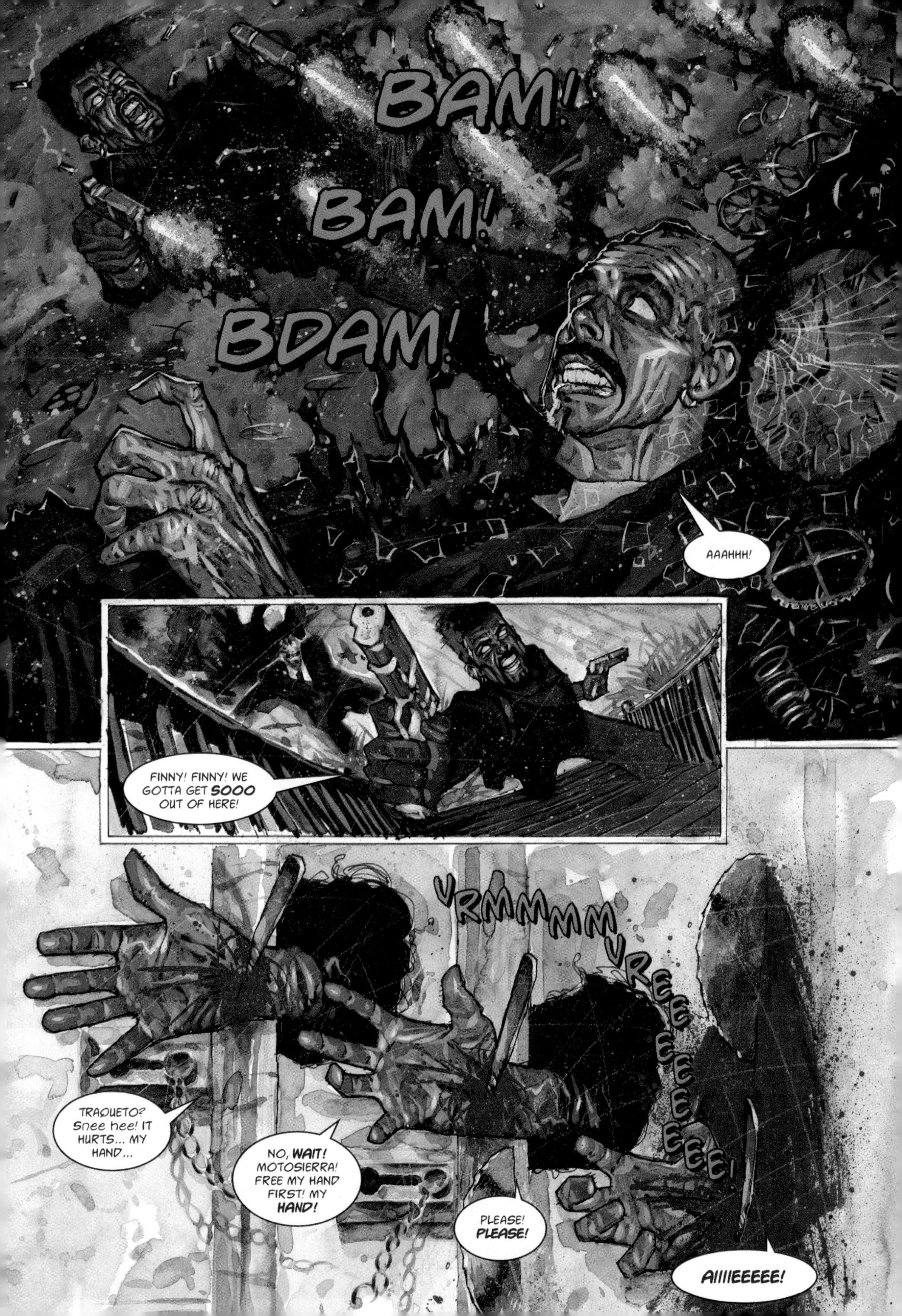
BAM!
BAM!
BDAM!
AAAHHH!
FINNY! FINNY! WE GOTTA GET SOOO OUT OF HERE!
VRMMMMMMVREEEEEEEEE!
TRAQUETO? Snee hee! IT HURTS... MY HAND...
NO, WAIT! MOTOSIERRA! FREE MY HAND FIRST! MY HAND!
PLEASE! PLEASE!
AIIIIEEEEE!

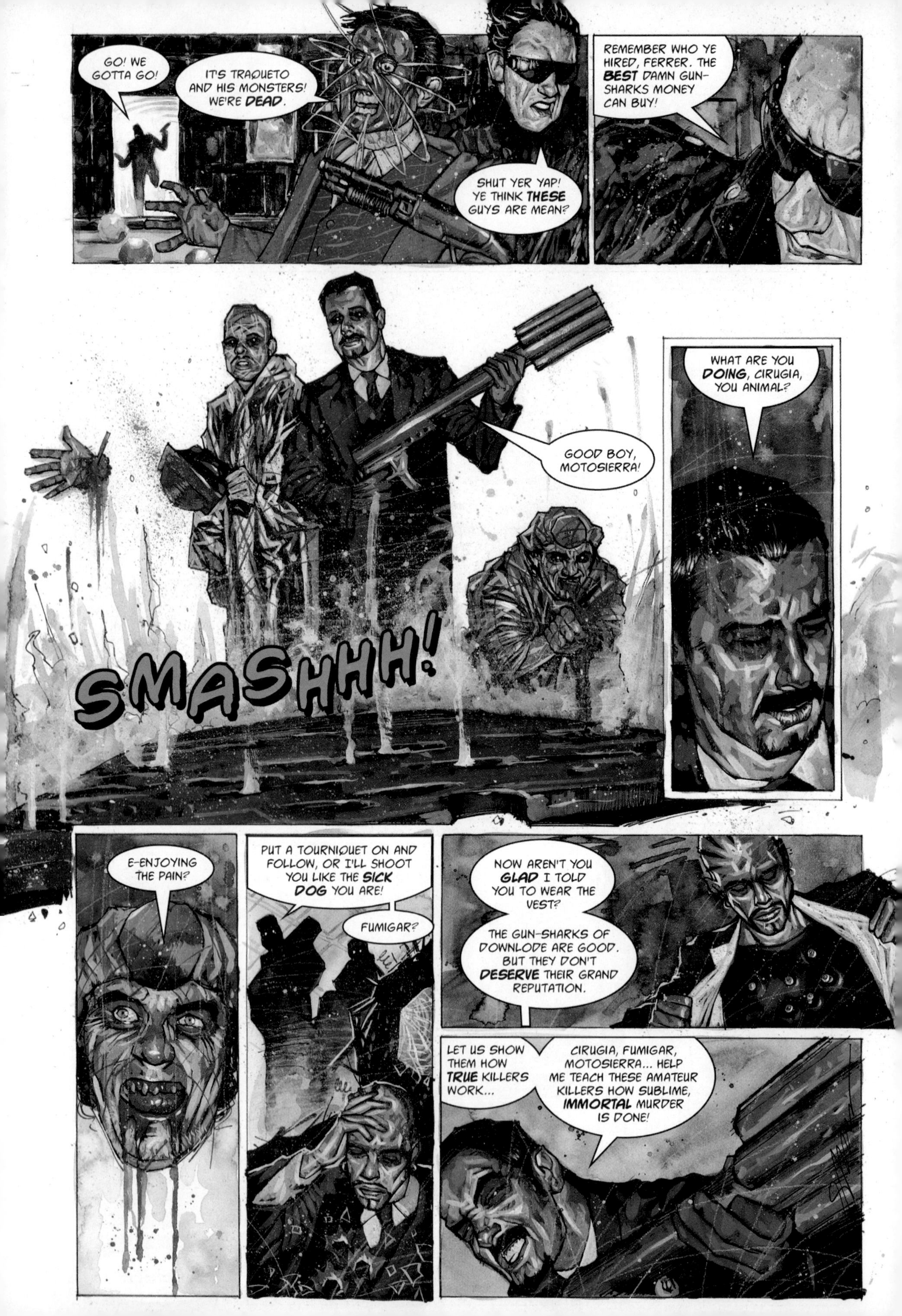
GO! WE GOTTA GO!
IT'S TRAQUETO AND HIS MONSTERS! WE'RE **DEAD**.
SHUT YER YAP! YE THINK **THESE** GUYS ARE MEAN?
REMEMBER WHO YE HIRED, FERRER. THE **BEST** DAMN GUN-SHARKS MONEY CAN BUY!
GOOD BOY, MOTOSIERRA!
SMASHHH!
WHAT ARE YOU **DOING**, CIRUGIA, YOU ANIMAL?
E-ENJOYING THE PAIN?
PUT A TOURNIQUET ON AND FOLLOW, OR I'LL SHOOT YOU LIKE THE **SICK DOG** YOU ARE!
FUMIGAR?
NOW AREN'T YOU **GLAD** I TOLD YOU TO WEAR THE VEST?
THE GUN-SHARKS OF DOWNLODE ARE GOOD. BUT THEY DON'T **DESERVE** THEIR GRAND REPUTATION.
LET US SHOW THEM HOW **TRUE** KILLERS WORK...
CIRUGIA, FUMIGAR, MOTOSIERRA... HELP ME TEACH THESE AMATEUR KILLERS HOW SUBLIME, **IMMORTAL** MURDER IS DONE!

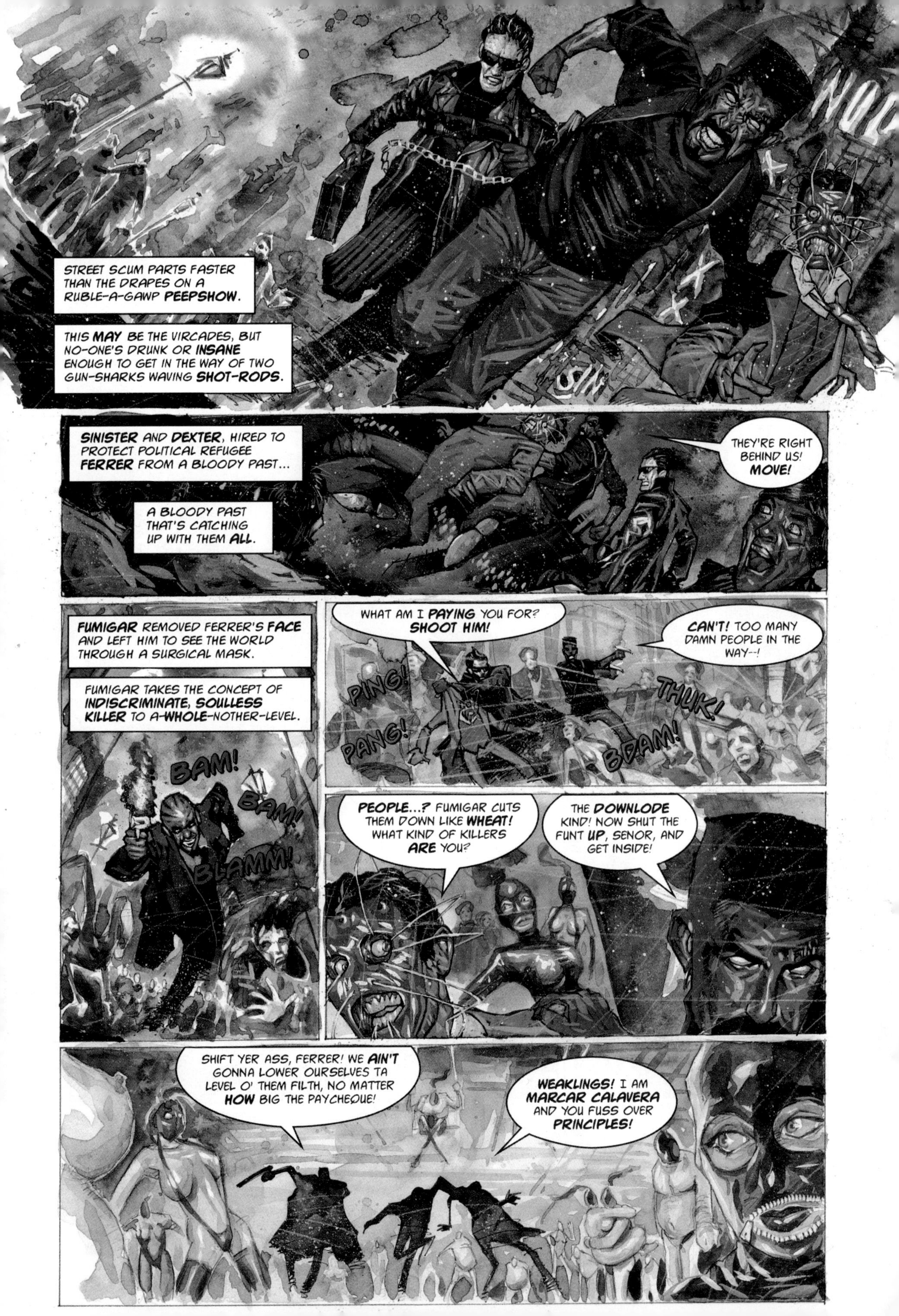
STREET SCUM PARTS FASTER THAN THE DRAPES ON A RUBLE-A-GAWP PEEPSHOW.
THIS MAY BE THE VIRCADES, BUT NO-ONE'S DRUNK OR INSANE ENOUGH TO GET IN THE WAY OF TWO GUN-SHARKS WAVING SHOT-RODS.
SINISTER AND DEXTER, HIRED TO PROTECT POLITICAL REFUGEE FERRER FROM A BLOODY PAST...
A BLOODY PAST THAT'S CATCHING UP WITH THEM ALL.
THEY'RE RIGHT BEHIND US! MOVE!
FUMIGAR REMOVED FERRER'S FACE AND LEFT HIM TO SEE THE WORLD THROUGH A SURGICAL MASK.
FUMIGAR TAKES THE CONCEPT OF INDISCRIMINATE, SOULLESS KILLER TO A-WHOLE-NOTHER-LEVEL.
BAM!
BAM!
BLAMM!
WHAT AM I PAYING YOU FOR? SHOOT HIM!
CAN'T! TOO MANY DAMN PEOPLE IN THE WAY--!
PING!
PANG!
THUK!
BDAM!
PEOPLE...? FUMIGAR CUTS THEM DOWN LIKE WHEAT! WHAT KIND OF KILLERS ARE YOU?
THE DOWNLODE KIND! NOW SHUT THE FUNT UP, SENOR, AND GET INSIDE!
SHIFT YER ASS, FERRER! WE AIN'T GONNA LOWER OURSELVES TA LEVEL O' THEM FILTH, NO MATTER HOW BIG THE PAYCHEQUE!
WEAKLINGS! I AM MARCAR CALAVERA AND YOU FUSS OVER PRINCIPLES!

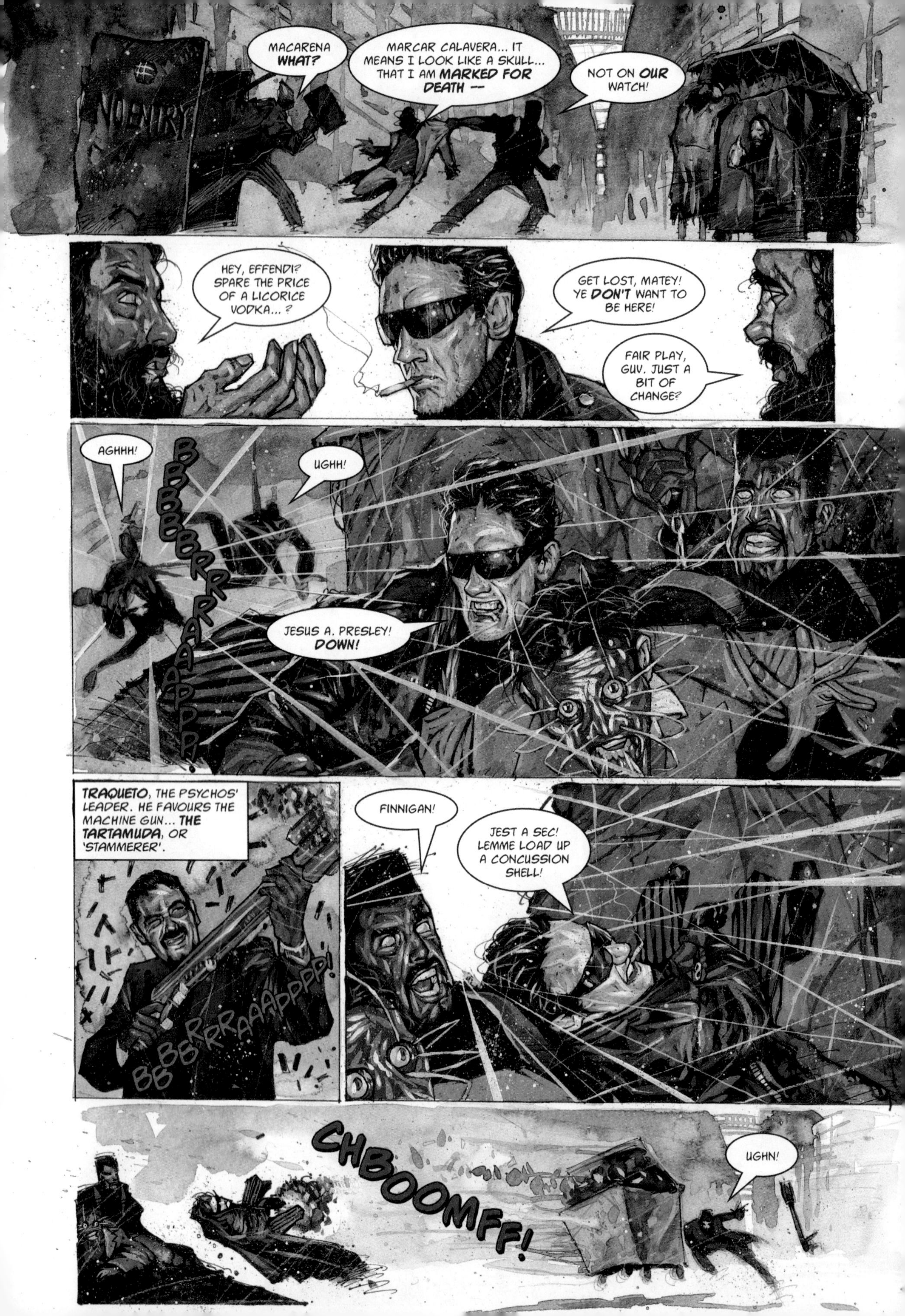
MACARENA WHAT?
MARCAR CALAVERA... IT MEANS I LOOK LIKE A SKULL... THAT I AM MARKED FOR DEATH --
NOT ON OUR WATCH!
HEY, EFFENDI? SPARE THE PRICE OF A LICORICE VODKA... ?
GET LOST, MATEY! YE DON'T WANT TO BE HERE!
FAIR PLAY, GUV. JUST A BIT OF CHANGE?
AGHHH!
BBBBBRRRAAAPPP!
UGHH!
JESUS A. PRESLEY! DOWN!
TRAQUETO, THE PSYCHOS' LEADER. HE FAVOURS THE MACHINE GUN... THE TARTAMUDA, OR 'STAMMERER'.
BBBBRRRAAAPPPP!
FINNIGAN!
JEST A SEC! LEMME LOAD UP A CONCUSSION SHELL!
CHBOOMFF!
UGHN!

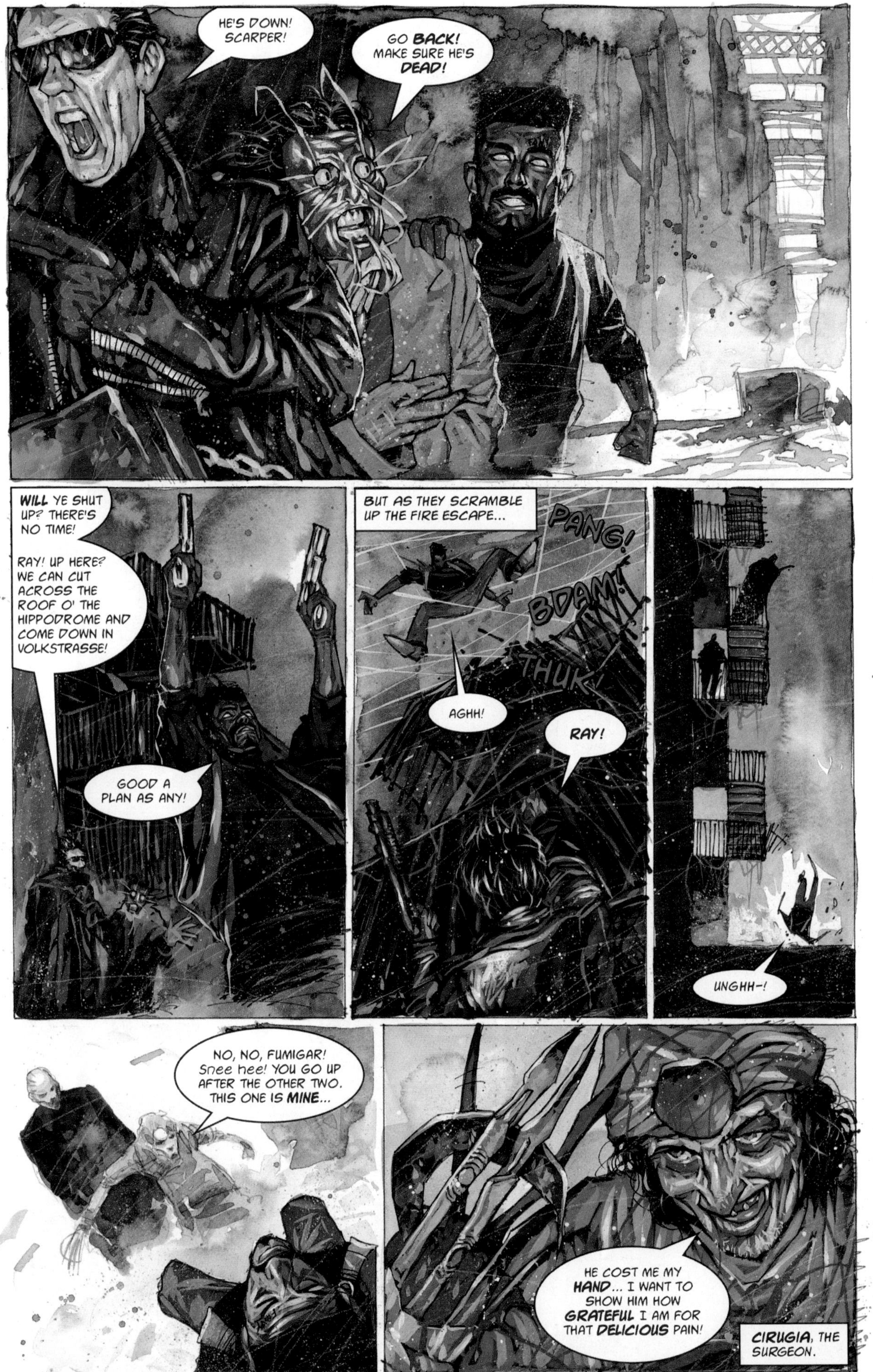
HE'S DOWN! SCARPER!
GO BACK! MAKE SURE HE'S DEAD!
WILL YE SHUT UP? THERE'S NO TIME!
RAY! UP HERE? WE CAN CUT ACROSS THE ROOF O' THE HIPPODROME AND COME DOWN IN VOLKSTRASSE!
GOOD A PLAN AS ANY!
BUT AS THEY SCRAMBLE UP THE FIRE ESCAPE...
PANG!
BDAM!
THUK!
AGHH!
RAY!
UNGHH-!
NO, NO, FUMIGAR! Snee hee! YOU GO UP AFTER THE OTHER TWO. THIS ONE IS MINE...
HE COST ME MY HAND... I WANT TO SHOW HIM HOW GRATEFUL I AM FOR THAT DELICIOUS PAIN!
CIRUGIA, THE SURGEON.

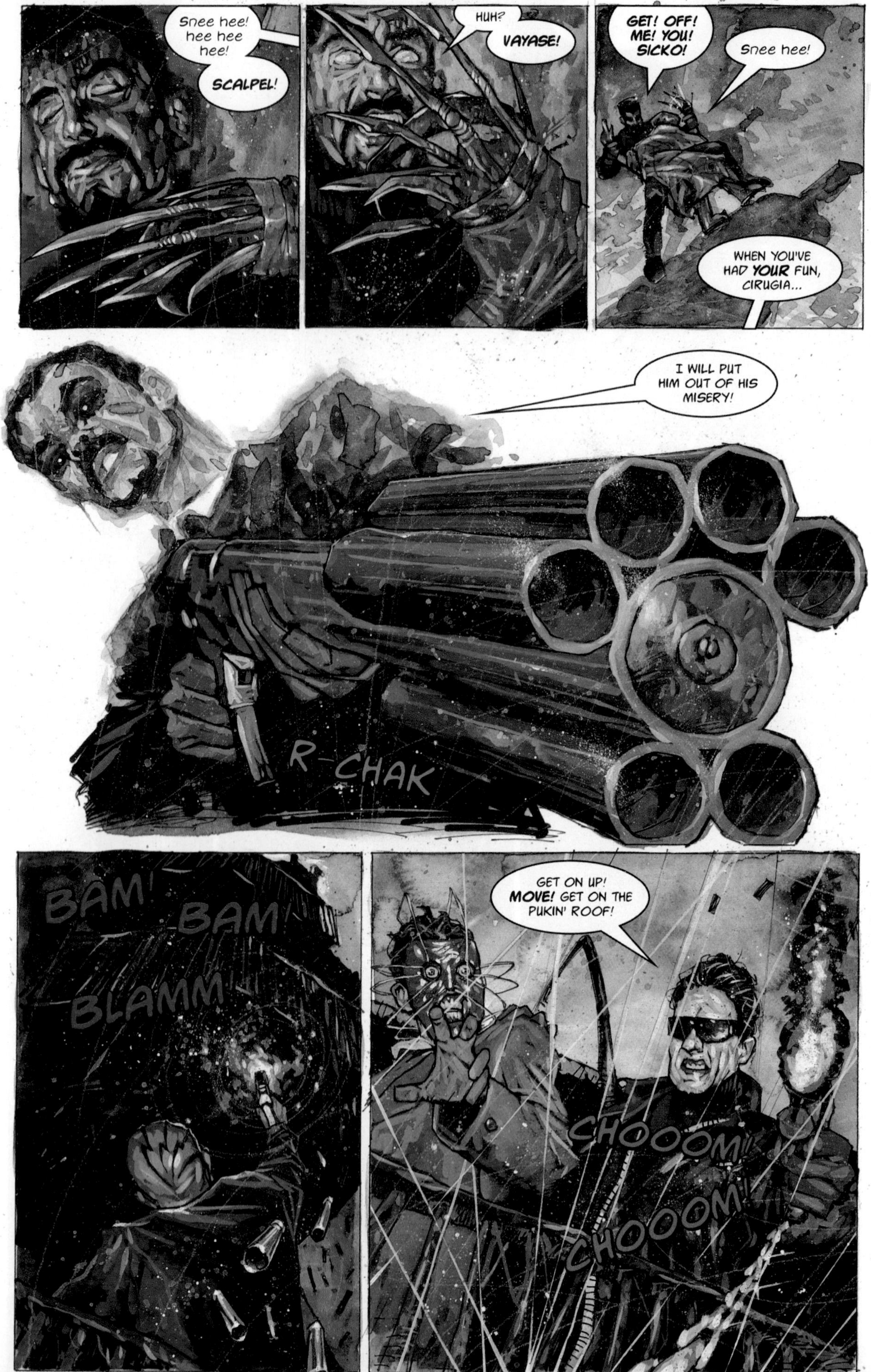
Snee hee! hee hee hee!
SCALPEL!
HUH?
VAYASE!
GET! OFF! ME! YOU! SICKO!
Snee hee!
WHEN YOU'VE HAD YOUR FUN, CIRUGIA...
I WILL PUT HIM OUT OF HIS MISERY!
R-CHAK
BAM!
BAM
BLAMM
GET ON UP! MOVE! GET ON THE PUKIN' ROOF!
CHOOOM!
CHOOOM!

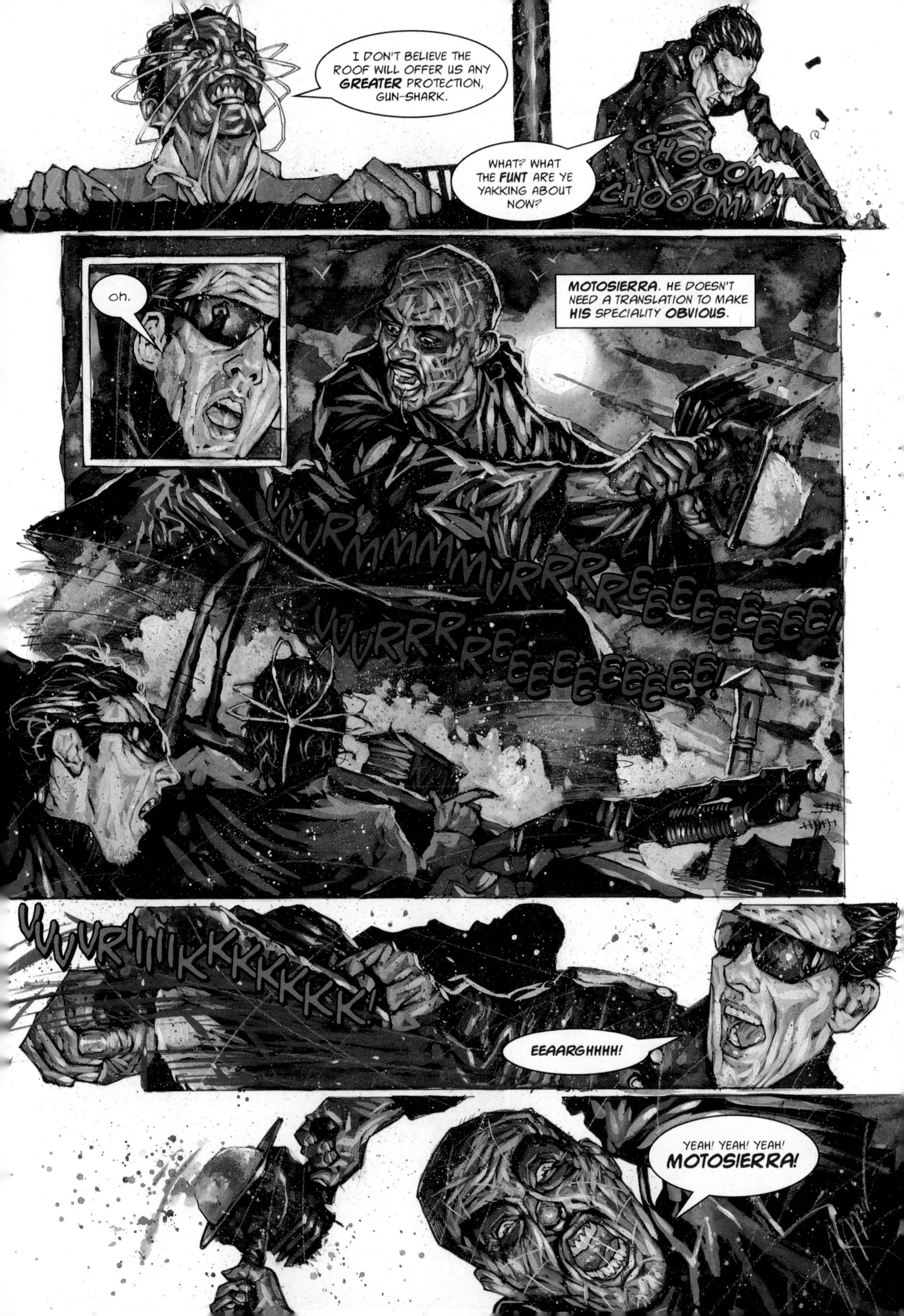
I DON'T BELIEVE THE ROOF WILL OFFER US ANY GREATER PROTECTION, GUN-SHARK.
WHAT? WHAT THE FUNT ARE YE YAKKING ABOUT NOW?
CHOOOM! CHOOOM!
oh.
MOTOSIERRA. HE DOESN'T NEED A TRANSLATION TO MAKE HIS SPECIALITY OBVIOUS.
VVVURMMMMMURRRRREEEEEEEEEEE!
VVVURRRREEEEEEEEEEEE!
VVVURIIIIIKKKKKKKK!
EEAARGHHHH!
YEAH! YEAH! YEAH! MOTOSIERRA!

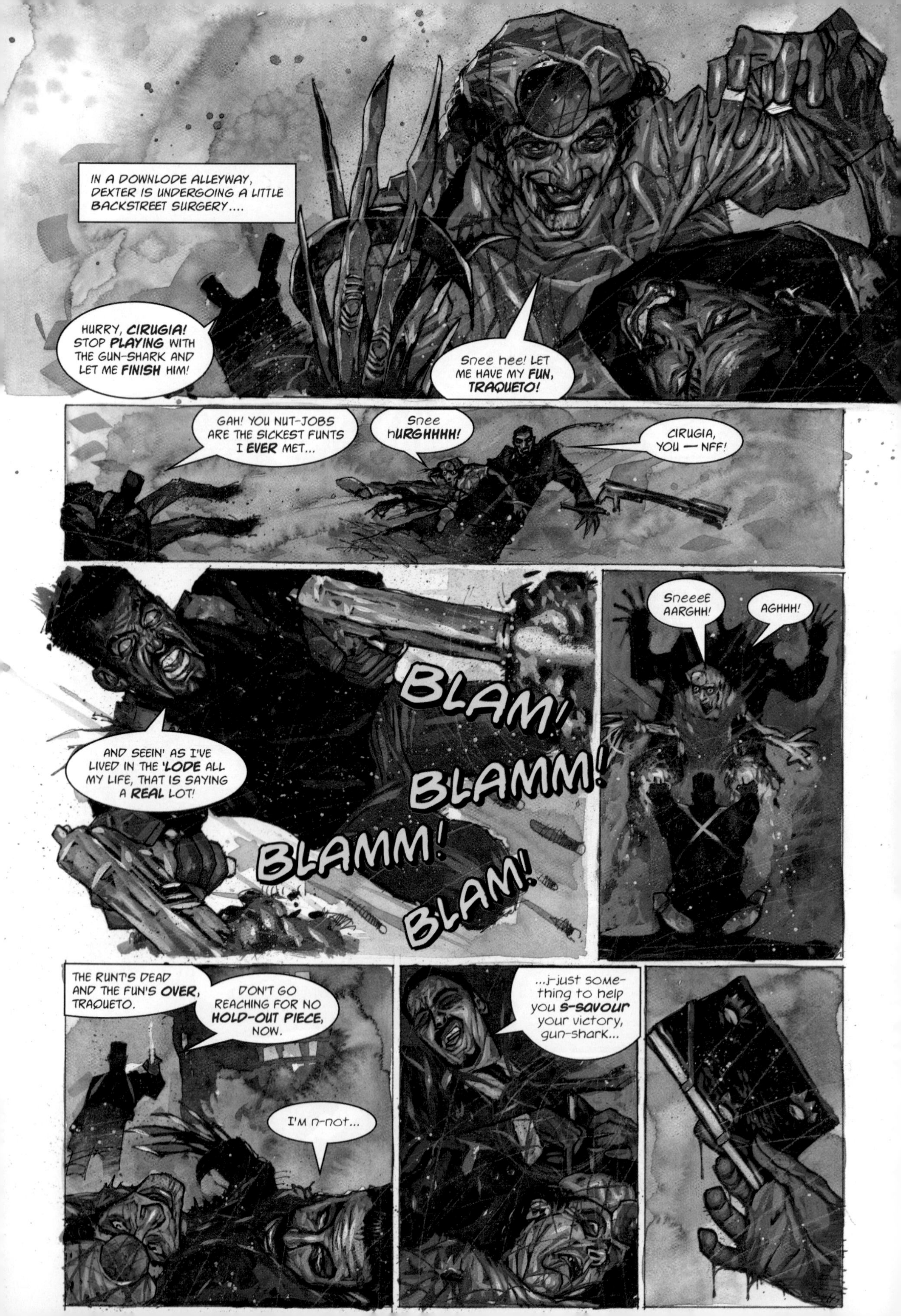

IN A DOWNLODE ALLEYWAY, DEXTER IS UNDERGOING A LITTLE BACKSTREET SURGERY....
HURRY, CIRUGIA! STOP PLAYING WITH THE GUN-SHARK AND LET ME FINISH HIM!
Snee hee! LET ME HAVE MY FUN, TRAQUETO!
GAH! YOU NUT-JOBS ARE THE SICKEST FUNTS I EVER MET...
Snee hURGHHHH!
CIRUGIA, YOU — NFF!
AND SEEIN' AS I'VE LIVED IN THE 'LODE ALL MY LIFE, THAT IS SAYING A REAL LOT!
BLAM!
BLAMM!
BLAMM!
BLAM!
SneeeE AARGHH!
AGHHH!
THE RUNT'S DEAD AND THE FUN'S OVER, TRAQUETO.
DON'T GO REACHING FOR NO HOLD-OUT PIECE, NOW.
I'M n-not...
...i-just something to help you s-savour your victory, gun-shark...

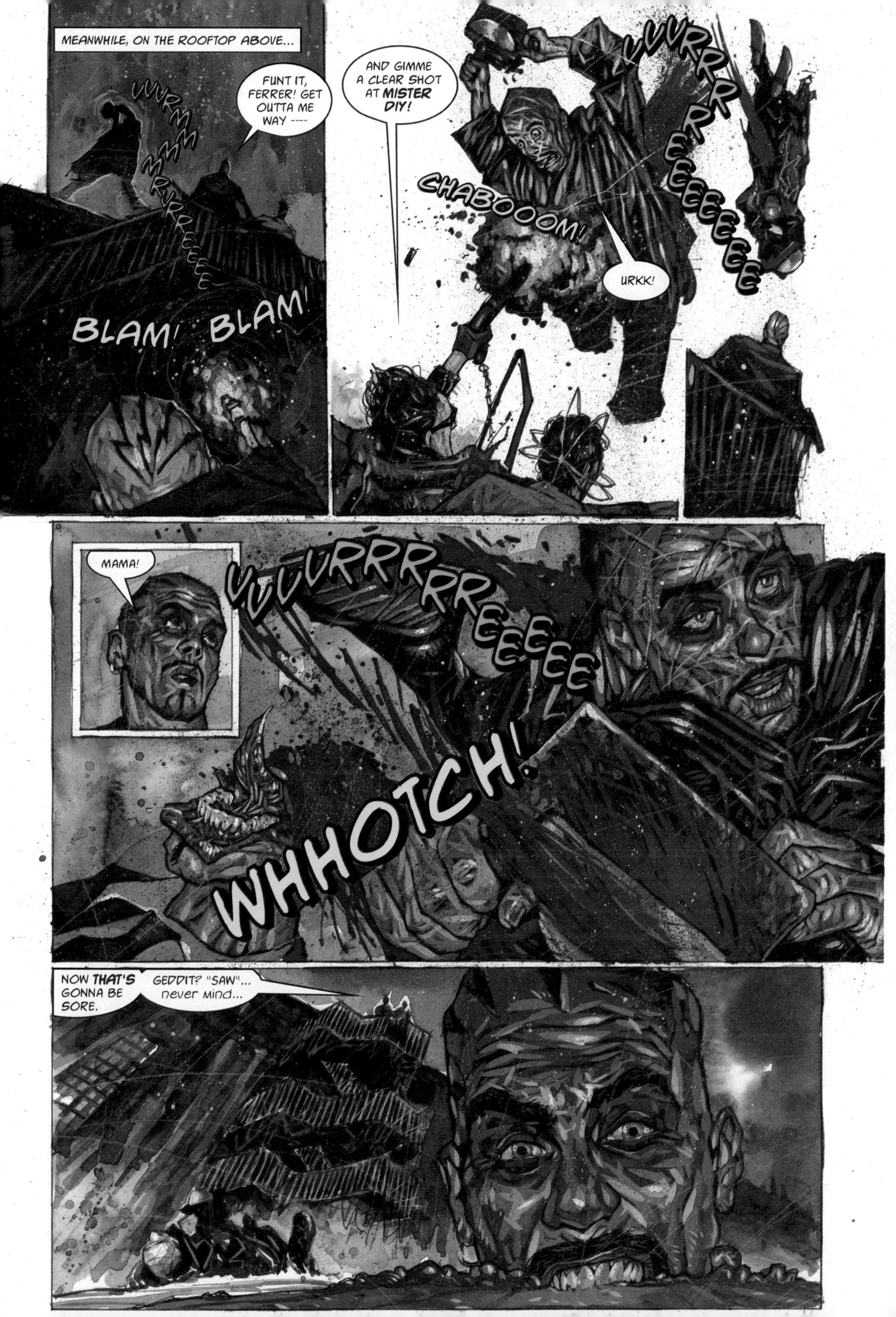
MEANWHILE, ON THE ROOFTOP ABOVE...
FUNT IT, FERRER! GET OUTTA ME WAY ----
VUURMMMMRRRREEEEE
BLAM! BLAM!
AND GIMME A CLEAR SHOT AT MISTER DIY!
VUURRRRREEEEEEEEE
CHABOOOOM!
URKK!
MAMA!
VUUURRRRREEEEEE
WHHOTCH!
NOW THAT'S GONNA BE SORE.
GEDDIT? "SAW"... never mind...

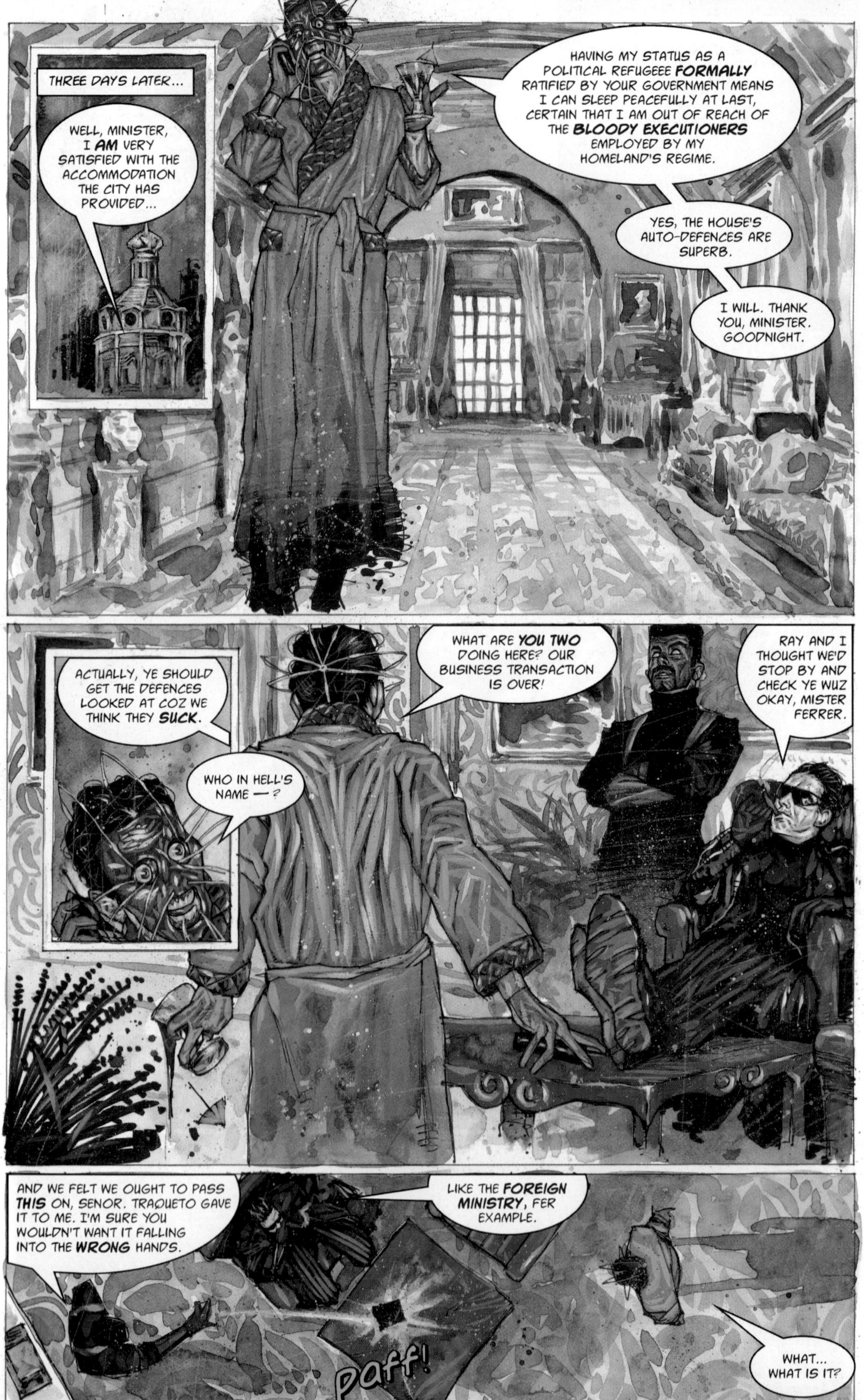
THREE DAYS LATER...
WELL, MINISTER, I **AM** VERY SATISFIED WITH THE ACCOMMODATION THE CITY HAS PROVIDED...
HAVING MY STATUS AS A POLITICAL REFUGEEE **FORMALLY** RATIFIED BY YOUR GOVERNMENT MEANS I CAN SLEEP PEACEFULLY AT LAST, CERTAIN THAT I AM OUT OF REACH OF THE **BLOODY EXECUTIONERS** EMPLOYED BY MY HOMELAND'S REGIME.
YES, THE HOUSE'S AUTO-DEFENCES ARE SUPERB.
I WILL. THANK YOU, MINISTER. GOODNIGHT.
ACTUALLY, YE SHOULD GET THE DEFENCES LOOKED AT COZ WE THINK THEY **SUCK**.
WHO IN HELL'S NAME — ?
WHAT ARE **YOU TWO** DOING HERE? OUR BUSINESS TRANSACTION IS OVER!
RAY AND I THOUGHT WE'D STOP BY AND CHECK YE WUZ OKAY, MISTER FERRER.
AND WE FELT WE OUGHT TO PASS **THIS** ON, SENOR. TRAQUETO GAVE IT TO ME. I'M SURE YOU WOULDN'T WANT IT FALLING INTO THE **WRONG** HANDS.
LIKE THE **FOREIGN MINISTRY**, FER EXAMPLE.
paff!
WHAT... WHAT IS IT?

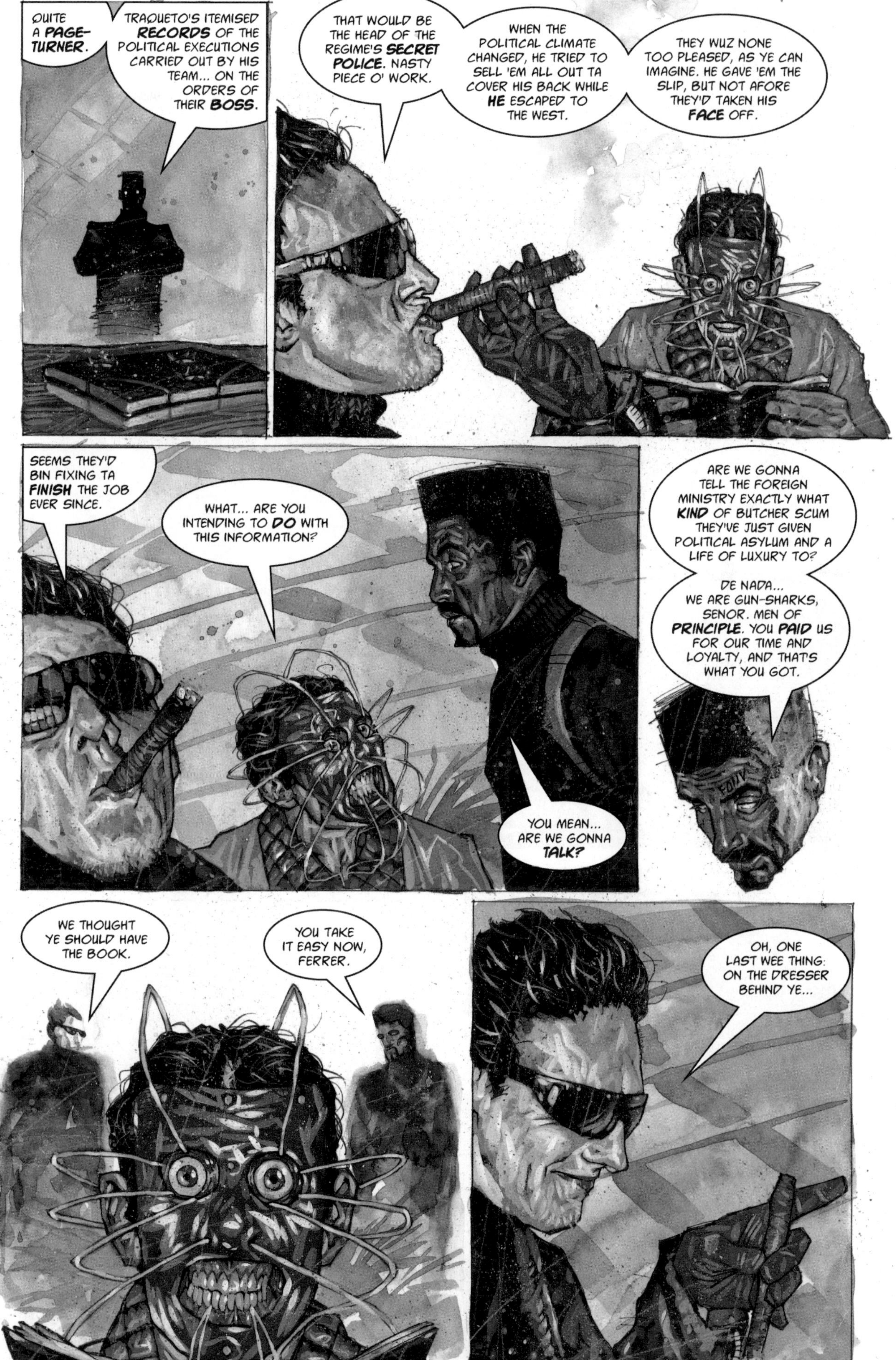
QUITE A **PAGE-TURNER**.
TRAQUETO'S ITEMISED **RECORDS** OF THE POLITICAL EXECUTIONS CARRIED OUT BY HIS TEAM... ON THE ORDERS OF THEIR **BOSS**.
THAT WOULD BE THE HEAD OF THE REGIME'S **SECRET POLICE**. NASTY PIECE O' WORK.
WHEN THE POLITICAL CLIMATE CHANGED, HE TRIED TO SELL 'EM ALL OUT TA COVER HIS BACK WHILE **HE** ESCAPED TO THE WEST.
THEY WUZ NONE TOO PLEASED, AS YE CAN IMAGINE. HE GAVE 'EM THE SLIP, BUT NOT AFORE THEY'D TAKEN HIS **FACE** OFF.
SEEMS THEY'D BIN FIXING TA **FINISH** THE JOB EVER SINCE.
WHAT... ARE YOU INTENDING TO **DO** WITH THIS INFORMATION?
YOU MEAN... ARE WE GONNA **TALK?**
ARE WE GONNA TELL THE FOREIGN MINISTRY EXACTLY WHAT **KIND** OF BUTCHER SCUM THEY'VE JUST GIVEN POLITICAL ASYLUM AND A LIFE OF LUXURY TO?
DE NADA... WE ARE GUN-SHARKS, SENOR. MEN OF **PRINCIPLE**. YOU **PAID** US FOR OUR TIME AND LOYALTY, AND THAT'S WHAT YOU GOT.
WE THOUGHT YE SHOULD HAVE THE BOOK.
YOU TAKE IT EASY NOW, FERRER.
OH, ONE LAST WEE THING: ON THE DRESSER BEHIND YE...

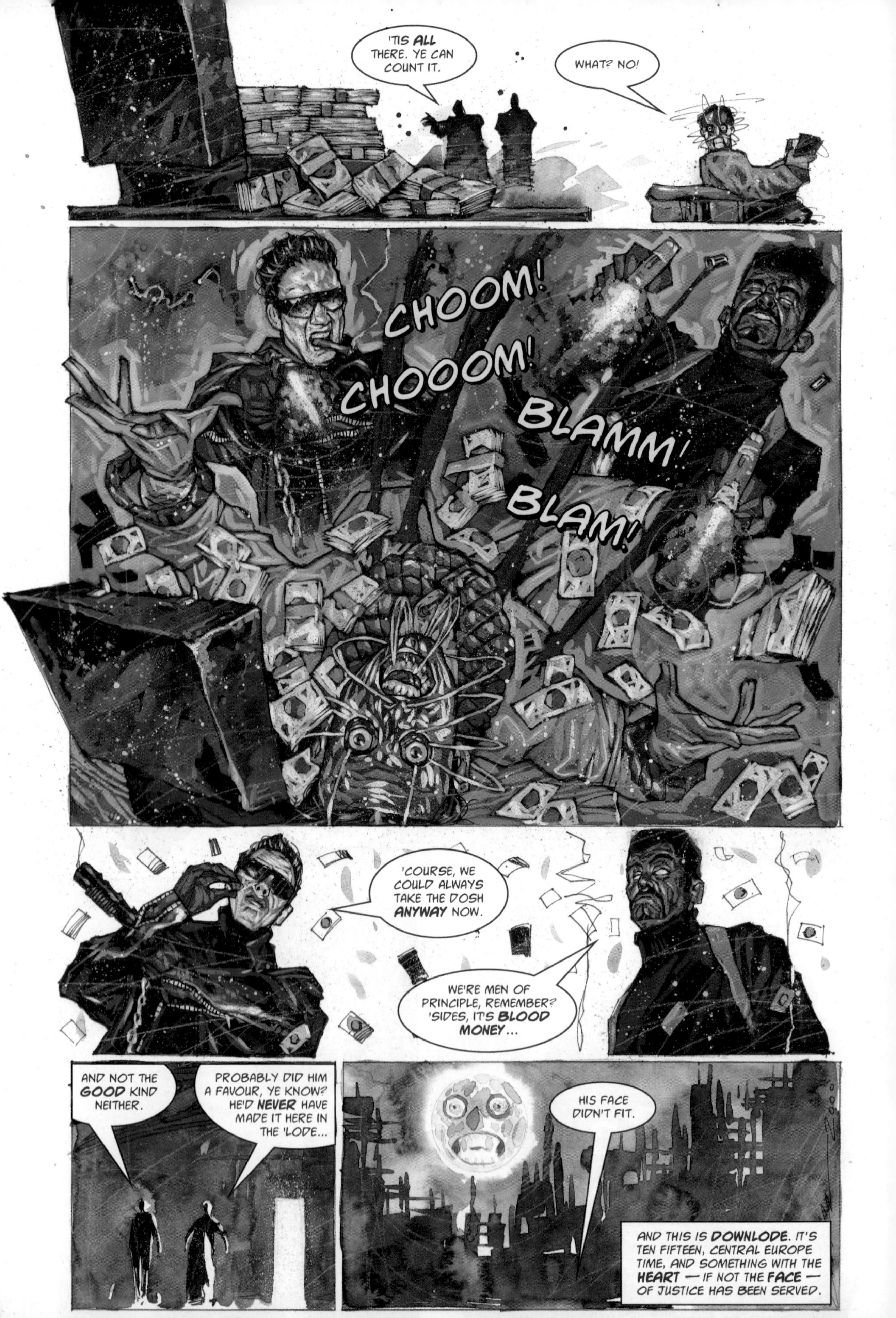
'TIS ALL THERE. YE CAN COUNT IT.
WHAT? NO!
CHOOOM!
CHOOOM!
BLAMM!
BLAM!
'COURSE, WE COULD ALWAYS TAKE THE DOSH ANYWAY NOW.
WE'RE MEN OF PRINCIPLE, REMEMBER? 'SIDES, IT'S BLOOD MONEY...
AND NOT THE GOOD KIND NEITHER.
PROBABLY DID HIM A FAVOUR, YE KNOW? HE'D NEVER HAVE MADE IT HERE IN THE 'LODE...
HIS FACE DIDN'T FIT.
AND THIS IS DOWNLODE. IT'S TEN FIFTEEN, CENTRAL EUROPE TIME, AND SOMETHING WITH THE HEART — IF NOT THE FACE — OF JUSTICE HAS BEEN SERVED.

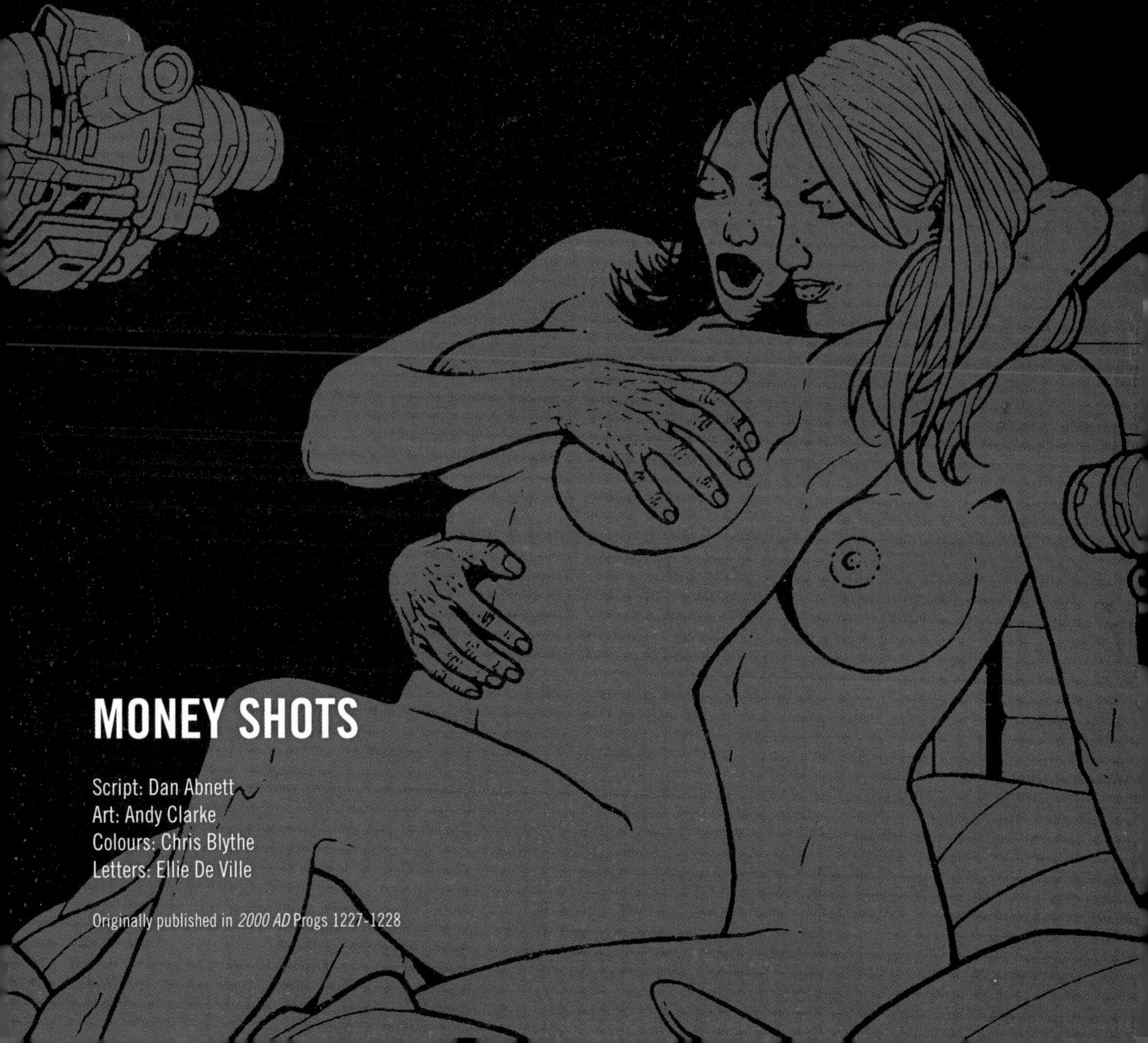

MONEY SHOTS

Script: Dan Abnett
Art: Andy Clarke
Colours: Chris Blythe
Letters: Ellie De Ville

Originally published in *2000 AD* Progs 1227-1228

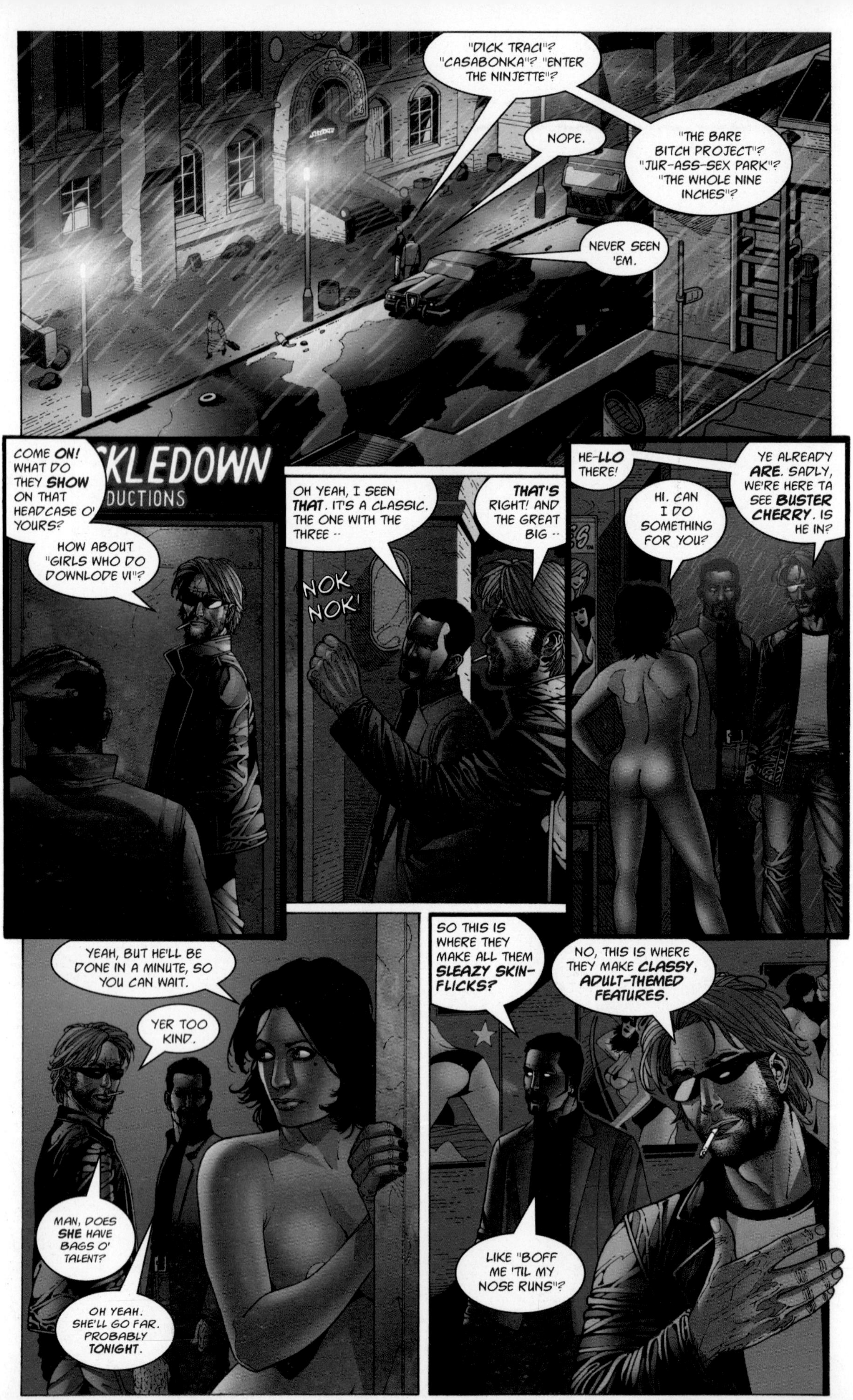

"DICK TRACI"? "CASABONKA"? "ENTER THE NINJETTE"?
NOPE.
"THE BARE BITCH PROJECT"? "JUR-ASS-SEX PARK"? "THE WHOLE NINE INCHES"?
NEVER SEEN 'EM.
COME ON! WHAT DO THEY SHOW ON THAT HEADCASE O' YOURS?
HOW ABOUT "GIRLS WHO DO DOWNLODE VI"?
OH YEAH, I SEEN THAT. IT'S A CLASSIC. THE ONE WITH THE THREE --
THAT'S RIGHT! AND THE GREAT BIG --
NOK NOK!
HE-LLO THERE!
HI. CAN I DO SOMETHING FOR YOU?
YE ALREADY ARE. SADLY, WE'RE HERE TA SEE BUSTER CHERRY. IS HE IN?
YEAH, BUT HE'LL BE DONE IN A MINUTE, SO YOU CAN WAIT.
YER TOO KIND.
MAN, DOES SHE HAVE BAGS O' TALENT?
OH YEAH. SHE'LL GO FAR. PROBABLY TONIGHT.
SO THIS IS WHERE THEY MAKE ALL THEM SLEAZY SKIN-FLICKS?
NO, THIS IS WHERE THEY MAKE CLASSY, ADULT-THEMED FEATURES.
LIKE "BOFF ME 'TIL MY NOSE RUNS"?

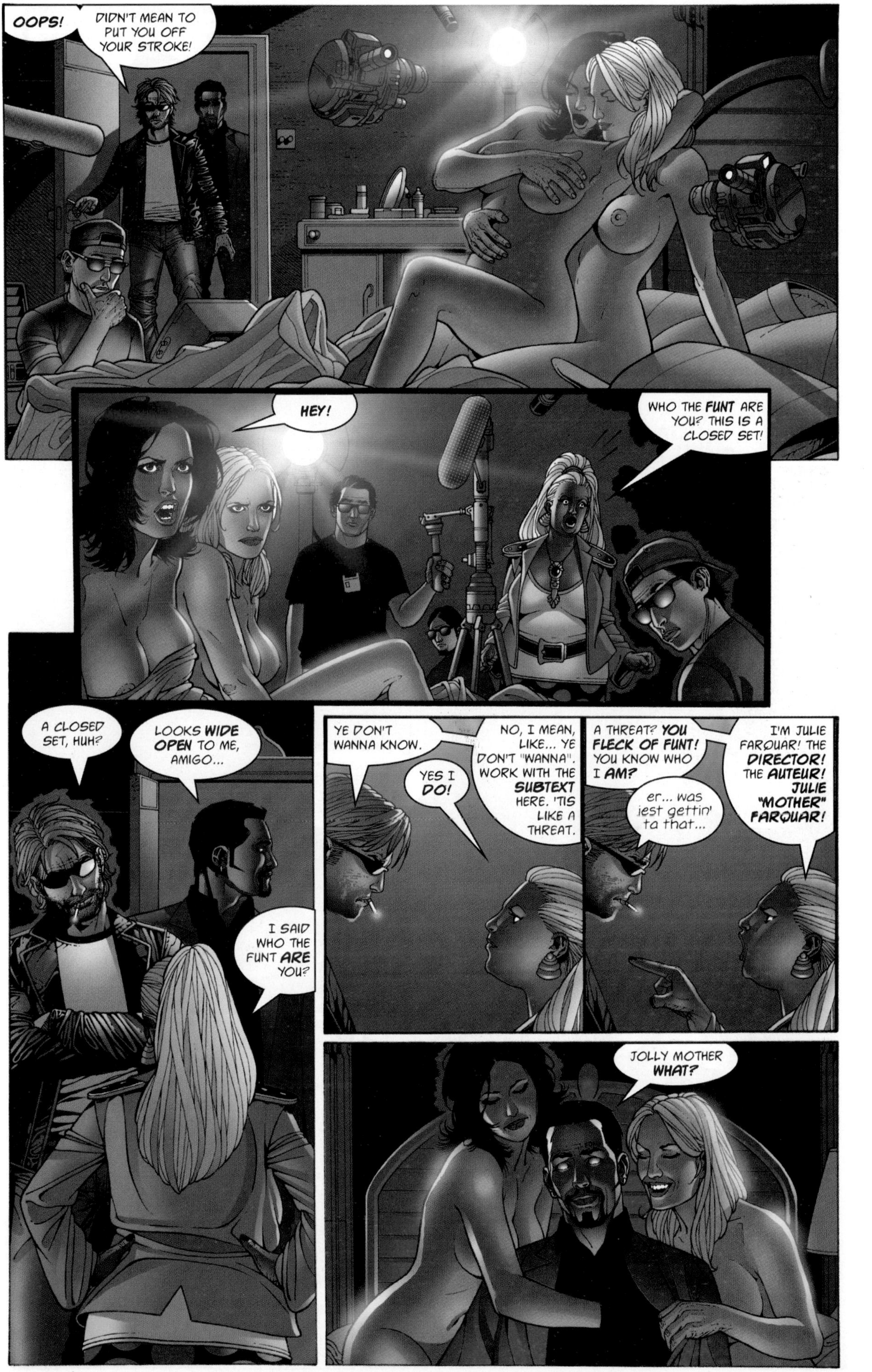
OOPS!
DIDN'T MEAN TO PUT YOU OFF YOUR STROKE!
HEY!
WHO THE FUNT ARE YOU? THIS IS A CLOSED SET!
A CLOSED SET, HUH?
LOOKS WIDE OPEN TO ME, AMIGO...
I SAID WHO THE FUNT ARE YOU?
YE DON'T WANNA KNOW.
YES I DO!
NO, I MEAN, LIKE... YE DON'T "WANNA". WORK WITH THE SUBTEXT HERE. 'TIS LIKE A THREAT.
A THREAT? YOU FLECK OF FUNT! YOU KNOW WHO I AM?
er... was jest gettin' ta that...
I'M JULIE FARQUAR! THE DIRECTOR! THE AUTEUR! JULIE "MOTHER" FARQUAR!
JOLLY MOTHER WHAT?

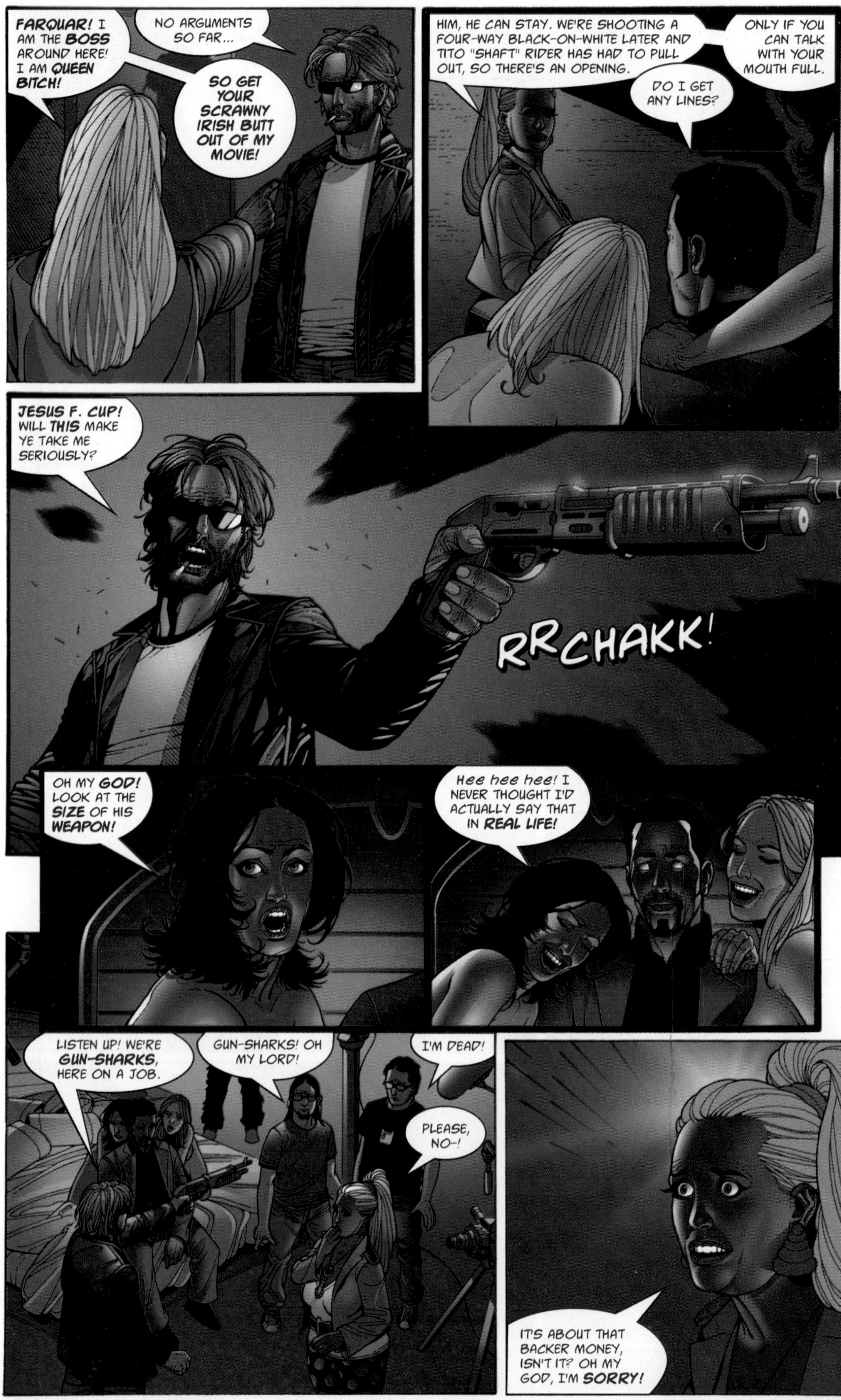
FARQUAR! I AM THE BOSS AROUND HERE! I AM QUEEN BITCH!
NO ARGUMENTS SO FAR...
SO GET YOUR SCRAWNY IRISH BUTT OUT OF MY MOVIE!
HIM, HE CAN STAY. WE'RE SHOOTING A FOUR-WAY BLACK-ON-WHITE LATER AND TITO "SHAFT" RIDER HAS HAD TO PULL OUT, SO THERE'S AN OPENING.
DO I GET ANY LINES?
ONLY IF YOU CAN TALK WITH YOUR MOUTH FULL.
JESUS F. CUP! WILL THIS MAKE YE TAKE ME SERIOUSLY?
RRCHAKK!
OH MY GOD! LOOK AT THE SIZE OF HIS WEAPON!
Hee hee hee! I NEVER THOUGHT I'D ACTUALLY SAY THAT IN REAL LIFE!
LISTEN UP! WE'RE GUN-SHARKS, HERE ON A JOB.
GUN-SHARKS! OH MY LORD!
I'M DEAD!
PLEASE, NO-!
IT'S ABOUT THAT BACKER MONEY, ISN'T IT? OH MY GOD, I'M SORRY!

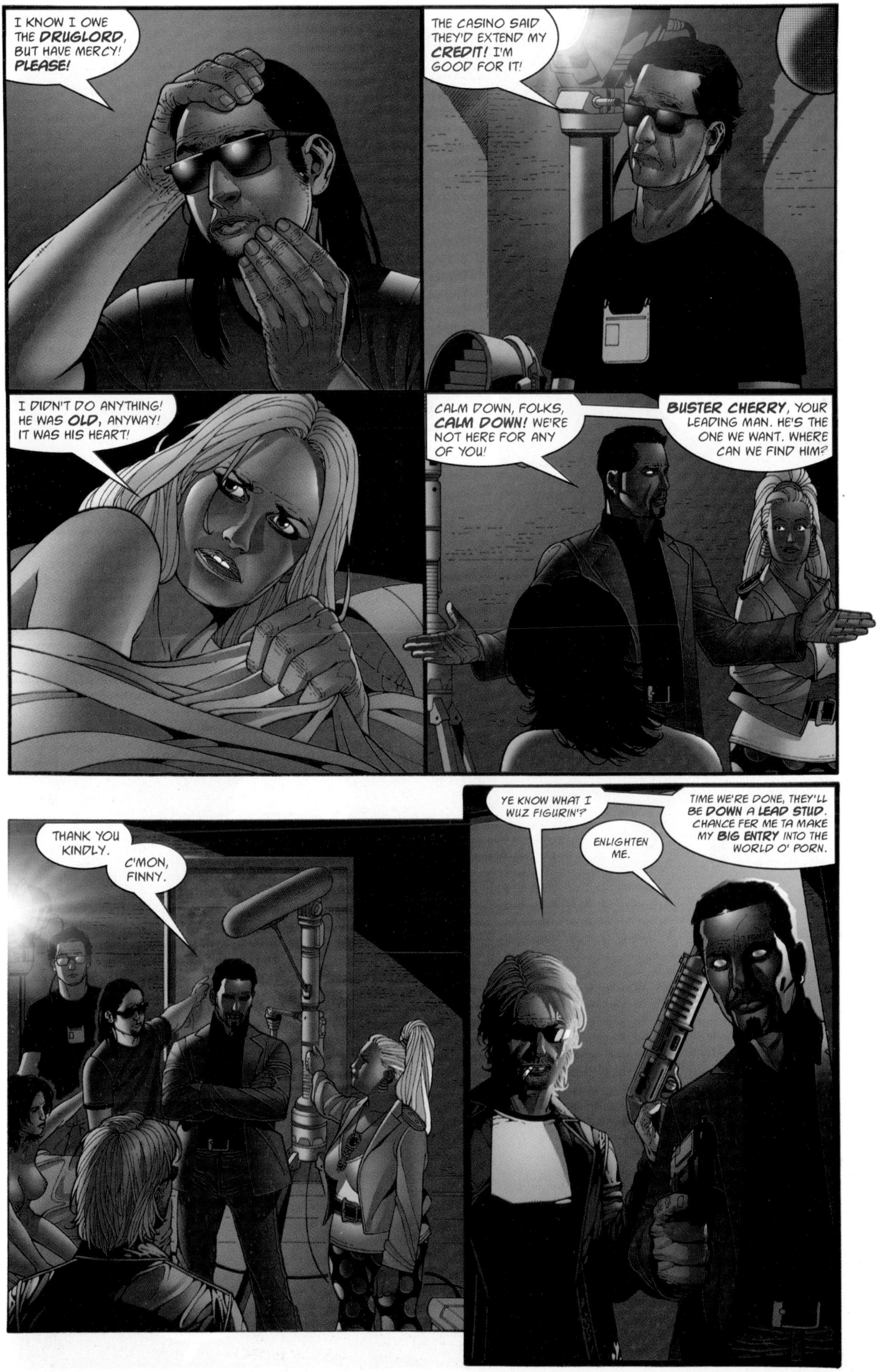
I KNOW I OWE THE DRUGLORD, BUT HAVE MERCY! PLEASE!
THE CASINO SAID THEY'D EXTEND MY CREDIT! I'M GOOD FOR IT!
I DIDN'T DO ANYTHING! HE WAS OLD, ANYWAY! IT WAS HIS HEART!
CALM DOWN, FOLKS, CALM DOWN! WE'RE NOT HERE FOR ANY OF YOU!
BUSTER CHERRY, YOUR LEADING MAN. HE'S THE ONE WE WANT. WHERE CAN WE FIND HIM?
THANK YOU KINDLY.
C'MON, FINNY.
YE KNOW WHAT I WUZ FIGURIN'?
ENLIGHTEN ME.
TIME WE'RE DONE, THEY'LL BE DOWN A LEAD STUD. CHANCE FER ME TA MAKE MY BIG ENTRY INTO THE WORLD O' PORN.

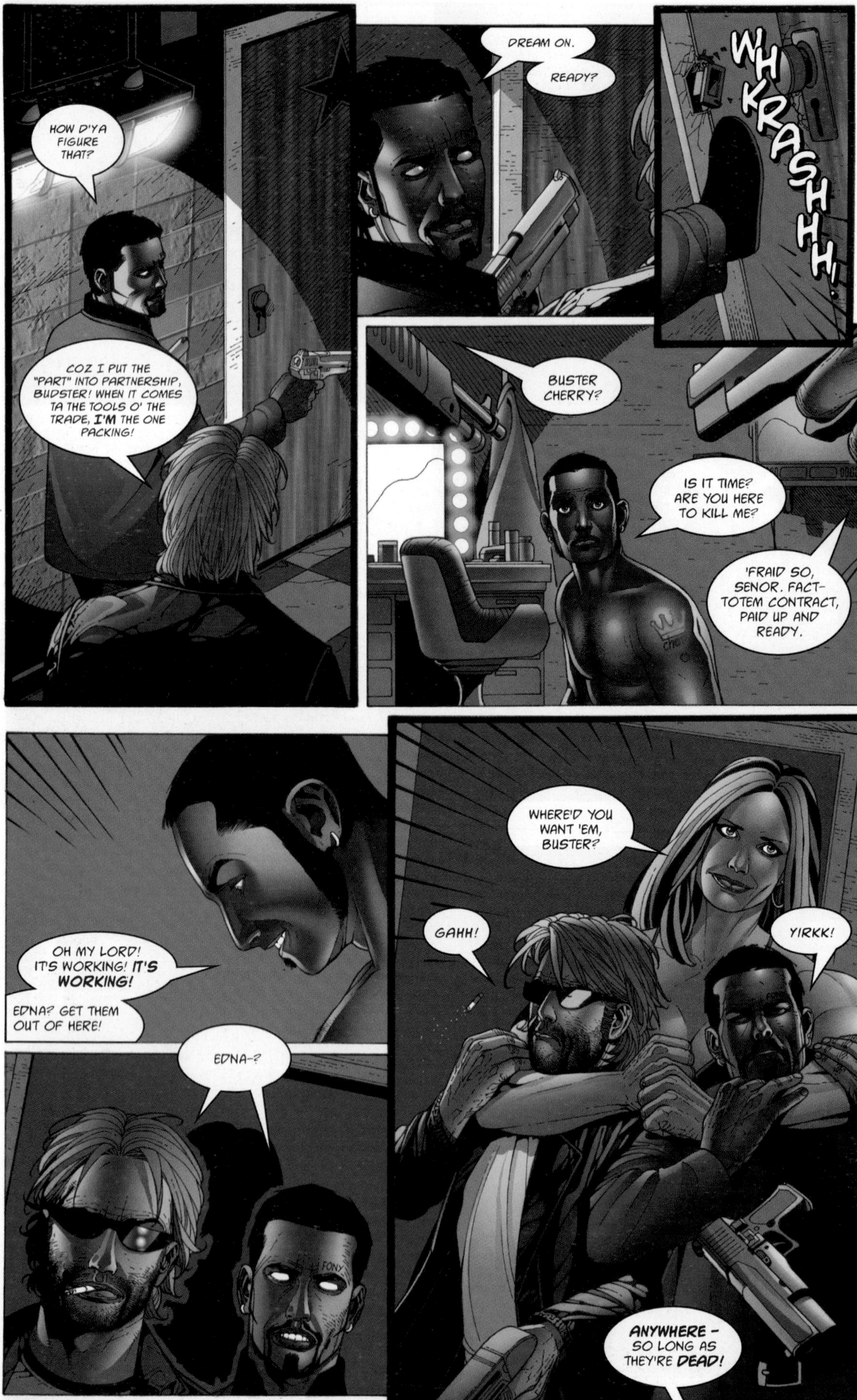
HOW D'YA FIGURE THAT?
COZ I PUT THE "PART" INTO PARTNERSHIP, BUDSTER! WHEN IT COMES TA THE TOOLS O' THE TRADE, I'M THE ONE PACKING!
DREAM ON.
READY?
WHKRASHHH!
BUSTER CHERRY?
IS IT TIME? ARE YOU HERE TO KILL ME?
'FRAID SO, SENOR. FACT-TOTEM CONTRACT, PAID UP AND READY.
OH MY LORD! IT'S WORKING! IT'S WORKING!
EDNA? GET THEM OUT OF HERE!
EDNA-?
WHERE'D YOU WANT 'EM, BUSTER?
GAHH!
YIRKK!
ANYWHERE - SO LONG AS THEY'RE DEAD!

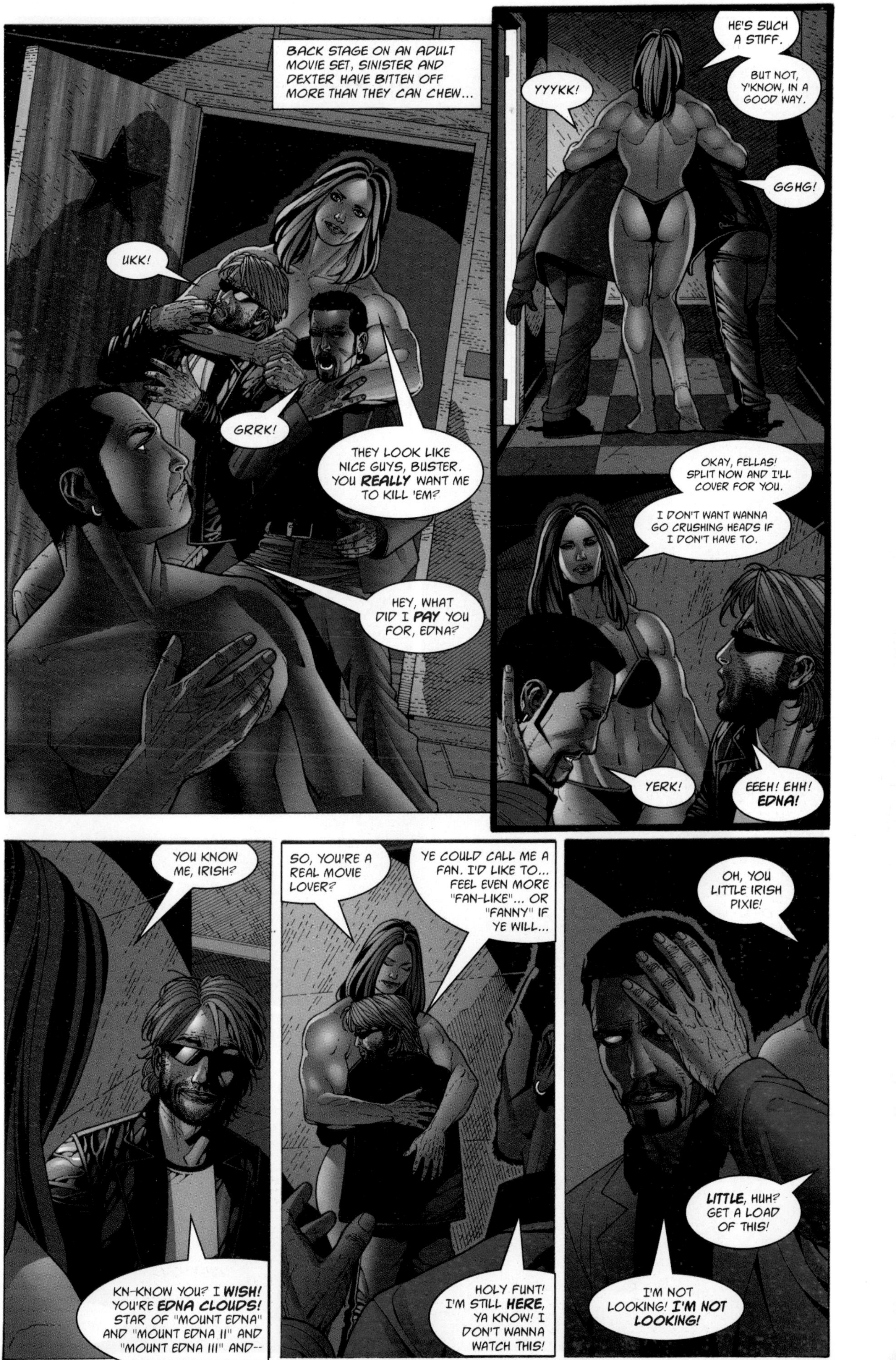
BACK STAGE ON AN ADULT MOVIE SET, SINISTER AND DEXTER HAVE BITTEN OFF MORE THAN THEY CAN CHEW...
UKK!
GRRK!
THEY LOOK LIKE NICE GUYS, BUSTER. YOU REALLY WANT ME TO KILL 'EM?
HEY, WHAT DID I PAY YOU FOR, EDNA?
HE'S SUCH A STIFF.
BUT NOT, Y'KNOW, IN A GOOD WAY.
YYYKK!
GGHG!
OKAY, FELLAS! SPLIT NOW AND I'LL COVER FOR YOU.
I DON'T WANT WANNA GO CRUSHING HEADS IF I DON'T HAVE TO.
YERK!
EEEH! EHH! EDNA!
YOU KNOW ME, IRISH?
KN-KNOW YOU? I WISH! YOU'RE EDNA CLOUDS! STAR OF "MOUNT EDNA" AND "MOUNT EDNA II" AND "MOUNT EDNA III" AND--
SO, YOU'RE A REAL MOVIE LOVER?
YE COULD CALL ME A FAN. I'D LIKE TO... FEEL EVEN MORE "FAN-LIKE"... OR "FANNY" IF YE WILL...
HOLY FUNT! I'M STILL HERE, YA KNOW! I DON'T WANNA WATCH THIS!
OH, YOU LITTLE IRISH PIXIE!
LITTLE, HUH? GET A LOAD OF THIS!
I'M NOT LOOKING! I'M NOT LOOKING!

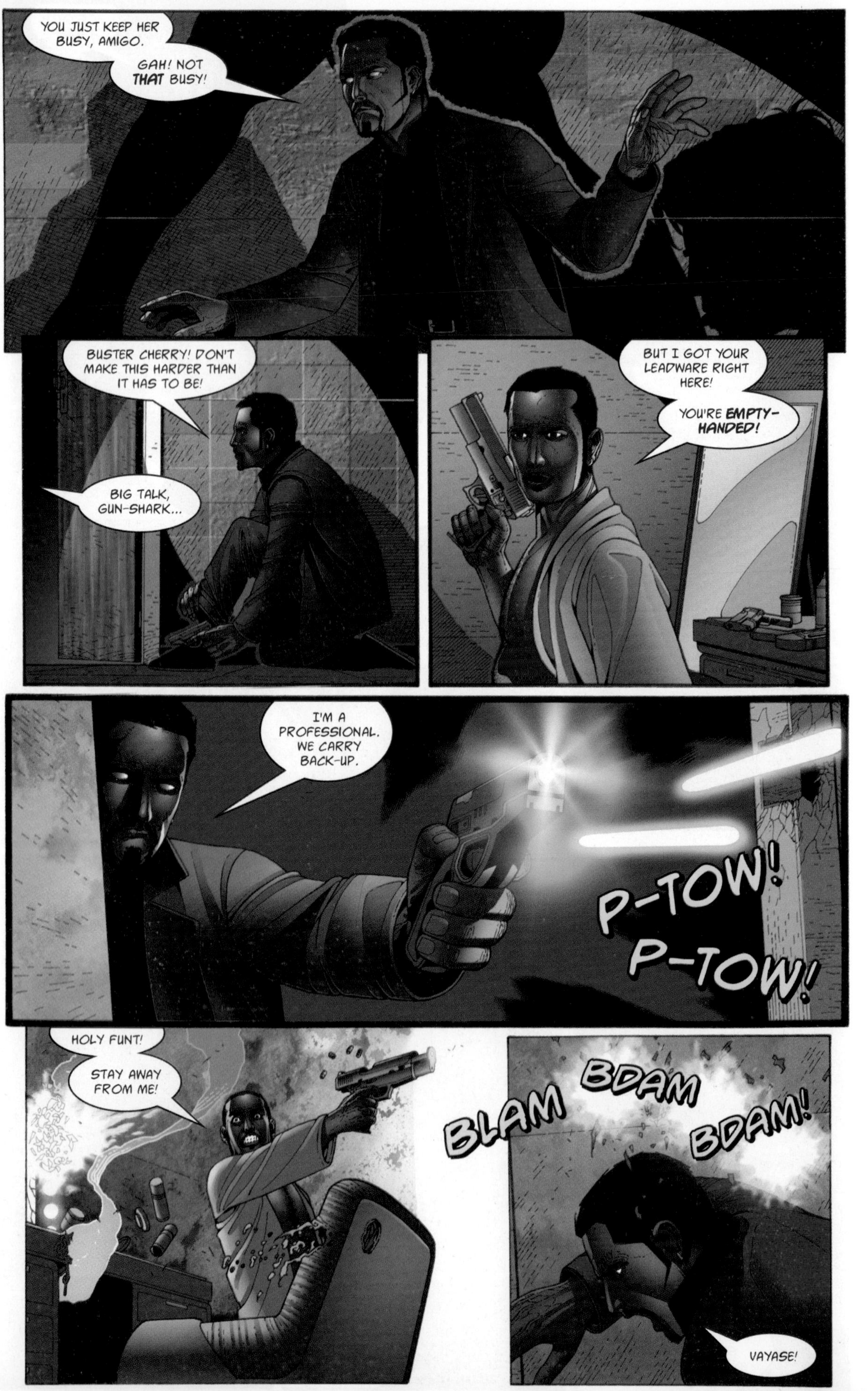
YOU JUST KEEP HER BUSY, AMIGO.
GAH! NOT THAT BUSY!
BUSTER CHERRY! DON'T MAKE THIS HARDER THAN IT HAS TO BE!
BIG TALK, GUN-SHARK...
BUT I GOT YOUR LEADWARE RIGHT HERE!
YOU'RE EMPTY-HANDED!
I'M A PROFESSIONAL. WE CARRY BACK-UP.
P-TOW!
P-TOW!
HOLY FUNT!
STAY AWAY FROM ME!
BLAM
BDAM
BDAM!
VAYASE!

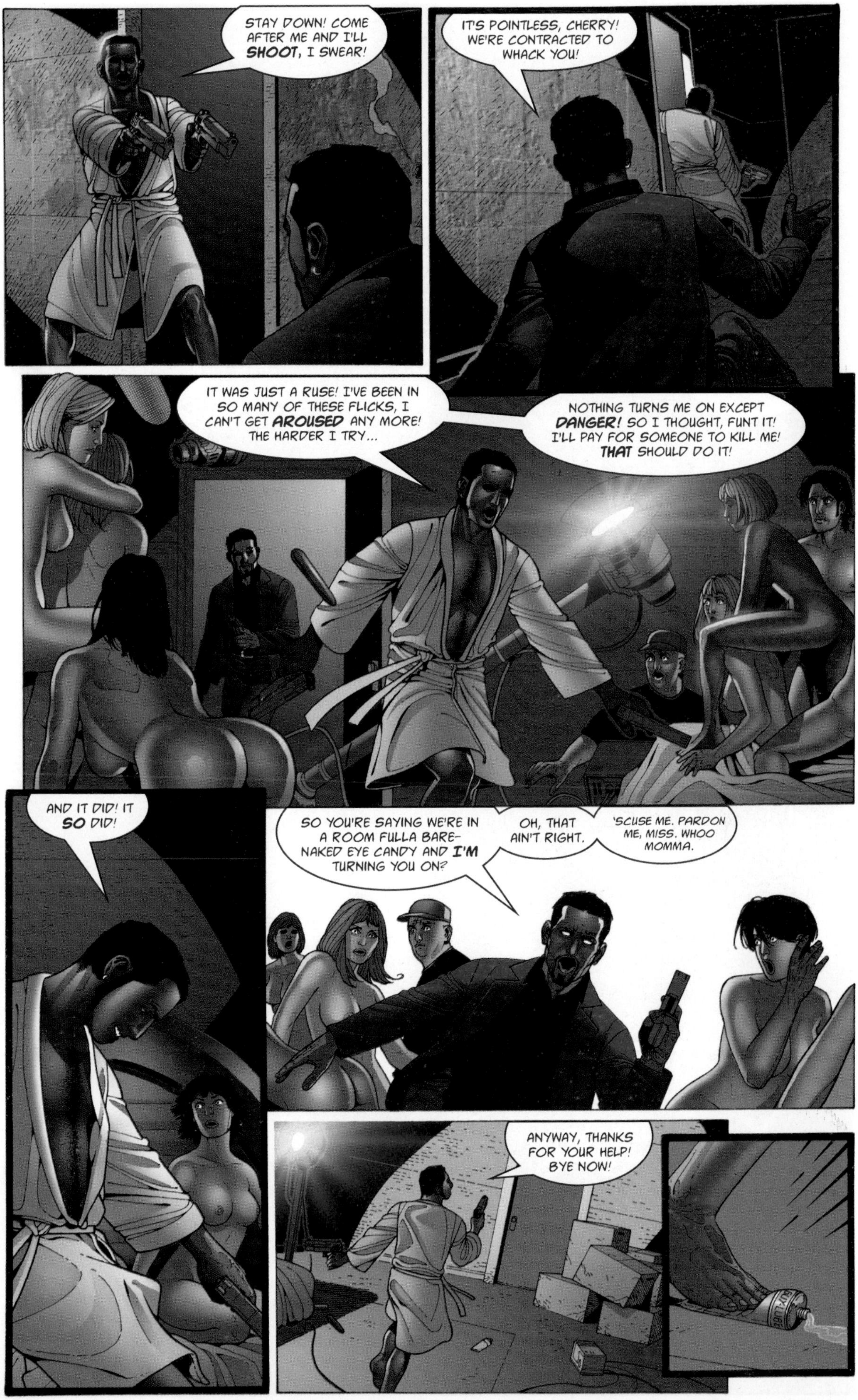
STAY DOWN! COME AFTER ME AND I'LL **SHOOT**, I SWEAR!
IT'S POINTLESS, CHERRY! WE'RE CONTRACTED TO WHACK YOU!
IT WAS JUST A RUSE! I'VE BEEN IN SO MANY OF THESE FLICKS, I CAN'T GET **AROUSED** ANY MORE! THE HARDER I TRY...
NOTHING TURNS ME ON EXCEPT **DANGER!** SO I THOUGHT, FUNT IT! I'LL PAY FOR SOMEONE TO KILL ME! **THAT** SHOULD DO IT!
AND IT DID! IT **SO** DID!
SO YOU'RE SAYING WE'RE IN A ROOM FULLA BARE-NAKED EYE CANDY AND **I'M** TURNING YOU ON?
OH, THAT AIN'T RIGHT.
'SCUSE ME. PARDON ME, MISS. WHOO MOMMA.
ANYWAY, THANKS FOR YOUR HELP! BYE NOW!

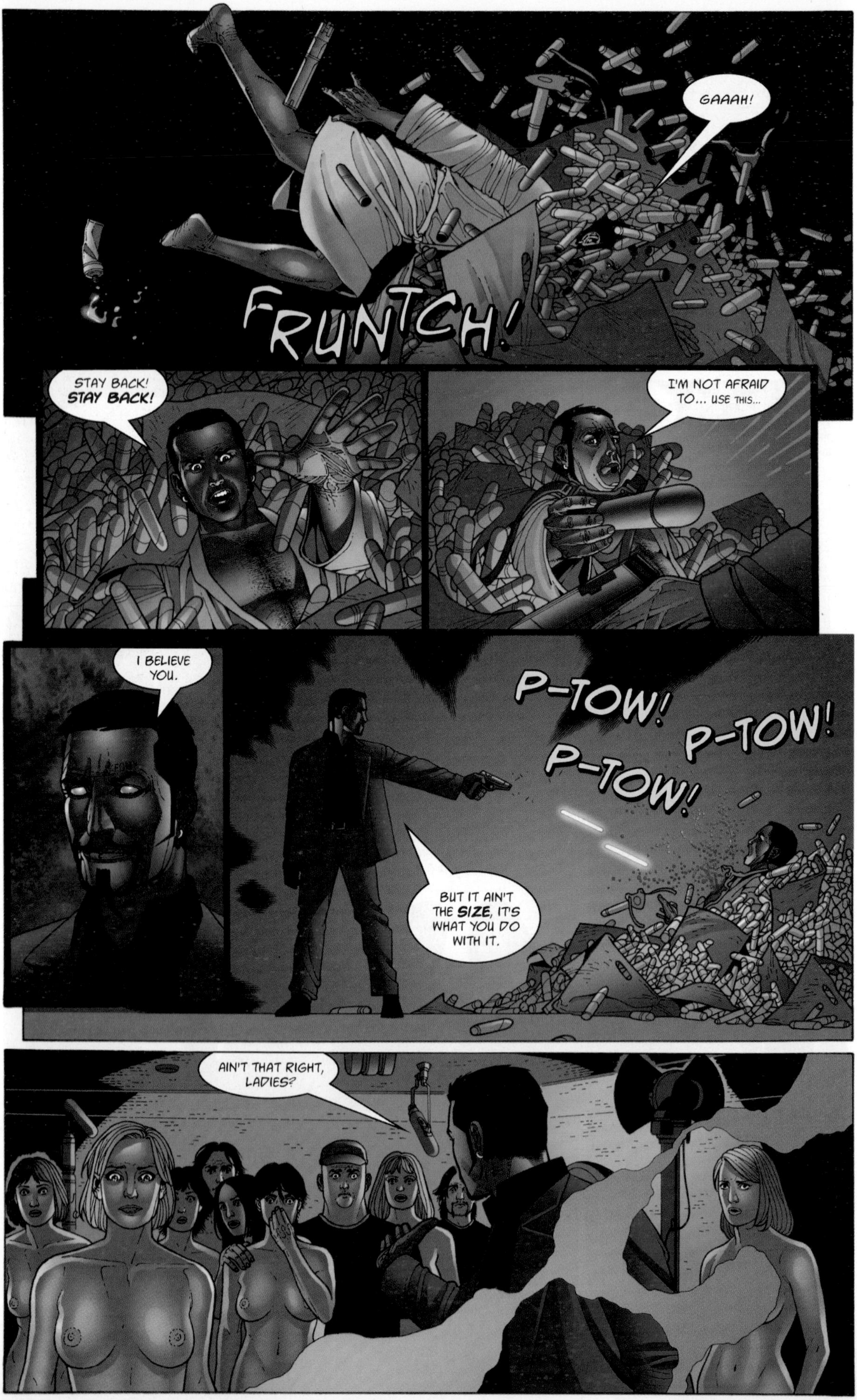
GAAAH!
FRUNTCH!
STAY BACK! STAY BACK!
I'M NOT AFRAID TO... USE THIS...
I BELIEVE YOU.
P-TOW!
P-TOW!
P-TOW!
BUT IT AIN'T THE SIZE, IT'S WHAT YOU DO WITH IT.
AIN'T THAT RIGHT, LADIES?

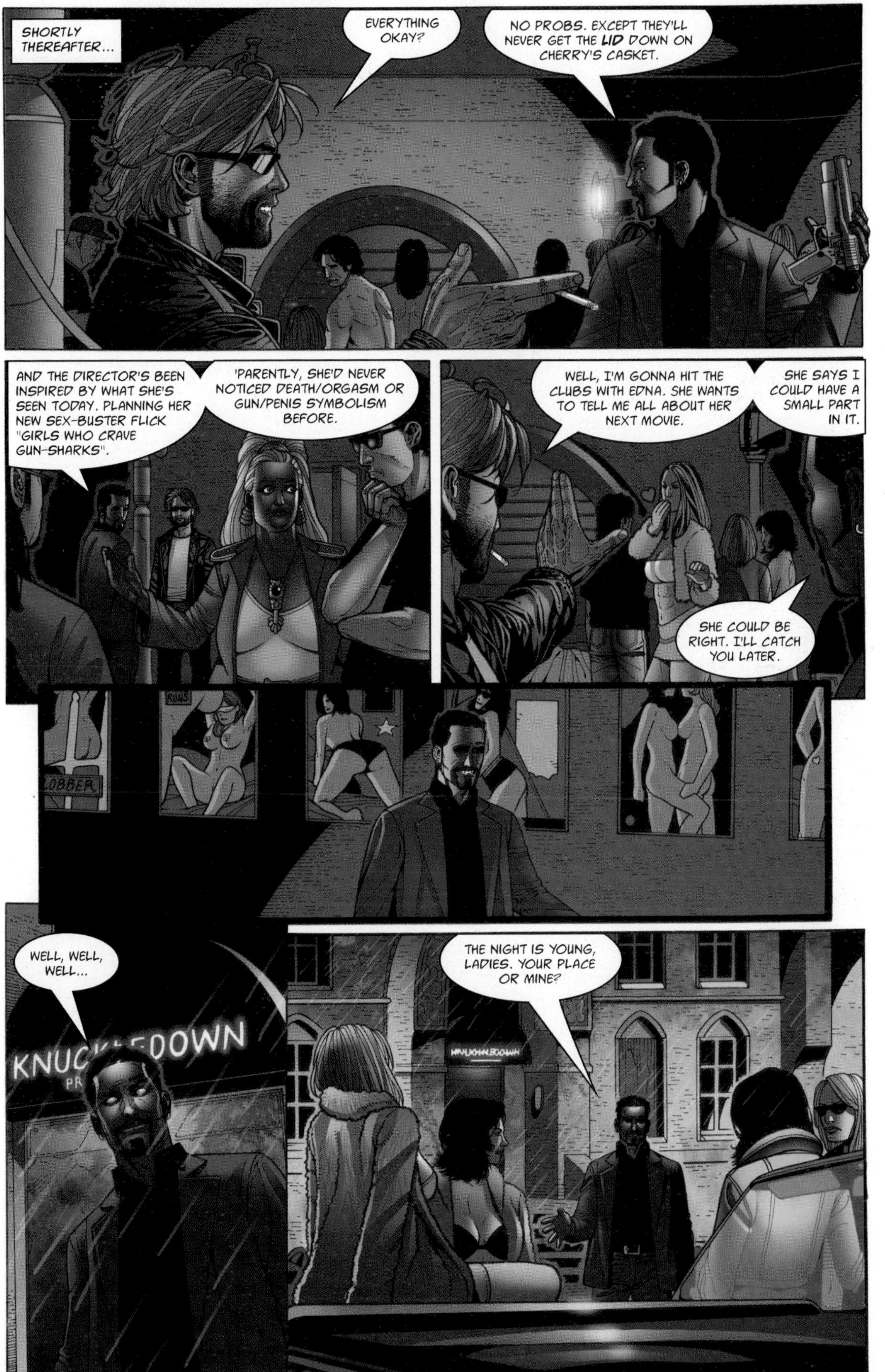
SHORTLY THEREAFTER...
EVERYTHING OKAY?
NO PROBS. EXCEPT THEY'LL NEVER GET THE **LID** DOWN ON CHERRY'S CASKET.
AND THE DIRECTOR'S BEEN INSPIRED BY WHAT SHE'S SEEN TODAY. PLANNING HER NEW SEX-BUSTER FLICK "GIRLS WHO CRAVE GUN-SHARKS".
'PARENTLY, SHE'D NEVER NOTICED DEATH/ORGASM OR GUN/PENIS SYMBOLISM BEFORE.
WELL, I'M GONNA HIT THE CLUBS WITH EDNA. SHE WANTS TO TELL ME ALL ABOUT HER NEXT MOVIE.
SHE SAYS I COULD HAVE A SMALL PART IN IT.
SHE COULD BE RIGHT. I'LL CATCH YOU LATER.
WELL, WELL, WELL...
THE NIGHT IS YOUNG, LADIES. YOUR PLACE OR MINE?

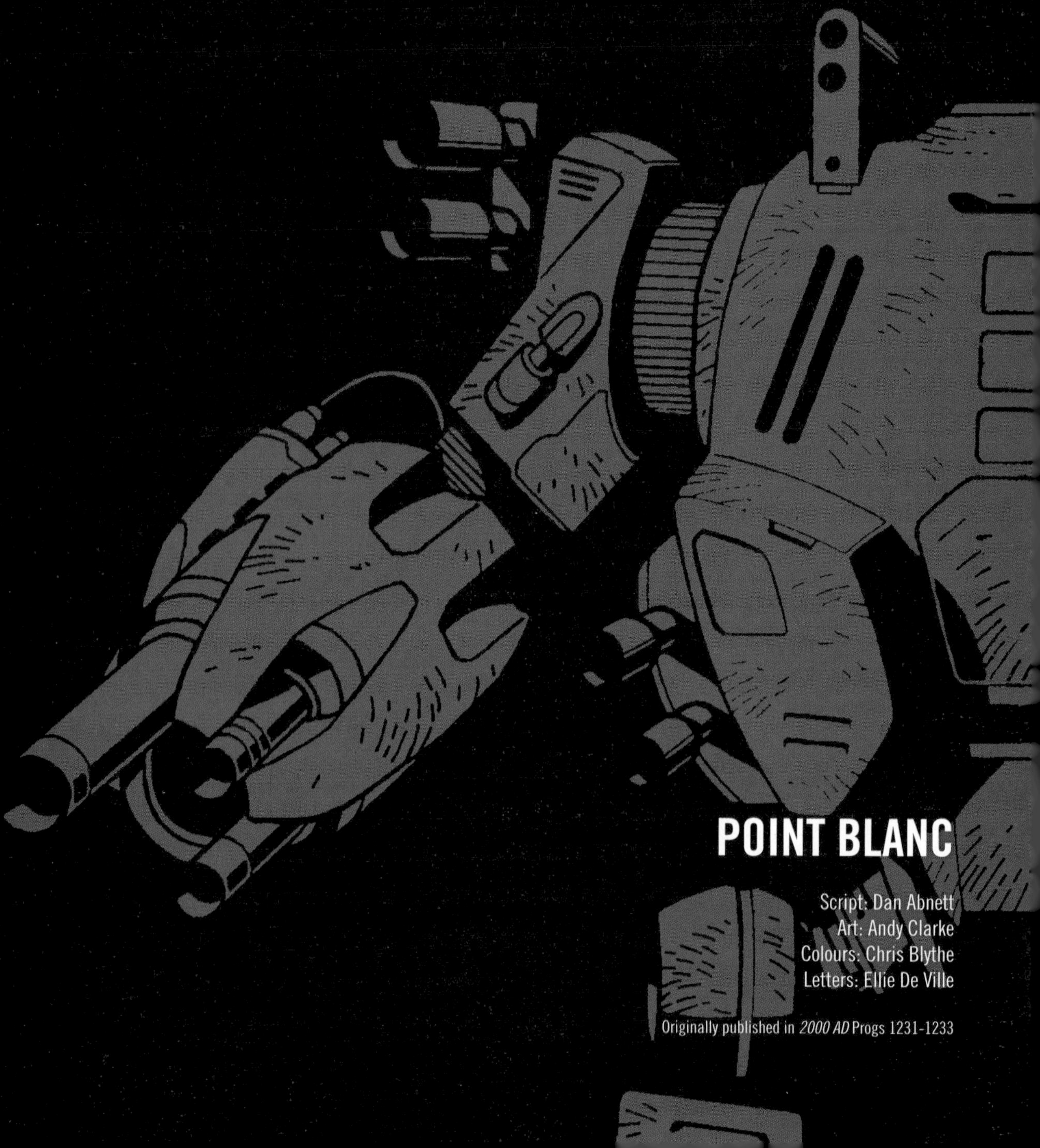

POINT BLANC

Script: Dan Abnett
Art: Andy Clarke
Colours: Chris Blythe
Letters: Ellie De Ville

Originally published in *2000 AD* Progs 1231-1233

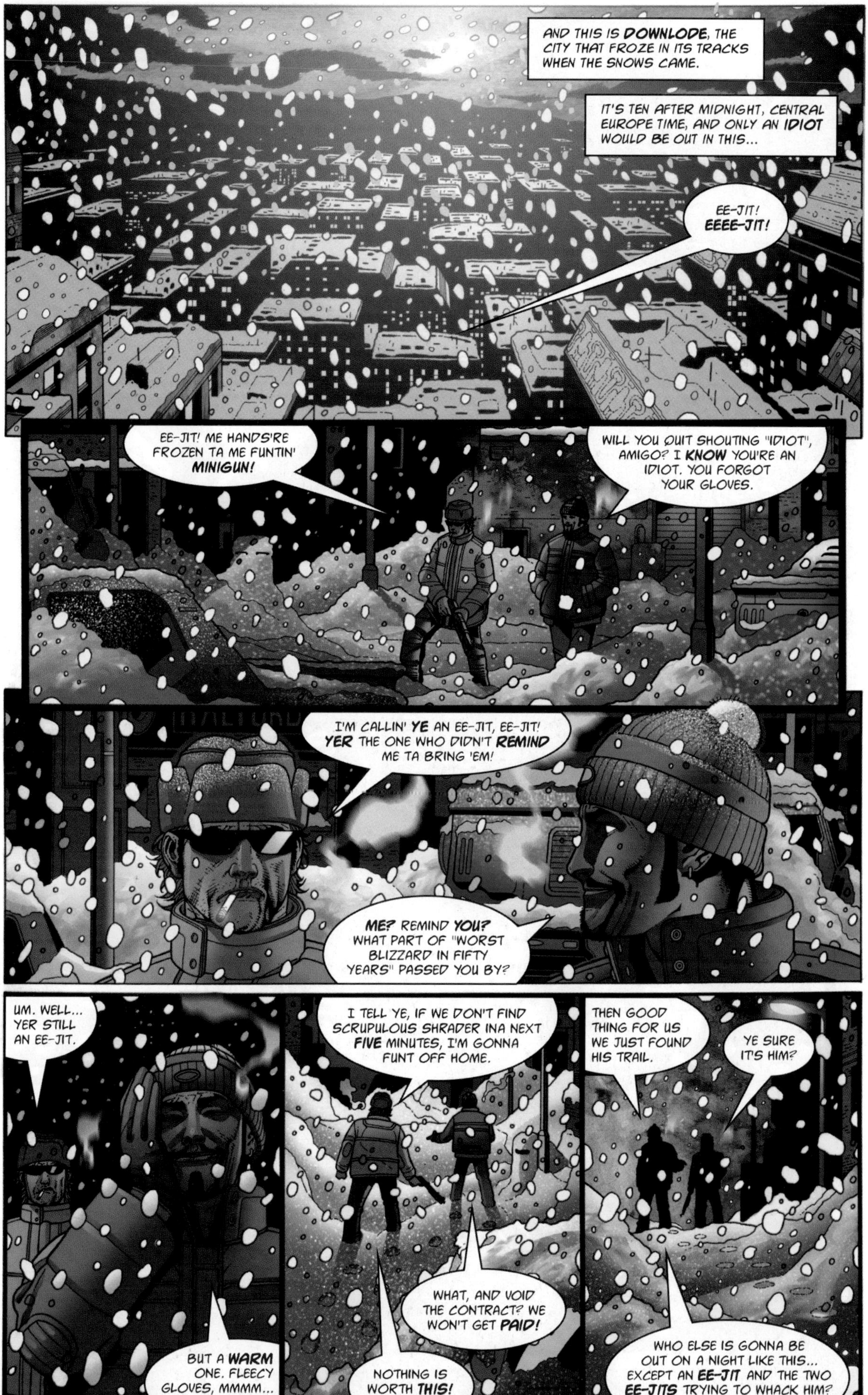

AND THIS IS **DOWNLODE**, THE CITY THAT FROZE IN ITS TRACKS WHEN THE SNOWS CAME.
IT'S TEN AFTER MIDNIGHT, CENTRAL EUROPE TIME, AND ONLY AN **IDIOT** WOULD BE OUT IN THIS...
EE-JIT! **EEEE-JIT!**
EE-JIT! ME HANDS'RE FROZEN TA ME FUNTIN' **MINIGUN!**
WILL YOU QUIT SHOUTING "IDIOT", AMIGO? I **KNOW** YOU'RE AN IDIOT. YOU FORGOT YOUR GLOVES.
I'M CALLIN' **YE** AN EE-JIT, EE-JIT! **YER** THE ONE WHO DIDN'T **REMIND** ME TA BRING 'EM!
ME? REMIND **YOU?** WHAT PART OF "WORST BLIZZARD IN FIFTY YEARS" PASSED YOU BY?
UM. WELL... YER STILL AN EE-JIT.
BUT A **WARM** ONE. FLEECY GLOVES, MMMM...
I TELL YE, IF WE DON'T FIND SCRUPULOUS SHRADER INA NEXT **FIVE** MINUTES, I'M GONNA FUNT OFF HOME.
WHAT, AND VOID THE CONTRACT? WE WON'T GET **PAID!**
NOTHING IS WORTH **THIS!**
THEN GOOD THING FOR US WE JUST FOUND HIS TRAIL.
YE SURE IT'S HIM?
WHO ELSE IS GONNA BE OUT ON A NIGHT LIKE THIS... EXCEPT AN **EE-JIT** AND THE TWO **EE-JITS** TRYING TO WHACK HIM?

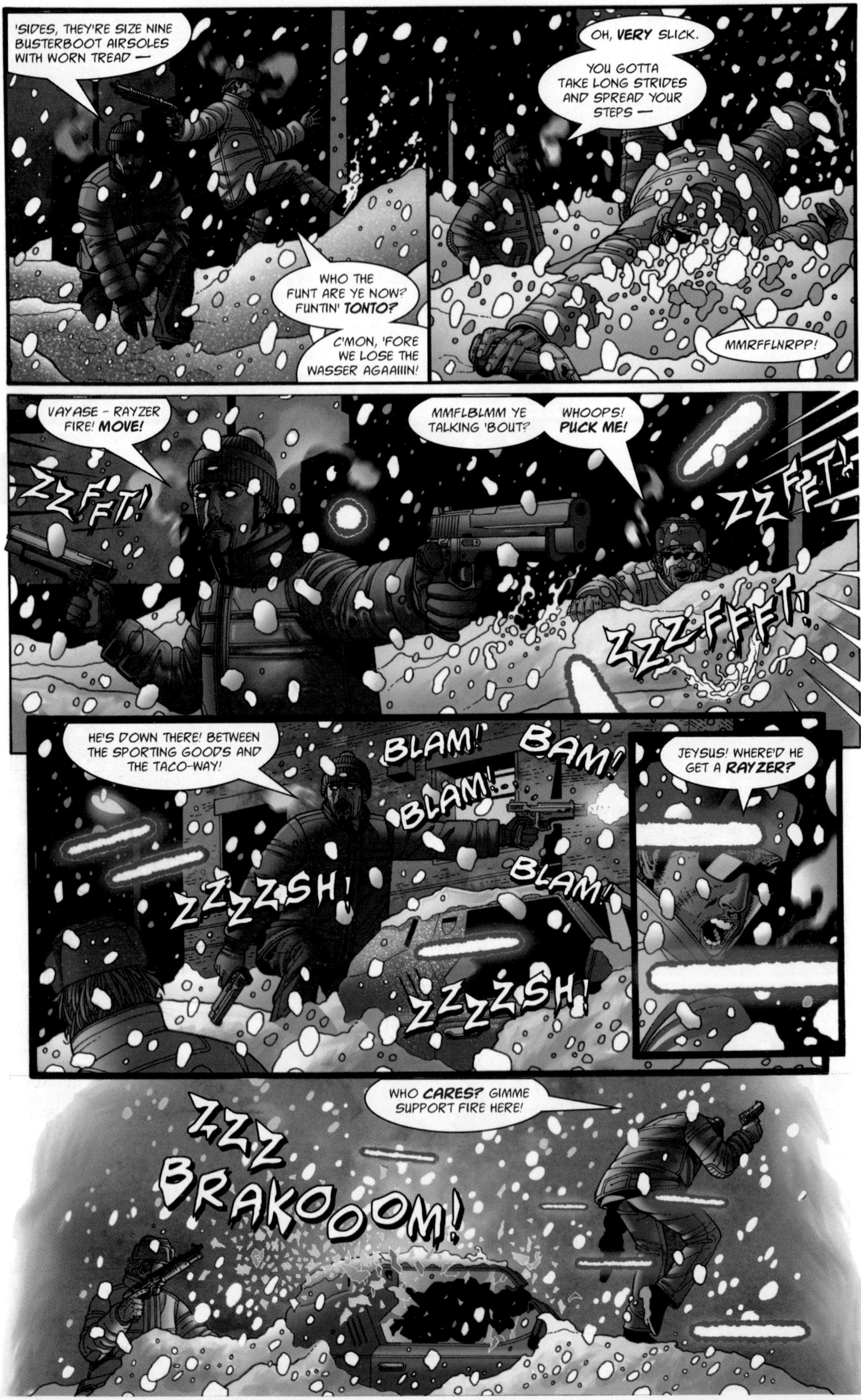
'SIDES, THEY'RE SIZE NINE BUSTERBOOT AIRSOLES WITH WORN TREAD —
WHO THE FUNT ARE YE NOW? FUNTIN' TONTO?
C'MON, 'FORE WE LOSE THE WASSER AGAAIIIN!
OH, VERY SLICK.
YOU GOTTA TAKE LONG STRIDES AND SPREAD YOUR STEPS —
MMRFFLNRPP!
VAYASE - RAYZER FIRE! MOVE!
ZZFFT!
MMFLBLMM YE TALKING 'BOUT?
WHOOPS! PUCK ME!
ZZFFT!
ZZZFFFT!
HE'S DOWN THERE! BETWEEN THE SPORTING GOODS AND THE TACO-WAY!
BLAM!
BAM!
BLAM!
BLAM!
ZZZZSH!
ZZZZSH!
JEYSUS! WHERE'D HE GET A RAYZER?
WHO CARES? GIMME SUPPORT FIRE HERE!
ZZZ BRAKOOOM!

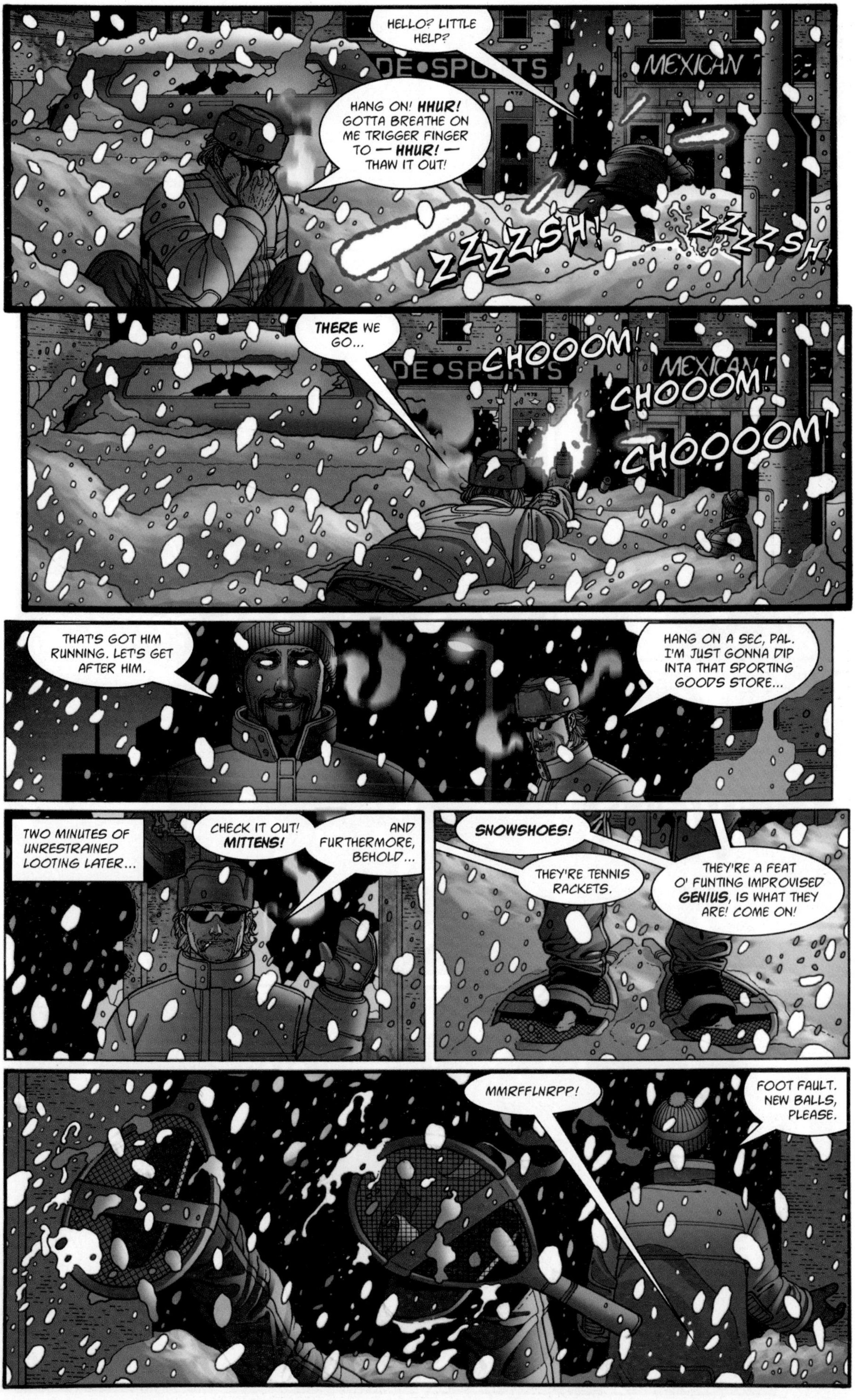

DE•SPORTS
MEXICAN
HELLO? LITTLE HELP?
HANG ON! **HHUR!** GOTTA BREATHE ON ME TRIGGER FINGER TO — **HHUR!** — THAW IT OUT!
ZZZZSH!
ZZZZSH!
THERE WE GO...
CHOOOM!
CHOOOM!
CHOOOOM!
THAT'S GOT HIM RUNNING. LET'S GET AFTER HIM.
HANG ON A SEC, PAL. I'M JUST GONNA DIP INTA THAT SPORTING GOODS STORE...
TWO MINUTES OF UNRESTRAINED LOOTING LATER...
CHECK IT OUT! **MITTENS!**
AND FURTHERMORE, BEHOLD...
SNOWSHOES!
THEY'RE TENNIS RACKETS.
THEY'RE A FEAT O' FUNTING IMPROVISED **GENIUS**, IS WHAT THEY ARE! COME ON!
MMRFFLNRPP!
FOOT FAULT. NEW BALLS, PLEASE.

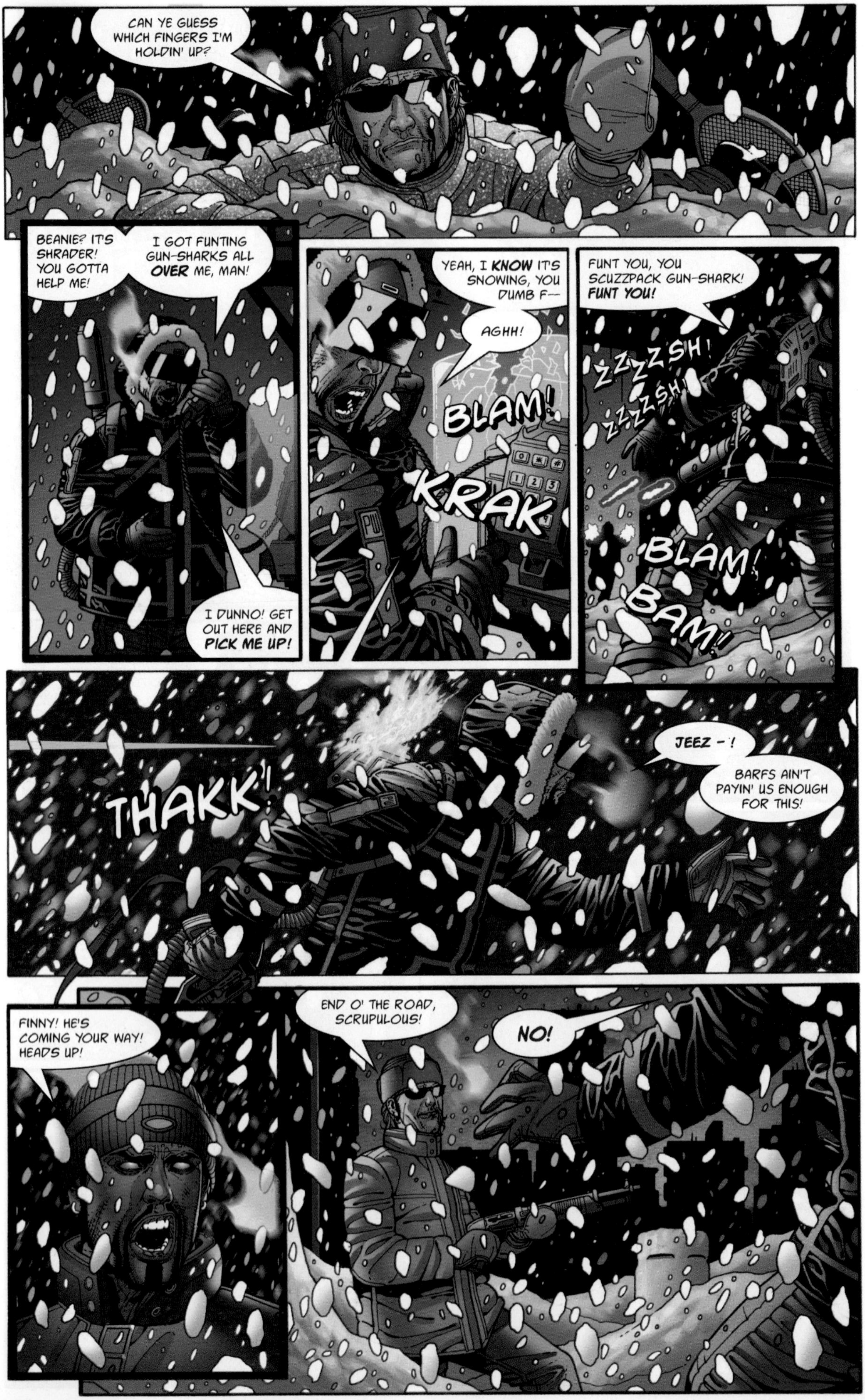
CAN YE GUESS WHICH FINGERS I'M HOLDIN' UP?
BEANIE? IT'S SHRADER! YOU GOTTA HELP ME!
I GOT FUNTING GUN-SHARKS ALL OVER ME, MAN!
I DUNNO! GET OUT HERE AND PICK ME UP!
YEAH, I KNOW IT'S SNOWING, YOU DUMB F--
AGHH!
BLAM!
KRAK
FUNT YOU, YOU SCUZZPACK GUN-SHARK! FUNT YOU!
ZZZZSH!
ZZZZSH!
BLAM!
BAM!
THAKK'!
JEEZ -'!
BARFS AIN'T PAYIN' US ENOUGH FOR THIS!
FINNY! HE'S COMING YOUR WAY! HEADS UP!
END O' THE ROAD, SCRUPULOUS!
NO!

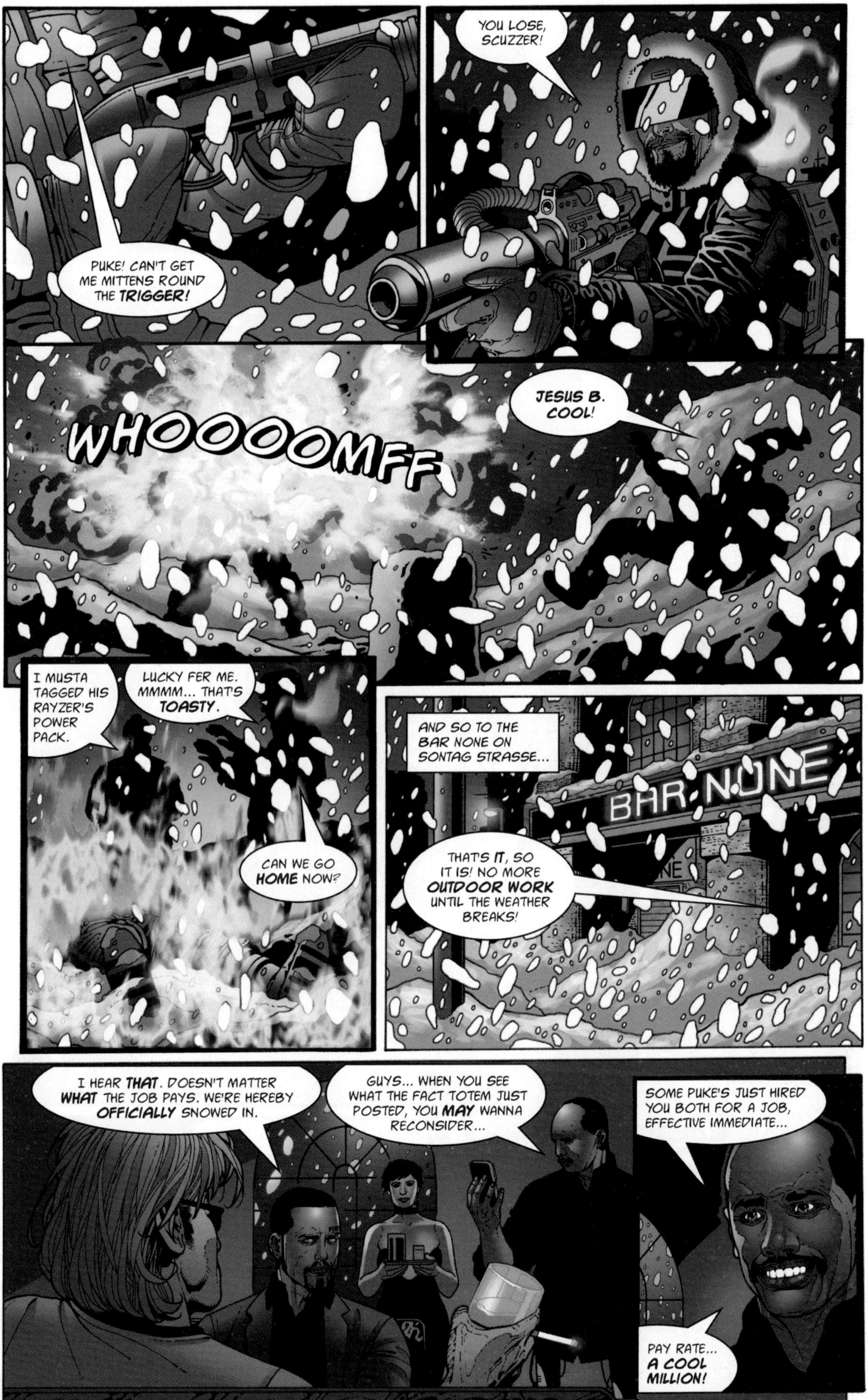
PUKE! CAN'T GET ME MITTENS ROUND THE TRIGGER!
YOU LOSE, SCUZZER!
WHOOOOOMFF
JESUS B. COOL!
I MUSTA TAGGED HIS RAYZER'S POWER PACK.
LUCKY FER ME. MMMM... THAT'S TOASTY.
CAN WE GO HOME NOW?
AND SO TO THE BAR NONE ON SONTAG STRASSE...
BAR NONE
THAT'S IT, SO IT IS! NO MORE OUTDOOR WORK UNTIL THE WEATHER BREAKS!
I HEAR THAT. DOESN'T MATTER WHAT THE JOB PAYS. WE'RE HEREBY OFFICIALLY SNOWED IN.
GUYS... WHEN YOU SEE WHAT THE FACT TOTEM JUST POSTED, YOU MAY WANNA RECONSIDER...
SOME PUKE'S JUST HIRED YOU BOTH FOR A JOB, EFFECTIVE IMMEDIATE...
PAY RATE... A COOL MILLION!

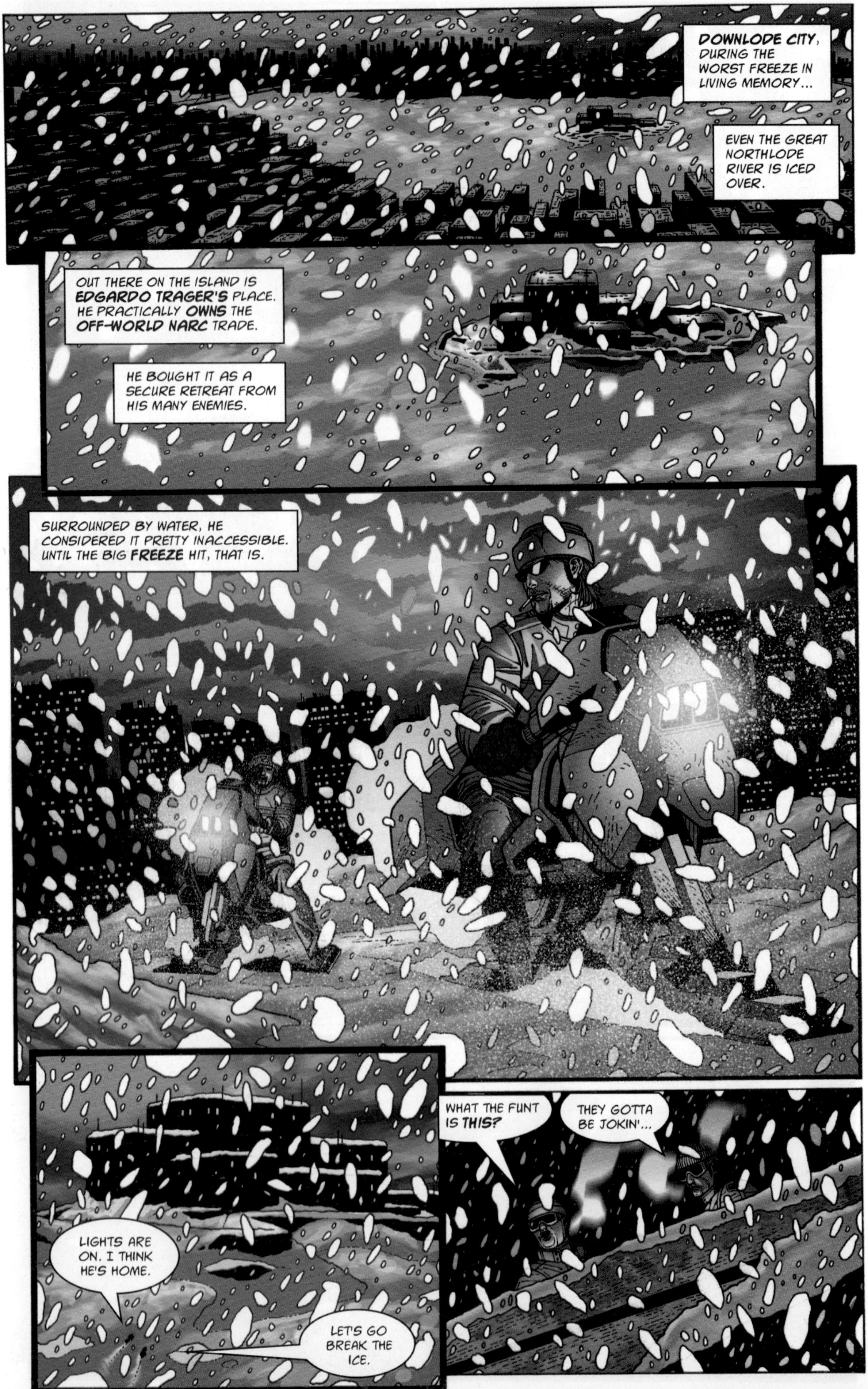
DOWNLODE CITY, DURING THE WORST FREEZE IN LIVING MEMORY...
EVEN THE GREAT NORTHLODE RIVER IS ICED OVER.
OUT THERE ON THE ISLAND IS EDGARDO TRAGER'S PLACE. HE PRACTICALLY OWNS THE OFF-WORLD NARC TRADE.
HE BOUGHT IT AS A SECURE RETREAT FROM HIS MANY ENEMIES.
SURROUNDED BY WATER, HE CONSIDERED IT PRETTY INACCESSIBLE. UNTIL THE BIG FREEZE HIT, THAT IS.
LIGHTS ARE ON. I THINK HE'S HOME.
LET'S GO BREAK THE ICE.
WHAT THE FUNT IS THIS?
THEY GOTTA BE JOKIN'...

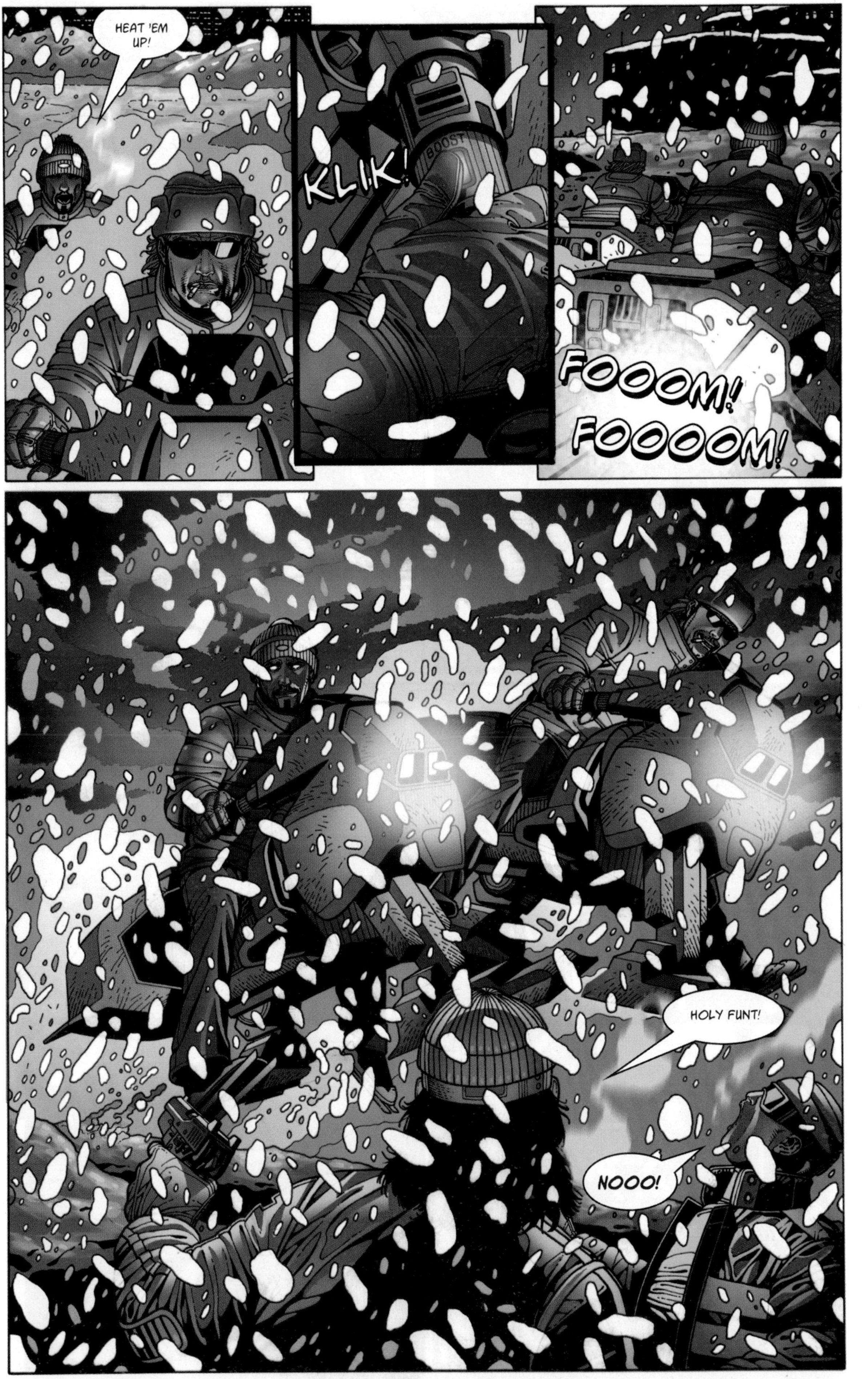
HEAT 'EM UP!
KLIK!
BOOST
FOOOOM! FOOOOM!
HOLY FUNT!
NOOO!

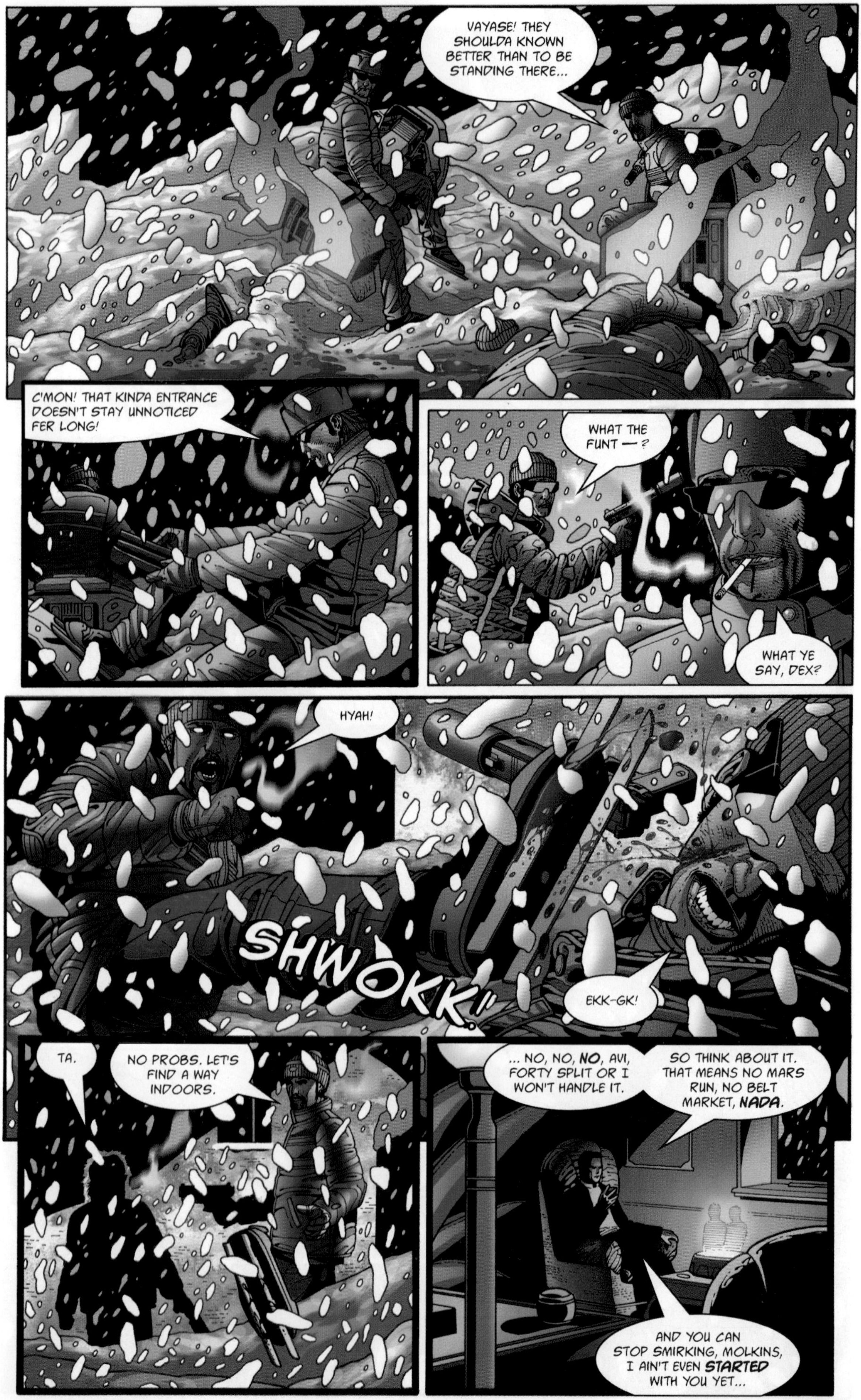
VAYASE! THEY SHOULDA KNOWN BETTER THAN TO BE STANDING THERE...
C'MON! THAT KINDA ENTRANCE DOESN'T STAY UNNOTICED FER LONG!
WHAT THE FUNT — ?
WHAT YE SAY, DEX?
HYAH!
SHWOKK!
EKK-GK!
TA.
NO PROBS. LET'S FIND A WAY INDOORS.
... NO, NO, NO, AVI, FORTY SPLIT OR I WON'T HANDLE IT.
SO THINK ABOUT IT. THAT MEANS NO MARS RUN, NO BELT MARKET, NADA.
AND YOU CAN STOP SMIRKING, MOLKINS, I AIN'T EVEN STARTED WITH YOU YET...

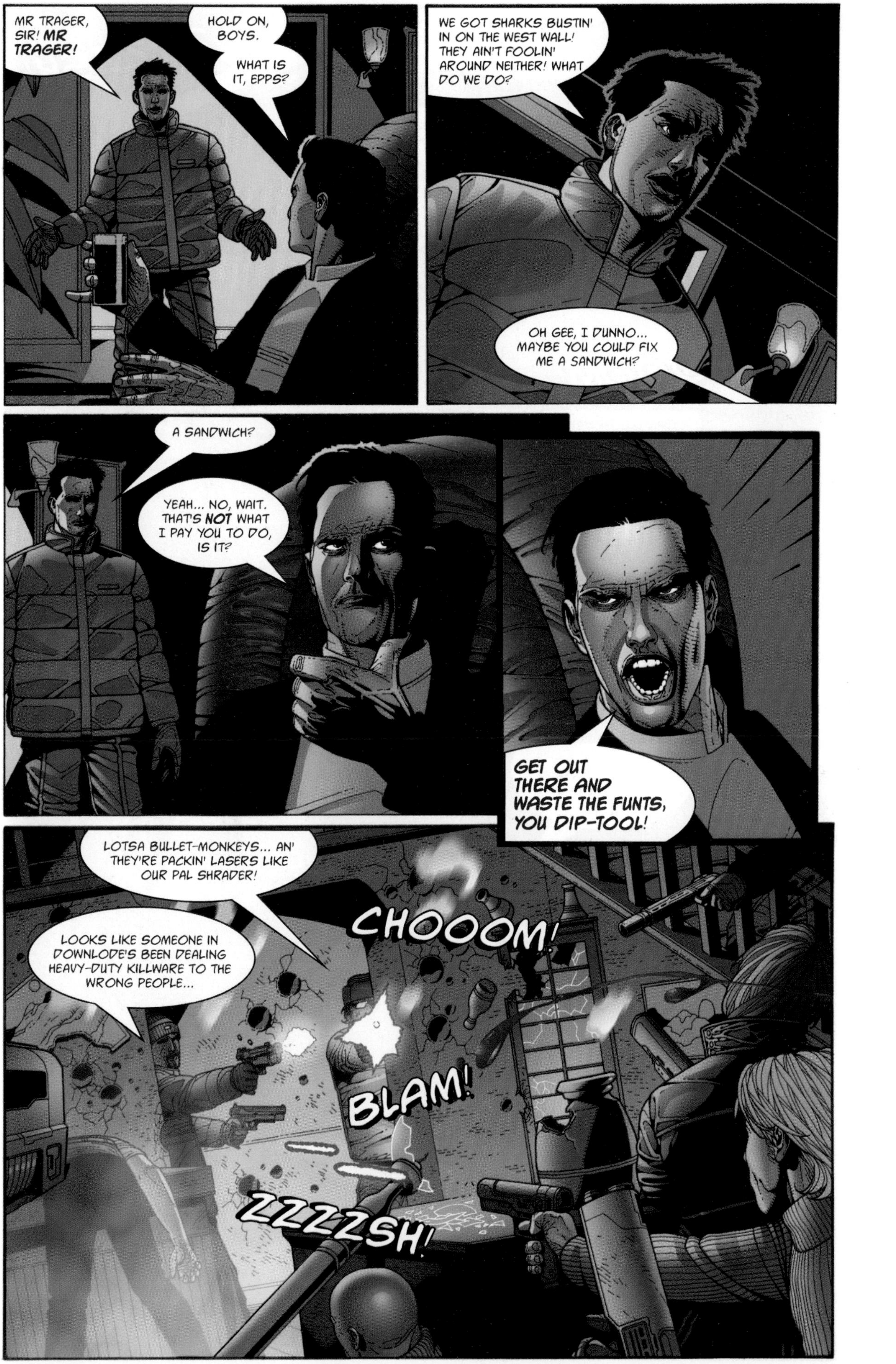
MR TRAGER, SIR! MR TRAGER!
HOLD ON, BOYS.
WHAT IS IT, EPPS?
WE GOT SHARKS BUSTIN' IN ON THE WEST WALL! THEY AIN'T FOOLIN' AROUND NEITHER! WHAT DO WE DO?
OH GEE, I DUNNO... MAYBE YOU COULD FIX ME A SANDWICH?
A SANDWICH?
YEAH... NO, WAIT. THAT'S NOT WHAT I PAY YOU TO DO, IS IT?
GET OUT THERE AND WASTE THE FUNTS, YOU DIP-TOOL!
LOTSA BULLET-MONKEYS... AN' THEY'RE PACKIN' LASERS LIKE OUR PAL SHRADER!
LOOKS LIKE SOMEONE IN DOWNLODE'S BEEN DEALING HEAVY-DUTY KILLWARE TO THE WRONG PEOPLE...
CHOOOM!
BLAM!
ZZZZZSH!

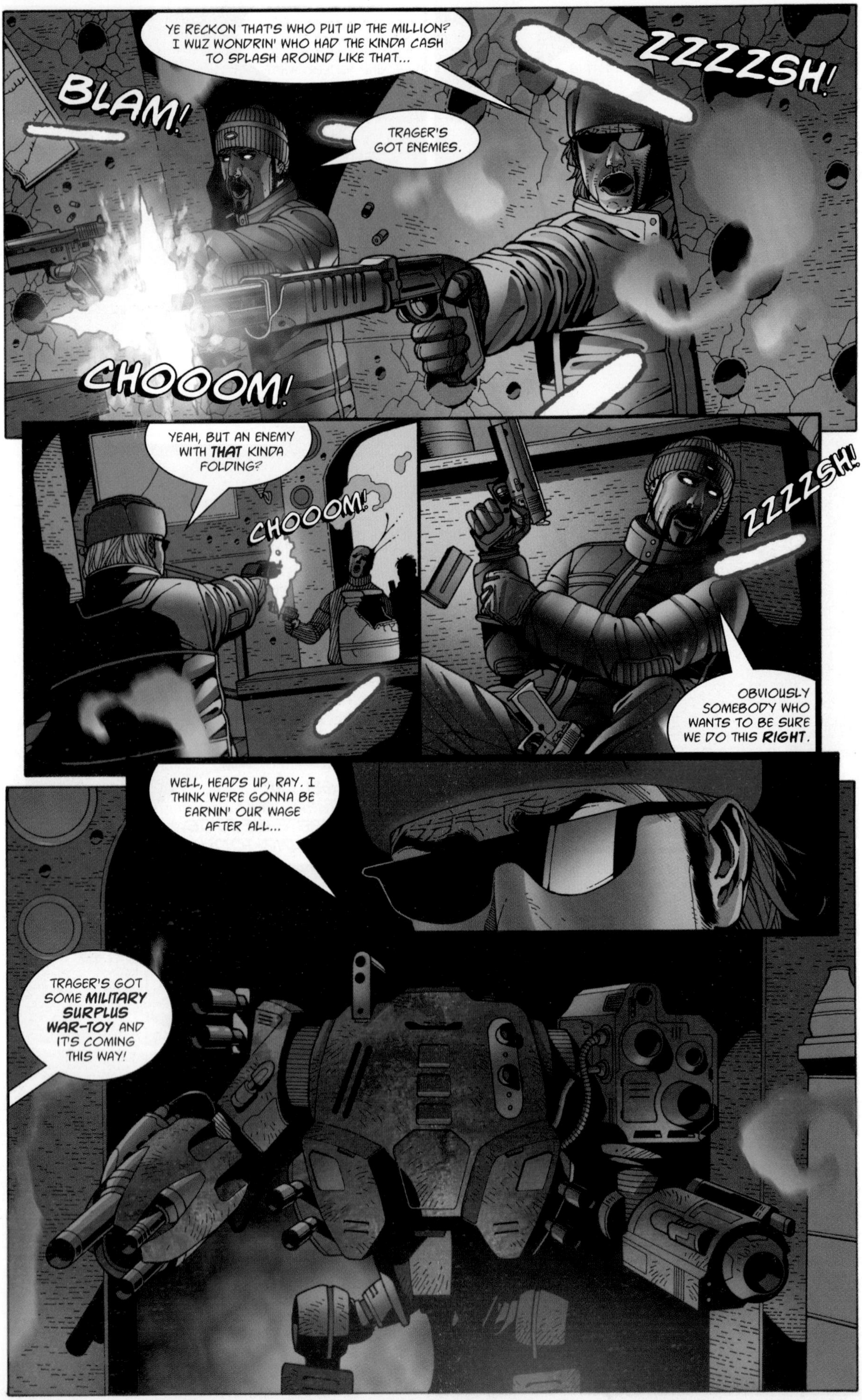
YE RECKON THAT'S WHO PUT UP THE MILLION? I WUZ WONDRIN' WHO HAD THE KINDA CASH TO SPLASH AROUND LIKE THAT...
ZZZZSH!
BLAM!
TRAGER'S GOT ENEMIES.
CHOOOM!
YEAH, BUT AN ENEMY WITH **THAT** KINDA FOLDING?
CHOOOM!
ZZZZSH!
OBVIOUSLY SOMEBODY WHO WANTS TO BE SURE WE DO THIS **RIGHT**.
WELL, HEADS UP, RAY. I THINK WE'RE GONNA BE EARNIN' OUR WAGE AFTER ALL...
TRAGER'S GOT SOME **MILITARY SURPLUS WAR-TOY** AND IT'S COMING THIS WAY!

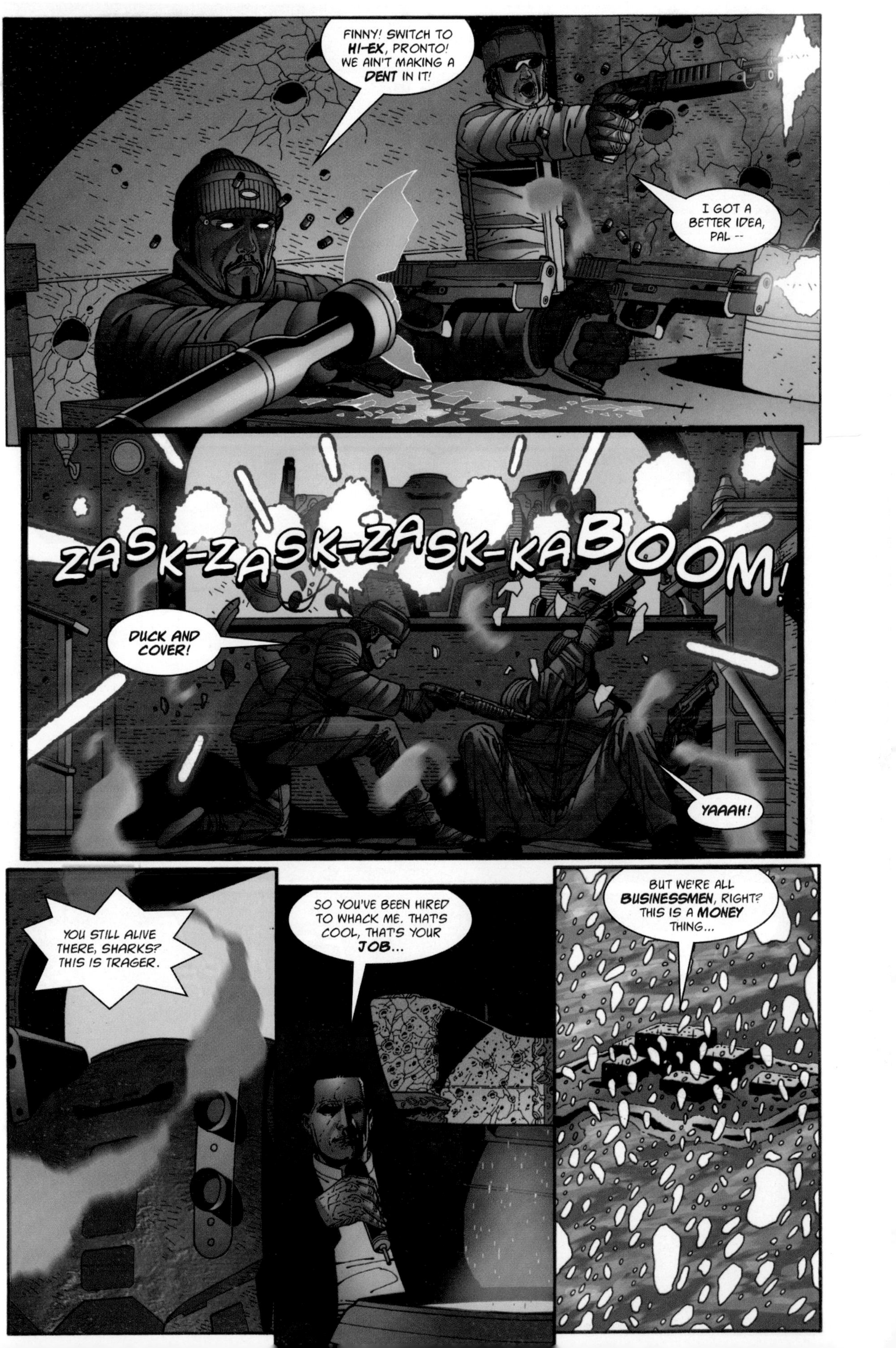
FINNY! SWITCH TO HI-EX, PRONTO! WE AIN'T MAKING A DENT IN IT!
I GOT A BETTER IDEA, PAL --
ZASK-ZASK-ZASK-KABOOM!
DUCK AND COVER!
YAAAH!
YOU STILL ALIVE THERE, SHARKS? THIS IS TRAGER.
SO YOU'VE BEEN HIRED TO WHACK ME. THAT'S COOL, THAT'S YOUR JOB...
BUT WE'RE ALL BUSINESSMEN, RIGHT? THIS IS A MONEY THING...

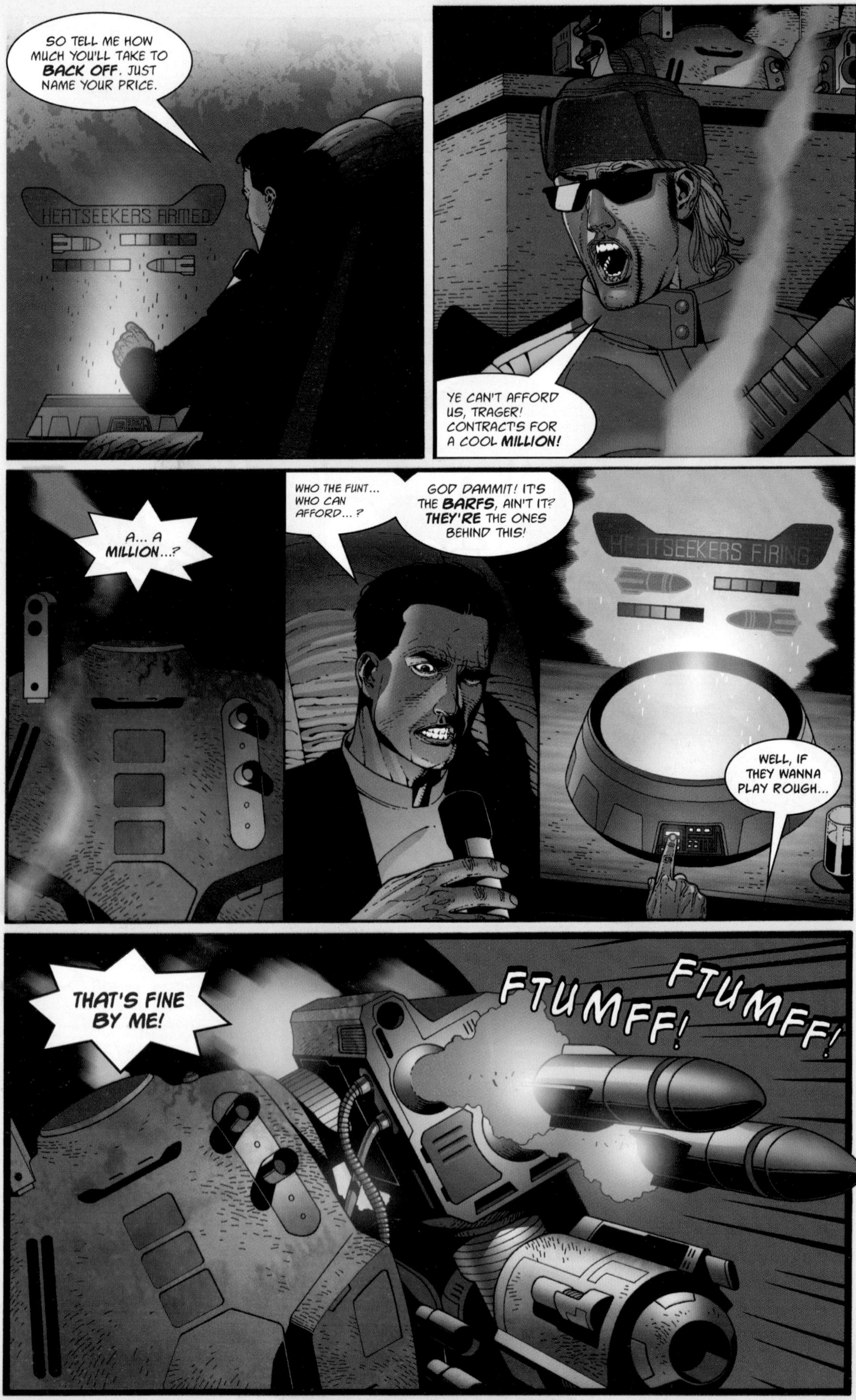

SO TELL ME HOW MUCH YOU'LL TAKE TO BACK OFF. JUST NAME YOUR PRICE.
HEATSEEKERS ARMED
YE CAN'T AFFORD US, TRAGER! CONTRACT'S FOR A COOL MILLION!
A... A MILLION...?
WHO THE FUNT... WHO CAN AFFORD...?
GOD DAMMIT! IT'S THE BARFS, AIN'T IT? THEY'RE THE ONES BEHIND THIS!
HEATSEEKERS FIRING
WELL, IF THEY WANNA PLAY ROUGH...
THAT'S FINE BY ME!
FTUMFF!
FTUMFF!

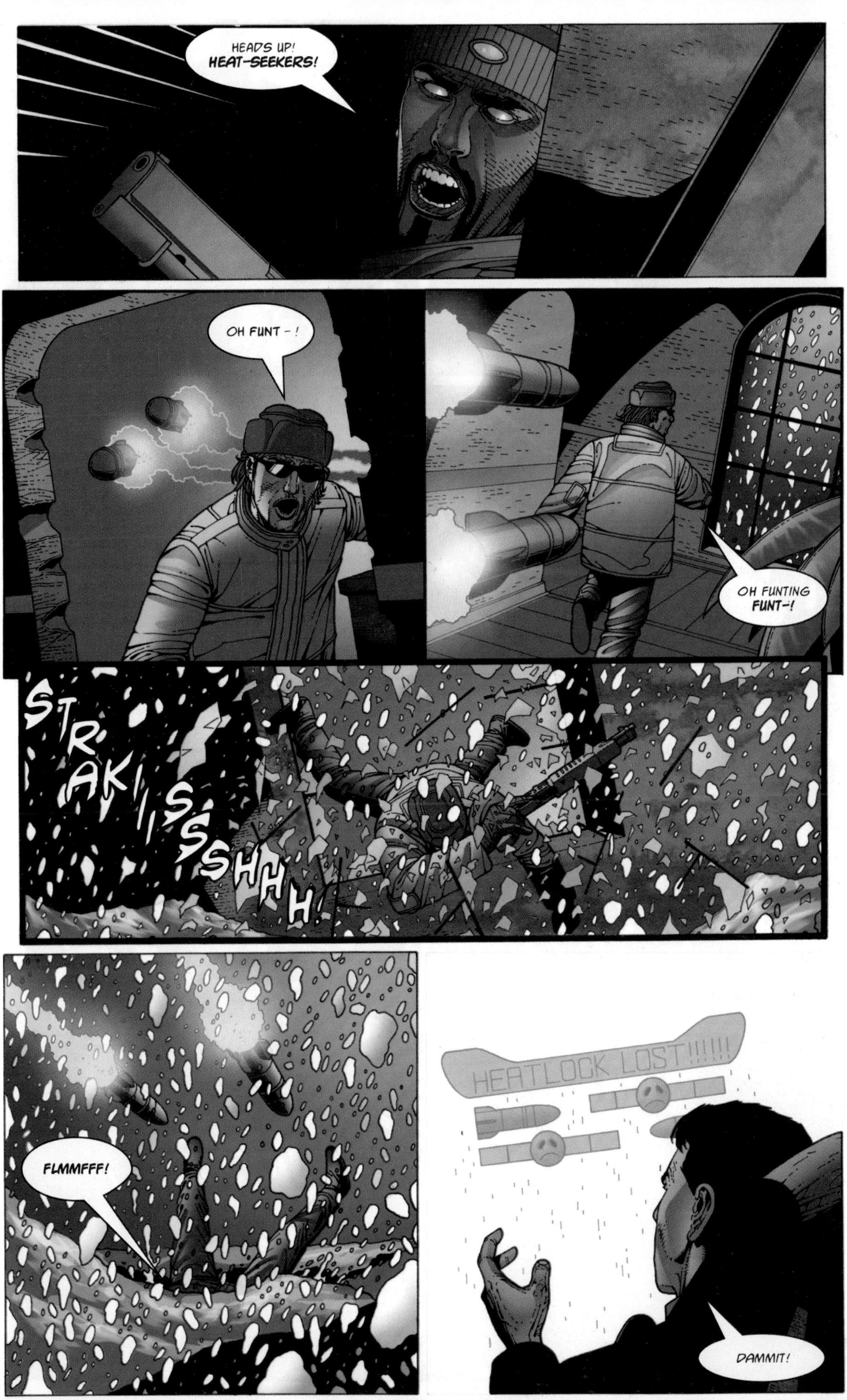
HEADS UP!
HEAT-SEEKERS!
OH FUNT -!
OH FUNTING
FUNT-!
STRAKIISSSHHHH!
FLMMFFF!
HEATLOCK LOST!!!!!!
DAMMIT!

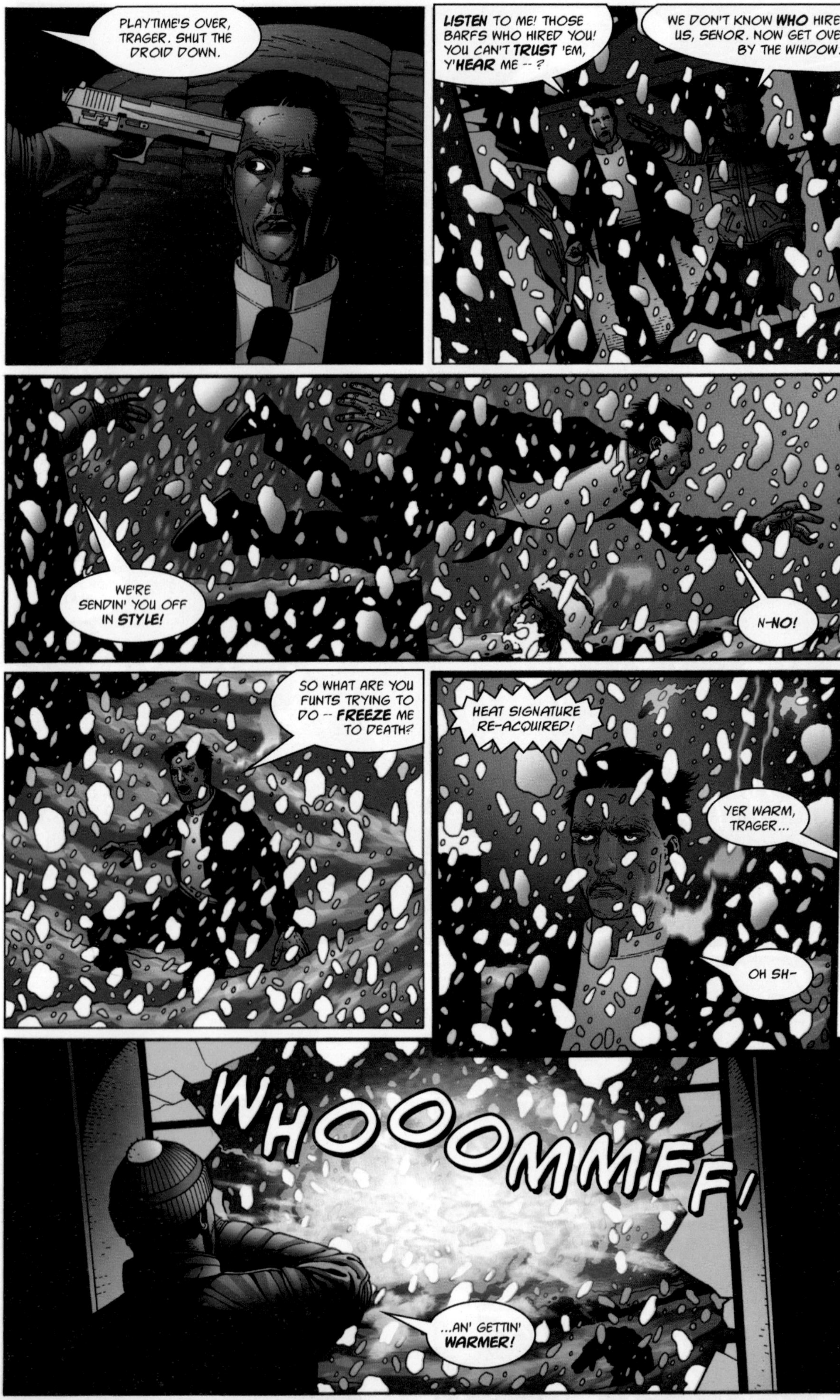
PLAYTIME'S OVER, TRAGER. SHUT THE DROID DOWN.
LISTEN TO ME! THOSE BARFS WHO HIRED YOU! YOU CAN'T TRUST 'EM, Y'HEAR ME -- ?
WE DON'T KNOW WHO HIRED US, SENOR. NOW GET OVER BY THE WINDOW...
WE'RE SENDIN' YOU OFF IN STYLE!
N-NO!
SO WHAT ARE YOU FUNTS TRYING TO DO -- FREEZE ME TO DEATH?
HEAT SIGNATURE RE-ACQUIRED!
YER WARM, TRAGER...
OH SH-
WHOOOMMFF!
...AN' GETTIN' WARMER!

LATER...

YE SURE THIS IS THE PLACE FER THE PAY-OFF?

S'WHAT THE FACT TOTEM SAID.

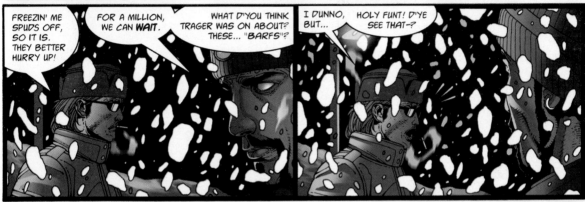

FREEZIN' ME SPUDS OFF, SO IT IS. THEY BETTER HURRY UP!

FOR A MILLION, WE CAN WAIT.

WHAT D'YOU THINK TRAGER WAS ON ABOUT? THESE... "BARFS"?

I DUNNO, BUT...

HOLY FUNT! D'YE SEE THAT-?

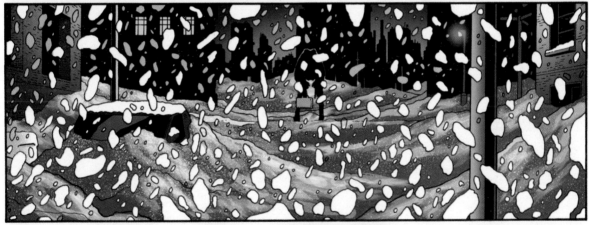

IT'S ALL HERE.

YEAH, BUT... I MEAN... WHAT THE FUNT WAS THAT?

I DON'T KNOW...

BUT YOU NOTICE HOW IT'S SUDDENLY STOPPED SNOWING...?

... LET'S GET OUT OF HERE, DEX... I GOT CHILLS EVEN A STRAIGHT MILL AIN'T WARMIN'!

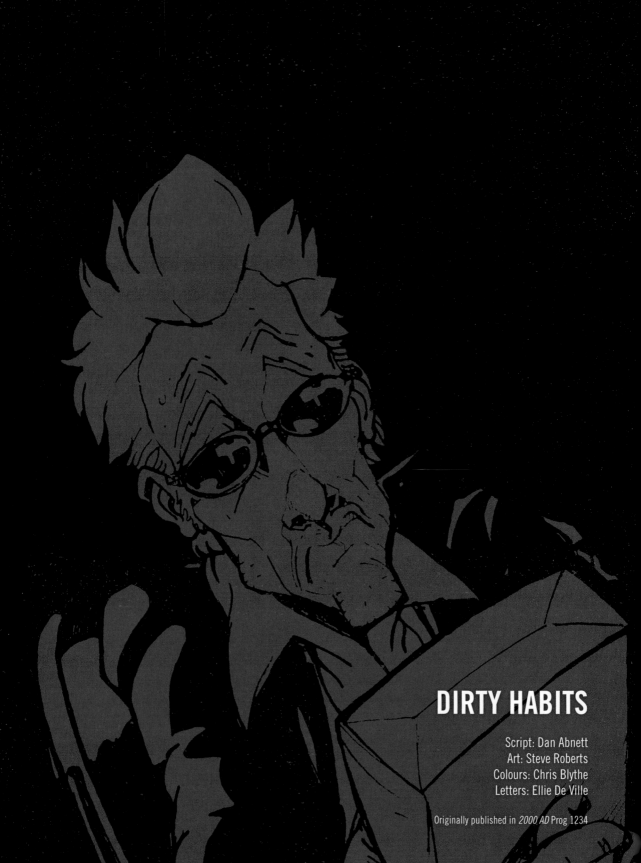

DIRTY HABITS

Script: Dan Abnett
Art: Steve Roberts
Colours: Chris Blythe
Letters: Ellie De Ville

Originally published in *2000 AD* Prog 1234

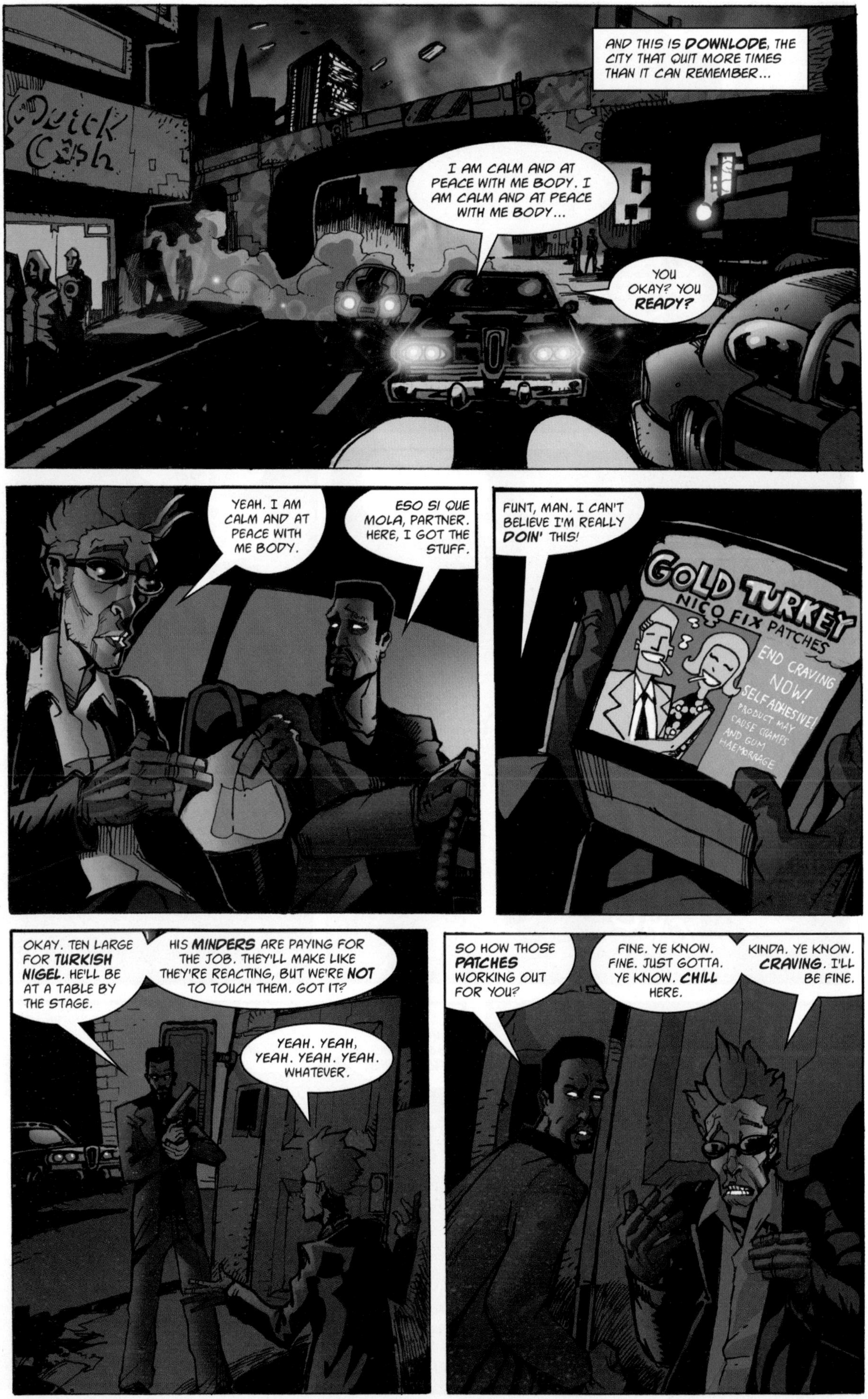
AND THIS IS DOWNLODE, THE CITY THAT QUIT MORE TIMES THAN IT CAN REMEMBER...
Quick Cash
I AM CALM AND AT PEACE WITH ME BODY. I AM CALM AND AT PEACE WITH ME BODY...
YOU OKAY? YOU READY?
YEAH. I AM CALM AND AT PEACE WITH ME BODY.
ESO SI QUE MOLA, PARTNER. HERE, I GOT THE STUFF.
FUNT, MAN. I CAN'T BELIEVE I'M REALLY DOIN' THIS!
GOLD TURKEY
NICO FIX PATCHES
END CRAVING NOW!
SELFADHESIVE!
PRODUCT MAY CAUSE CRAMPS AND GUM HAEMORRAGE
OKAY. TEN LARGE FOR TURKISH NIGEL. HE'LL BE AT A TABLE BY THE STAGE.
HIS MINDERS ARE PAYING FOR THE JOB. THEY'LL MAKE LIKE THEY'RE REACTING, BUT WE'RE NOT TO TOUCH THEM. GOT IT?
YEAH. YEAH, YEAH. YEAH. YEAH. WHATEVER.
SO HOW THOSE PATCHES WORKING OUT FOR YOU?
FINE. YE KNOW. FINE. JUST GOTTA. YE KNOW. CHILL HERE.
KINDA. YE KNOW. CRAVING. I'LL BE FINE.

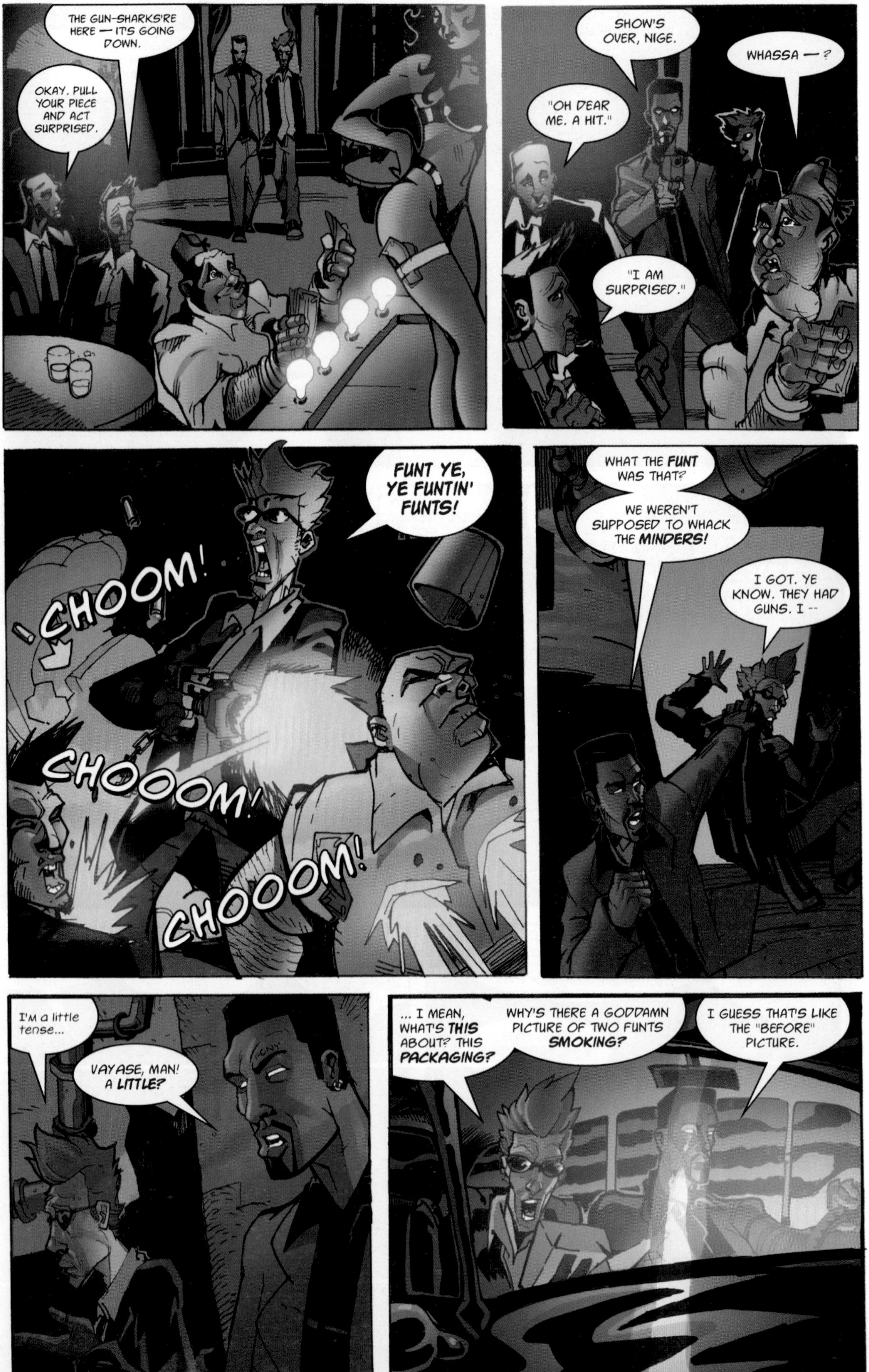
THE GUN-SHARKS'RE HERE — IT'S GOING DOWN.
OKAY. PULL YOUR PIECE AND ACT SURPRISED.
SHOW'S OVER, NIGE.
WHASSA — ?
"OH DEAR ME. A HIT."
"I AM SURPRISED."
FUNT YE, YE FUNTIN' FUNTS!
CHOOM!
CHOOOM!
CHOOOM!
WHAT THE FUNT WAS THAT?
WE WEREN'T SUPPOSED TO WHACK THE MINDERS!
I GOT. YE KNOW. THEY HAD GUNS. I --
I'm a little tense...
VAYASE, MAN! A LITTLE?
... I MEAN, WHAT'S THIS ABOUT? THIS PACKAGING?
WHY'S THERE A GODDAMN PICTURE OF TWO FUNTS SMOKING?
I GUESS THAT'S LIKE THE "BEFORE" PICTURE.

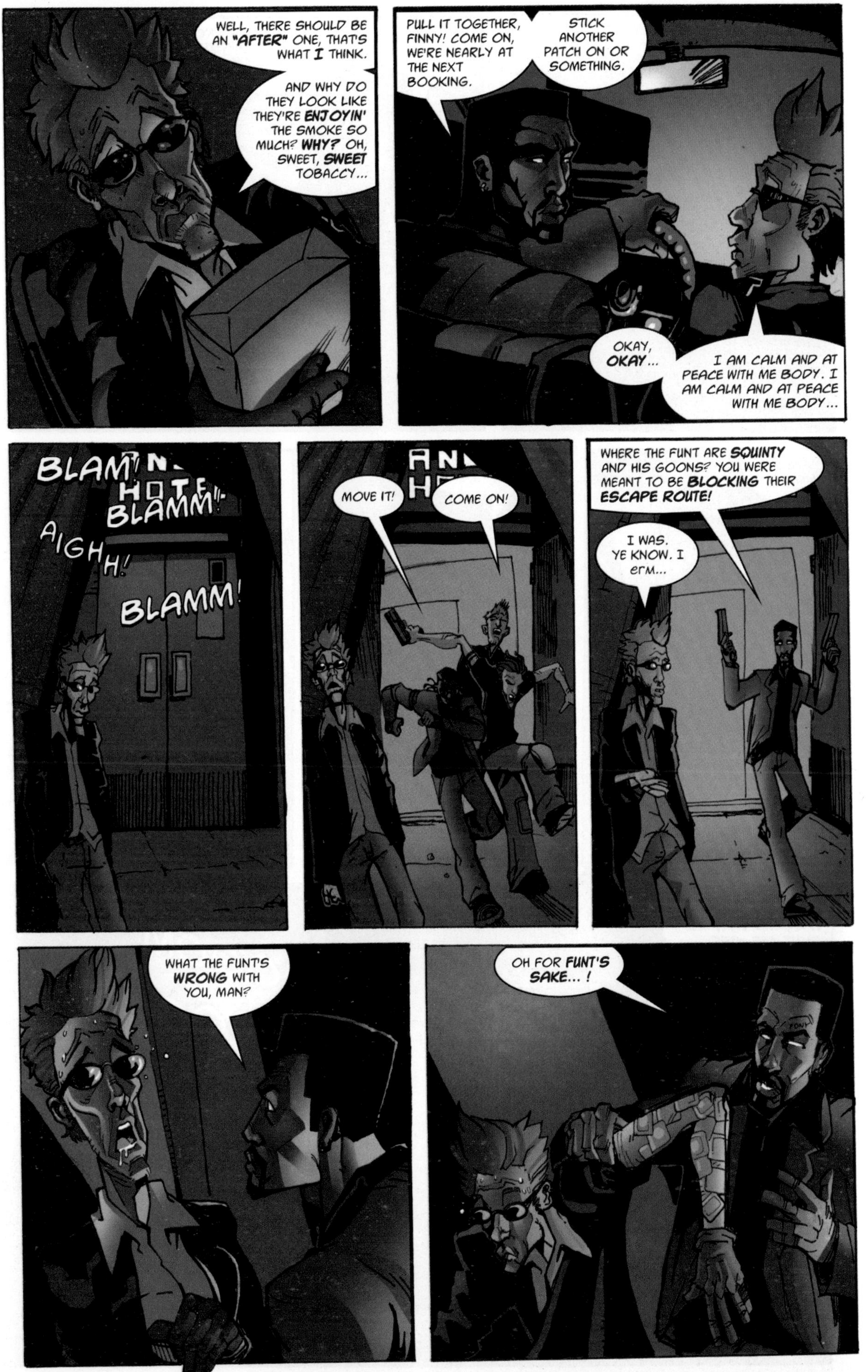

WELL, THERE SHOULD BE AN **"AFTER"** ONE, THAT'S WHAT **I** THINK.
AND WHY DO THEY LOOK LIKE THEY'RE **ENJOYIN'** THE SMOKE SO MUCH? **WHY?** OH, SWEET, **SWEET** TOBACCY...
PULL IT TOGETHER, FINNY! COME ON, WE'RE NEARLY AT THE NEXT BOOKING.
STICK ANOTHER PATCH ON OR SOMETHING.
OKAY, **OKAY**...
I AM CALM AND AT PEACE WITH ME BODY. I AM CALM AND AT PEACE WITH ME BODY...
BLAM!
BLAMM!
AIGHH!
BLAMM!
MOVE IT!
COME ON!
WHERE THE FUNT ARE **SQUINTY** AND HIS GOONS? YOU WERE MEANT TO BE **BLOCKING** THEIR **ESCAPE ROUTE!**
I WAS. YE KNOW. I erm...
WHAT THE FUNT'S **WRONG** WITH YOU, MAN?
OH FOR **FUNT'S SAKE**... !

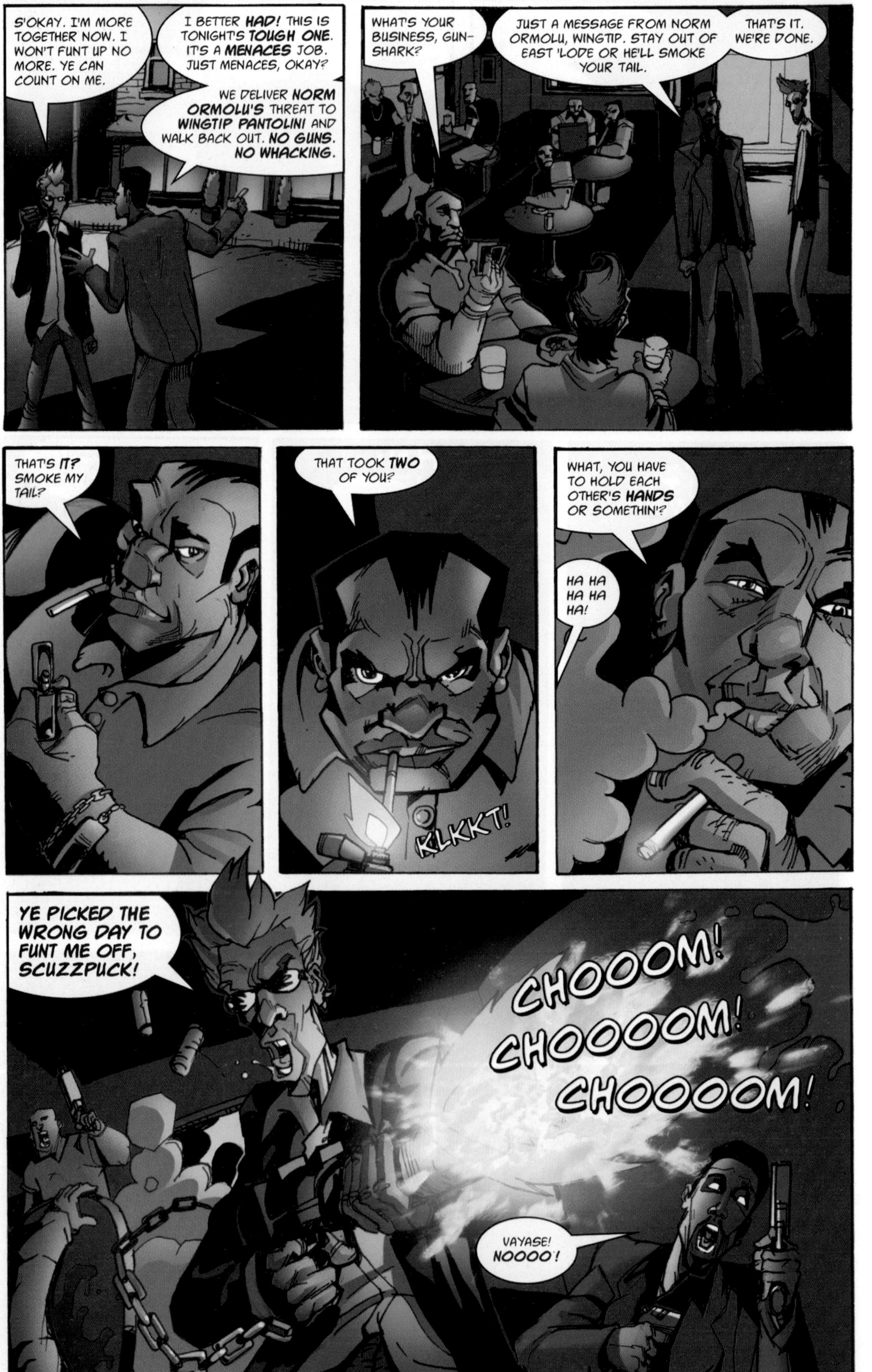

S'OKAY. I'M MORE TOGETHER NOW. I WON'T FUNT UP NO MORE. YE CAN COUNT ON ME.
I BETTER **HAD!** THIS IS TONIGHT'S **TOUGH ONE**. IT'S A **MENACES** JOB. JUST MENACES, OKAY?
WE DELIVER **NORM ORMOLU'S** THREAT TO **WINGTIP PANTOLINI** AND WALK BACK OUT. **NO GUNS. NO WHACKING**.
WHAT'S YOUR BUSINESS, GUN-SHARK?
JUST A MESSAGE FROM NORM ORMOLU, WINGTIP. STAY OUT OF EAST 'LODE OR HE'LL SMOKE YOUR TAIL.
THAT'S IT. WE'RE DONE.
THAT'S **IT?** SMOKE MY TAIL?
THAT TOOK **TWO** OF YOU?
KLKKT!
WHAT, YOU HAVE TO HOLD EACH OTHER'S **HANDS** OR SOMETHIN'?
HA HA HA HA HA!
YE PICKED THE WRONG DAY TO FUNT ME OFF, SCUZZPUCK!
CHOOOOM!
CHOOOOOM!
CHOOOOOM!
VAYASE! NOOOO!

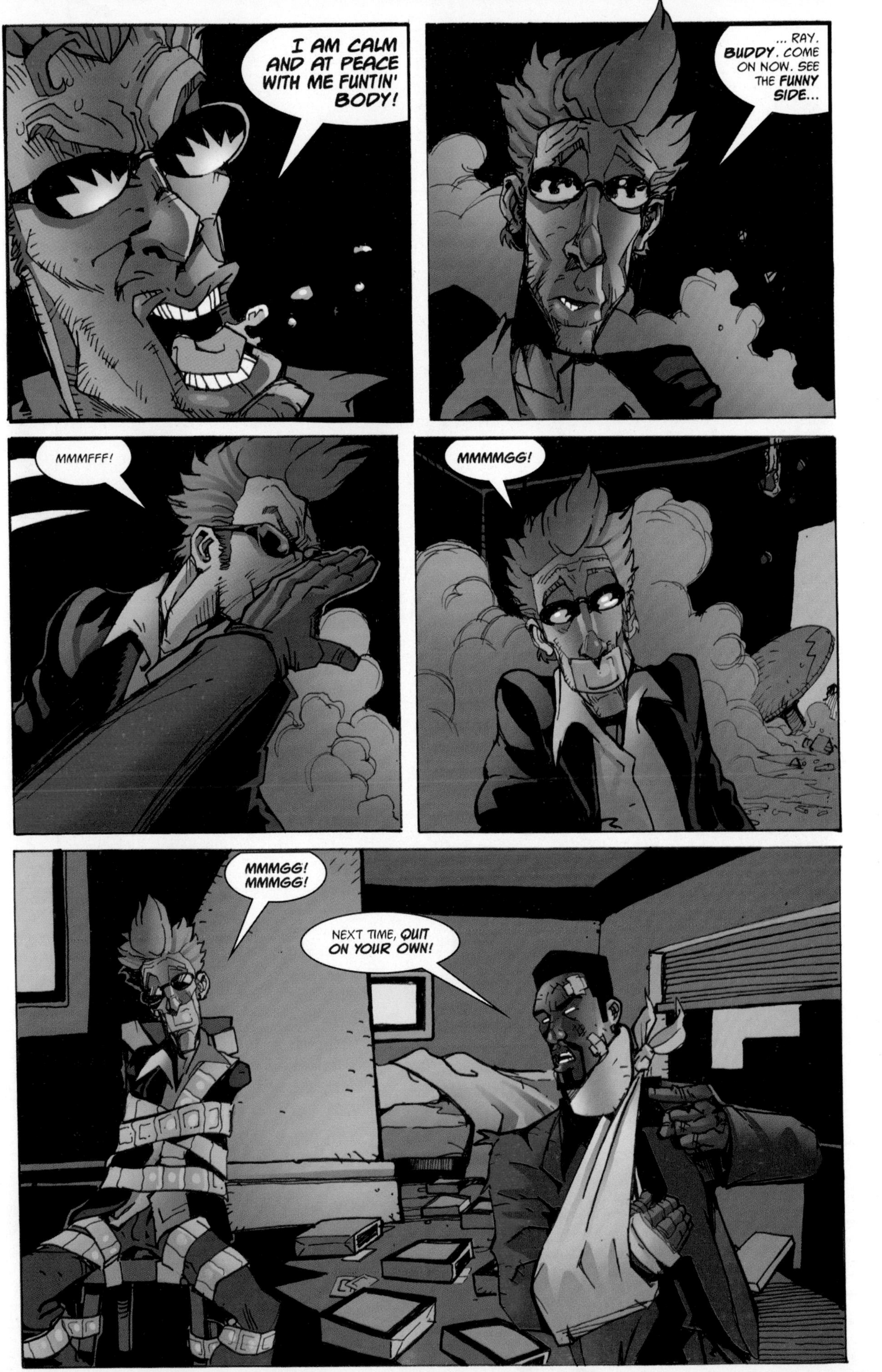
I AM CALM AND AT PEACE WITH ME FUNTIN' BODY!
... RAY. BUDDY. COME ON NOW. SEE THE FUNNY SIDE...
MMMFFF!
MMMMGG!
MMMGG! MMMGG!
NEXT TIME, QUIT ON YOUR OWN!

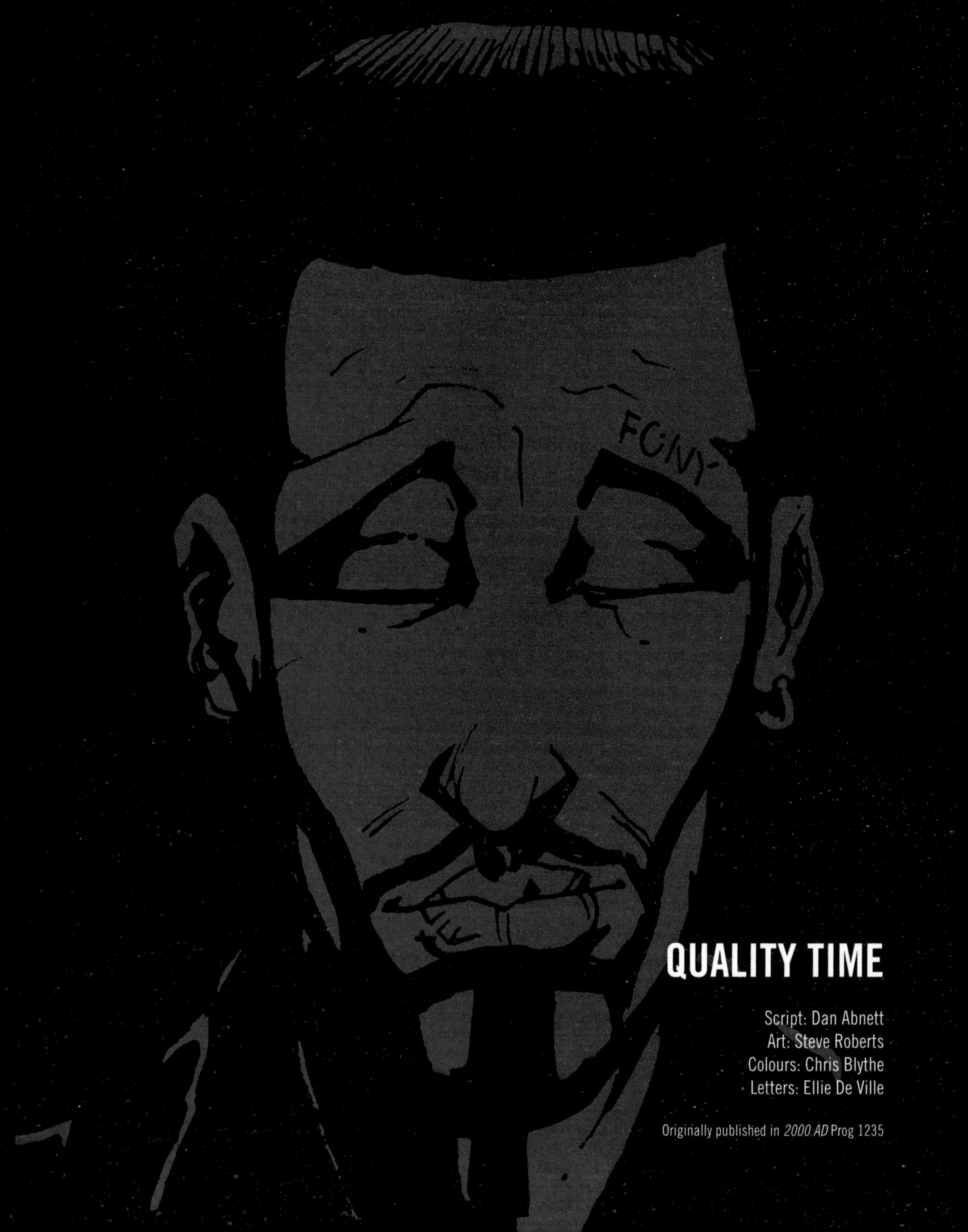

QUALITY TIME

Script: Dan Abnett
Art: Steve Roberts
Colours: Chris Blythe
Letters: Ellie De Ville

Originally published in *2000 AD* Prog 1235

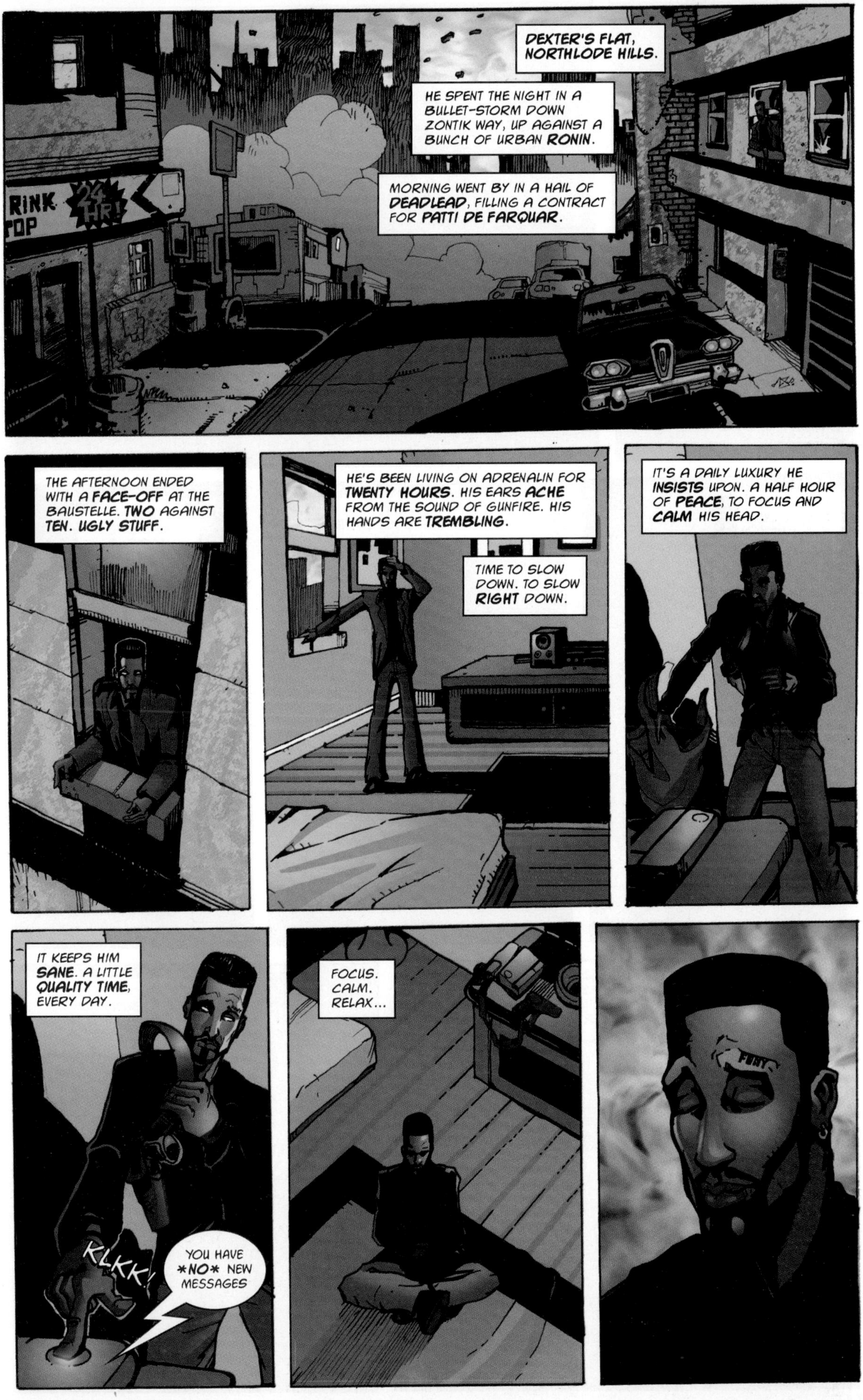
DEXTER'S FLAT, NORTHLODE HILLS.
HE SPENT THE NIGHT IN A BULLET-STORM DOWN ZONTIK WAY, UP AGAINST A BUNCH OF URBAN RONIN.
MORNING WENT BY IN A HAIL OF DEADLEAD, FILLING A CONTRACT FOR PATTI DE FARQUAR.
24 HR
THE AFTERNOON ENDED WITH A FACE-OFF AT THE BAUSTELLE. TWO AGAINST TEN. UGLY STUFF.
HE'S BEEN LIVING ON ADRENALIN FOR TWENTY HOURS. HIS EARS ACHE FROM THE SOUND OF GUNFIRE. HIS HANDS ARE TREMBLING.
TIME TO SLOW DOWN. TO SLOW RIGHT DOWN.
IT'S A DAILY LUXURY HE INSISTS UPON. A HALF HOUR OF PEACE, TO FOCUS AND CALM HIS HEAD.
IT KEEPS HIM SANE. A LITTLE QUALITY TIME, EVERY DAY.
KLKK!
YOU HAVE *NO* NEW MESSAGES
FOCUS. CALM. RELAX...

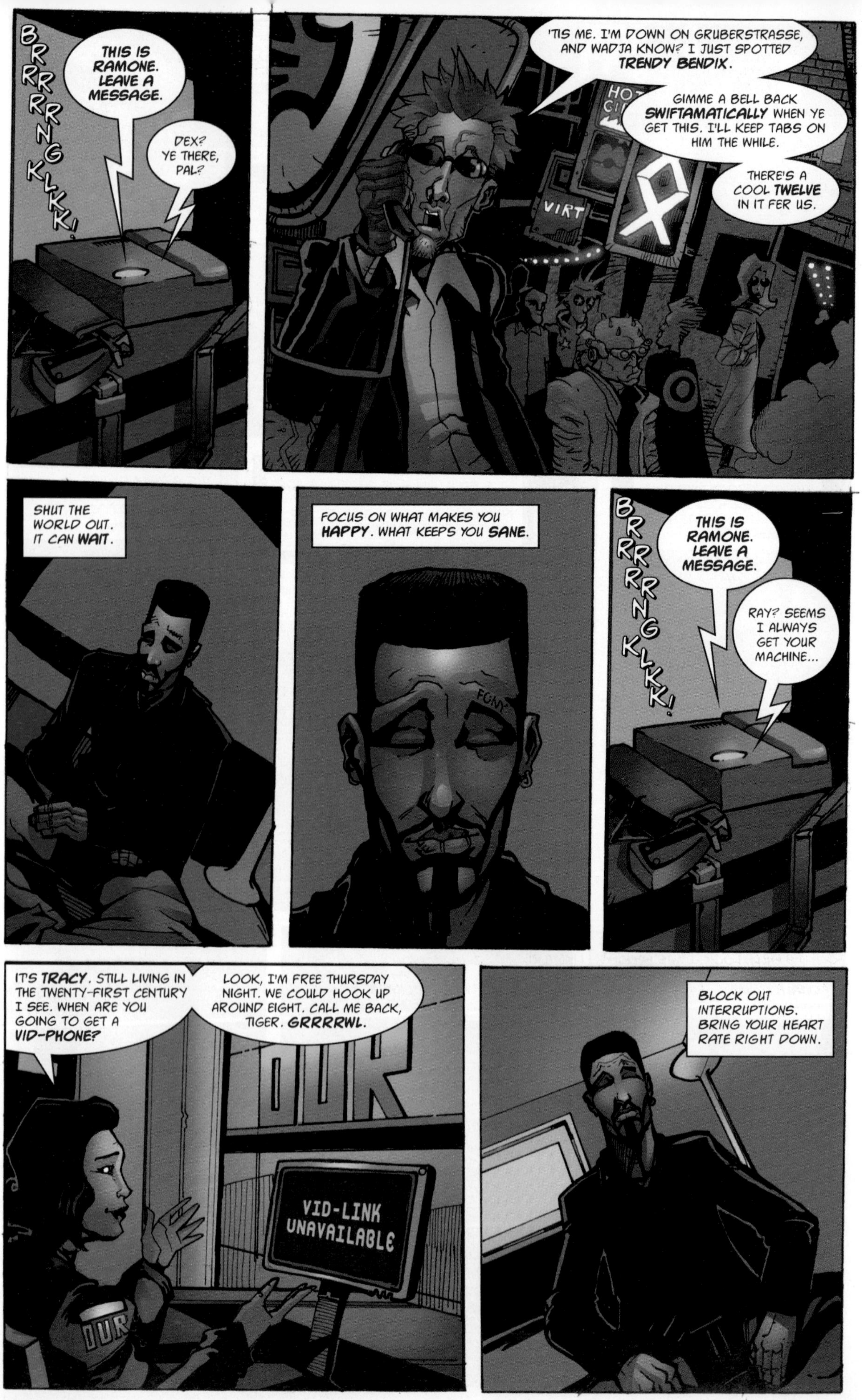
BRRRRNGKLKK!
THIS IS RAMONE. LEAVE A MESSAGE.
DEX? YE THERE, PAL?
'TIS ME. I'M DOWN ON GRUBERSTRASSE, AND WADJA KNOW? I JUST SPOTTED TRENDY BENDIX.
GIMME A BELL BACK SWIFTAMATICALLY WHEN YE GET THIS. I'LL KEEP TABS ON HIM THE WHILE.
THERE'S A COOL TWELVE IN IT FER US.
VIRT
SHUT THE WORLD OUT. IT CAN WAIT.
FOCUS ON WHAT MAKES YOU HAPPY. WHAT KEEPS YOU SANE.
BRRRRNGKLKK!
THIS IS RAMONE. LEAVE A MESSAGE.
RAY? SEEMS I ALWAYS GET YOUR MACHINE...
IT'S TRACY. STILL LIVING IN THE TWENTY-FIRST CENTURY I SEE. WHEN ARE YOU GOING TO GET A VID-PHONE?
LOOK, I'M FREE THURSDAY NIGHT. WE COULD HOOK UP AROUND EIGHT. CALL ME BACK, TIGER. GRRRRWL.
VID-LINK UNAVAILABLE
BLOCK OUT INTERRUPTIONS. BRING YOUR HEART RATE RIGHT DOWN.

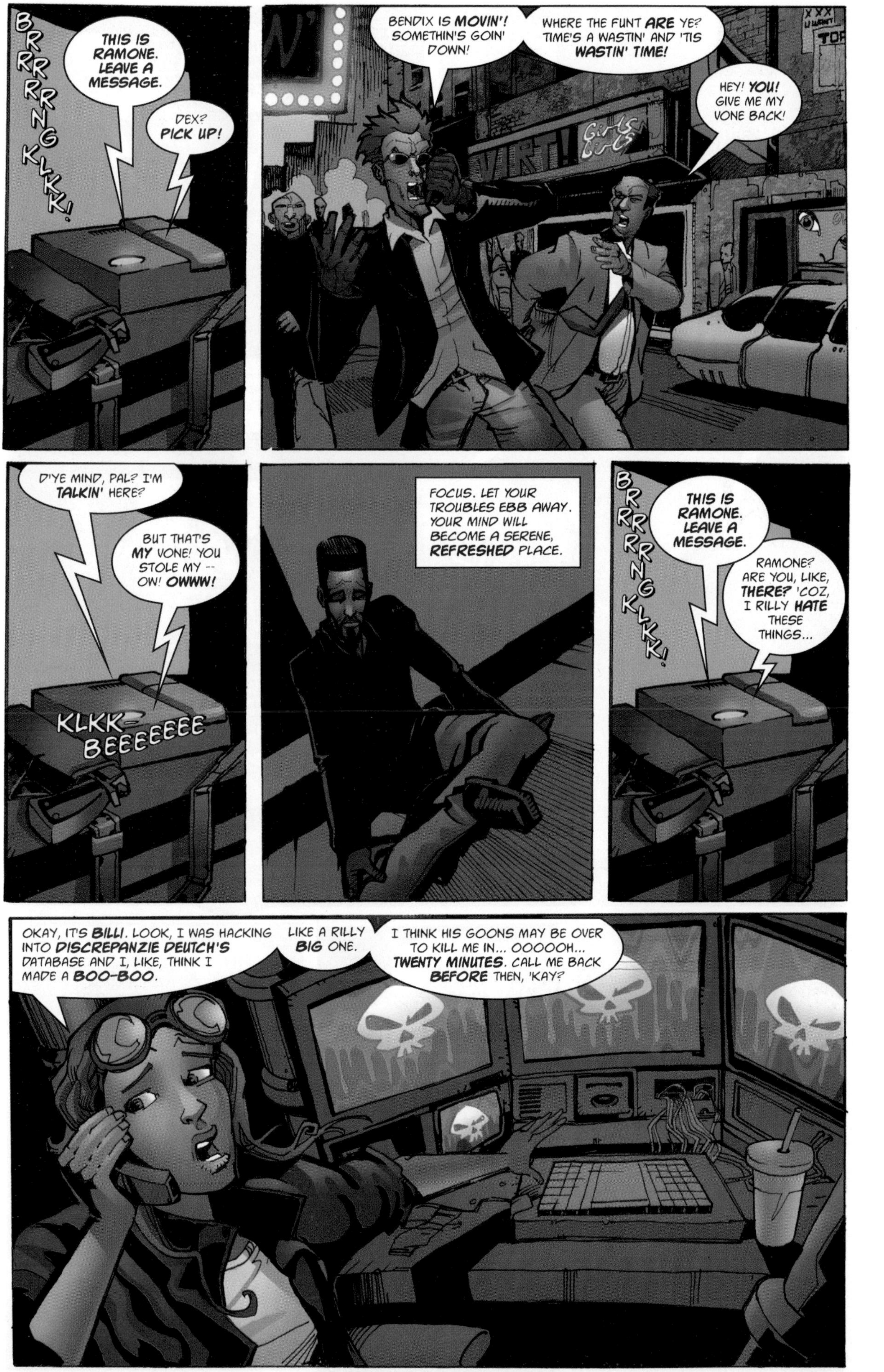
BRRRRRNGKLKK!
THIS IS RAMONE. LEAVE A MESSAGE.
DEX? PICK UP!
BENDIX IS MOVIN'! SOMETHIN'S GOIN' DOWN!
WHERE THE FUNT ARE YE? TIME'S A WASTIN' AND 'TIS WASTIN' TIME!
HEY! YOU! GIVE ME MY VONE BACK!
D'YE MIND, PAL? I'M TALKIN' HERE?
BUT THAT'S MY VONE! YOU STOLE MY -- OW! OWWW!
KLKK-BEEEEEEEE
FOCUS. LET YOUR TROUBLES EBB AWAY. YOUR MIND WILL BECOME A SERENE, REFRESHED PLACE.
BRRRRRNGKLKK!
THIS IS RAMONE. LEAVE A MESSAGE.
RAMONE? ARE YOU, LIKE, THERE? 'COZ, I RILLY HATE THESE THINGS...
OKAY, IT'S BILLI. LOOK, I WAS HACKING INTO DISCREPANZIE DEUTCH'S DATABASE AND I, LIKE, THINK I MADE A BOO-BOO.
LIKE A RILLY BIG ONE.
I THINK HIS GOONS MAY BE OVER TO KILL ME IN... OOOOOH... TWENTY MINUTES. CALL ME BACK BEFORE THEN, 'KAY?

MAKE THE
CALM YOUR
FR—

BRRRRNGKLKK!

THIS IS
RAMONE.
LEAVE A
MESSAGE.

MR DEXTER?
IT'S WENDY GO
AT THE BAR
NONE...

ROCKY ASKED ME TO
CALL. HE WAS WONDERING
IF YOU COULD —

HAI-AH!

OOOFF!

PARDON ME. ROCKY WAS WONDERING
IF YOU COULD STOP BY. THERE'S KIND
OF A SITUATION.

WHH-
KRAKKK!

TRY AND SHUT
OUT TH—

BRRRRNGKLKK!

THIS IS
RAMONE.
LEAVE A
MESSAGE.

DEXTER!
DEEEEEX!
PICK UP!
FUNTIN'
PICK UP!

DAH!
VAYASE!

WHERE ARE
YE? IT'S GOIN' ALL
ARSE-SHAPED,
DEX!

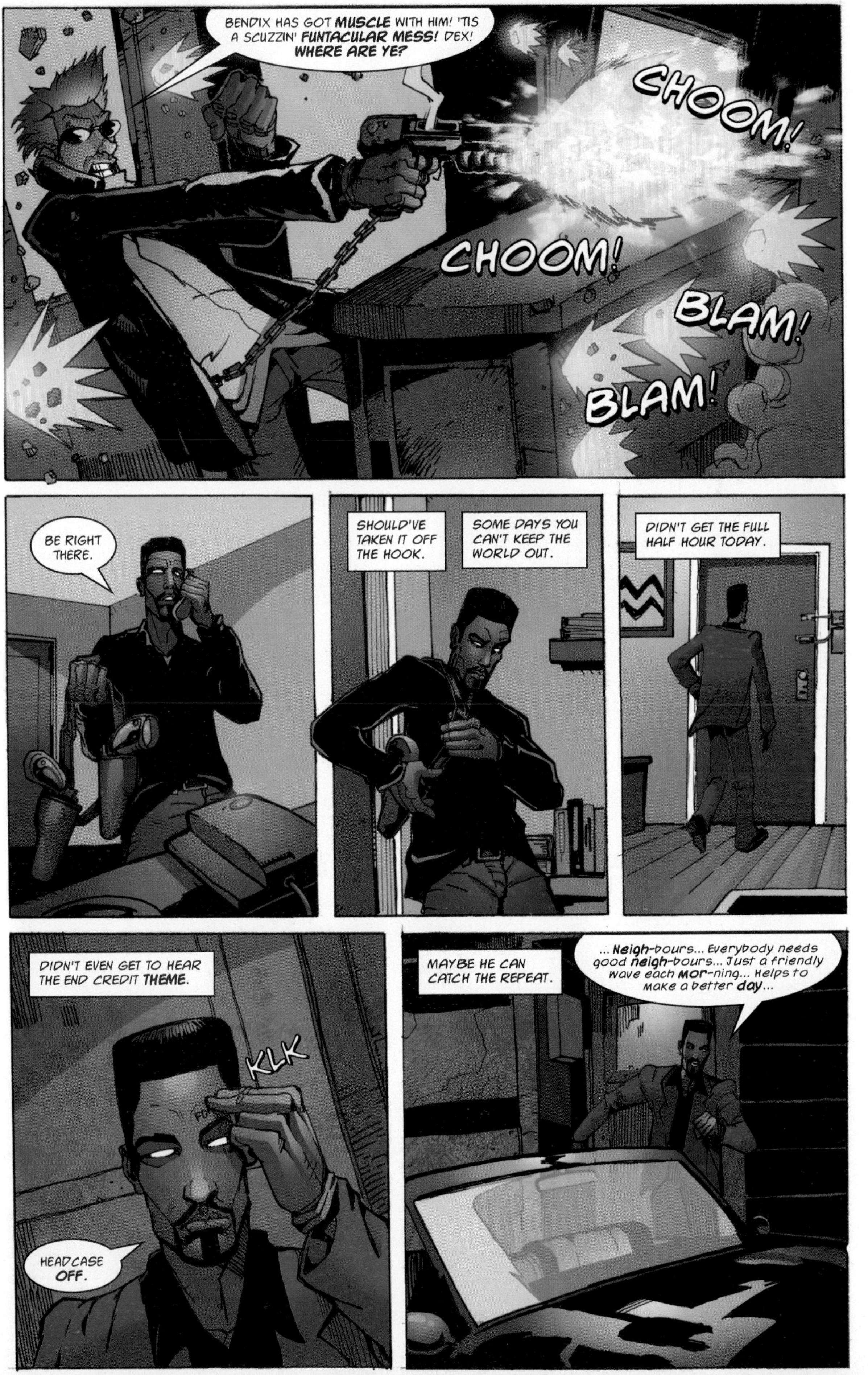

BENDIX HAS GOT MUSCLE WITH HIM! 'TIS A SCUZZIN' FUNTACULAR MESS! DEX! WHERE ARE YE?
CHOOM!
CHOOM!
BLAM!
BLAM!
BE RIGHT THERE.
SHOULD'VE TAKEN IT OFF THE HOOK.
SOME DAYS YOU CAN'T KEEP THE WORLD OUT.
DIDN'T GET THE FULL HALF HOUR TODAY.
DIDN'T EVEN GET TO HEAR THE END CREDIT THEME.
KLK
HEADCASE OFF.
MAYBE HE CAN CATCH THE REPEAT.
... Neigh-bours... Everybody needs good neigh-bours... Just a friendly wave each MOR-ning... Helps to make a better day...

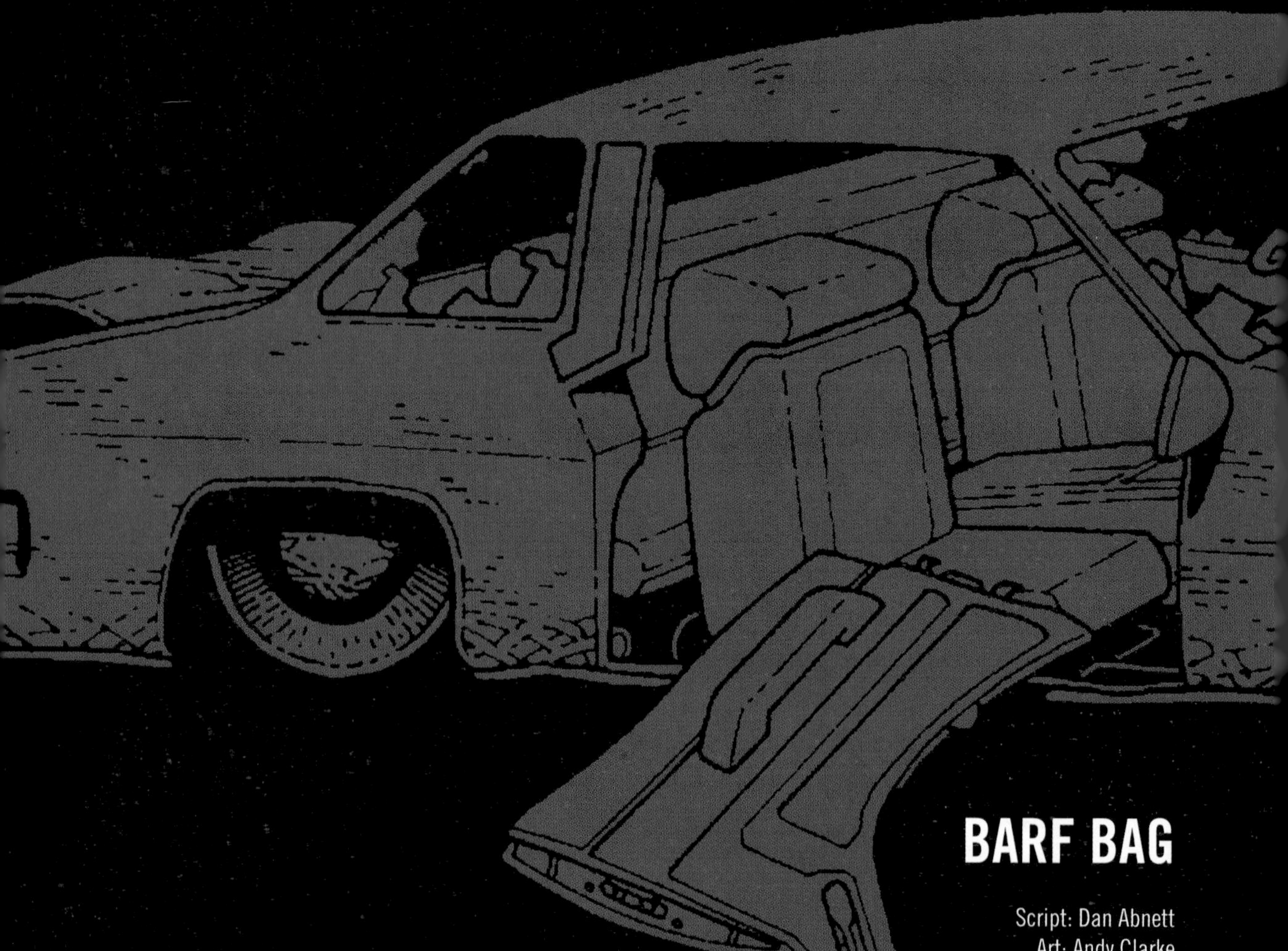

BARF BAG

Script: Dan Abnett
Art: Andy Clarke
Colours: Len O' Grady
Letters: Ellie De Ville

Originally published in *2000 AD* Progs 1243-1245

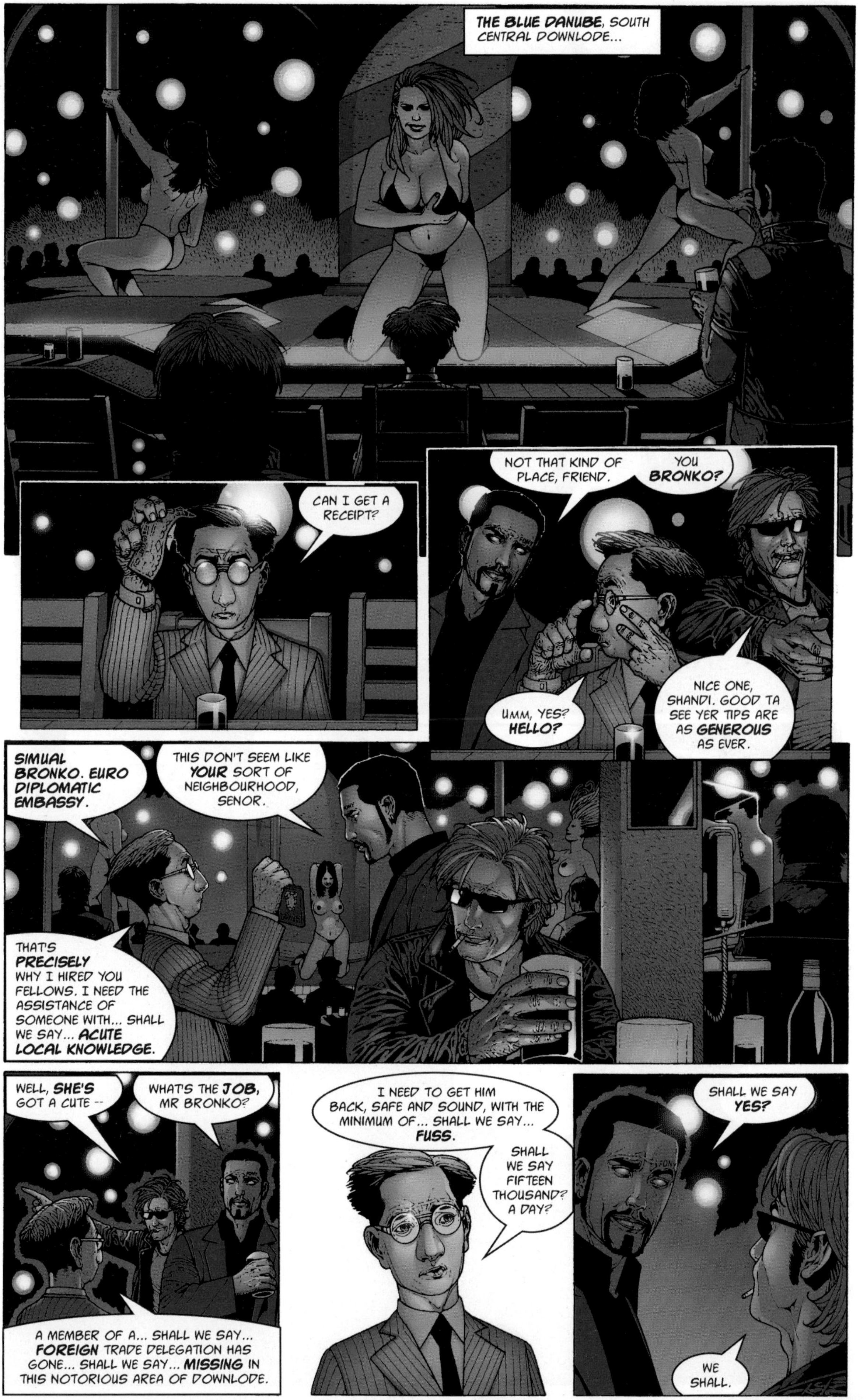
THE BLUE DANUBE, SOUTH CENTRAL DOWNLODE...
CAN I GET A RECEIPT?
NOT THAT KIND OF PLACE, FRIEND.
YOU BRONKO?
UMM, YES? HELLO?
NICE ONE, SHANDI. GOOD TA SEE YER TIPS ARE AS GENEROUS AS EVER.
SIMUAL BRONKO. EURO DIPLOMATIC EMBASSY.
THIS DON'T SEEM LIKE YOUR SORT OF NEIGHBOURHOOD, SENOR.
THAT'S PRECISELY WHY I HIRED YOU FELLOWS. I NEED THE ASSISTANCE OF SOMEONE WITH... SHALL WE SAY... ACUTE LOCAL KNOWLEDGE.
WELL, SHE'S GOT A CUTE --
WHAT'S THE JOB, MR BRONKO?
A MEMBER OF A... SHALL WE SAY... FOREIGN TRADE DELEGATION HAS GONE... SHALL WE SAY... MISSING IN THIS NOTORIOUS AREA OF DOWNLODE.
I NEED TO GET HIM BACK, SAFE AND SOUND, WITH THE MINIMUM OF... SHALL WE SAY... FUSS.
SHALL WE SAY FIFTEEN THOUSAND? A DAY?
SHALL WE SAY YES?
WE SHALL.

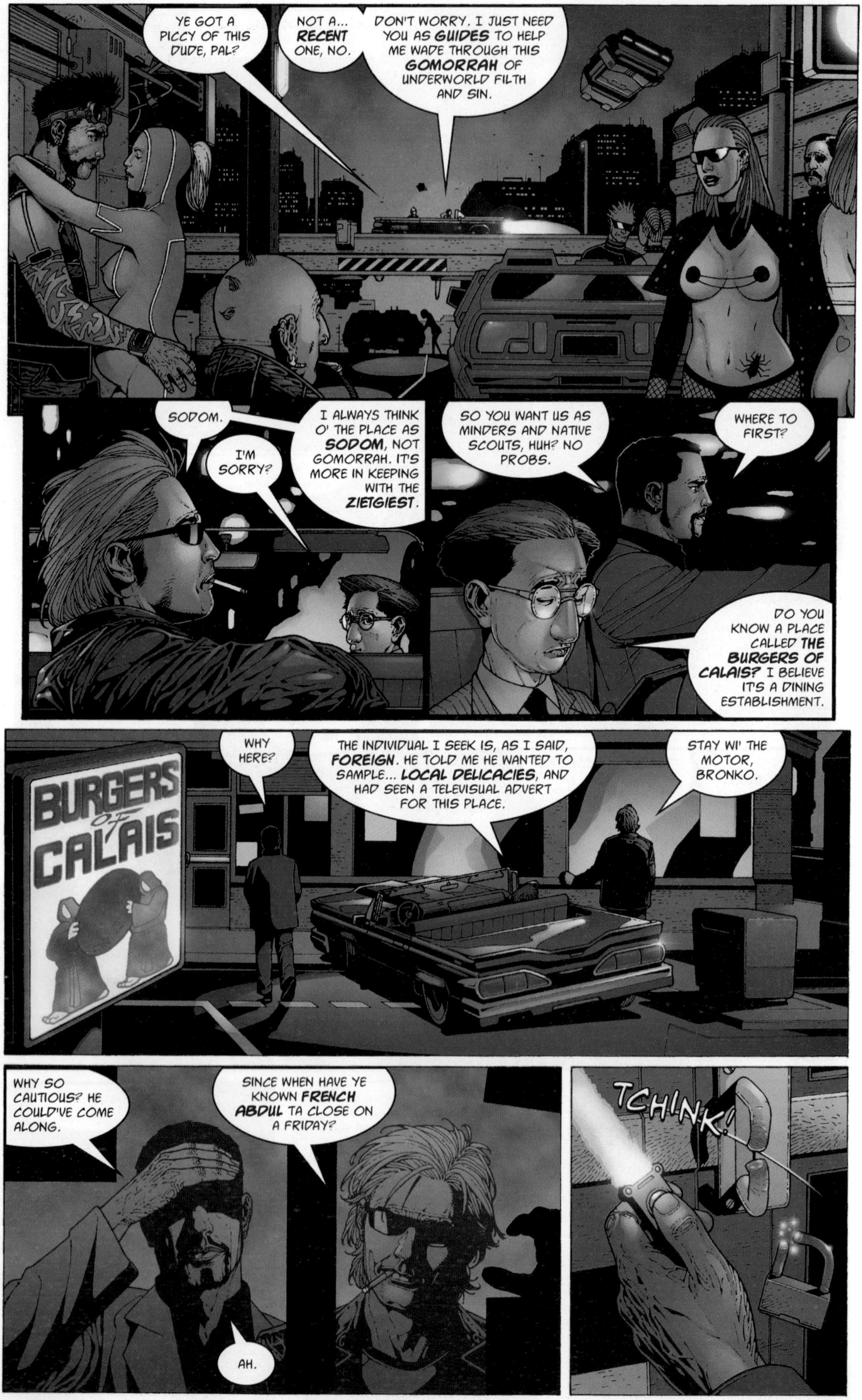
YE GOT A PICCY OF THIS DUDE, PAL?
NOT A... RECENT ONE, NO.
DON'T WORRY. I JUST NEED YOU AS GUIDES TO HELP ME WADE THROUGH THIS GOMORRAH OF UNDERWORLD FILTH AND SIN.
SODOM.
I'M SORRY?
I ALWAYS THINK O' THE PLACE AS SODOM, NOT GOMORRAH. IT'S MORE IN KEEPING WITH THE ZIETGIEST.
SO YOU WANT US AS MINDERS AND NATIVE SCOUTS, HUH? NO PROBS.
WHERE TO FIRST?
DO YOU KNOW A PLACE CALLED THE BURGERS OF CALAIS? I BELIEVE IT'S A DINING ESTABLISHMENT.
BURGERS OF CALAIS
WHY HERE?
THE INDIVIDUAL I SEEK IS, AS I SAID, FOREIGN. HE TOLD ME HE WANTED TO SAMPLE... LOCAL DELICACIES, AND HAD SEEN A TELEVISUAL ADVERT FOR THIS PLACE.
STAY WI' THE MOTOR, BRONKO.
WHY SO CAUTIOUS? HE COULD'VE COME ALONG.
SINCE WHEN HAVE YE KNOWN FRENCH ABDUL TA CLOSE ON A FRIDAY?
AH.
TCHINK!

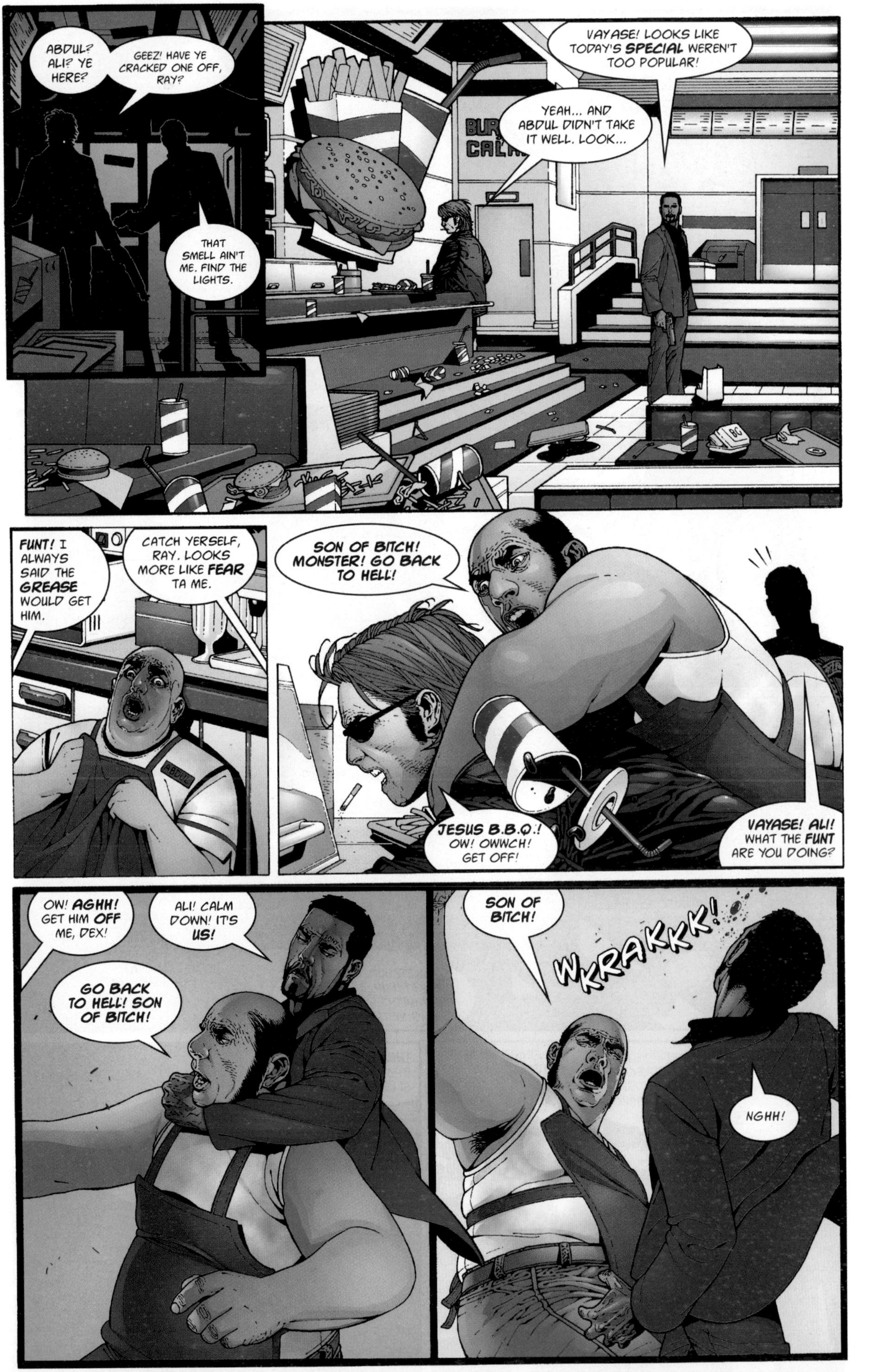
ABDUL? ALI? YE HERE?
GEEZ! HAVE YE CRACKED ONE OFF, RAY?
THAT SMELL AIN'T ME. FIND THE LIGHTS.
VAYASE! LOOKS LIKE TODAY'S SPECIAL WEREN'T TOO POPULAR!
YEAH... AND ABDUL DIDN'T TAKE IT WELL. LOOK...
FUNT! I ALWAYS SAID THE GREASE WOULD GET HIM.
CATCH YERSELF, RAY. LOOKS MORE LIKE FEAR TA ME.
SON OF BITCH! MONSTER! GO BACK TO HELL!
JESUS B.B.Q.! OW! OWWCH! GET OFF!
VAYASE! ALI! WHAT THE FUNT ARE YOU DOING?
OW! AGHH! GET HIM OFF ME, DEX!
ALI! CALM DOWN! IT'S US!
GO BACK TO HELL! SON OF BITCH!
SON OF BITCH!
WKRAKKK!
NGHH!

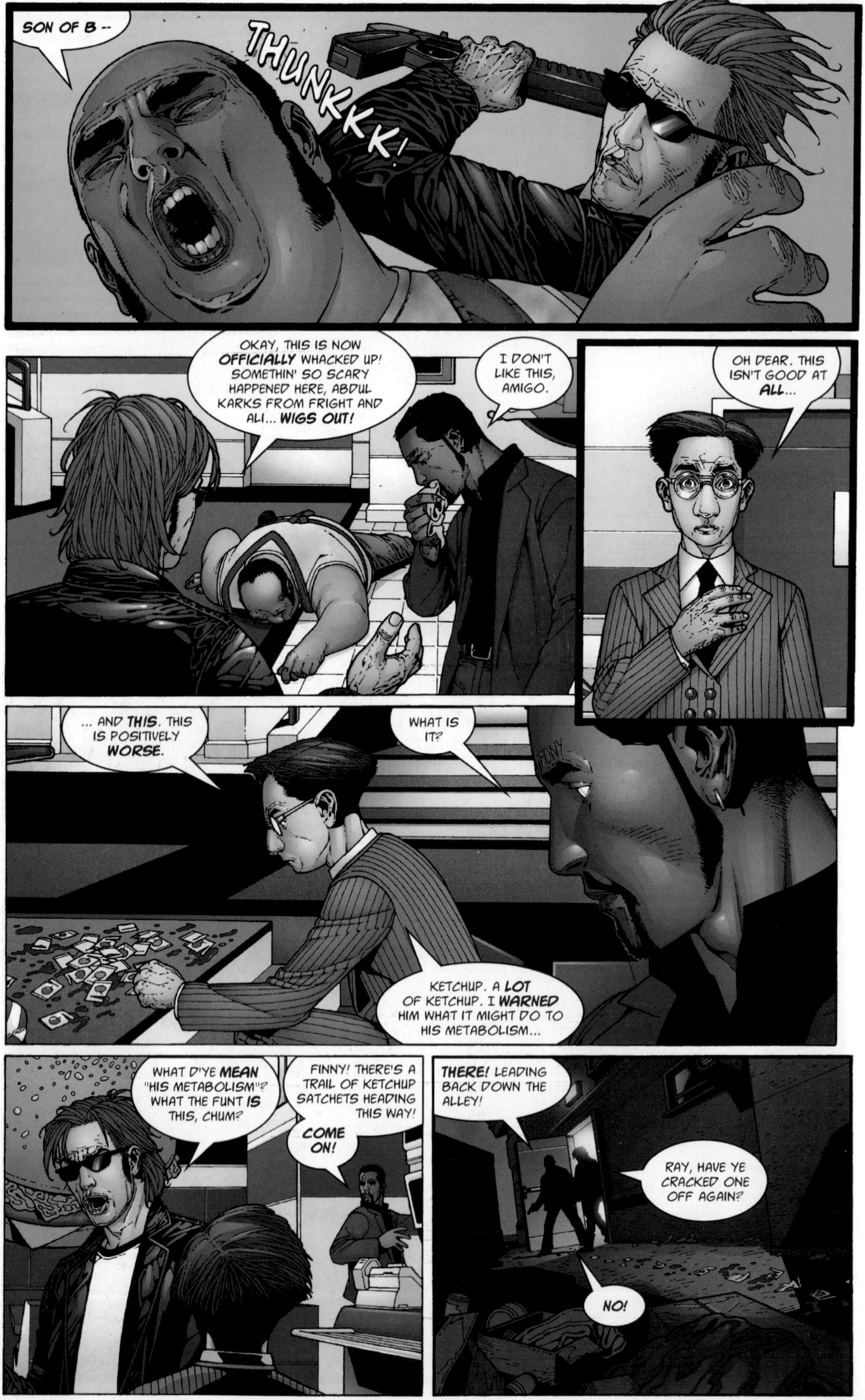
SON OF B --
THUNKKKK!
OKAY, THIS IS NOW OFFICIALLY WHACKED UP! SOMETHIN' SO SCARY HAPPENED HERE, ABDUL KARKS FROM FRIGHT AND ALI... WIGS OUT!
I DON'T LIKE THIS, AMIGO.
OH DEAR. THIS ISN'T GOOD AT ALL...
... AND THIS. THIS IS POSITIVELY WORSE.
WHAT IS IT?
KETCHUP. A LOT OF KETCHUP. I WARNED HIM WHAT IT MIGHT DO TO HIS METABOLISM...
WHAT D'YE MEAN "HIS METABOLISM"? WHAT THE FUNT IS THIS, CHUM?
FINNY! THERE'S A TRAIL OF KETCHUP SATCHETS HEADING THIS WAY!
COME ON!
THERE! LEADING BACK DOWN THE ALLEY!
RAY, HAVE YE CRACKED ONE OFF AGAIN?
NO!

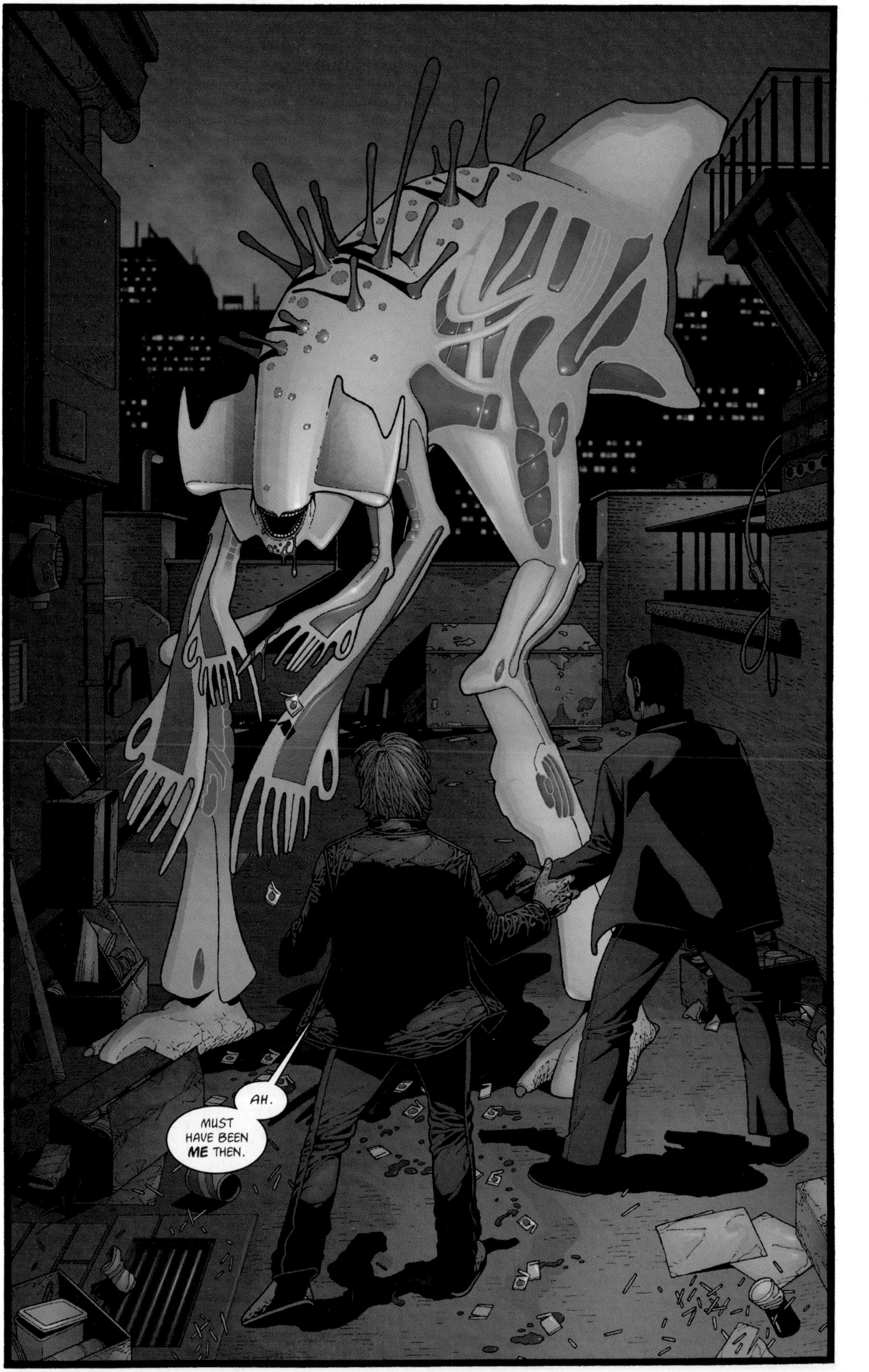
AH.
MUST HAVE BEEN ME THEN.

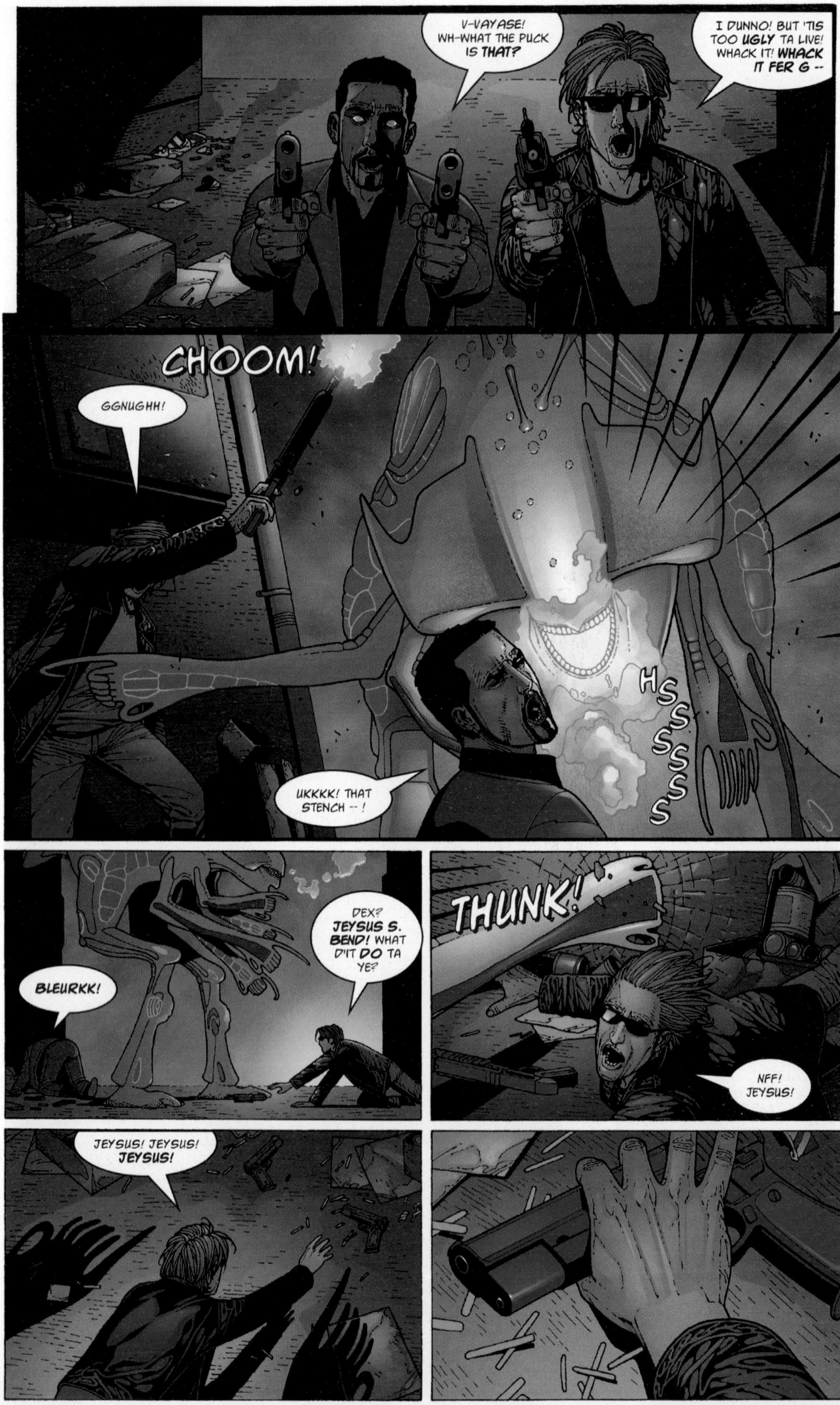
V-VAYASE! WH-WHAT THE PUCK IS THAT?
I DUNNO! BUT 'TIS TOO UGLY TA LIVE! WHACK IT! WHACK IT FER G --
CHOOM!
GGNUGHH!
HSSSSSS
UKKKK! THAT STENCH -- !
DEX? JEYSUS S. BEND! WHAT D'IT DO TA YE?
BLEURKK!
THUNK!
NFF! JEYSUS!
JEYSUS! JEYSUS! JEYSUS!

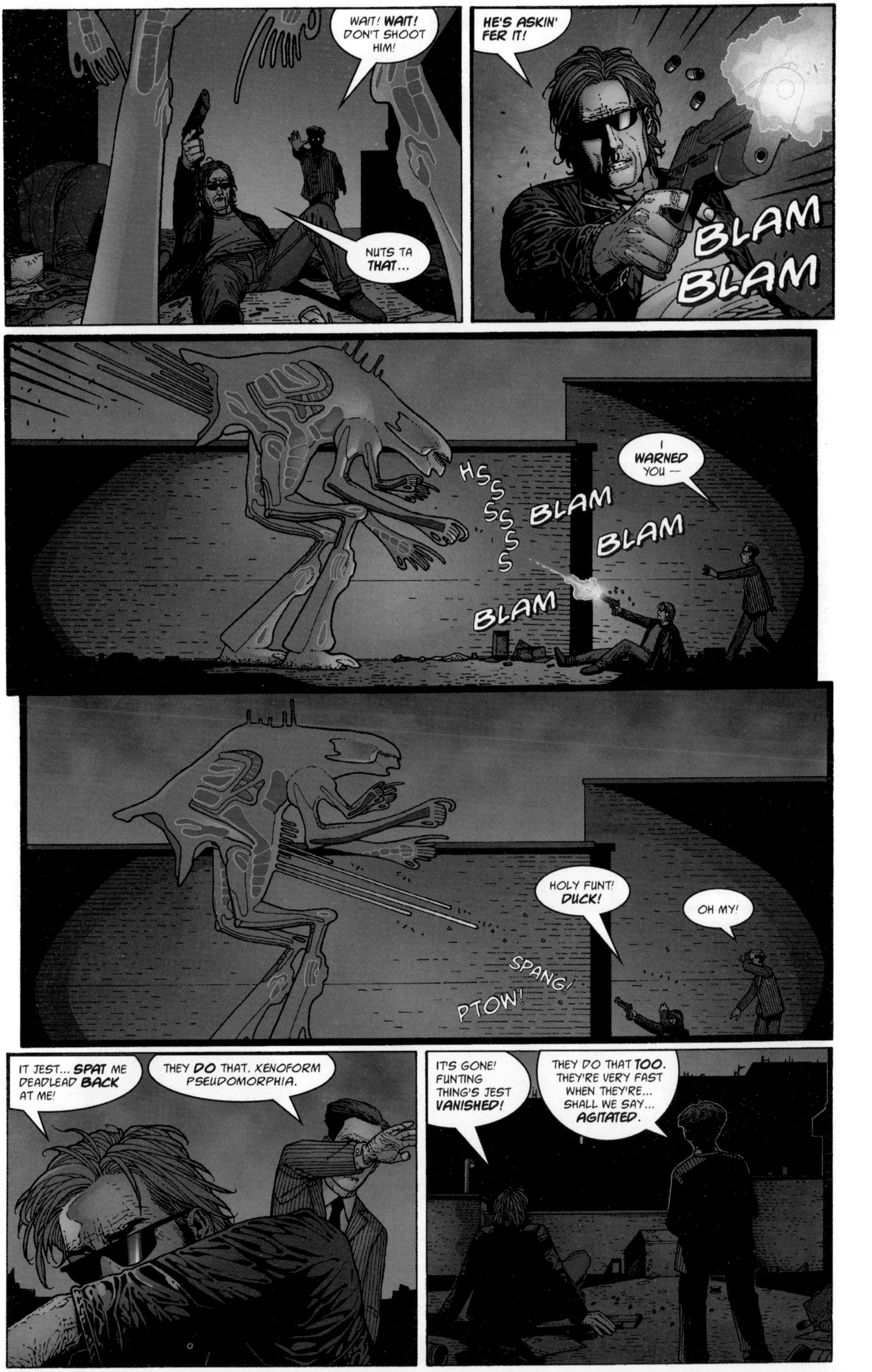
WAIT! WAIT! DON'T SHOOT HIM!
NUTS TA THAT...
HE'S ASKIN' FER IT!
BLAM
BLAM
HSSSSSS
I WARNED YOU --
BLAM
BLAM
BLAM
HOLY FUNT! DUCK!
OH MY!
SPANG!
PTOW!
IT JEST... SPAT ME DEADLEAD BACK AT ME!
THEY DO THAT. XENOFORM PSEUDOMORPHIA.
IT'S GONE! FUNTING THING'S JEST VANISHED!
THEY DO THAT TOO. THEY'RE VERY FAST WHEN THEY'RE... SHALL WE SAY... AGITATED.

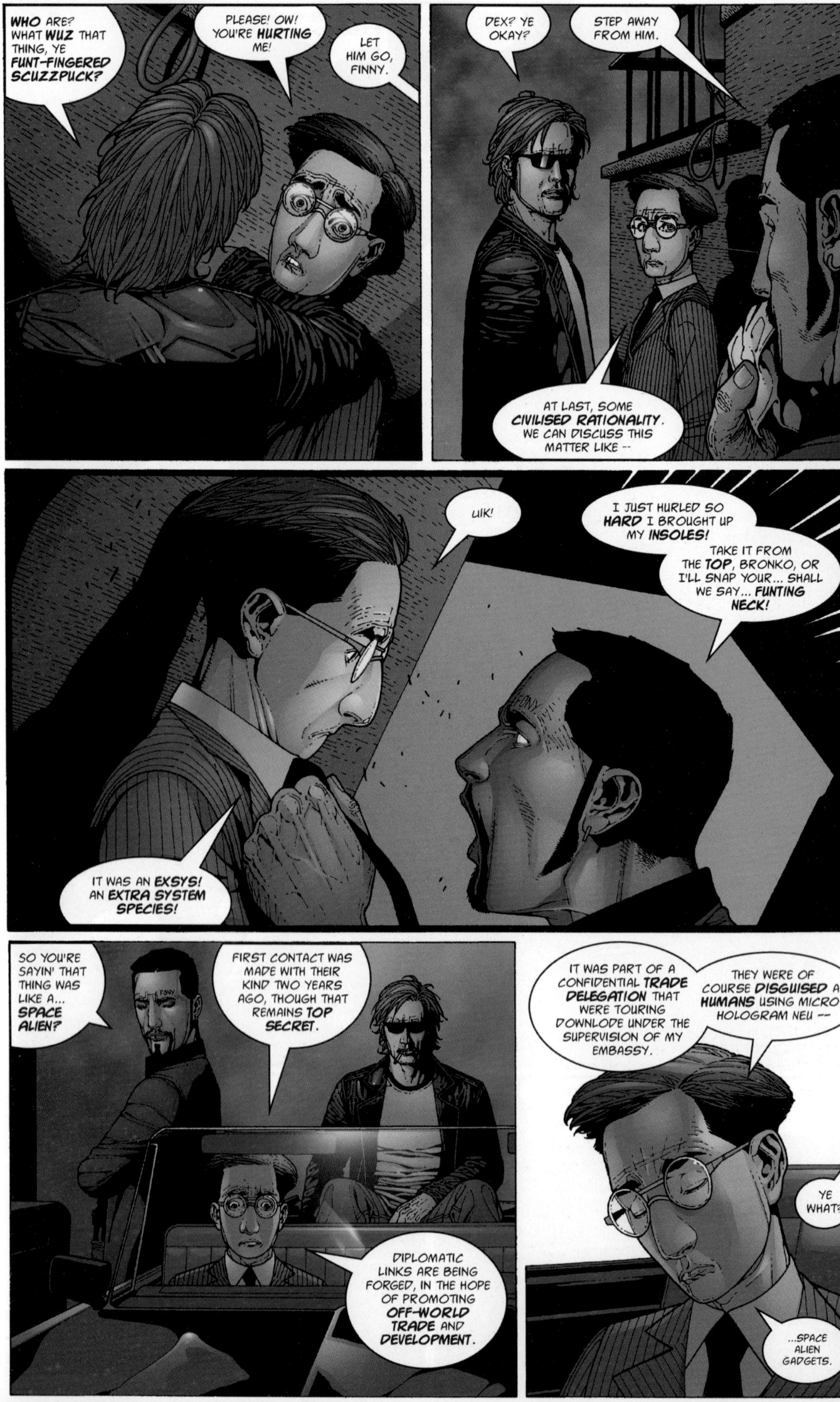

WHO ARE? WHAT WUZ THAT THING, YE FUNT-FINGERED SCUZZPUCK?
PLEASE! OW! YOU'RE HURTING ME!
LET HIM GO, FINNY.
DEX? YE OKAY?
STEP AWAY FROM HIM.
AT LAST, SOME CIVILISED RATIONALITY. WE CAN DISCUSS THIS MATTER LIKE --
UIK!
I JUST HURLED SO HARD I BROUGHT UP MY INSOLES!
TAKE IT FROM THE TOP, BRONKO, OR I'LL SNAP YOUR... SHALL WE SAY... FUNTING NECK!
IT WAS AN EXSYS! AN EXTRA SYSTEM SPECIES!
SO YOU'RE SAYIN' THAT THING WAS LIKE A... SPACE ALIEN?
FIRST CONTACT WAS MADE WITH THEIR KIND TWO YEARS AGO, THOUGH THAT REMAINS TOP SECRET.
DIPLOMATIC LINKS ARE BEING FORGED, IN THE HOPE OF PROMOTING OFF-WORLD TRADE AND DEVELOPMENT.
IT WAS PART OF A CONFIDENTIAL TRADE DELEGATION THAT WERE TOURING DOWNLODE UNDER THE SUPERVISION OF MY EMBASSY.
THEY WERE OF COURSE DISGUISED AS HUMANS USING MICRO-HOLOGRAM NEU --
YE WHAT?
...SPACE ALIEN GADGETS.

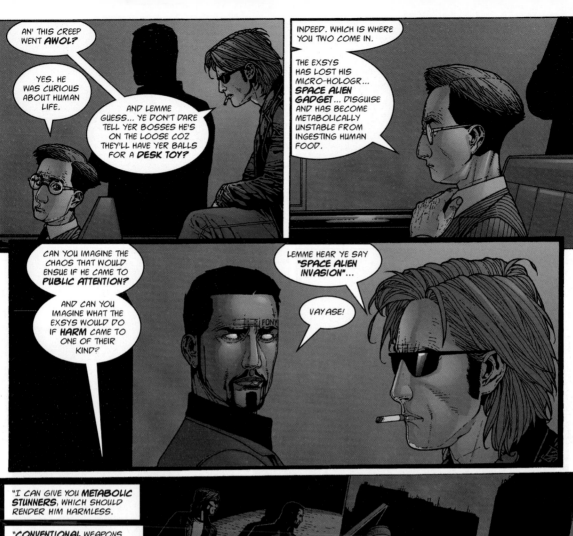

AN' THIS CREEP WENT **AWOL**?

YES. HE WAS CURIOUS ABOUT HUMAN LIFE.

AND LEMME GUESS... YE DON'T DARE TELL YER BOSSES HE'S ON THE LOOSE COZ THEY'LL HAVE YER BALLS FOR A **DESK TOY**?

INDEED. WHICH IS WHERE YOU TWO COME IN.

THE EXSYS HAS LOST HIS MICRO-HOLOGR... **SPACE ALIEN GADGET**... DISGUISE AND HAS BECOME METABOLICALLY UNSTABLE FROM INGESTING HUMAN FOOD.

CAN YOU IMAGINE THE CHAOS THAT WOULD ENSUE IF HE CAME TO **PUBLIC ATTENTION**?

AND CAN YOU IMAGINE WHAT THE EXSYS WOULD DO IF **HARM** CAME TO ONE OF THEIR KIND?

LEMME HEAR YE SAY "**SPACE ALIEN INVASION**"...

VAYASE!

"I CAN GIVE YOU **METABOLIC STUNNERS**, WHICH SHOULD RENDER HIM HARMLESS.

"**CONVENTIONAL** WEAPONS ARE USELESS... AND OF COURSE, I CAN'T ALLOW HIM TO BE **INJURED** OR **KILLED**.

"AS MR DEXTER HAS ALREADY FOUND, THE EXSYS CAN EXHALE AN EXTREMELY NOXIOUS **PHEROMONAL DEFENCE**...

"AND THANKS TO THE HUMAN NOURISHMENT CONTAMINATING HIS SYSTEM, HE IS **DELUSIONAL** AND **DANGEROUS**.

"THE REST IS DOWN TO YOU."

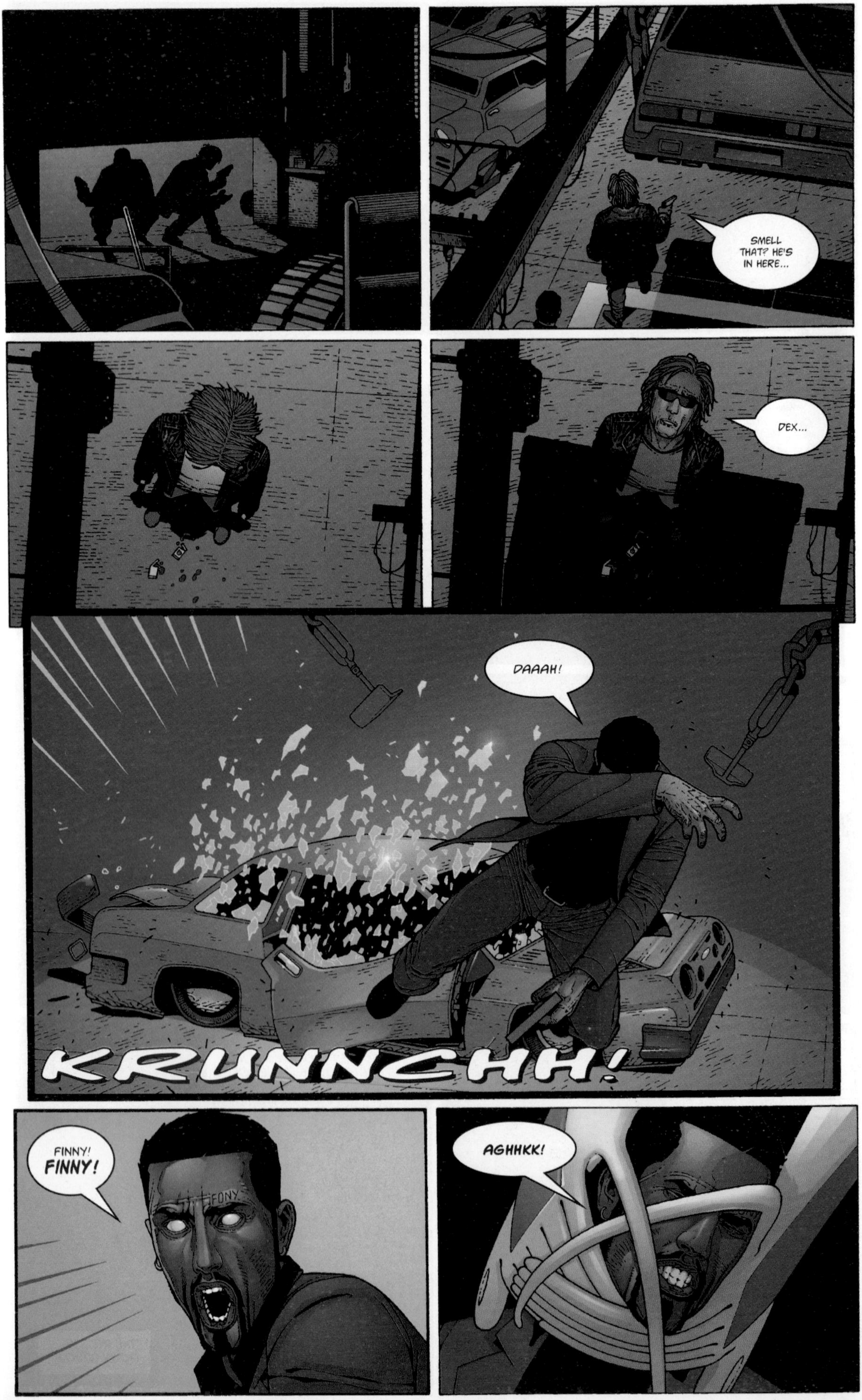
SMELL THAT? HE'S IN HERE...
DEX...
DAAAH!
KRUNNCHH!
FINNY! FINNY!
AGHHKK!

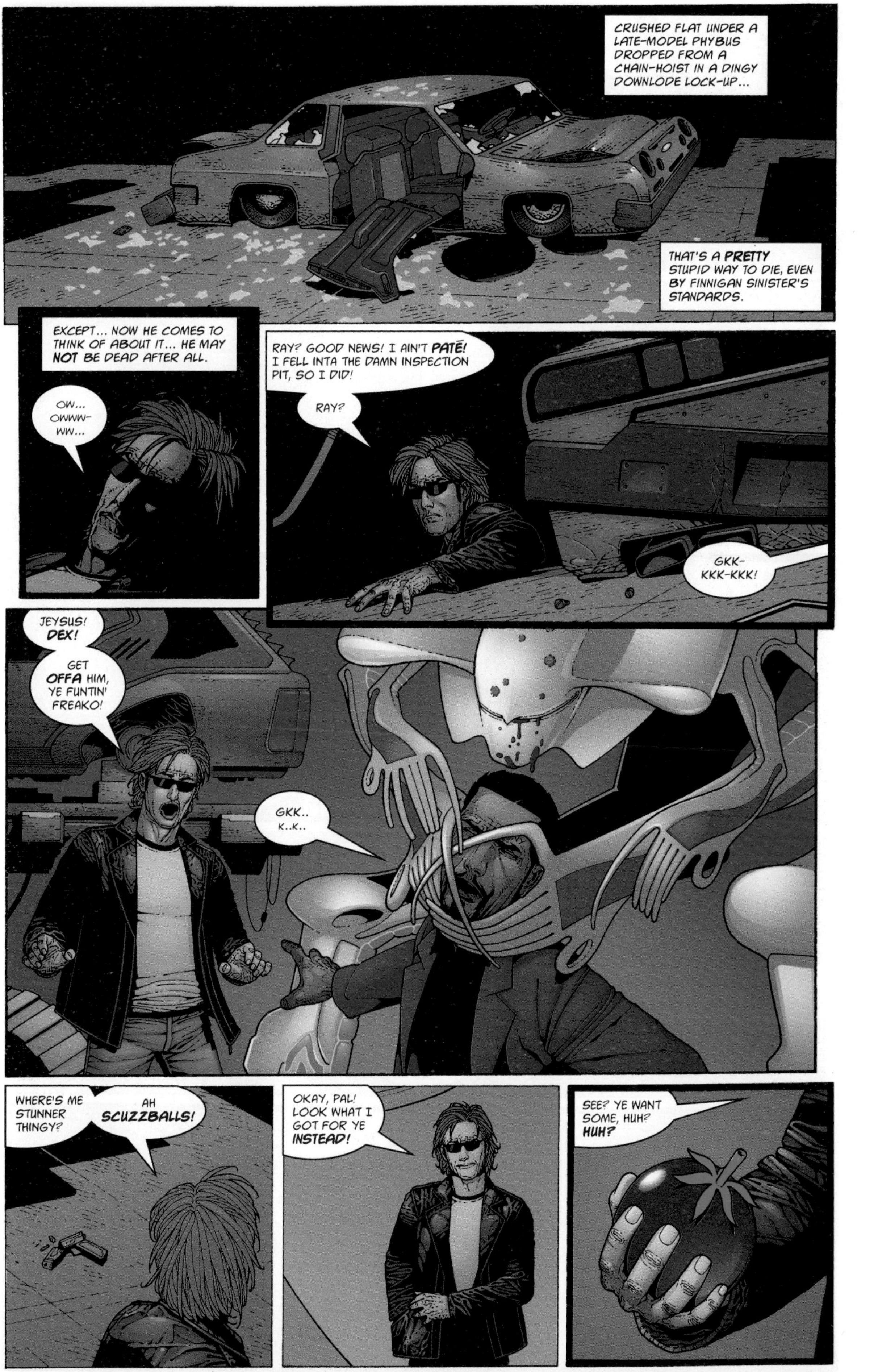

CRUSHED FLAT UNDER A LATE-MODEL PHYBUS DROPPED FROM A CHAIN-HOIST IN A DINGY DOWNLODE LOCK-UP...
THAT'S A **PRETTY** STUPID WAY TO DIE, EVEN BY FINNIGAN SINISTER'S STANDARDS.
EXCEPT... NOW HE COMES TO THINK OF ABOUT IT... HE MAY **NOT** BE DEAD AFTER ALL.
OW... OWWW-WW...
RAY? GOOD NEWS! I AIN'T **PATÉ!** I FELL INTA THE DAMN INSPECTION PIT, SO I DID!
RAY?
GKK-KKK-KKK!
JEYSUS! **DEX!**
GET **OFFA** HIM, YE FUNTIN' FREAKO!
GKK.. K..K..
WHERE'S ME STUNNER THINGY?
AH **SCUZZBALLS!**
OKAY, PAL! LOOK WHAT I GOT FOR YE **INSTEAD!**
SEE? YE WANT SOME, HUH? **HUH?**

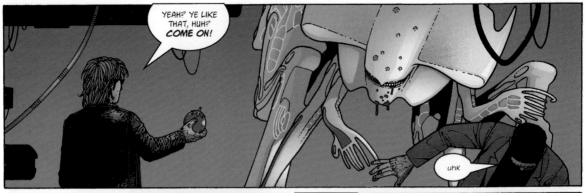

YEAH? YE LIKE THAT, HUH? **COME ON!**

uhK

LOOK! *THAT'S* THE STUFF, HUH?

OH, YEAH! THAT'S *GOOD!* MMM–HMMM!

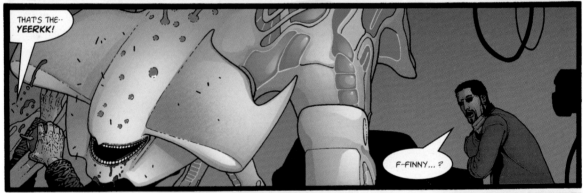

THAT'S THE·· YEERKK!

F-FINNY...?

VAYASE!

FFFZZ ZZAAAKKK!

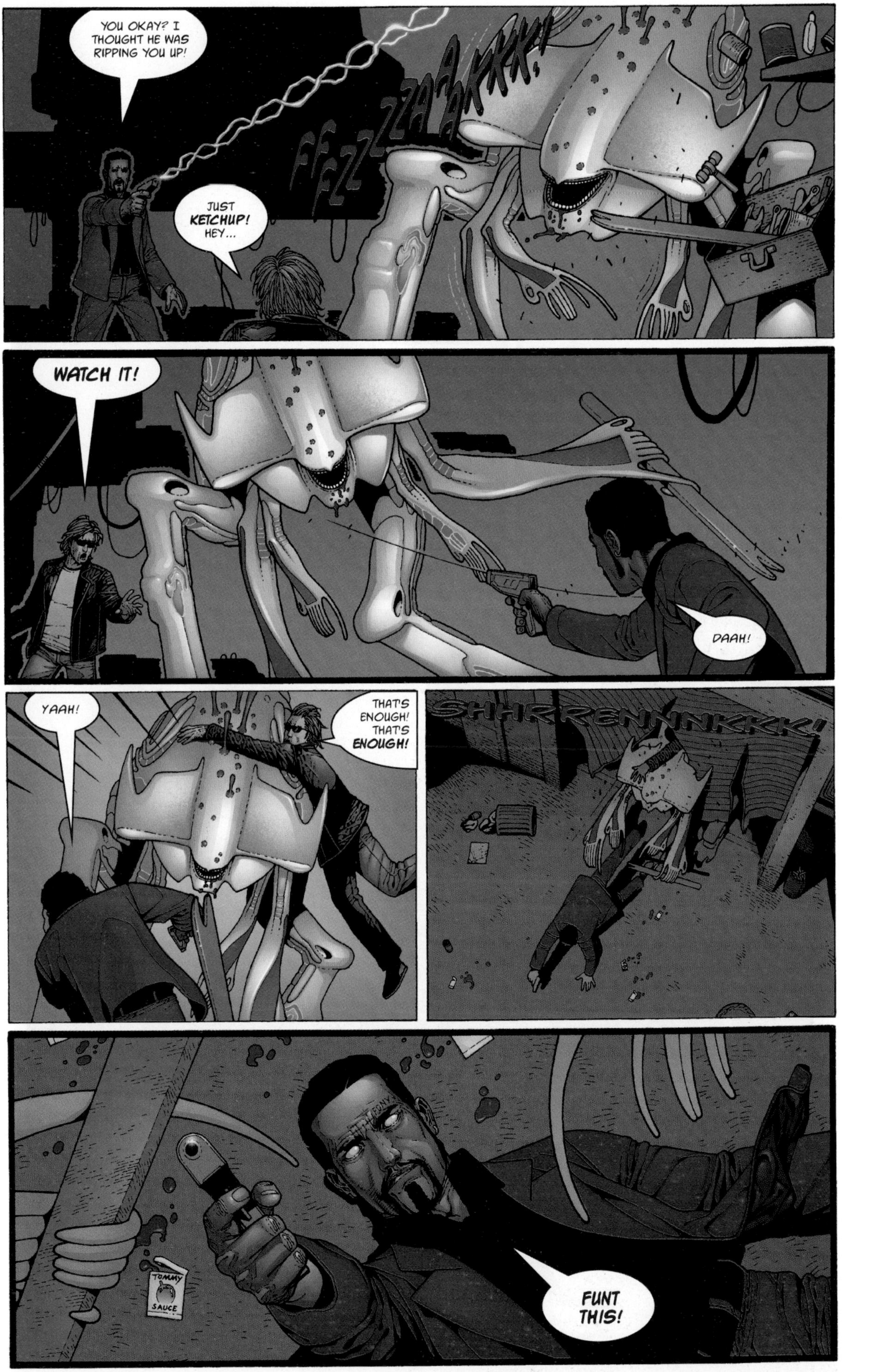
YOU OKAY? I THOUGHT HE WAS RIPPING YOU UP!
FFZZZZZAAAAKKKK!
JUST KETCHUP! HEY...
WATCH IT!
DAAH!
YAAH!
THAT'S ENOUGH! THAT'S ENOUGH!
SHHRRENNNKKK!
TOMMY SAUCE
FUNT THIS!

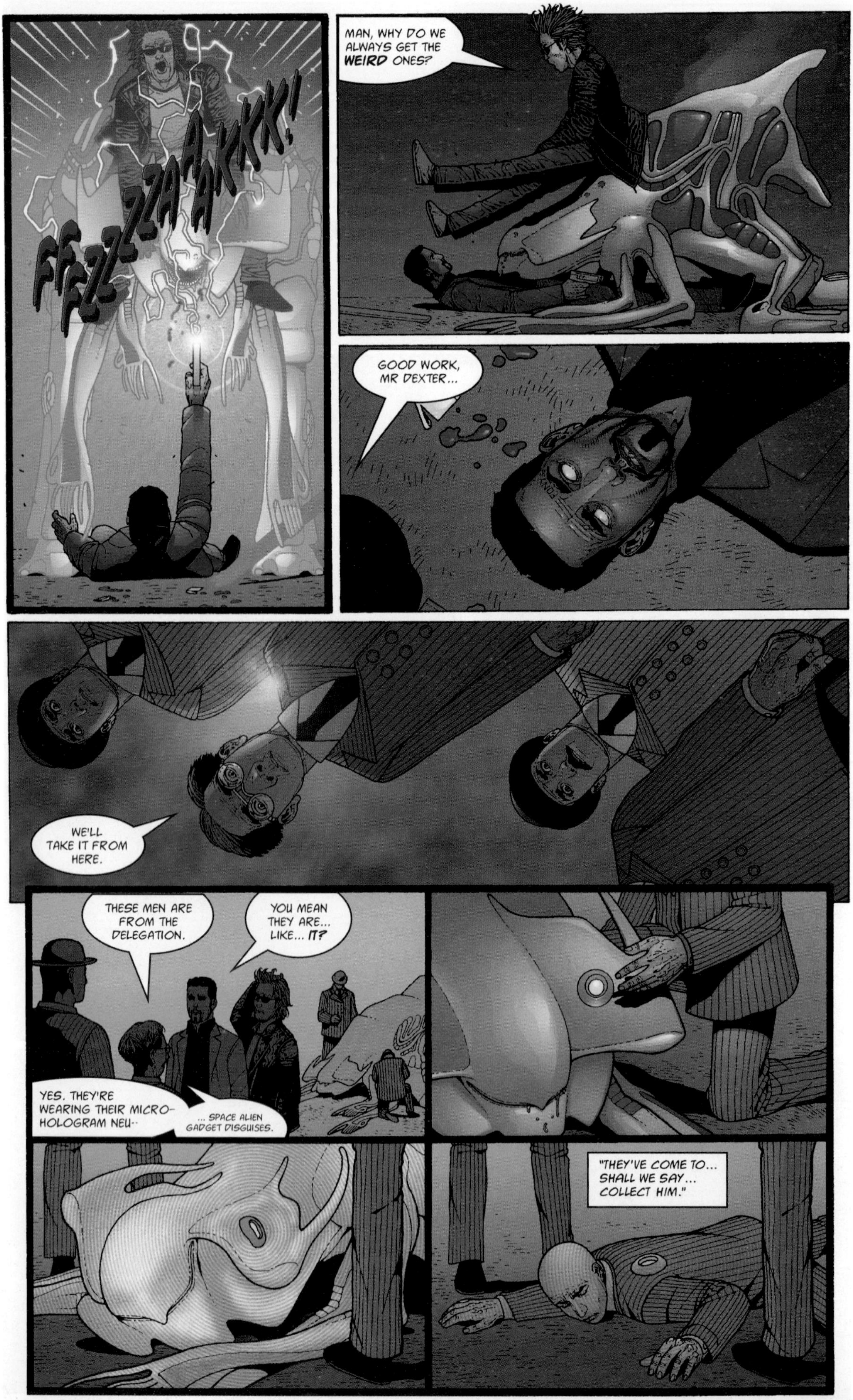
FFFZZZZZAAAKKK!
MAN, WHY DO WE ALWAYS GET THE **WEIRD** ONES?
GOOD WORK, MR DEXTER...
WE'LL TAKE IT FROM HERE.
THESE MEN ARE FROM THE DELEGATION.
YOU MEAN THEY ARE... LIKE... **IT?**
YES. THEY'RE WEARING THEIR MICRO-HOLOGRAM NEU--
... SPACE ALIEN GADGET DISGUISES.
"THEY'VE COME TO... SHALL WE SAY... COLLECT HIM."

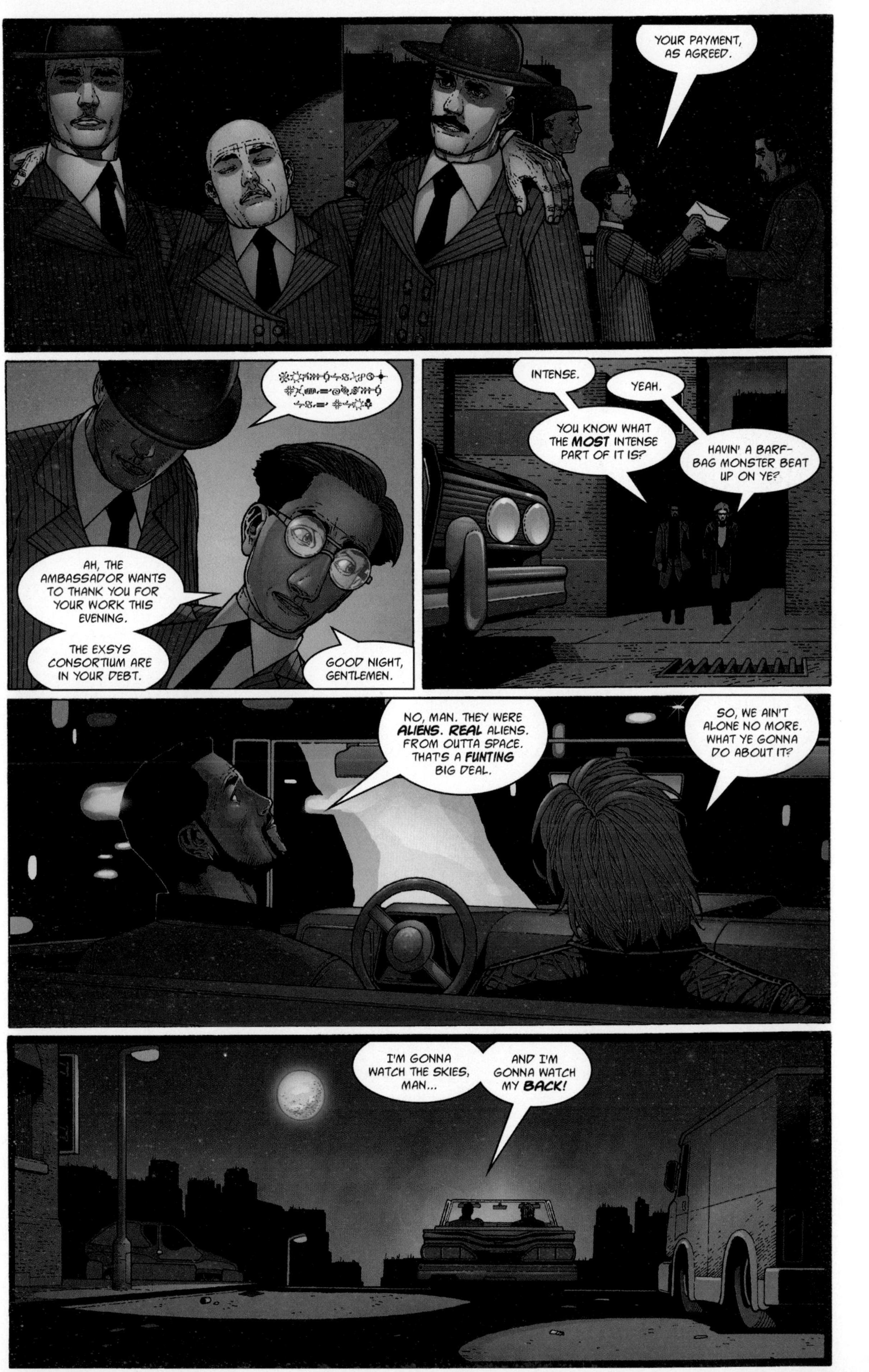
YOUR PAYMENT, AS AGREED.
AH, THE AMBASSADOR WANTS TO THANK YOU FOR YOUR WORK THIS EVENING.
THE EXSYS CONSORTIUM ARE IN YOUR DEBT.
GOOD NIGHT, GENTLEMEN.
INTENSE.
YEAH.
YOU KNOW WHAT THE **MOST** INTENSE PART OF IT IS?
HAVIN' A BARF-BAG MONSTER BEAT UP ON YE?
NO, MAN. THEY WERE **ALIENS**. **REAL** ALIENS. FROM OUTTA SPACE. THAT'S A **FUNTING** BIG DEAL.
SO, WE AIN'T ALONE NO MORE. WHAT YE GONNA DO ABOUT IT?
I'M GONNA WATCH THE SKIES, MAN...
AND I'M GONNA WATCH MY **BACK**!

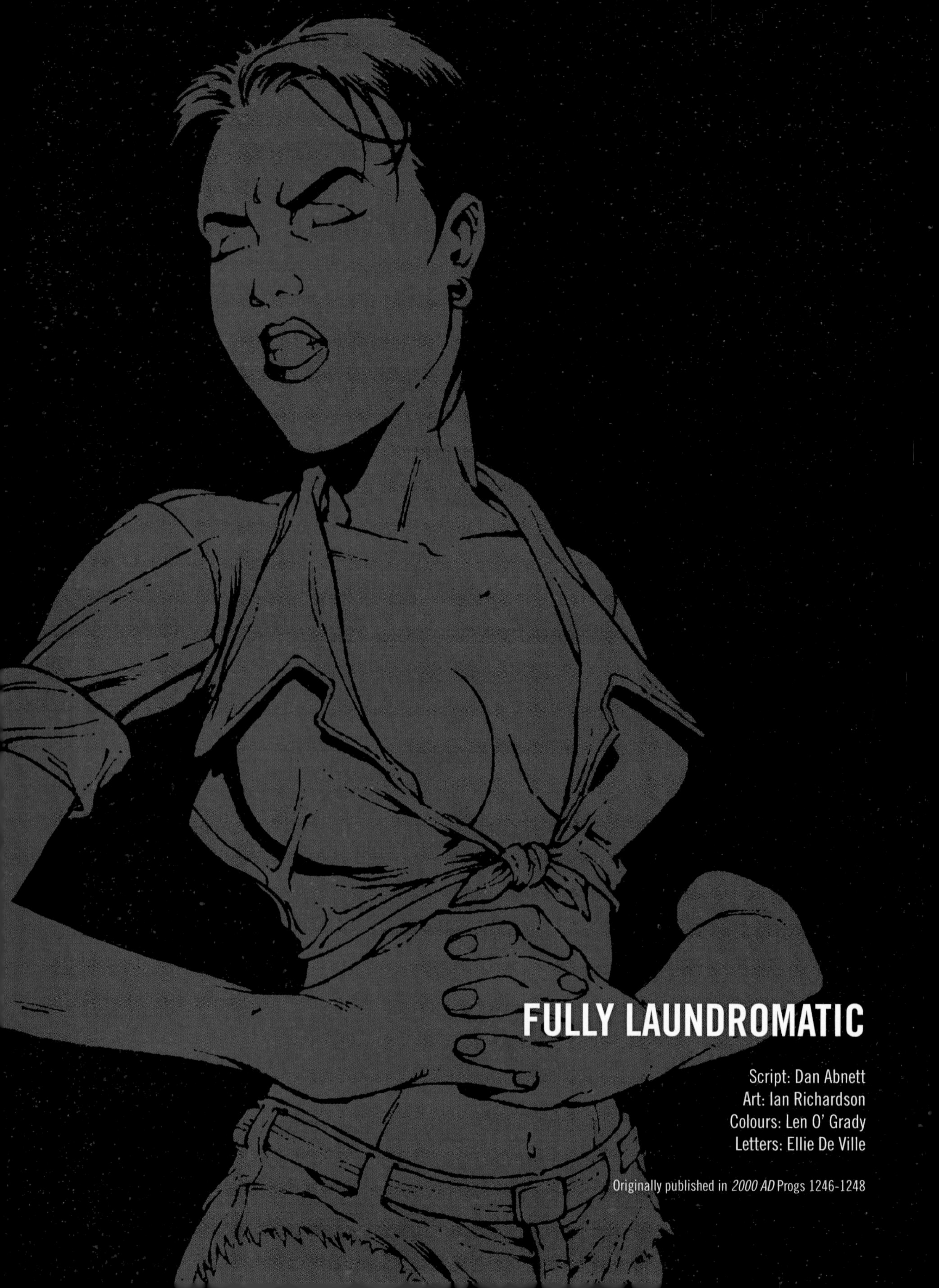

FULLY LAUNDROMATIC

Script: Dan Abnett
Art: Ian Richardson
Colours: Len O' Grady
Letters: Ellie De Ville

Originally published in *2000 AD* Progs 1246-1248

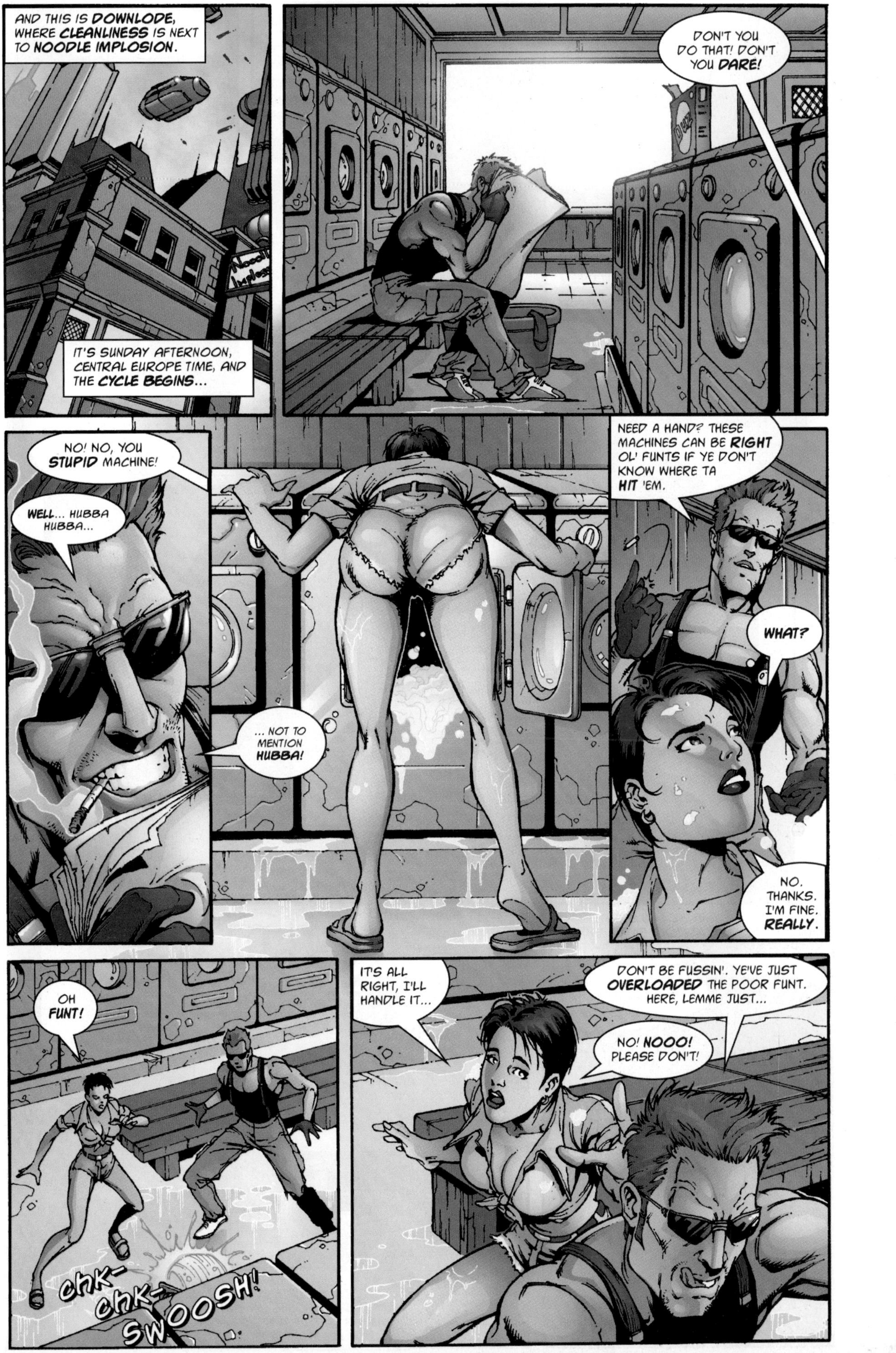
AND THIS IS **DOWNLODE**, WHERE **CLEANLINESS** IS NEXT TO **NOODLE IMPLOSION**.
IT'S SUNDAY AFTERNOON, CENTRAL EUROPE TIME, AND THE **CYCLE BEGINS...**
DON'T YOU DO THAT! DON'T YOU **DARE!**
NO! NO, YOU **STUPID** MACHINE!
WELL... HUBBA HUBBA...
...NOT TO MENTION **HUBBA!**
NEED A HAND? THESE MACHINES CAN BE **RIGHT** OL' FUNTS IF YE DON'T KNOW WHERE TA **HIT** 'EM.
WHAT?
NO. THANKS. I'M FINE. **REALLY.**
OH **FUNT!**
CHK-CHK-SWOOSH!
IT'S ALL RIGHT, I'LL HANDLE IT...
DON'T BE FUSSIN'. YE'VE JUST **OVERLOADED** THE POOR FUNT. HERE, LEMME JUST...
NO! **NOOO!** PLEASE DON'T!

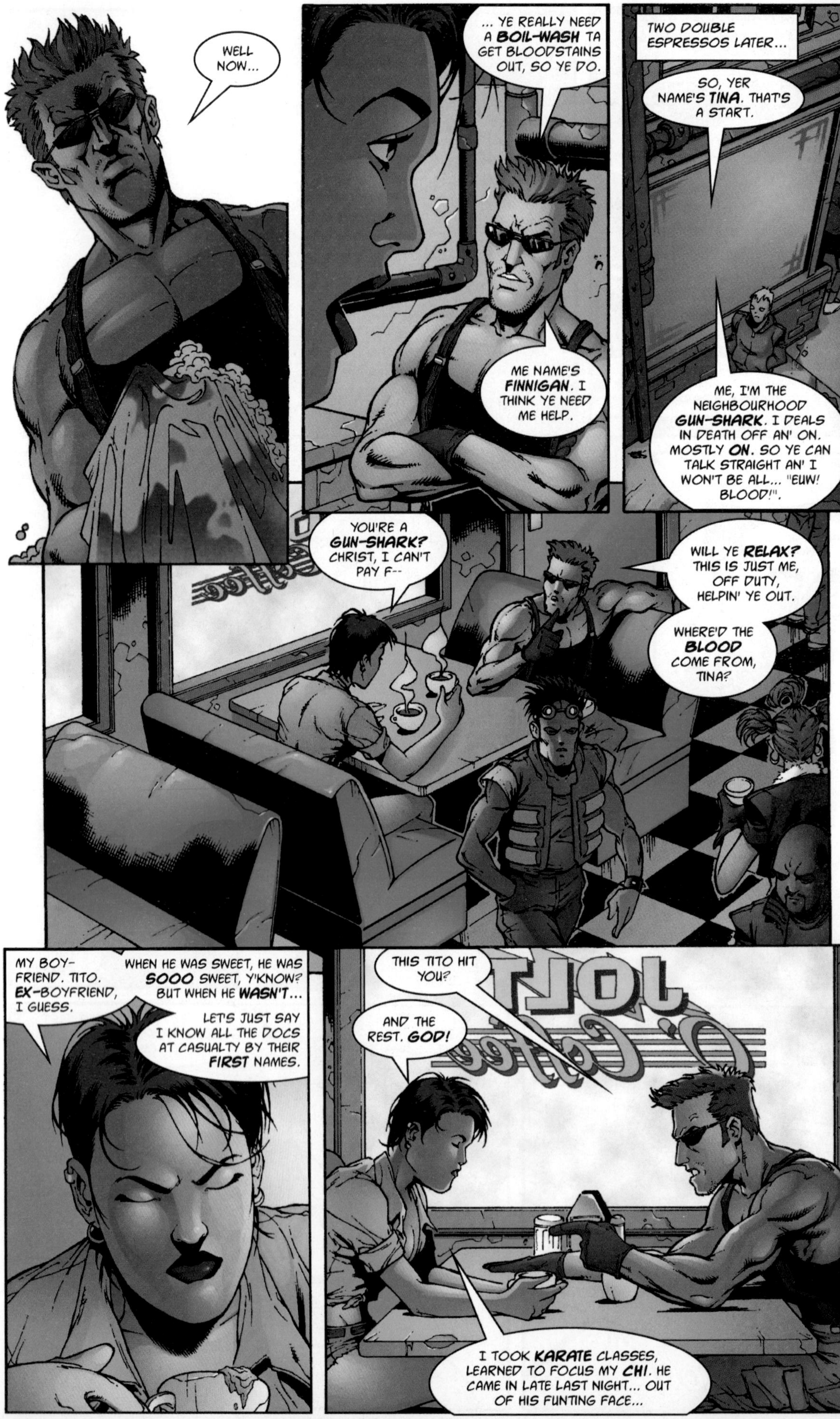
WELL NOW...
... YE REALLY NEED A BOIL-WASH TA GET BLOODSTAINS OUT, SO YE DO.
ME NAME'S FINNIGAN. I THINK YE NEED ME HELP.
TWO DOUBLE ESPRESSOS LATER...
SO, YER NAME'S TINA. THAT'S A START.
ME, I'M THE NEIGHBOURHOOD GUN-SHARK. I DEALS IN DEATH OFF AN' ON. MOSTLY ON. SO YE CAN TALK STRAIGHT AN' I WON'T BE ALL... "EUW! BLOOD!".
YOU'RE A GUN-SHARK? CHRIST, I CAN'T PAY F--
WILL YE RELAX? THIS IS JUST ME, OFF DUTY, HELPIN' YE OUT.
WHERE'D THE BLOOD COME FROM, TINA?
MY BOY-FRIEND. TITO. EX-BOYFRIEND, I GUESS.
WHEN HE WAS SWEET, HE WAS SOOO SWEET, Y'KNOW? BUT WHEN HE WASN'T...
LET'S JUST SAY I KNOW ALL THE DOCS AT CASUALTY BY THEIR FIRST NAMES.
THIS TITO HIT YOU?
AND THE REST. GOD!
I TOOK KARATE CLASSES, LEARNED TO FOCUS MY CHI. HE CAME IN LATE LAST NIGHT... OUT OF HIS FUNTING FACE...

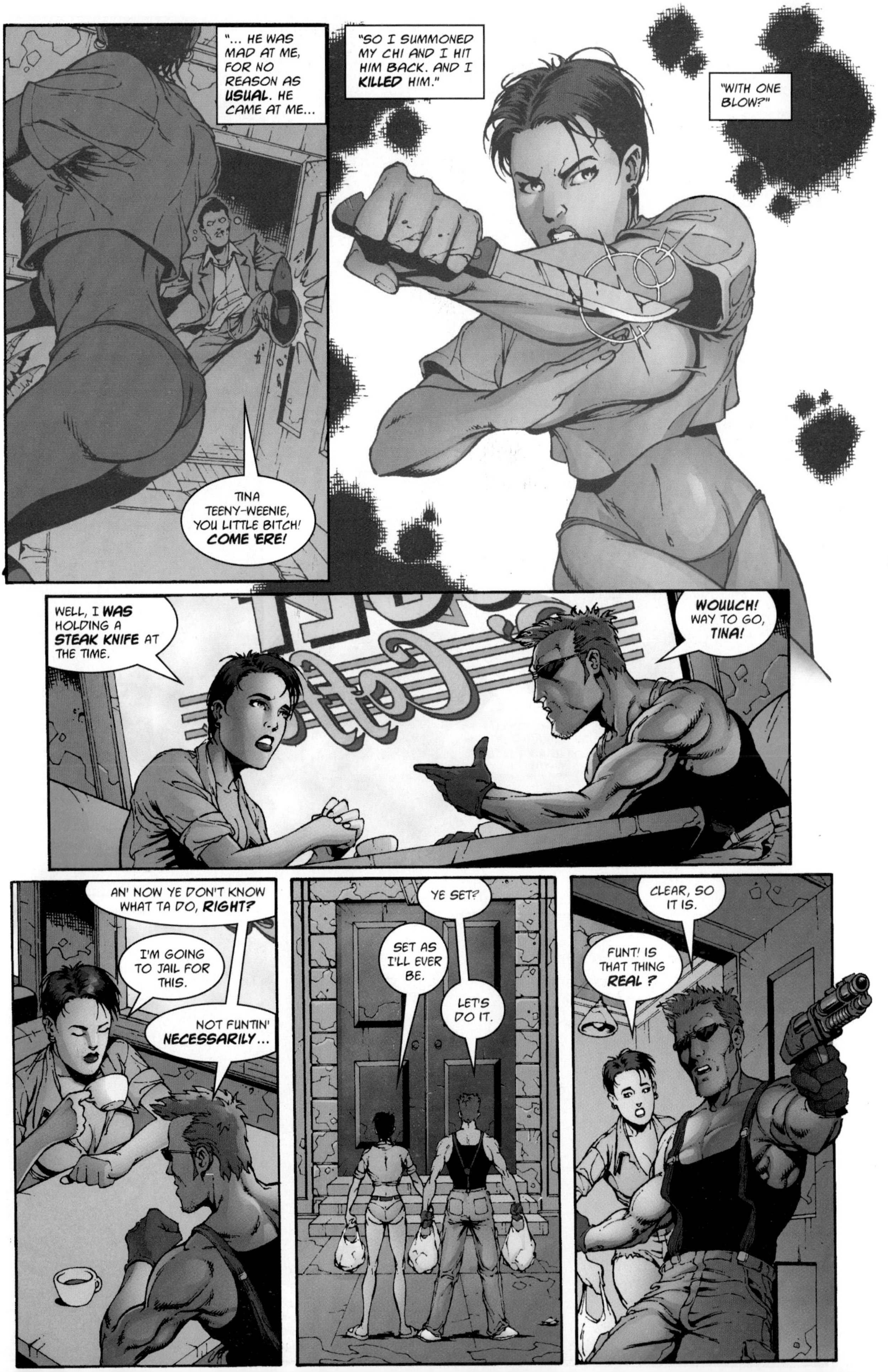
"... HE WAS MAD AT ME, FOR NO REASON AS **USUAL**. HE CAME AT ME...
TINA TEENY-WEENIE, YOU LITTLE BITCH! **COME 'ERE!**
"SO I SUMMONED MY CHI AND I HIT HIM BACK. AND I **KILLED** HIM."
"WITH ONE BLOW?"
WELL, I **WAS** HOLDING A **STEAK KNIFE** AT THE TIME.
WOUUCH! WAY TO GO, **TINA!**
AN' NOW YE DON'T KNOW WHAT TA DO, **RIGHT?**
I'M GOING TO JAIL FOR THIS.
NOT FUNTIN' **NECESSARILY**...
YE SET?
SET AS I'LL EVER BE.
LET'S DO IT.
CLEAR, SO IT IS.
FUNT! IS THAT THING **REAL ?**

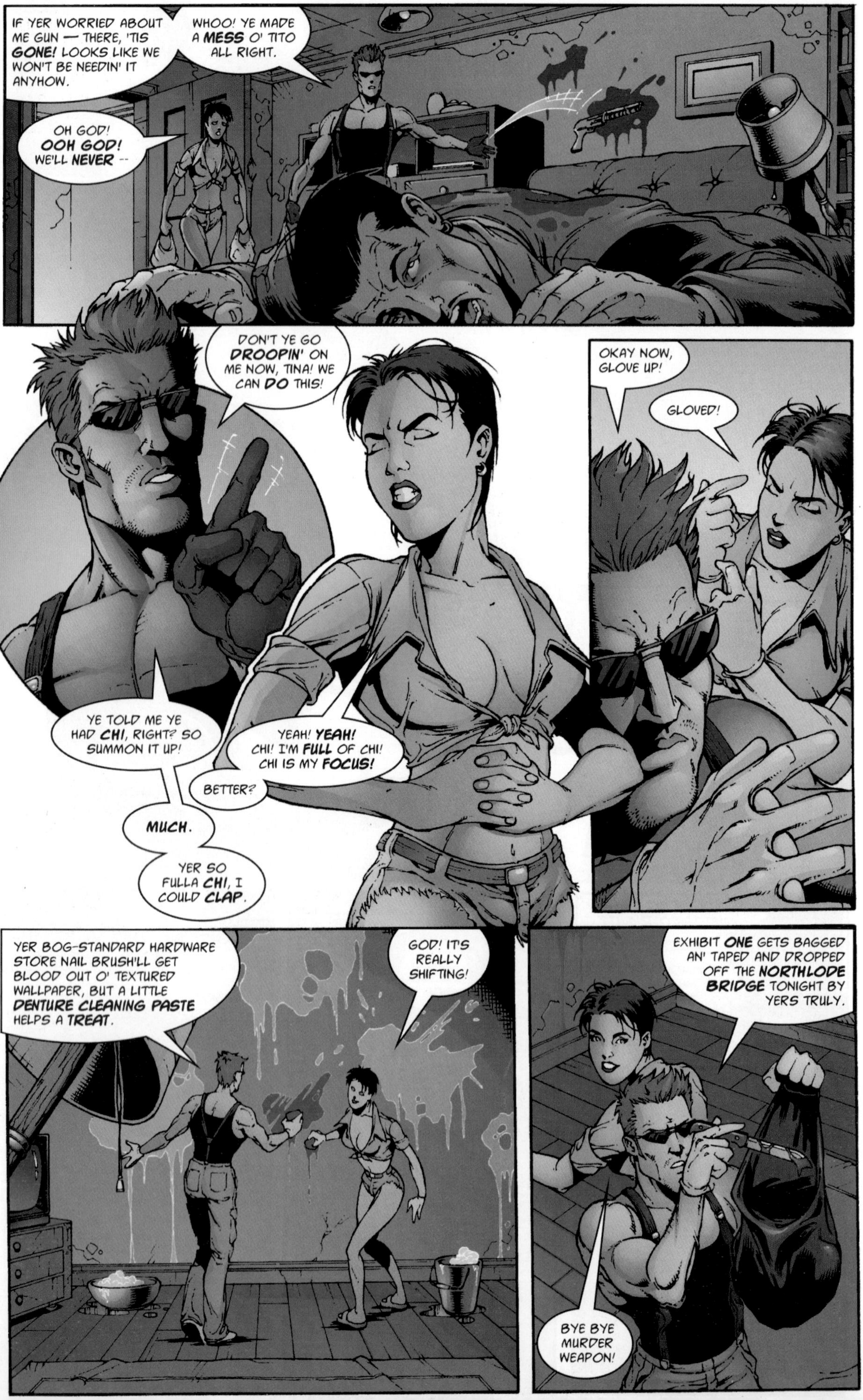
IF YER WORRIED ABOUT ME GUN — THERE, 'TIS GONE! LOOKS LIKE WE WON'T BE NEEDIN' IT ANYHOW.
WHOO! YE MADE A MESS O' TITO ALL RIGHT.
OH GOD! OOH GOD! WE'LL NEVER --
DON'T YE GO DROOPIN' ON ME NOW, TINA! WE CAN DO THIS!
YE TOLD ME YE HAD CHI, RIGHT? SO SUMMON IT UP!
YEAH! YEAH! CHI! I'M FULL OF CHI! CHI IS MY FOCUS!
BETTER?
MUCH.
YER SO FULLA CHI, I COULD CLAP.
OKAY NOW, GLOVE UP!
GLOVED!
YER BOG-STANDARD HARDWARE STORE NAIL BRUSH'LL GET BLOOD OUT O' TEXTURED WALLPAPER, BUT A LITTLE DENTURE CLEANING PASTE HELPS A TREAT.
GOD! IT'S REALLY SHIFTING!
EXHIBIT ONE GETS BAGGED AN' TAPED AND DROPPED OFF THE NORTHLODE BRIDGE TONIGHT BY YERS TRULY.
BYE BYE MURDER WEAPON!

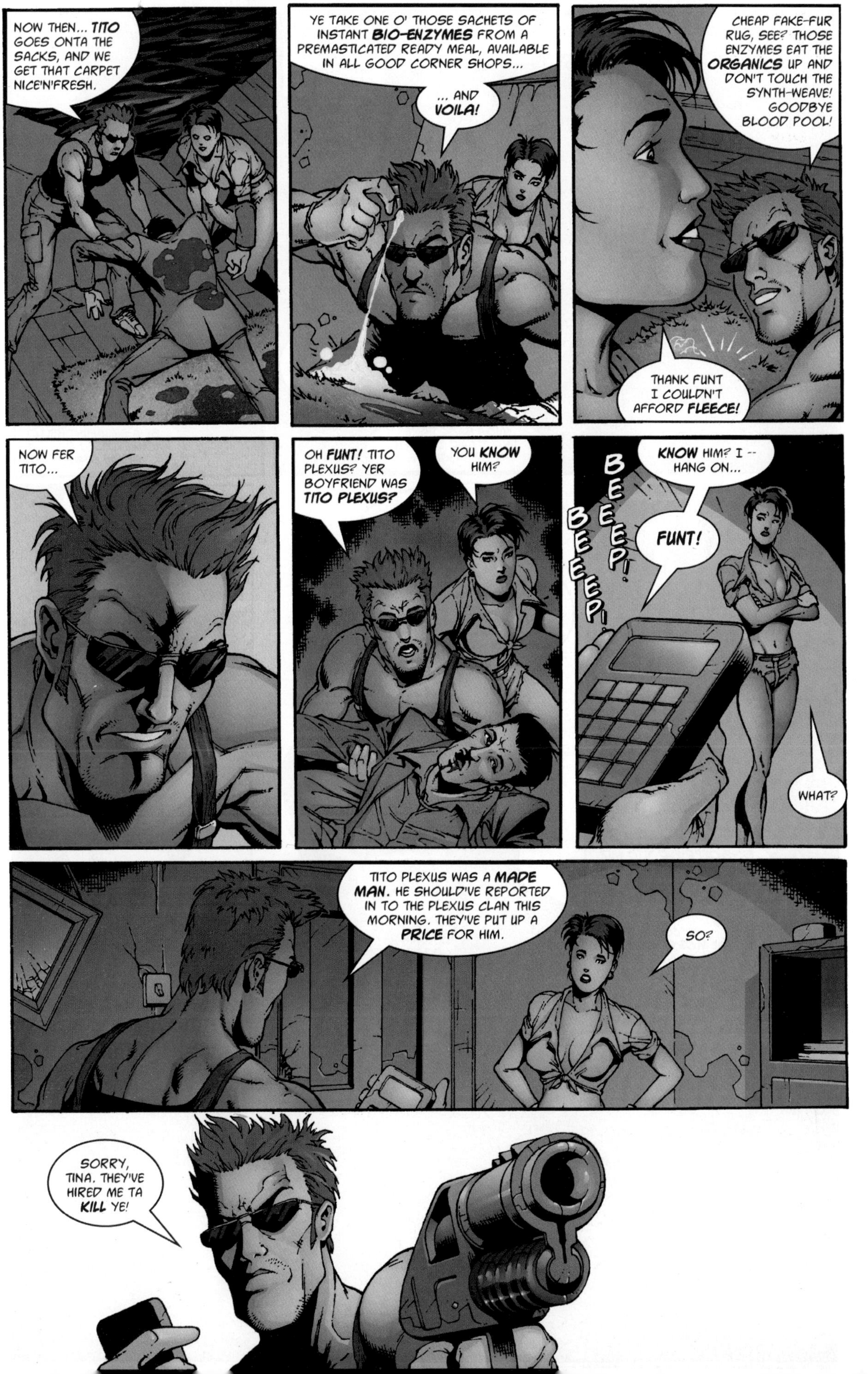

NOW THEN... TITO GOES ONTA THE SACKS, AND WE GET THAT CARPET NICE'N'FRESH.
YE TAKE ONE O' THOSE SACHETS OF INSTANT BIO-ENZYMES FROM A PREMASTICATED READY MEAL, AVAILABLE IN ALL GOOD CORNER SHOPS...
... AND VOILA!
CHEAP FAKE-FUR RUG, SEE? THOSE ENZYMES EAT THE ORGANICS UP AND DON'T TOUCH THE SYNTH-WEAVE! GOODBYE BLOOD POOL!
THANK FUNT I COULDN'T AFFORD FLEECE!
NOW FER TITO...
OH FUNT! TITO PLEXUS? YER BOYFRIEND WAS TITO PLEXUS?
YOU KNOW HIM?
BEEEP! BEEEP!
KNOW HIM? I -- HANG ON...
FUNT!
WHAT?
TITO PLEXUS WAS A MADE MAN. HE SHOULD'VE REPORTED IN TO THE PLEXUS CLAN THIS MORNING. THEY'VE PUT UP A PRICE FOR HIM.
SO?
SORRY, TINA. THEY'VE HIRED ME TA KILL YE!

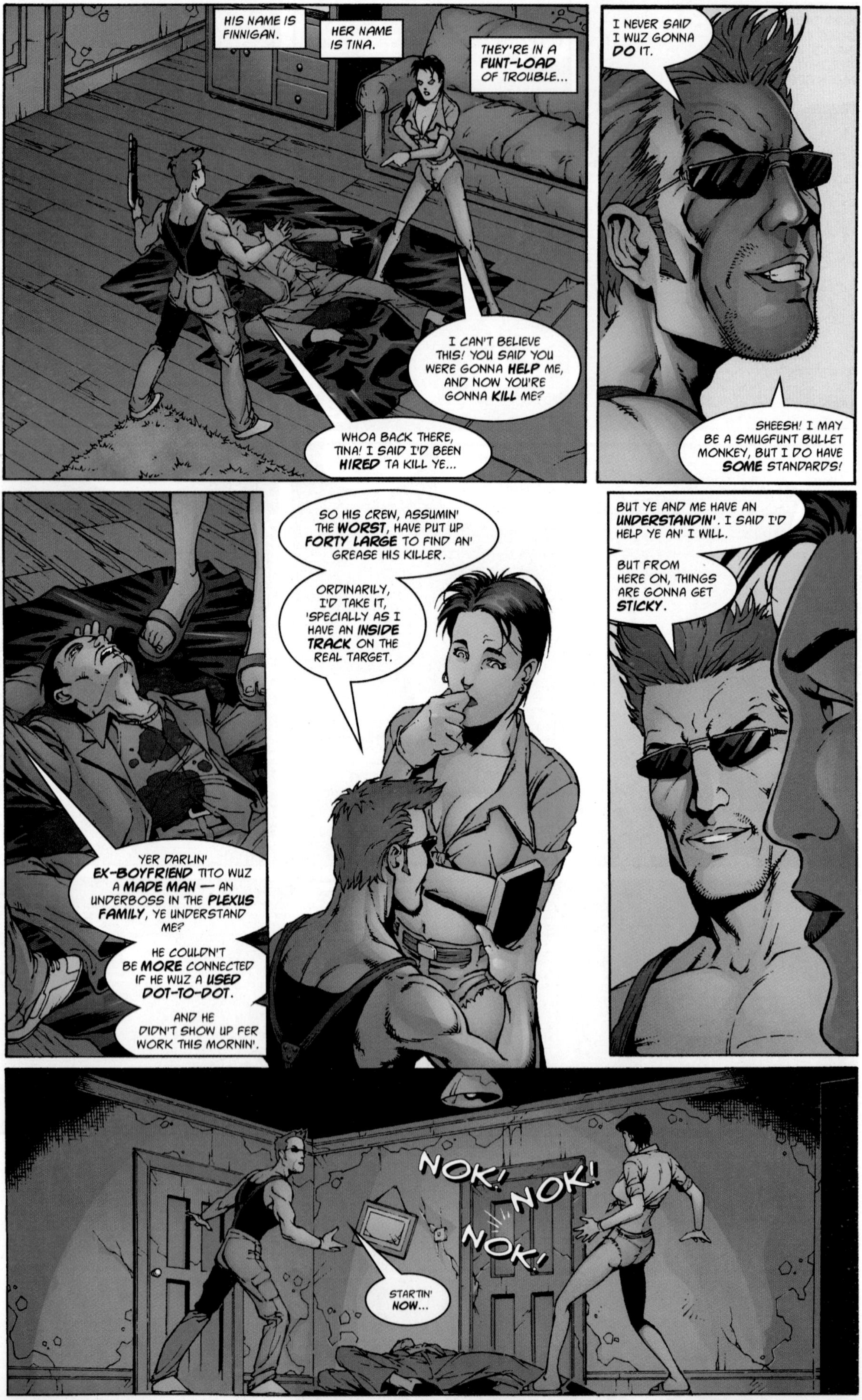
HIS NAME IS FINNIGAN.
HER NAME IS TINA.
THEY'RE IN A FUNT-LOAD OF TROUBLE...
I CAN'T BELIEVE THIS! YOU SAID YOU WERE GONNA HELP ME, AND NOW YOU'RE GONNA KILL ME?
WHOA BACK THERE, TINA! I SAID I'D BEEN HIRED TA KILL YE...
I NEVER SAID I WUZ GONNA DO IT.
SHEESH! I MAY BE A SMUGFUNT BULLET MONKEY, BUT I DO HAVE SOME STANDARDS!
YER DARLIN' EX-BOYFRIEND TITO WUZ A MADE MAN — AN UNDERBOSS IN THE PLEXUS FAMILY, YE UNDERSTAND ME?
HE COULDN'T BE MORE CONNECTED IF HE WUZ A USED DOT-TO-DOT.
AND HE DIDN'T SHOW UP FER WORK THIS MORNIN'.
SO HIS CREW, ASSUMIN' THE WORST, HAVE PUT UP FORTY LARGE TO FIND AN' GREASE HIS KILLER.
ORDINARILY, I'D TAKE IT, 'SPECIALLY AS I HAVE AN INSIDE TRACK ON THE REAL TARGET.
BUT YE AND ME HAVE AN UNDERSTANDIN'. I SAID I'D HELP YE AN' I WILL.
BUT FROM HERE ON, THINGS ARE GONNA GET STICKY.
NOK! NOK! NOK!
STARTIN' NOW...

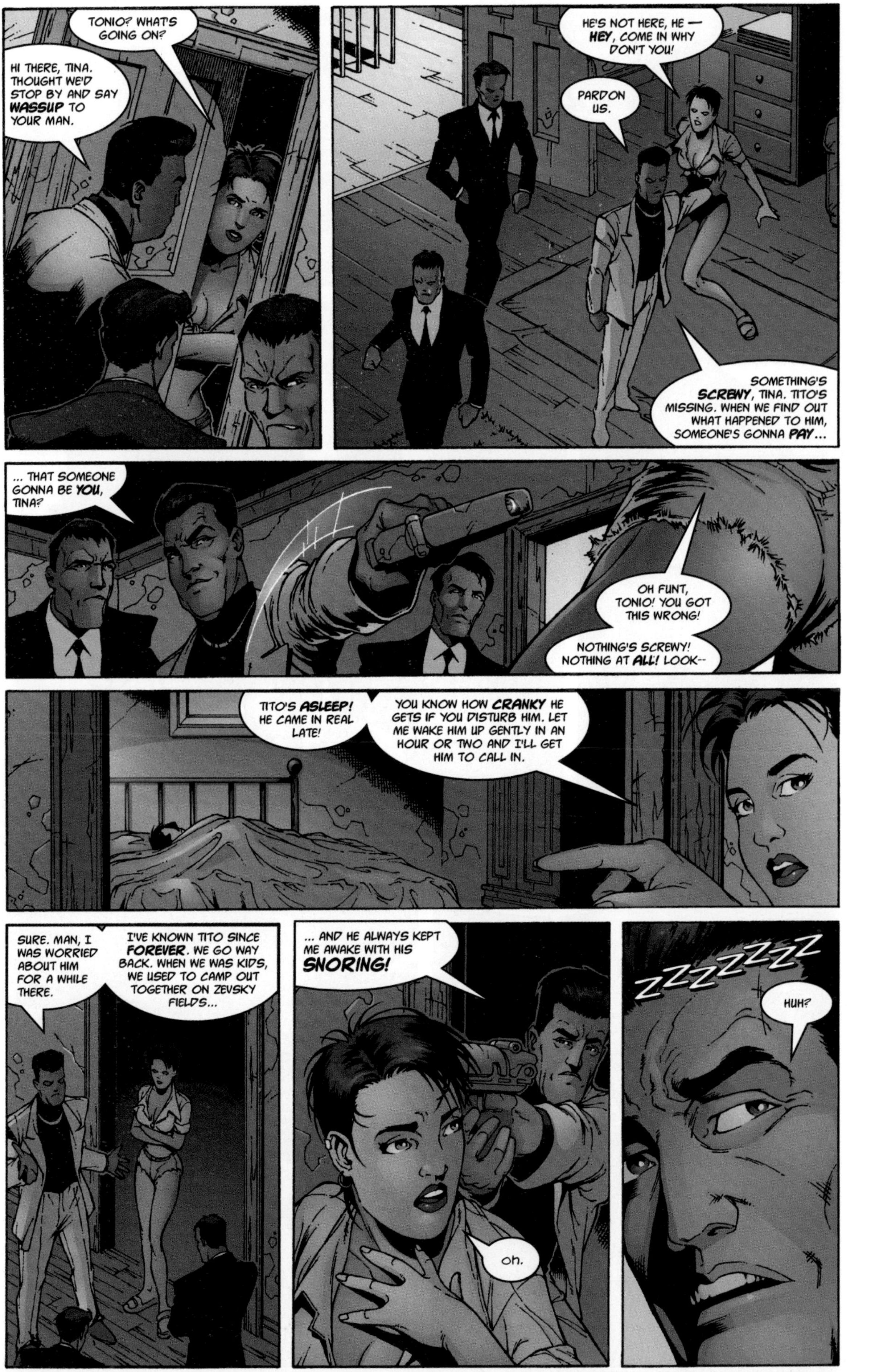
TONIO? WHAT'S GOING ON?
HI THERE, TINA. THOUGHT WE'D STOP BY AND SAY WASSUP TO YOUR MAN.
HE'S NOT HERE, HE — HEY, COME IN WHY DON'T YOU!
PARDON US.
SOMETHING'S SCRBNY, TINA. TITO'S MISSING. WHEN WE FIND OUT WHAT HAPPENED TO HIM, SOMEONE'S GONNA PAY...
... THAT SOMEONE GONNA BE YOU, TINA?
OH FUNT, TONIO! YOU GOT THIS WRONG!
NOTHING'S SCREWY! NOTHING AT ALL! LOOK--
TITO'S ASLEEP! HE CAME IN REAL LATE!
YOU KNOW HOW CRANKY HE GETS IF YOU DISTURB HIM. LET ME WAKE HIM UP GENTLY IN AN HOUR OR TWO AND I'LL GET HIM TO CALL IN.
SURE. MAN, I WAS WORRIED ABOUT HIM FOR A WHILE THERE.
I'VE KNOWN TITO SINCE FOREVER. WE GO WAY BACK. WHEN WE WAS KIDS, WE USED TO CAMP OUT TOGETHER ON ZEVSKY FIELDS...
... AND HE ALWAYS KEPT ME AWAKE WITH HIS SNORING!
oh.
ZZZZZZZZZ
HUH?

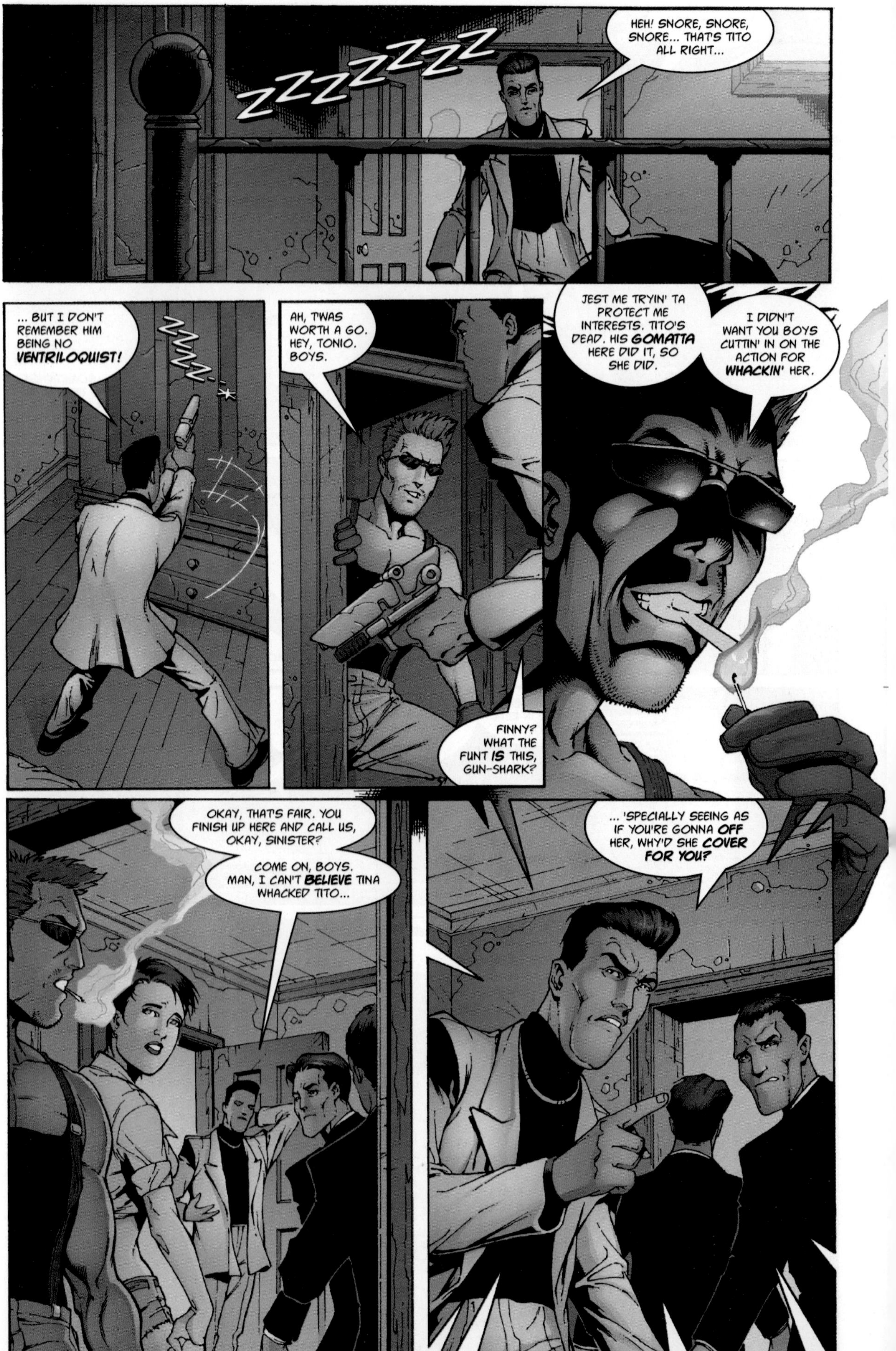

ZZZZZZZZ
HEH! SNORE, SNORE, SNORE... THAT'S TITO ALL RIGHT...
... BUT I DON'T REMEMBER HIM BEING NO VENTRILOQUIST!
ZZZZ--
AH, T'WAS WORTH A GO. HEY, TONIO. BOYS.
FINNY? WHAT THE FUNT IS THIS, GUN-SHARK?
JEST ME TRYIN' TA PROTECT ME INTERESTS. TITO'S DEAD. HIS GOMATTA HERE DID IT, SO SHE DID.
I DIDN'T WANT YOU BOYS CUTTIN' IN ON THE ACTION FOR WHACKIN' HER.
OKAY, THAT'S FAIR. YOU FINISH UP HERE AND CALL US, OKAY, SINISTER?
COME ON, BOYS. MAN, I CAN'T BELIEVE TINA WHACKED TITO...
... 'SPECIALLY SEEING AS IF YOU'RE GONNA OFF HER, WHY'D SHE COVER FOR YOU?

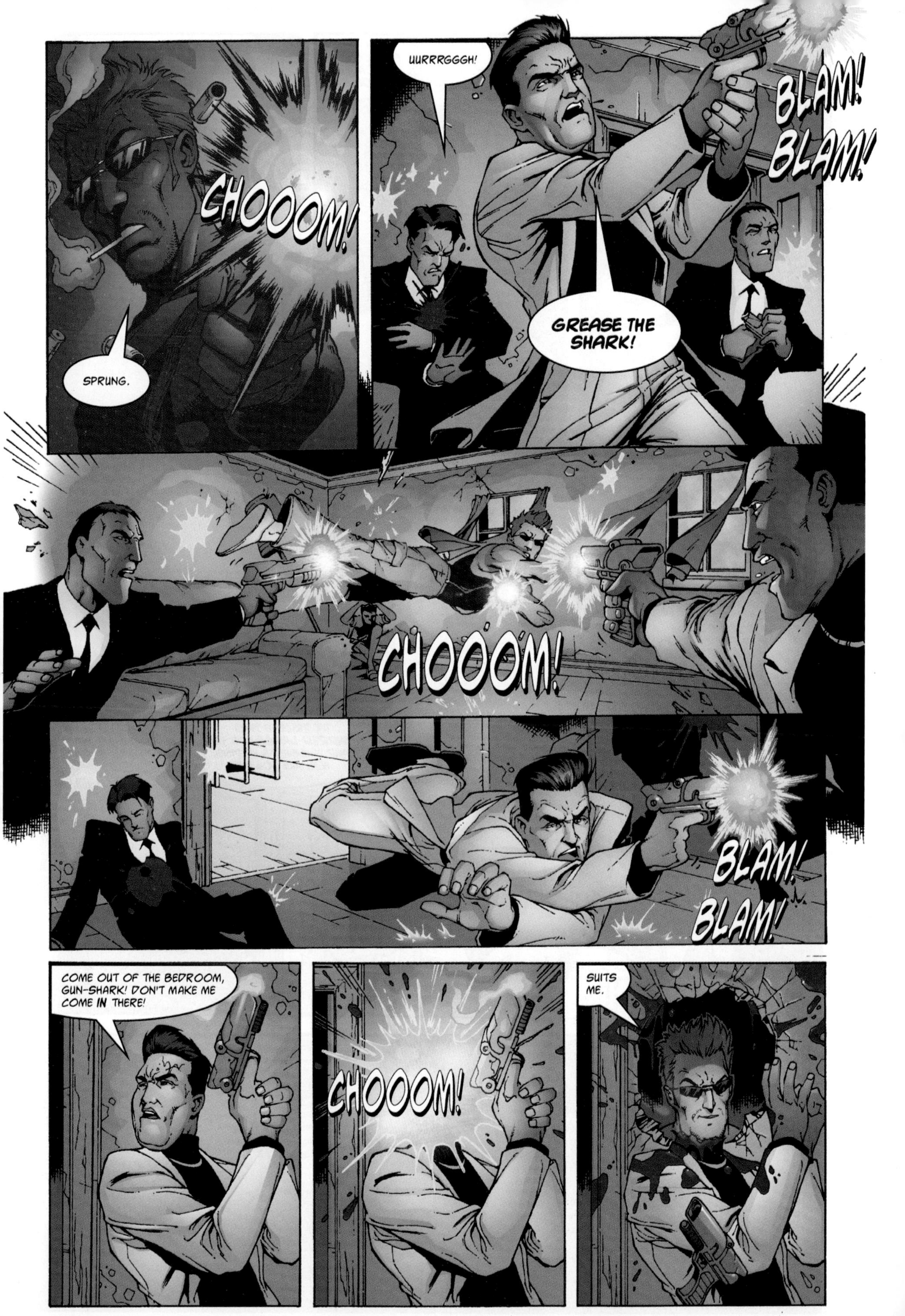
CHOOOM!
SPRUNG.
UURRRGGGH!
GREASE THE SHARK!
BLAM! BLAM!
CHOOOM!
BLAM! BLAM!
COME OUT OF THE BEDROOM, GUN-SHARK! DON'T MAKE ME COME IN THERE!
CHOOOM!
SUITS ME.

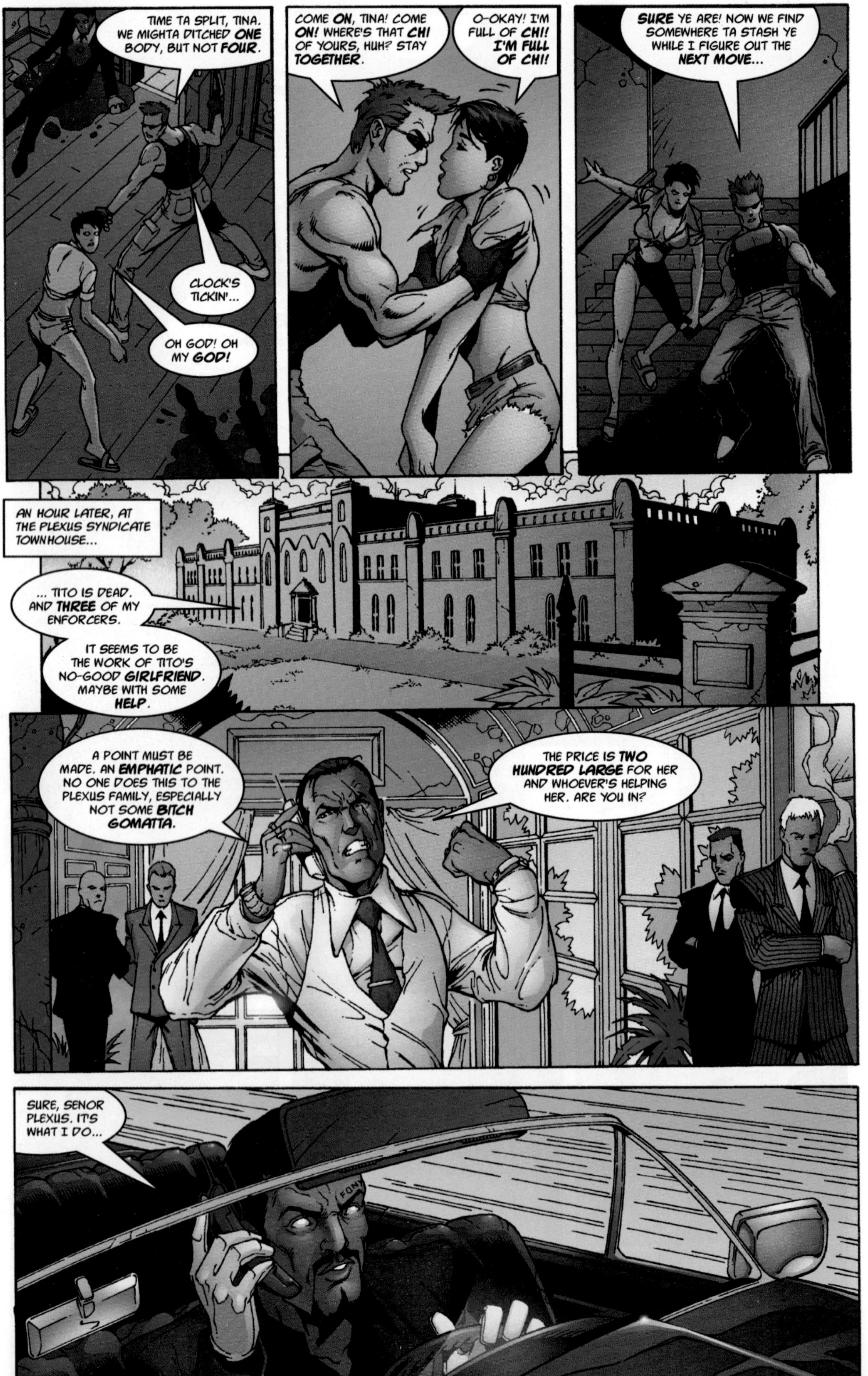
TIME TA SPLIT, TINA. WE MIGHTA DITCHED **ONE** BODY, BUT NOT **FOUR**.
CLOCK'S TICKIN'...
OH GOD! OH MY **GOD!**
COME **ON**, TINA! COME **ON!** WHERE'S THAT **CHI** OF YOURS, HUH? STAY **TOGETHER**.
O-OKAY! I'M FULL OF **CHI!** **I'M FULL OF CHI!**
SURE YE ARE! NOW WE FIND SOMEWHERE TA STASH YE WHILE I FIGURE OUT THE **NEXT MOVE**...
AN HOUR LATER, AT THE PLEXUS SYNDICATE TOWNHOUSE...
... TITO IS DEAD. AND **THREE** OF MY ENFORCERS.
IT SEEMS TO BE THE WORK OF TITO'S NO-GOOD **GIRLFRIEND**. MAYBE WITH SOME **HELP**.
A POINT MUST BE MADE. AN **EMPHATIC** POINT. NO ONE DOES THIS TO THE PLEXUS FAMILY, ESPECIALLY NOT SOME **BITCH GOMATTA**.
THE PRICE IS **TWO HUNDRED LARGE** FOR HER AND WHOEVER'S HELPING HER. ARE YOU IN?
SURE, SENOR PLEXUS. IT'S WHAT I DO...

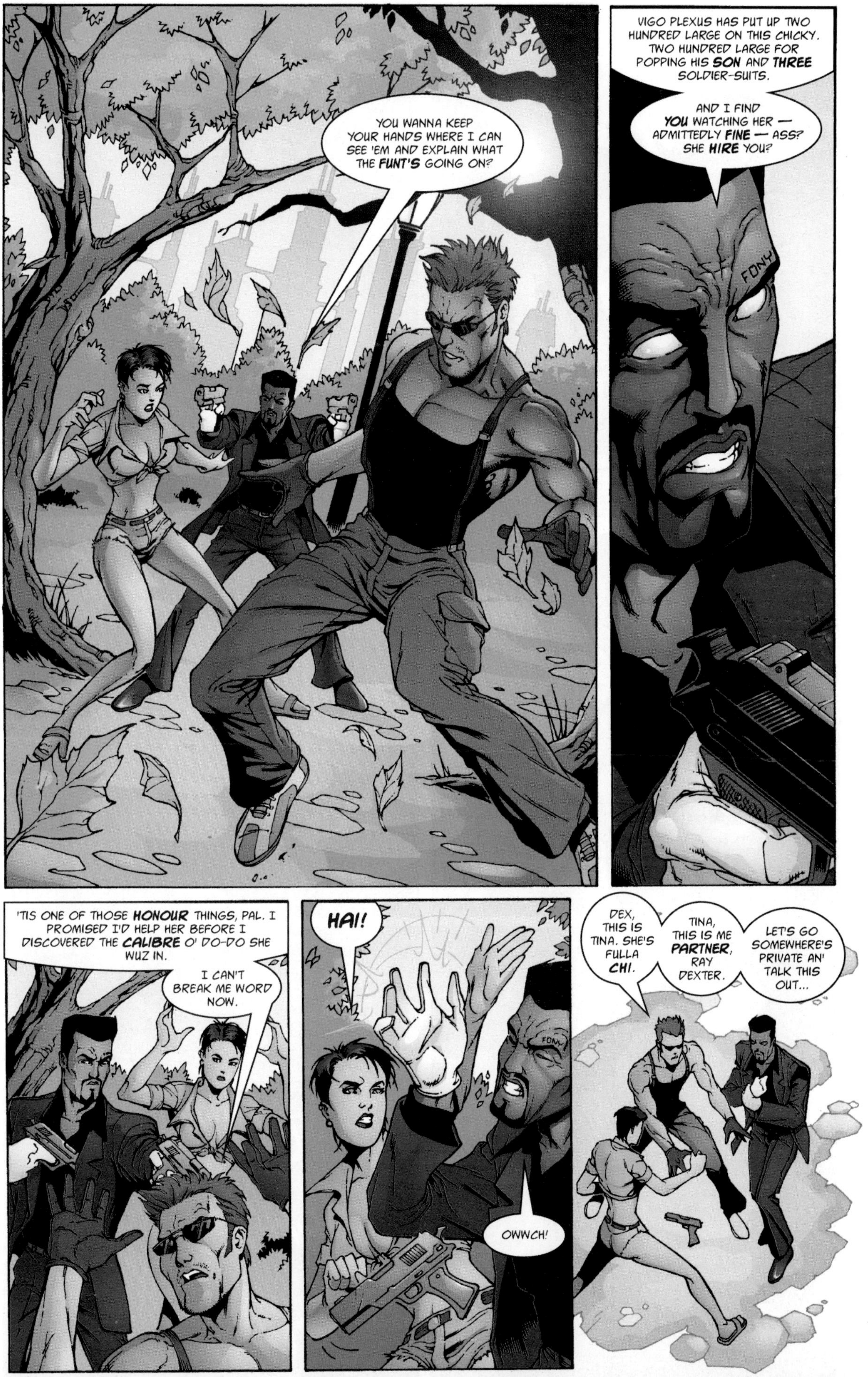
YOU WANNA KEEP YOUR HANDS WHERE I CAN SEE 'EM AND EXPLAIN WHAT THE FUNT'S GOING ON?
VIGO PLEXUS HAS PUT UP TWO HUNDRED LARGE ON THIS CHICKY. TWO HUNDRED LARGE FOR POPPING HIS SON AND THREE SOLDIER-SUITS.
AND I FIND YOU WATCHING HER — ADMITTEDLY FINE — ASS? SHE HIRE YOU?
FONY
'TIS ONE OF THOSE HONOUR THINGS, PAL. I PROMISED I'D HELP HER BEFORE I DISCOVERED THE CALIBRE O' DO-DO SHE WUZ IN.
I CAN'T BREAK ME WORD NOW.
HAI!
OWWCH!
DEX, THIS IS TINA. SHE'S FULLA CHI.
TINA, THIS IS ME PARTNER, RAY DEXTER.
LET'S GO SOMEWHERE'S PRIVATE AN' TALK THIS OUT...

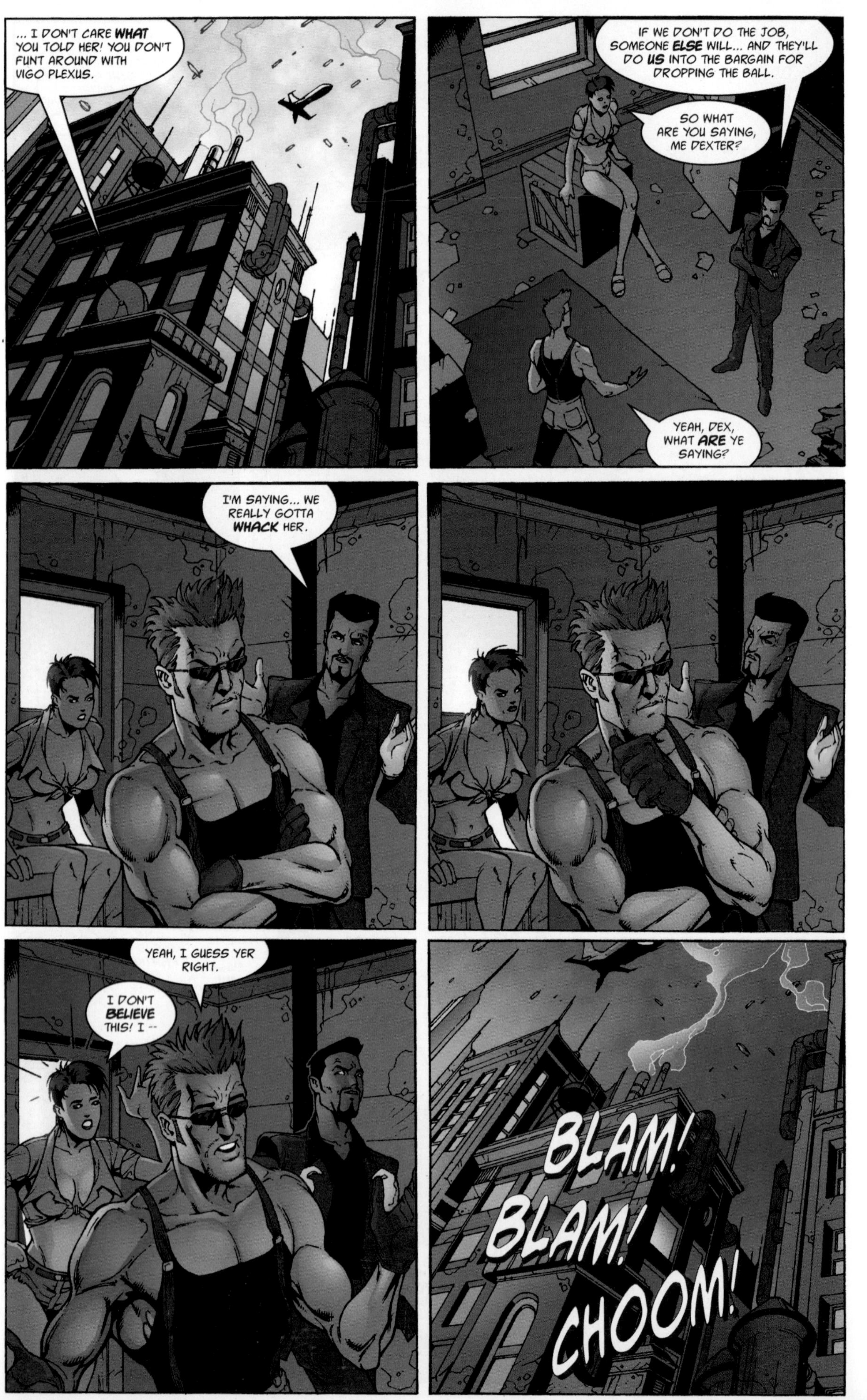
... I DON'T CARE **WHAT** YOU TOLD HER! YOU DON'T FUNT AROUND WITH VIGO PLEXUS.
IF WE DON'T DO THE JOB, SOMEONE **ELSE** WILL... AND THEY'LL DO **US** INTO THE BARGAIN FOR DROPPING THE BALL.
SO WHAT ARE YOU SAYING, ME DEXTER?
YEAH, DEX, WHAT **ARE** YE SAYING?
I'M SAYING... WE REALLY GOTTA **WHACK** HER.
YEAH, I GUESS YER RIGHT.
I DON'T **BELIEVE** THIS! I --
BLAM! BLAM! CHOOM!

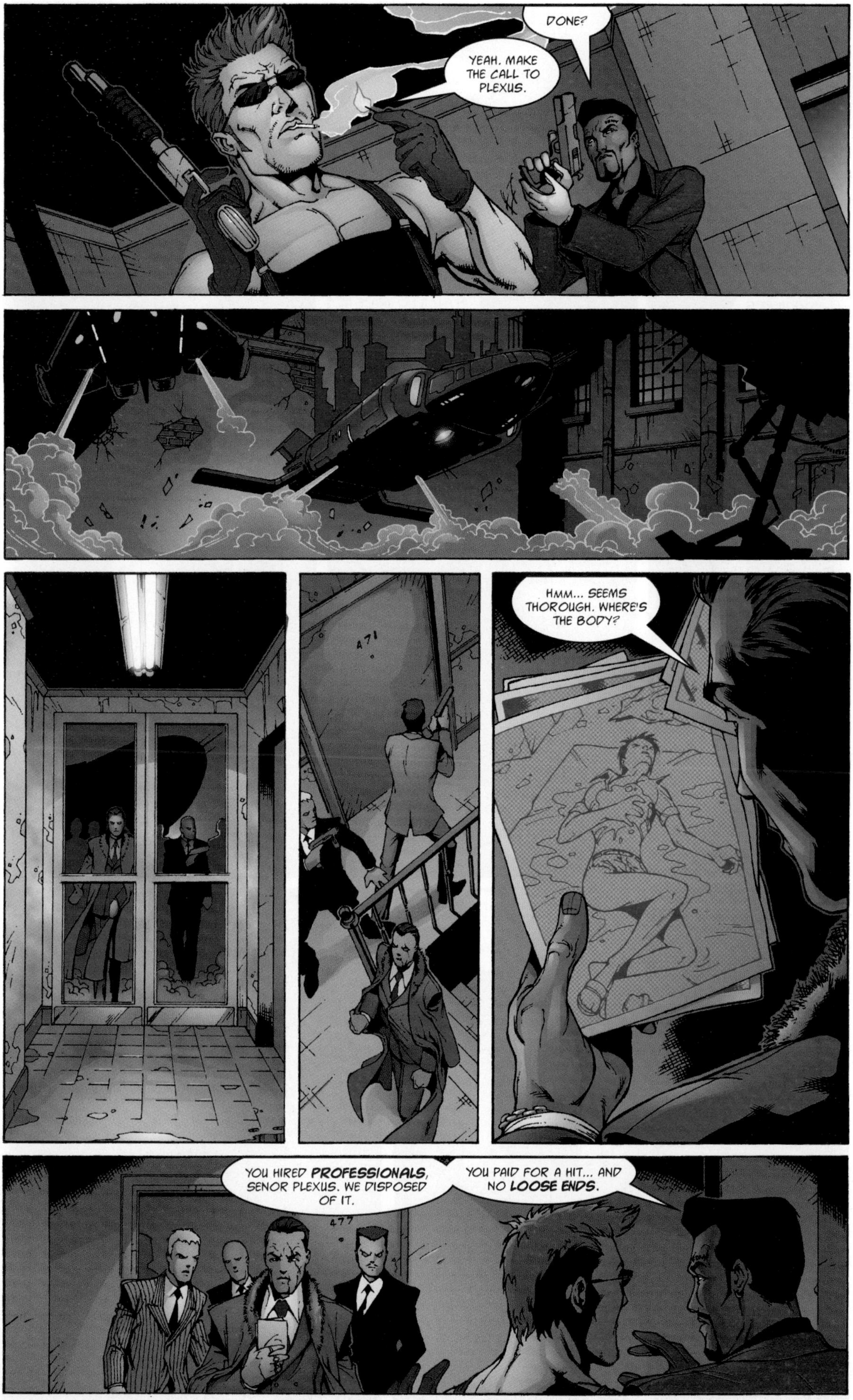
DONE?
YEAH. MAKE THE CALL TO PLEXUS.
HMM... SEEMS THOROUGH. WHERE'S THE BODY?
YOU HIRED **PROFESSIONALS**, SENOR PLEXUS. WE DISPOSED OF IT.
YOU PAID FOR A HIT... AND NO **LOOSE ENDS**.

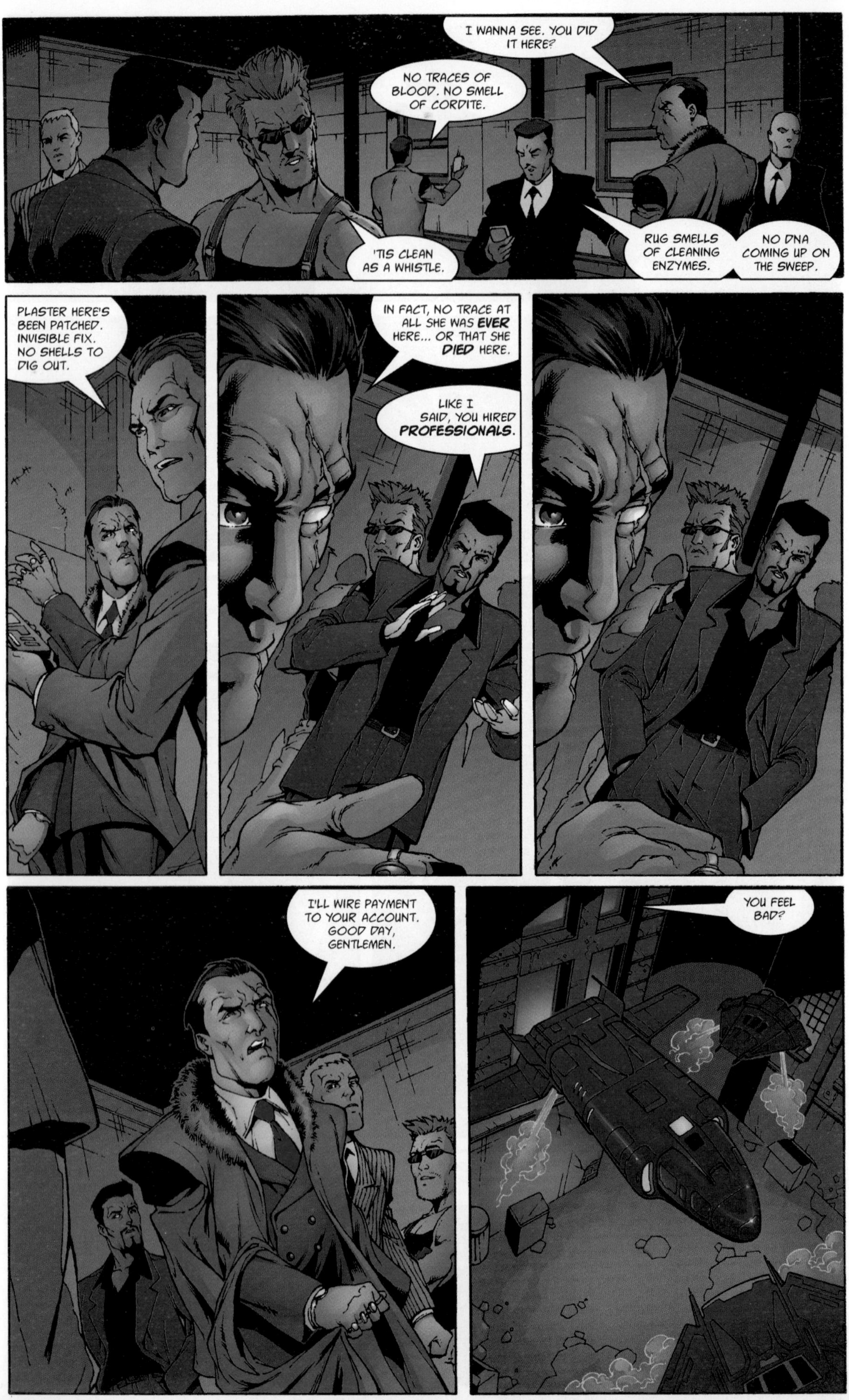
I WANNA SEE. YOU DID IT HERE?
NO TRACES OF BLOOD. NO SMELL OF CORDITE.
'TIS CLEAN AS A WHISTLE.
RUG SMELLS OF CLEANING ENZYMES.
NO DNA COMING UP ON THE SWEEP.
PLASTER HERE'S BEEN PATCHED. INVISIBLE FIX. NO SHELLS TO DIG OUT.
IN FACT, NO TRACE AT ALL SHE WAS EVER HERE... OR THAT SHE DIED HERE.
LIKE I SAID, YOU HIRED PROFESSIONALS.
I'LL WIRE PAYMENT TO YOUR ACCOUNT. GOOD DAY, GENTLEMEN.
YOU FEEL BAD?

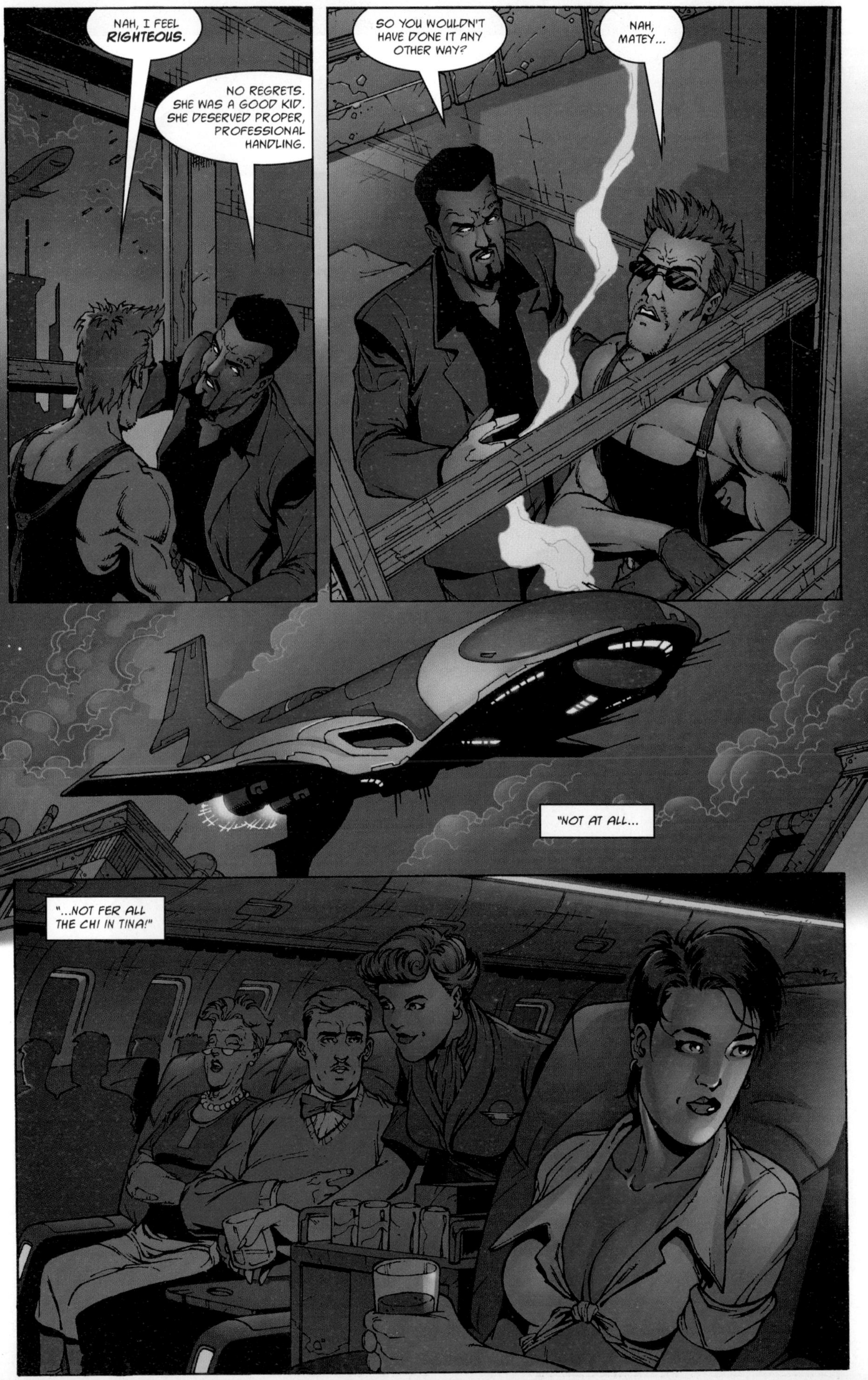

NAH, I FEEL **RIGHTEOUS**.
NO REGRETS. SHE WAS A GOOD KID. SHE DESERVED PROPER, PROFESSIONAL HANDLING.
SO YOU WOULDN'T HAVE DONE IT ANY OTHER WAY?
NAH, MATEY...
"NOT AT ALL...
"...NOT FER ALL THE CHI IN TINA!"

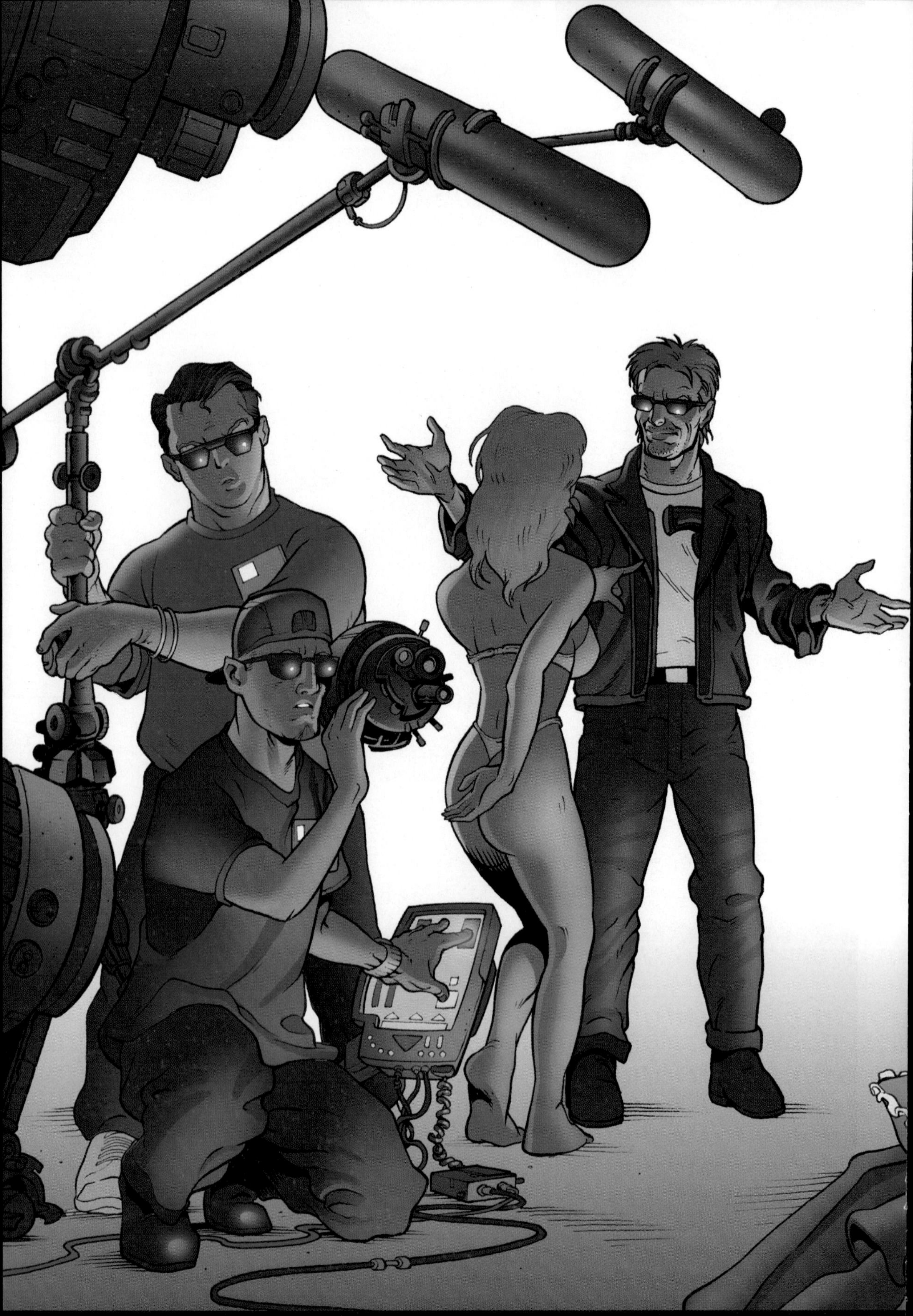

2000 AD Prog 1228: Cover by **Richard Elson**

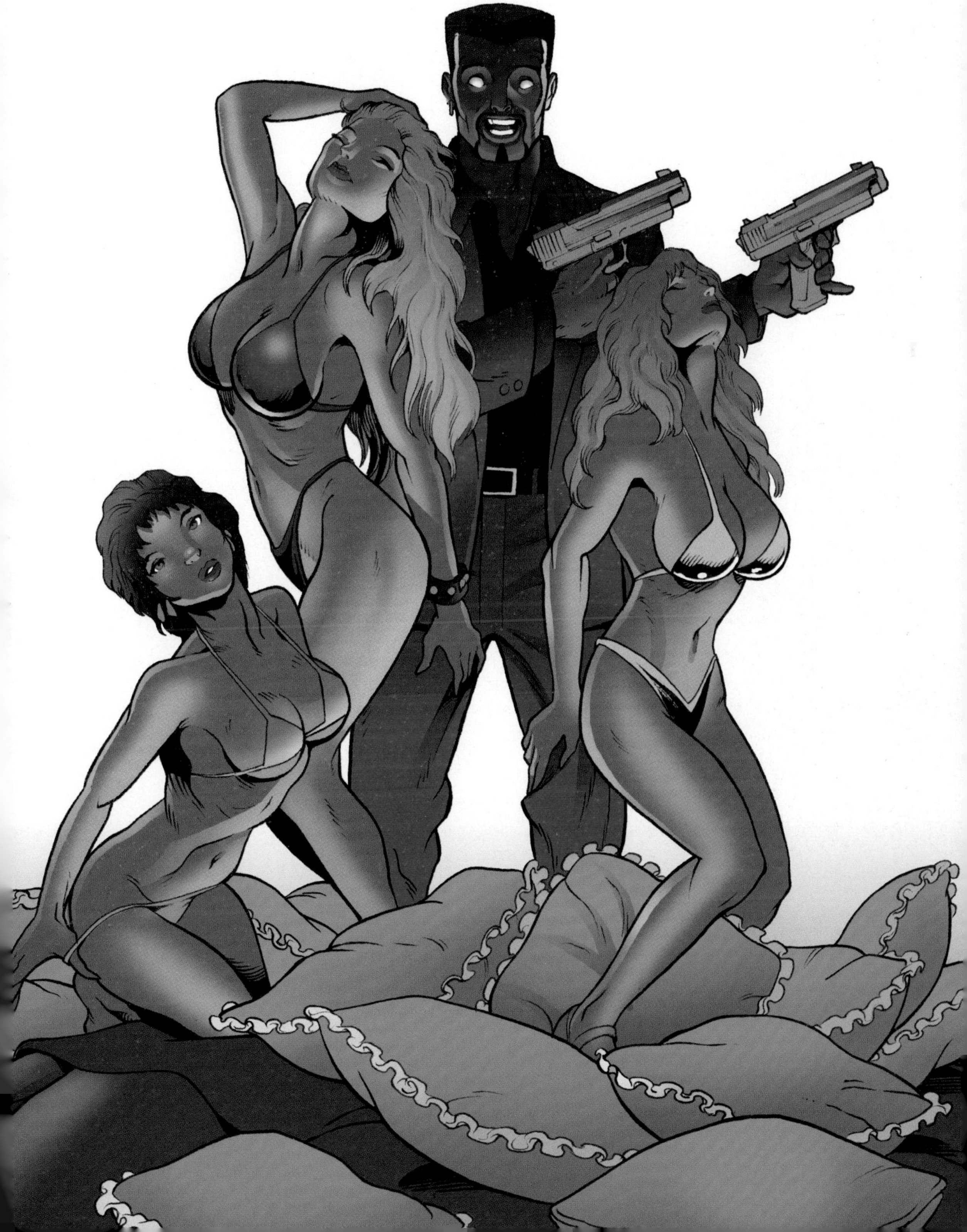

DAN ABNETT

Dan Abnett is the co-creator of *2000 AD* series *Atavar*, *Badlands*, *Sancho Panzer* and *Sinister Dexter*. He has also written *Black Light*, *Downlode Tales*, *Durham Red*, *Flesh*, *Future Shocks*, *Judge Dredd*, *Pulp Sci-Fi*, *Roadkill*, *Rogue Trooper*, *The VCs*, *Vector 13* and *Venus Bluegenes*, as well as *The Scarlet Apocrypha* and *Wardog* for the *Megazine*. A prolific creator, Abnett has also written for Marvel, Dark Horse and DC Comics. He is the author of more than thirty novels, including the bestselling *Gaunt's Ghosts* and *Horus Heresy* series for Black Library, and *Torchwood: Border Princes* and *Doctor Who: The Story of Martha* for the BBC. His most recent work outside the Galaxy's Greatest Comic includes *Nova* and *Guardians of The Galaxy* for Marvel, and *The Authority* for Wildstorm. Dan's website can be found at www.danabnett.com

ANDY CLARKE

Andy Clarke is a rising star of *2000 AD*. Making his debut on *Sinister Dexter*, he quickly gained in popularity thanks to his highly detailed and realistic artwork, which falls in style somewhere between that of John Cassaday and Whilce Portacio. Stints on *Judge Dredd*, *Nikolai Dante*, *Rose O' Rion* and *Pulp Sci-Fi* led to Clarke moving on to his first co-created series, punk psychic thriller *Thirteen*. The success of the latter saw Clarke teamed with Andy Diggle on *Snow/Tiger*, an acclaimed military thriller which represents his most recent *2000 AD* work.

SIMON DAVIS

Simon Davis' unique, angular painted style has been a fixture of *Sinister Dexter* for some years now, since his *2000 AD* debut on the series. He has also found the time to create *B.L.A.I.R. 1* and *Black Siddha*, as well as contributing to *Downlode Tales*, *Judge Dredd*, *Missionary Man*, *Outlaw*, *Plagues of Necropolis*, *Tales of Telguuth*, *Tharg the Mighty* and *Vector 13*. His most recent non-*2000 AD* work was on DC's *JLA: Riddle of the Beast*.

PATRICK GODDARD

Patrick Goddard is has worked extensively for the Galaxy's Greatest Comic. Co-creator of the *Megazine* series *Wardog*, he has pencilled *Judge Dredd*, *Mean Machine*, *Middenface McNulty* and *Sinister Dexter*.

NIGEL RAYNOR

Nigel Raynor is the co-creator of *Pussyfoot 5* and *Repo-Mex*, and has also illustrated *Future Shocks*, *Pulp Sci-Fi* and *Sinister Dexter*.

IAN RICHARDSON

Ian Richardson has provided the art for various *2000 AD* strips, including *Future Shocks*, *Past Imperfect* and *Sinister Dexter*.

STEVE ROBERTS

Steve Roberts is, relatively speaking, a *2000 AD* newcomer, but his bright cartooning has illuminated both gun-loving criminals *Sinister Dexter* and no-good students *Bec and Kawl*, which he co-created with Simon Spurrier.